Rose Hilton

'Something to Keep the Balance'

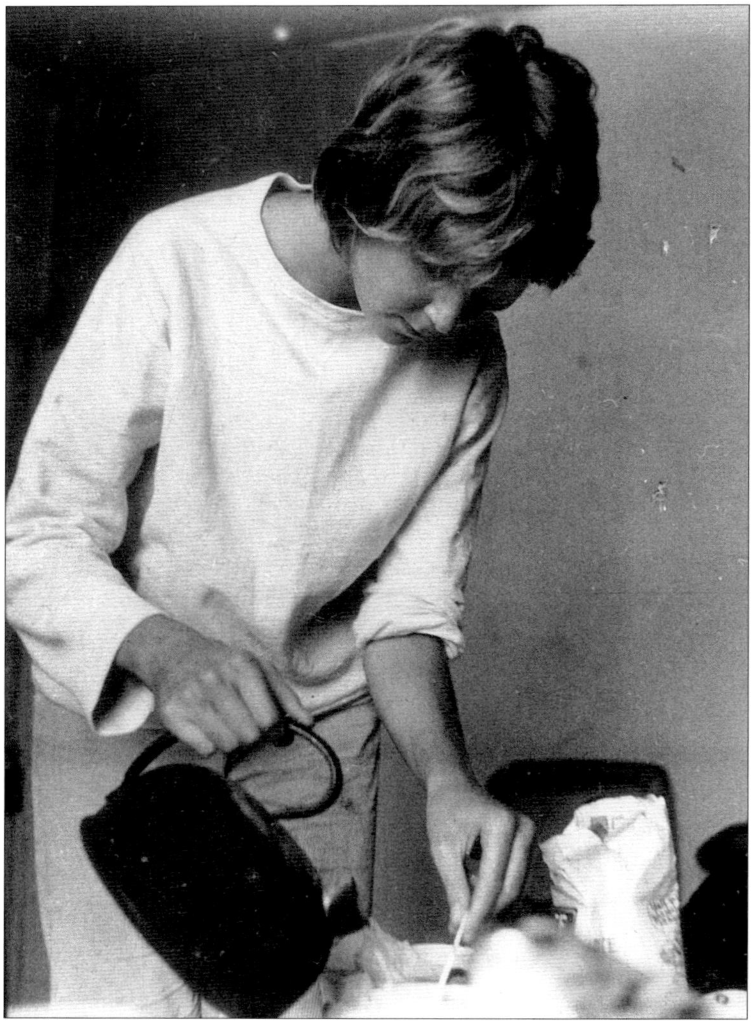

ROSE HILTON

‘Something to Keep the Balance’

ANDREW LAMBIRTH

LUND HUMPHRIES

First published in 2009 by Lund Humphries,
in association with Messum's

Lund Humphries
Wey Court East
Union Road
Farnham
Surrey GU9 7PT
UK

Lund Humphries
Suite 420
101 Cherry Street
Burlington
VT 05401-4405
USA

www.lundhumphries.com

Lund Humphries is part of Ashgate Publishing

British Library Cataloguing-in-Publication Data:
Lambirth, Andrew, 1959–
Rose Hilton : something to keep the blalance
1. Hilton, Rose – Criticism and interpretation
I. Title
759.2

ISBN 9781848220089

Library of Congress Control Number: 2008940722

Edited by Slaney Begley
Designed by Nigel Soper

Design note: Extracts from interviews with Rose, conducted by the author, have been set in Scala. Extracts from Rose's diaries and other contemporary writings are set in Helvetica Neue.

Jacket front: *Undressing in the Kitchen,* 1996

Jacket back: *Red Window,* 2002

Frontispiece: Photograph of Rose at the Royal College of Art, 1957

Origination by MRM Graphics Ltd Winslow Bucks

Printed in Thailand

CONTENTS

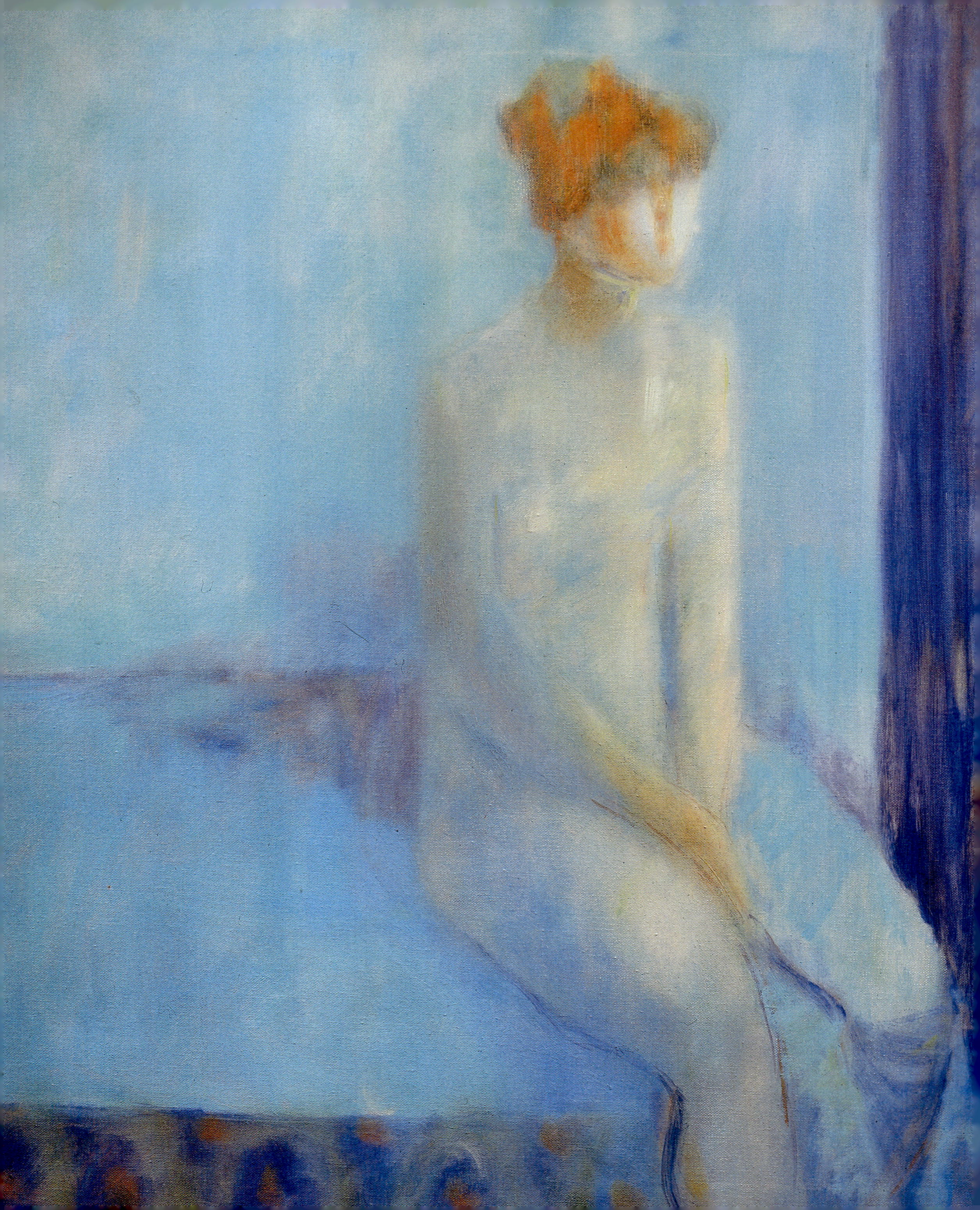

FOREWORD

I GOT TO KNOW ROSE HILTON through writing about her late husband, Roger. Initially I was asked to contribute a catalogue essay for an exhibition of Roger's drawings at Jonathan Clark's gallery in London in 2001. I met Rose at the Private View: a tall, elegant figure in black, she seemed rather daunting, though friendly. She approved of what I had written, and it was later agreed that I should write a full monograph on Roger's life and work. (This was published in 2007 after many vicissitudes as *Roger Hilton: The Figured Language of Thought*.)

In the process of researching that book I spent a lot of time talking to Rose and my liking for her deepened into admiring affection. I also liked her own work as a painter, though Rose was at first reticent about showing it to me. In due course, I wrote a catalogue essay for one of her shows at David Messum's London gallery. That friendship has led now to this book, which is Rose's story.

It was evident to me that there was a separate story to be told aside from the narrative of Roger Hilton's life – a story that explained the whole trajectory of Rose's life and its own particular triumph in art, in which the 16-year period with Roger was a crucial but relatively short-lived episode. I think it most appropriate that Rose's story should be told mostly in Rose's words. This book is a highly personal account and as such it seems fitting that it should be narrated in the first person. It is based on interviews I conducted with Rose and excerpts from the diaries she has kept over the years. The result is an intimate portrait of her life with Roger and a record of her own development as an artist and an individual.

Those two strands of her existence – Roger and art – are fairly inextricably entwined, so much so that it's difficult to decide where one ends and the other begins. They are the two most important elements in her life and the shaping factors of her fate. In many respects, painting has been Rose's lifeline. The sense of celebration she achieves through it makes a powerful contrast with her sometimes turbulent existence. Now her painting may be regarded as her greatest achievement. This book aims to set her art in the context of her life.

ANDREW LAMBIRTH
September 2008

FORMATIVE YEARS

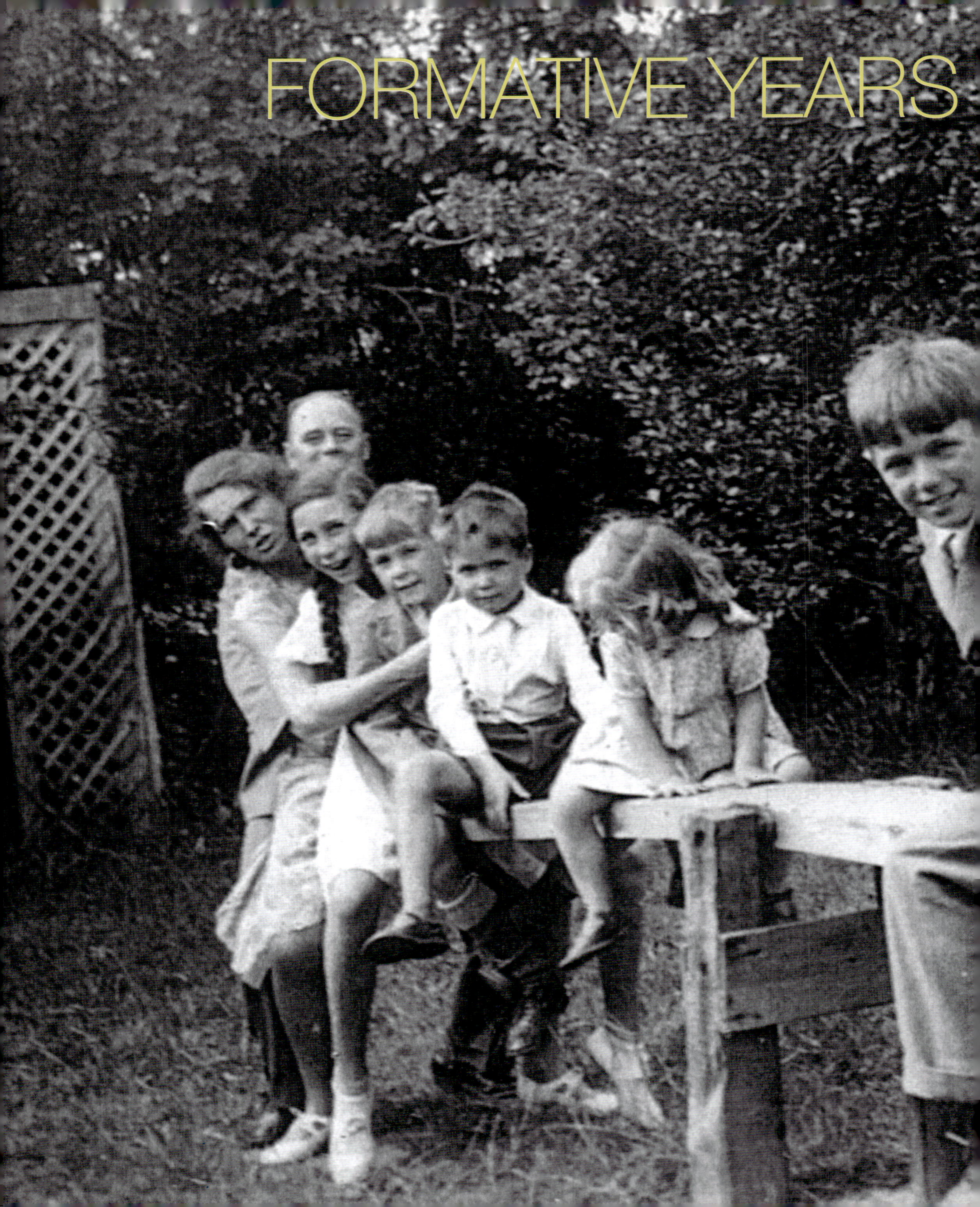

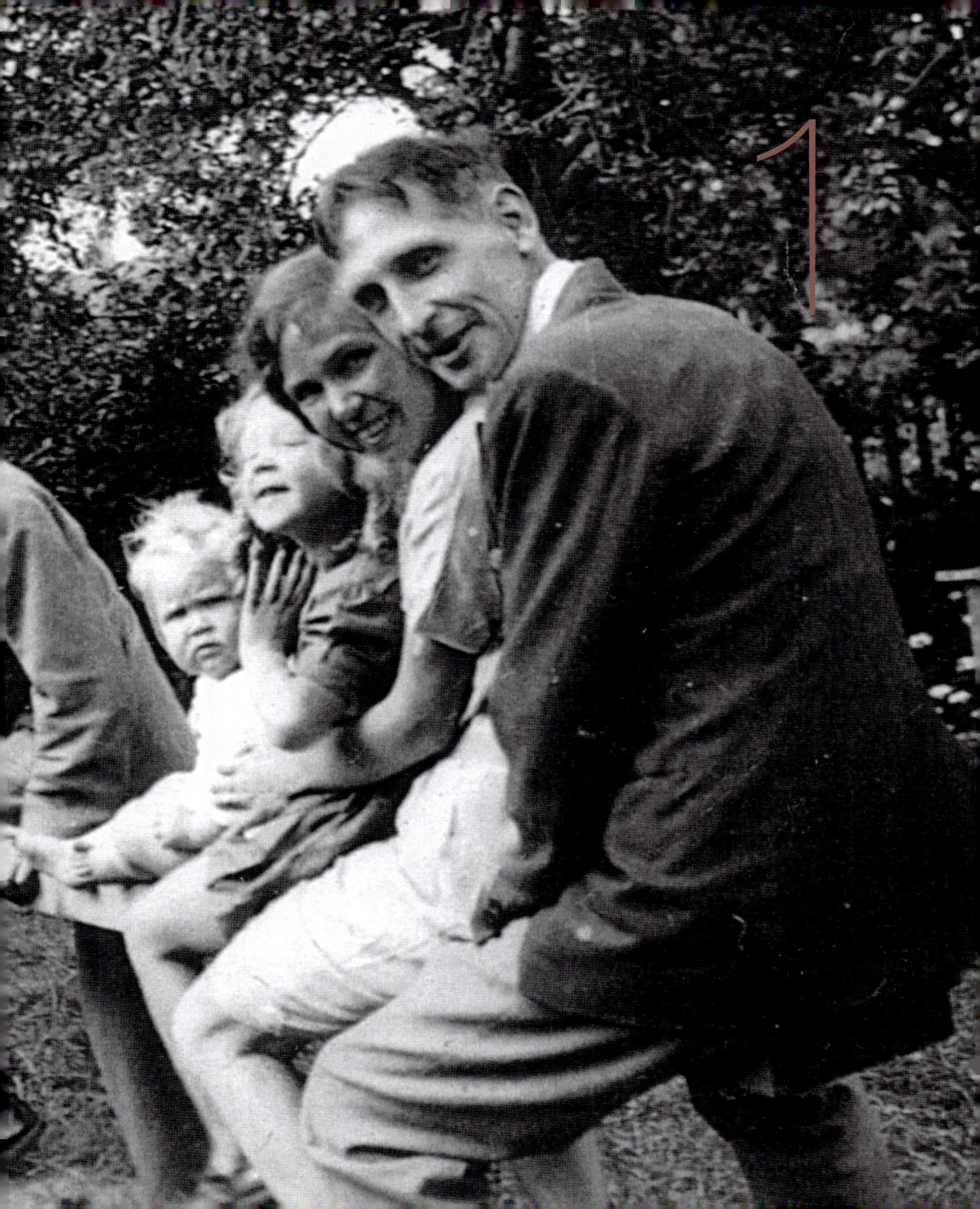

1

THE FAMILY

Rosemary Phipps was born on 15 August 1931 in the ancient village of Leigh (pronounced Lye), near Tonbridge in Kent. Her parents were Plymouth Brethren and her father, Robert Charles Phipps, was a master baker. Religion imbued her upbringing, which was comfortable but hard-working. The family was large and close-knit. Eventually, Rose's parents were to have eight children, but they were born in two tranches, as it were. Rose was the fourth child of the first five. There is a family photograph taken in 1933 (fig.2), with Rose on the extreme left, seated, her sister Moira standing next to her, then her brother David, while seated on the far right is Robert, the eldest. In amongst the group is their mother with the new baby, Patricia. This photo commemorates a happy moment before tragedy struck, and the baby died. Rose's mother, Louie, was devastated. Rose comments:

I think my mother was so very upset by it that she didn't have any more sex with my father for about five years. No more children were born in that period and I don't think they would have used contraceptives. Then they must have started again in the later 1930s, just before the war. My sister Priscilla was born in 1938, then there was Roger and Alan. Christopher Roger he was called, he became a doctor. He died in a car crash when I was with Roger Hilton, in 1965. And Alan was killed on a motorbike. Something went a bit wrong with our family. Roger Hilton, although he quite got on with my mum, used to say 'it's that mad religion, it unbalanced everybody'. Well it did in a way.

Nan [Jules] Knott, my mother's mother, was a Cockney really with Irish blood. That's where the religion came from. My parents met in Wimbledon. Old Tom, Nan's husband, was not very religious and liked whisky. He was always dapper and well-dressed. But they went to the Gospel Hall and so did my father's family and that's where they met. My dad was in love with my mother's sister, Maggie, who was a nurse, but she died when she was about 20. My mother, Louie, was younger, and he transferred his affections to her.

Religion certainly provided a structure and a discipline to the family life. As Rose recalls:

As children we were taken every Sunday to the Gospel Hall. I talked to my brother David about it and he says we were Open Brethren, which

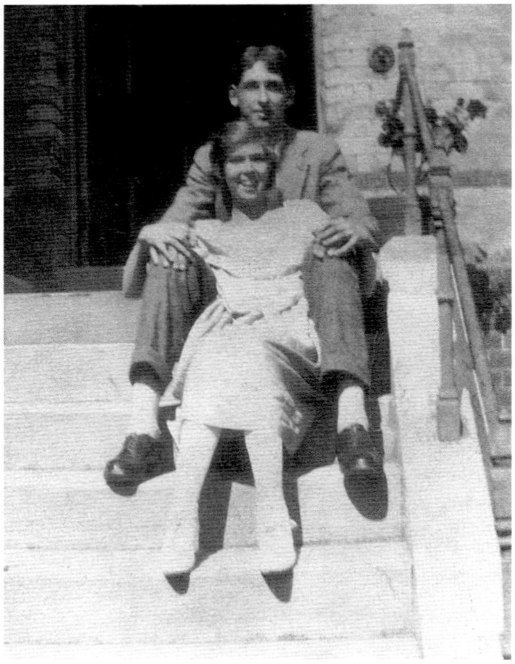

fig 1. Rose's parents, 1925

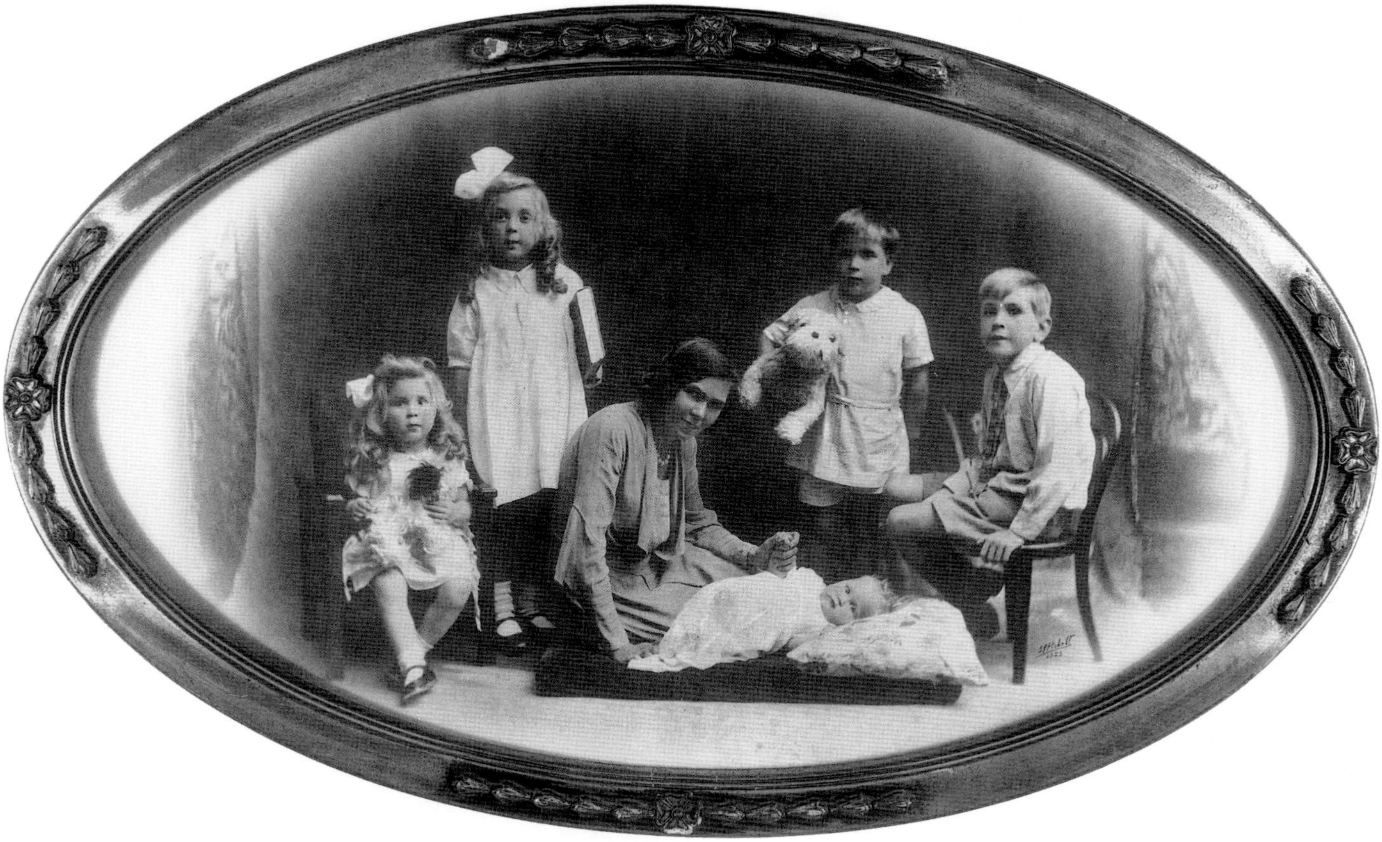

fig 2. Mrs Phipps and her children. Rose is on the left, 1933

were not quite so strict as the Plymouth Brethren. There wasn't an organ, only a tuning fork, because they didn't believe in any music with the singing. There were interminable long prayers off the cuff, interspersed with Alleluias. And lay preachers rather than ministers. It was all to do with the second coming and God's punishment. The second coming they took really literally. There was someone who came to our chapel who had skylights in their roof to make it easier.

My mother used to speak at women's meetings. My father was quieter. He'd been in the First World War. I adored my mother until I was about 17 because she was funny and she made us laugh a lot. She was good with the children, perhaps because she had two sides to her. She always reckoned if she wasn't such a devout Christian she'd be a very wicked woman. She secretly quite liked gambling. She used to go in for advertisement competitions – making up a rhyme for Heinz Baked Beans or whatever. She won a Mini car once. Even in those early days of chapel and Bible reading, because they ran an extensive business in the village, not just the bakery, she drove a van. Not many people – especially women – were doing that in the 1920s and 1930s. My father drove as well but she did deliveries to help out. She was very lively. As my brother says, we got mixed up who was the higher power – mum or God. When the children were born, she dedicated them to God to do His Work.

My father didn't come on so heavily with religion but he believed. He worked hard and was very conscientious. He was a tall, very kindly man with a nice face. We had a maid called Eve because my mother was always helping with the business and you could get somebody quite cheaply in those days to help with the children. And they had had four children within five years. The maid came in every day and put a little pinny on. We weren't a rich enough family to have maids really but we were quite well-to-do. My father was a baker by profession and made very good bread. He also ran the post office in Leigh and a grocer's store. He and my mother worked very hard and we were very much part of that life.

I remember clearly my first day at infants' school in Leigh. I was five. I just remember being left there and feeling upset. We had to lie down after lunch on little mats and have a rest. [A habit she enjoys these days once more.] In that 1933 photograph I have long curly golden locks. My mother would not let us cut our hair because of religion, so we had plaits. I hated it and I got them cut as soon as I was able. I've had short hair ever since. She was upset about that as she said I had the best hair of the family. It upset her that I chopped it about as soon as I went to art school.

Was there any painting in her family?

Yes. I had a great-uncle who was recognised as a very good chocolate box painter. He did marvellous designs for Victorian chocolate boxes. That's what he made his living by, although he trained at St Martins School of Art, London. My mother also drew rather well and had that kind of artistic temperament.

But it was far from being an artistic upbringing. The only books tended to be religious and there was no art on the walls, except one reproduction of a painting. Rose remembers it well:

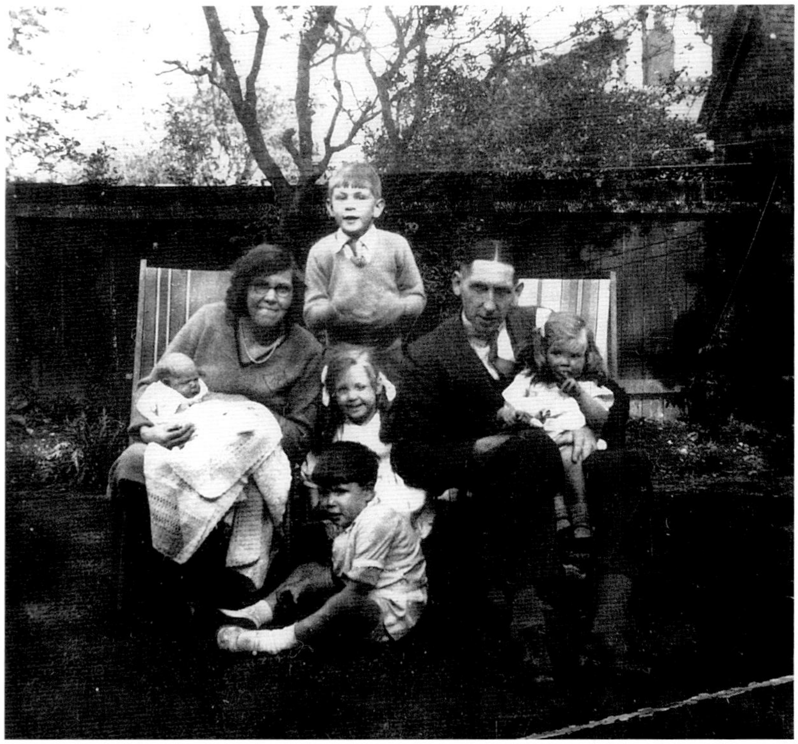

fig 3. The Phipps family, Rose on her father's knee, 1933

It was a war picture that my dad had brought with him, of a soldier saying goodbye to his horse. It was called *Goodbye, Old Man*. In those days, children's Bibles had pictures in them, so that's where your imagination went if you were drawn to pictures.

On Sundays we always had the visiting speaker to lunch. And I do remember people coming to call, though we were not allowed to play games on Sundays or even to skip. The children came out of chapel slightly earlier than the rest of the congregation. One day the four of us hid our skipping ropes in the stinging nettles – I always remember this – so that we could skip home. Of course it got reported back to our parents and we were all punished. Dad was a bit stricter with the boys – he whacked them – and with us he just sort of hit the skirt (we had our Scotch kilts on). We were organised by my elder brother, Robert. I don't think my mother ever really forgave him for being the rebel. She tried to dominate him and he wouldn't have it.

GROWING UP

IT WAS A SECURE childhood, I felt loved and happy with my brothers and sisters. If any of us had been an only child in a Plymouth Brethren household it would have been much more miserable, but it was actually good fun. I don't think I could have gone in for a difficult relationship like the one I had with Roger [Hilton] if I hadn't had that start in life.

My parents read the Bible every day, aloud in the morning after breakfast when we were young, and there were family prayers. Those were the idyllic years at Leigh, from one to eight. They were nice to us and we had swings in the big garden and two woolly sheep in a pen, which were our pets. And a huge sheepdog. Then when the war came that little routine got broken up a bit, though they went on with their daily readings. My father was too old to fight in the Second World War but he became an air-raid warden. I can remember him being called out to help every time there was a siren.

I was eight when the war broke out, and we moved to Tunbridge Wells for a short time. Then my father arranged to buy a similar business in Downe, near Farnborough [part of the Bromley Rural District in north-west Kent]. It was quite

fig 4. The Phipps family (uncle and aunt on left) in the garden at Leigh, 1933

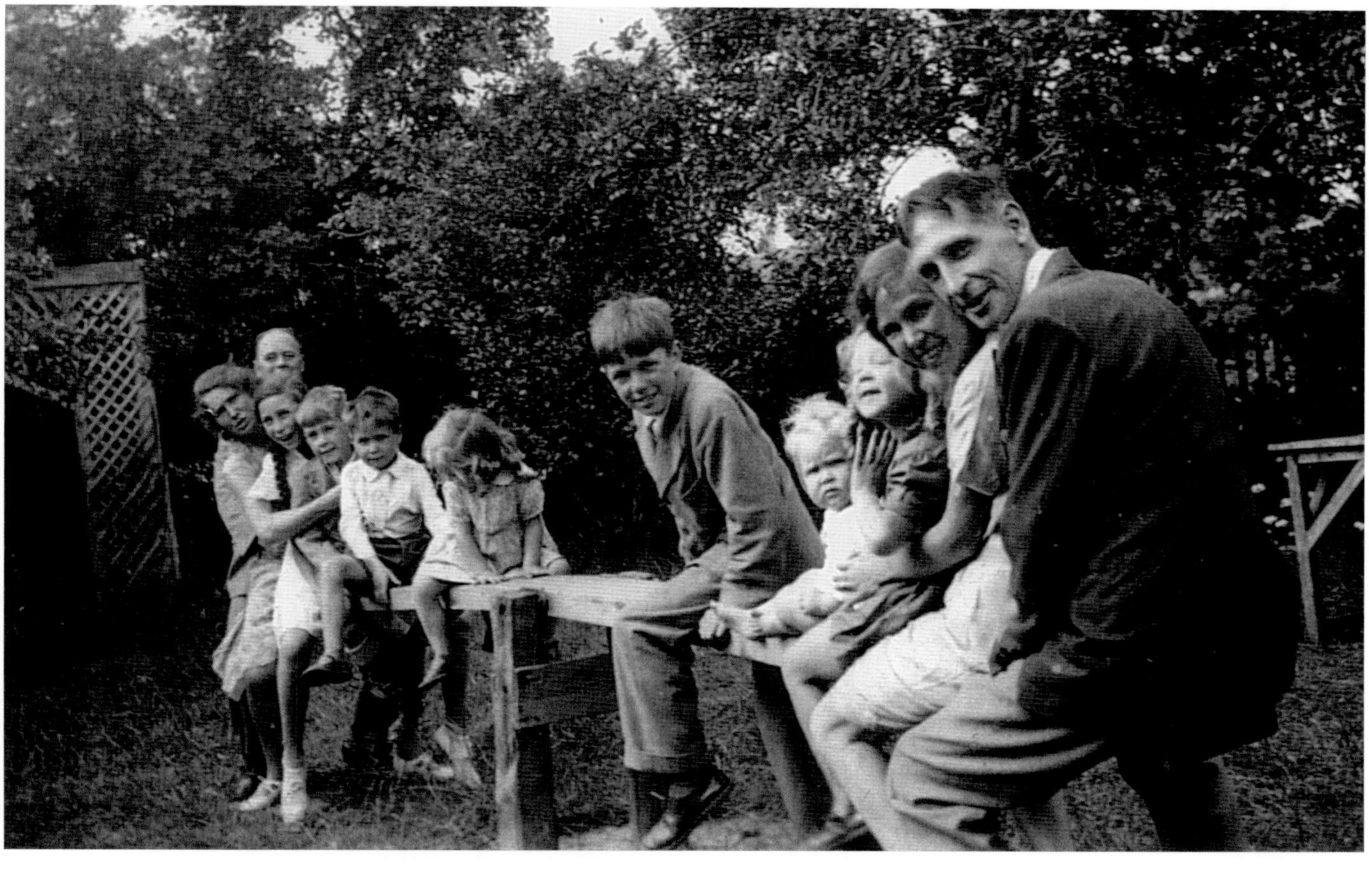

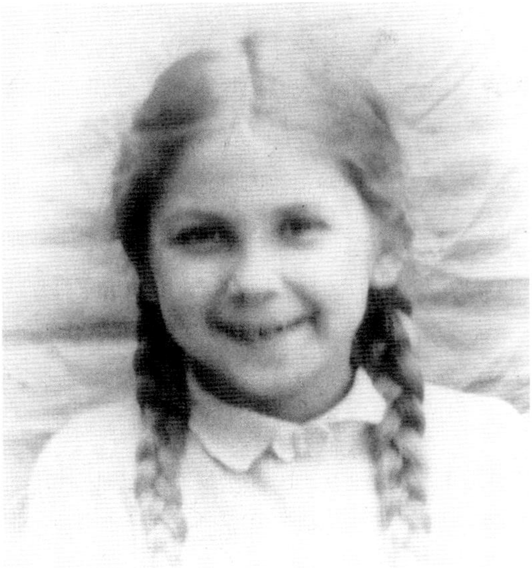

fig 5. Rose's school photograph, 1936

substantial enterprise and they employed people to help in the bake-house. My mother worked in the post office bit and did the ledger and the accounts. There was also room for two or three tables in the shop and my mum used to do morning coffee. There was one old boy called Mr Bennell, who used to come in and have coffee, who was particularly interested that I wanted to study art. He took a huge interest in me and eventually left me some money. He was obviously lonely, and it was fate that he came into my life. He took me to London to see *Aida*, and to art galleries. I remember going to the National Gallery with him really clearly, and seeing the Piero della Francescas – *The Baptism* and *The Nativity*.

Religion was still extremely important, but it dominated life less. As Rose remembers:

When we got to Downe the Gospel Hall gradually shut up after a year because there weren't enough people going. So we then switched to the Baptist Chapel. I liked the Sunday School and the Youth Club. All the children were expected to help a lot in the shop. We didn't ever have Saturdays off, and were expected to work in the holidays too. We were popular: a big family in the centre of the village. We lived at the bakery at first and then we rented rather a smart-looking house called Dunedin, in High Elms Road, which had a place where we kept pigs. My parents didn't ever go to pubs or anything like that and they were tremendously energetic. There were texts on the walls, like 'Christ is the Head of this House', but no pictures.

In those days before wall-to-wall television and computer screens, children made their own entertainment and sharpened their imaginations through invention, both in terms of story-telling and games. There was no chance to read fiction or expand the mind in that way, for Mrs Phipps was not exactly tolerant in her approach to freedom of thought. Downe was also famous for being the former home of Charles Darwin, who had lived in Down House on the edge of the village. Rose recalls:

There was a picture of Darwin, an old man with a big beard and big hat on, in the Village Hall and everybody was very proud of it. Everybody except my mother, who used to shake her fist at him when she went past.

Then came another move, a temporary one this time, but again dictated by the war. In 1944 the family was evacuated to North Wales, as Rose recounts:

It was the last bit of bombing of the war, with the doodlebugs coming over, and in Downe we were very near Biggin Hill aerodrome. It was very dangerous and children were to be evacuated,

fig 6. Rose the student

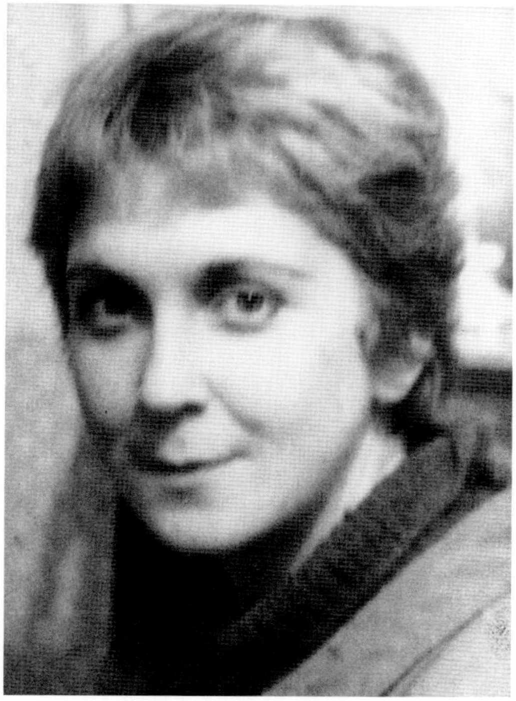

and because my mother had quite a lot of children, she was made a warden. She took us to North Wales, and it was great – I liked it a lot. Moira stayed behind to look after my father and Robert was already doing his first year with the Royal Electrical Mechanical Engineers. It was David and me and the three younger ones. We were billeted for about four months on a funny old farmer, quite near Hell's Mouth, which is a lovely big bay where I learnt to swim. Italian prisoners of war were working on the farms and singing away. We went to chapel on Sundays as usual, and sometimes it was totally in Welsh. I remember learning a whole chunk of Romans from the New Testament in Welsh. I can recite it now. What goes in at that age really stays. There was only one sad bit, when our mother went off for a walk to get away from us all and didn't come back for hours. We got really worried, but she'd only fallen asleep on the mountain.

Back in England, I went to school in Orpington. I liked it there, particularly art and music. Right from the start, because of all the hymn-singing, I could harmonise and sing alto to anybody's soprano. We always had a piano in the house. Robert played very well. My brother David and I used to cycle to Orpington school and back, eight miles a day. I was always keen on the art classes, and I loved reading all the books – like Thomas Hardy – we didn't have at home. We didn't really have books in the house except religious ones. My mum liked C.S. Lewis – *The Screwtape Letters*. When I left Orpington I went for a short while to Bromley Art School, two terms. Then my parents said if I was to do art, which seemed to be my bent, I must get my school certificate so I could teach.

So they took me away from Bromley Art School, much to my disgust, and sent me to a school at Bickley, also near Bromley, when I was 15. It was a girls' technical college spread between Bickley, Chislehurst and Sidcup, so I used to travel a lot. I got my school certificate then. My first art teacher was a Mr Greenwood at Chislehurst, the only male on the staff. He was encouraging, he believed in it all. He was called Ernest Greenwood and I wrote to him recently – he was almost a hundred – as I saw a watercolour by him at the Bankside Gallery. He remembered me. I still have red chalk drawings I did in his class.

Rose developed the habit of keeping a diary early on in life, to record important events and feelings, and to try to make sense of some of the new experiences that bombarded her. The first diary to survive dates from 1948, when Rose was 17, and begins with the serious injunction: 'THIS IS PRIVATE PROPERTY AND MUST NOT BE READ'. It is full of schoolgirl notes, of meetings with friends, her mother's activities, her father's health, and what her brothers and sisters got up to. The pervading tone is very religious and extends to appreciative remarks about preachers heard on a Sunday. In the intervals between homework, music, choir and helping out in the family store, Rose also manages a paper round. But more worrying states of mind keep breaking in. On 10 January she notes: 'Unhappy thinking', February 14: 'No Valentine's Card', and on July 4: 'Very lonely.' But she was fit and well (18 June: 'Had a medical today – 5 ft 9 in in height and 10 stone 7 lbs in weight, healthy I think everywhere except teeth'), and there were other preoccupations, chiefly art.

On 12 January she records: 'Went to the van Gogh painting exhibition at the Tate Gallery with the School', and when it snows hard in February, she not only goes tobogganing, but also paints a snow scene with a cedar tree. Gradually the focus draws closer. 13 July: 'Didn't go swimming. Drew in the evening.' But there are pangs of conscience the next month: 'Very disappointed because I can't have Geography with Miss Godly. Still I have Art. Oh dear I'm not a good Christian.' By 23 September she is writing: 'Art with Mr Greenwood. He really is a very serious and attractive person. I like him'. The next month she notes that she has been copying a Michelangelo male figure, and on 21 October, 'Mr Greenwood told me about my picture getting a certificate.' By mid-November: 'Art with Mr G. I'm starting a big piece of work with nudes. I'm so excited about it.'

But it was not all good news and record achievements. The entry for 3 February 1949 reads: 'Art with Mr Greenwood. Plant drawing not very good.' Just three days later, other thoughts burst their bounds: 'Oh dear, my heart is blackened with sin – all sorts and my mind seems so often to doubt but I do believe but I lack assurance. Dear Jesus do help me I pray.' She doesn't feel she is progressing much in art, perhaps because she is set to such tasks as drawing a pair of scales. By the end of March exam results have come through, and the figures are suggestive. Rose got 50 per cent for life drawing, but the following week only got 33 per cent in art as against 70 per cent in scripture. She reports on 9 May: 'Art with Mr Greenwood. Good but my life drawing is not very good.'

Nevertheless, with continual application and the encouragement of Mr Greenwood, Rose did manage a distinction in art. At this point, Mr Greenwood advised Mr and Mrs Phipps not to send Rose back to Bromley, as the teaching was not very distinguished there, but to choose Beckenham instead. As Rose remembers:

> For some reason they agreed, and I was sent to Beckenham Art School, when I was about 18. They probably regretted it afterwards, as it was the teachers at Beckenham who got me into the Royal College and launched me as an artist.

plate 1. ***Assembled sheet of studies***, 1948, ink and wash on paper, various sizes

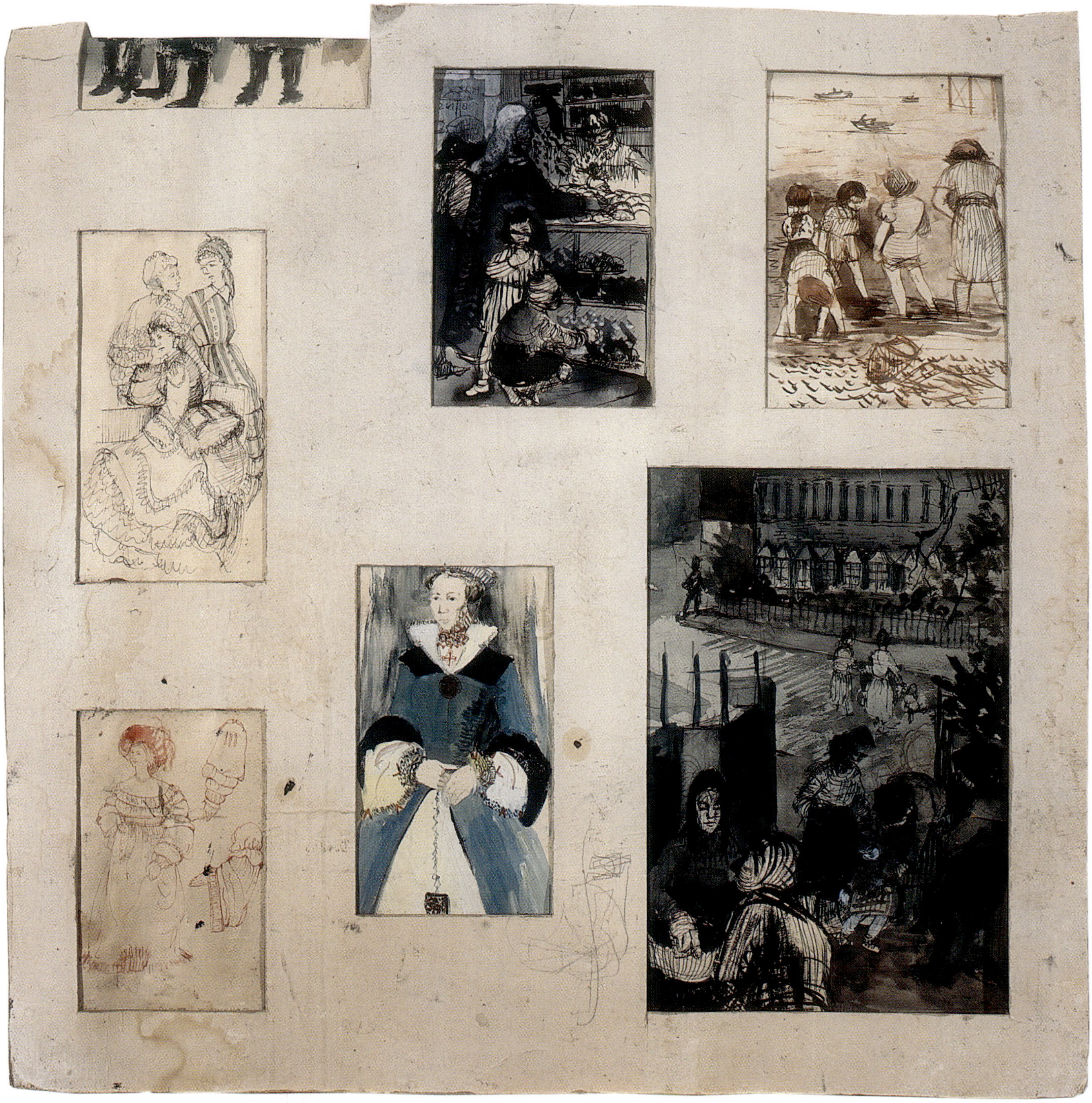

BECKENHAM ART SCHOOL

Art school was the real beginning of Rose's move away from the values of her upbringing, and her time at Beckenham (1949–53) marked the first stages of her rebellion. She continued to live at home, but each day she was subjected to a range of new feelings and emotions quite outside her experience. Her eyes were swiftly opened to a side of life never previously dreamt about. Rose comments:

I was still very under my parents' thumb and I still believed, but it was already beginning to perplex me. There was an ex-serviceman at Beckenham who was rather horrible, a bit older than us, who said 'what does your father do?' I replied 'oh, he's a baker' and he said to me 'no wonder you look like a doughnut', or something really scathing. I thought well … how does that fit with my religious beliefs?

It was a real shock to Rose when people were habitually unpleasant to each other. She tried not to think too much about this and instead buried herself in the great adventure of being finally at art school.

I studied illustration and calligraphy for the first year at Beckenham and then I specialised in painting. There was life drawing in a studio with a coke-burning stove, and the excitement of drawing the naked figure. Both men and women were nude. I remember going home on the bus and making sure my nude drawings didn't show – it was still considered a bit naughty. And we did anatomy, and got to know all the bones and muscles. There was not much difference between that and a medical training really. I enjoyed that – I've always taken to the figure. I also painted still-lifes, from set-ups in the studio or you could bring your own. I did a bit of each. For instance, I brought in rhododendrons to put in a white metal bowl in the studio, on a block, with a screen behind. I could have done a very academic painting of that but somehow I didn't. I did the space business instead. Not landscapes so much at that time.

This is a description of one of Rose's best early paintings, *Interior, Beckenham Art School* (1950, plate 2):

I could have attempted an academic painting of this subject, instead my feeling for objects in space predominated. This must have been instinctive as I had not seen many other pictures that could have influenced me. The use of thin paint to divide the painting, and the tilt of the screen to give tension within the work, make this a key painting in my development. I always have it on my walls at home.

Beckenham was a much smaller school than Bromley, and perhaps because of that the teaching really was much better. Rose thought the teachers were brilliant, particularly Mr Freeth, who taught her, and Wolfie Cohen, who taught her friend and graphic design student Alan Green (plate 3).

I remember Tom Freeth coming round. He didn't say much, and it meant a lot to be praised ever. On one occasion I thought I'd made a rather formless mess and he said 'I think we'll make a

plate 2. ***Interior, Beckenham Art School***, 1950, oil on canvas, 91.4 x 71.1 cm (36 x 28 in)

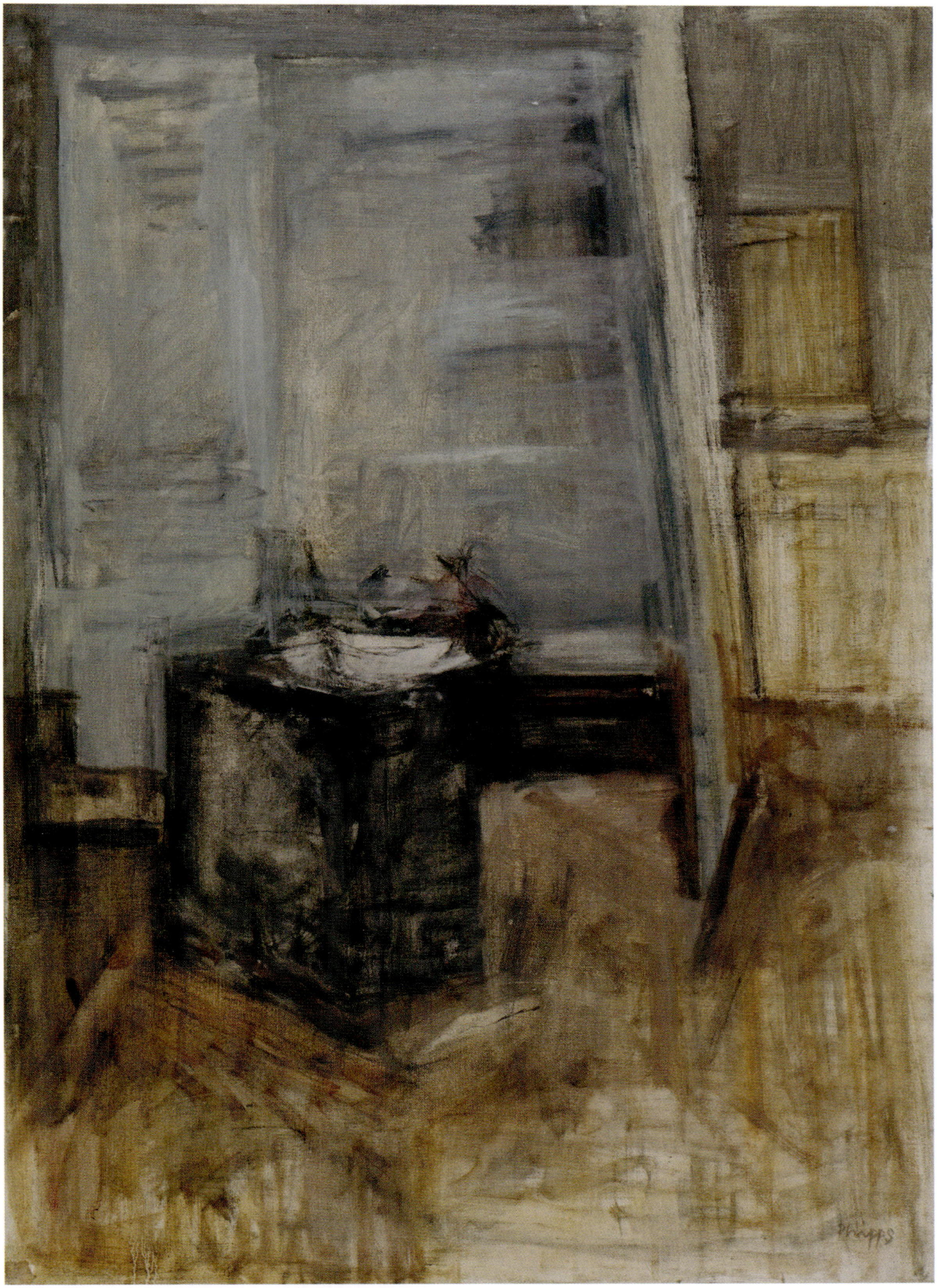

painter out of you'. I'm sure he said it because my picture wasn't tight, but somehow free. That was something I did intuitively and he must have recognised that. I had to do a thesis while I was there, which I wrote on the relationship between Dutch drawings and paintings. I was looking at those funny old landscape painters, the de Hoochs and all that, and Rembrandt as well. And Flemish painting I was interested in – their lovely small nudes. It's a long time ago, I wish I'd kept more from then.

Rose was learning not just about art, but also about people and the way she affected them. Her natural enthusiasm and good nature has always made it easy for her to find friends, and it was no different in the new context of art school. She recalls:

Alan Green was my first boyfriend, when I was 18, at Beckenham. I was trying to get him to come to chapel with me and get converted and he I suppose was trying to get me to go to bed with him, which I would have considered very sinful at that time. I don't think I even allowed him to kiss me. We used to go around together and have our coffee breaks together and I'd draw him. We didn't go up to London much but I did get to meet his mum and dad.

Rose and Alan actually remained close friends for some years and exchanged letters regularly, especially when Alan went off to do his National Service in Korea and Rose was sent to a sanatorium to be treated for tuberculosis. The tone of Alan's letters (which Rose kept) is high-minded and respectful. He addresses his friend quite formally as 'Dear Rosemary' and confides his enthusiasms and self-doubts. They discuss books, art, their ambitions and changing states of mind. Youthful, serious letters, they are touching in their affectionate earnestness.

At the time Rose wrote of how excited she was by Freeth's lectures about artistic interpretation. In 1951 she noted: 'Painting is an isolation, a concentration.' All very high-minded and in keeping with the tone of Alan Green's letters. With reference to her thesis subject, Rose wrote: 'The modern painter in fact has to be more courageous [than a Dutch seventeenth-century one] in the face of the public, because 9 out of 10 people just regard it as fanatical without trying to see what really made the painter arrive at that stage.' This even applied to her own family apparently, for in January 1952 she had a big argument about money with them. In her diary she writes: '"Art is fanatical" – I suppose according to Daddy (though I love him dearly).'

In a note on the back page of her 1952 diary, Rose has quoted Dostoevsky: 'If you love you belong to God. Love redeems everything, saves everything.' It's not clear whether she was thinking of spiritual love or its more physical manifestation in connection with this, but from another note it's clear that she was striving to keep her work on a high level. She evidently believed in praising the wonders of the world: 'I will give back of these things, their soul – their relation in space – their relation to each other – their colour, deepness and shape.' If the expression is exalted, the ambition is evident, and it's one that has continued to sustain her to this day.

plate 3. ***Alan Green*** (sketchbook), 1950, ink on paper, 31.1 x 21 cm ($12\frac{1}{4}$ x $8\frac{1}{4}$ in)

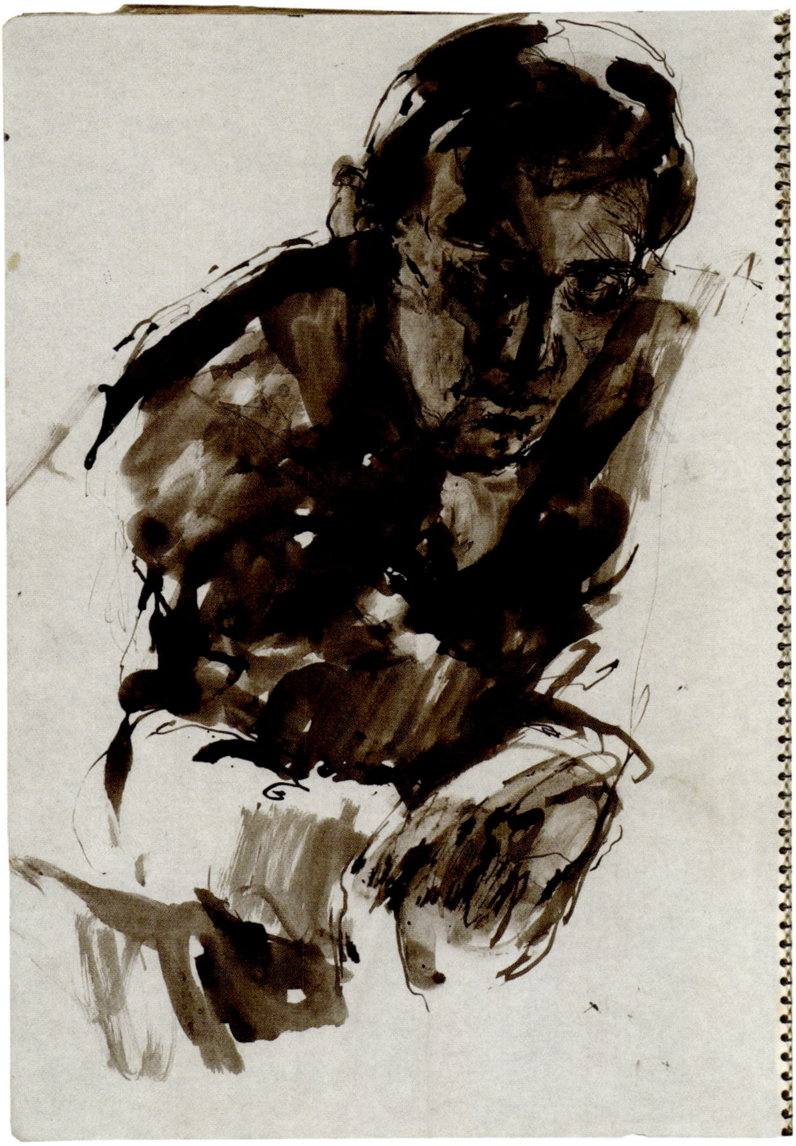

Rose's time at Beckenham was like walking a tightrope. Exposed to many and tempting new influences, she nevertheless wanted to please her parents, who were, after all, making this training possible. To spare their anxieties, Rose refused to attend any of the art school parties, but her mind was roaming freely among the thoughts and doctrines then fashionable. She recalls:

It was fascinating really. My friend Rozanne Palmer was reading all these existential books, like Sartre and Kafka, which I started to read too. I took them home and my mother put them in the summer-house, wouldn't have them indoors. But I took to them all. I was probably a great worry to her and heartless, too, by that time. It was a question of going for what I wanted and I'm really glad I had that in me. So I did Intermediate and studied graphic design and then went on to the Painting School and did my NTD there [National Teachers' Diploma]. My poor parents were still thinking it was OK, I was going to be an art teacher. Then unknown to them I took the Royal College Entrance Exam.

My eldest brother, Robert, was a good influence on me. He was five years older and adored me. He died quite young. He argued with my parents all the time about me and his own beliefs. He wouldn't be baptised – he was the only one of us. I was baptised when I was 14. He kept an eye on me. When I got accepted by the Royal College and my parents thought it was too much, that I shouldn't go, then he said: 'If you don't let her go, you'll have to deal with me. I won't have any more relationship with you.' He was a really important person in my life.

ROYAL COLLEGE

THE GREATEST CHALLENGE facing Rose was the reconciliation of her religious beliefs – or at least the residue of her strict religious upbringing – with the new world and very different type of life she was now entering. Her determination to go to the Royal College at all costs indicated the seriousness of her commitment to becoming an artist. But she felt she had to justify to herself her decision. As she says:

I tried desperately to believe that whatever I had in the way of talent was a giving. Not whether I was good or bad, but just to do it and be dedicated about doing it and quite disciplined. Having got that bit straight, what follows is that you develop by doing it. You don't have ideas about what you want to do, you just do it.

She wasn't theory driven at all, but relied upon practice – the making of art.

I won a scholarship to the Royal College. Under the Labour Government my college fees were paid and I got a weekly allowance, which wasn't very much, but everything was really cheap, and you were expected to work in the holidays as a waitress or something. I worked at Lyons Corner House, but I wasn't very good.

There was a selection committee for the Royal College. You had to submit six pictures, which you sent in and they looked at. Then you were either invited for an interview or not. The still-life I did at Beckenham was one of them and probably some life paintings. So I was asked for interview. There were Robert Buhler, Carel Weight, Ruskin Spear, Rodrigo Moynihan all sitting in a row. At the time I was still on this truth thing and talking about Christ. Buhler teased me about it much much later at the Chelsea Arts Club, saying they had doubts. I think that to get in you either had to be incredibly beautiful or else slightly eccentric, and I probably passed muster as the second. The real beauties were girls like Pauline Boty. People who wore make-up. At that time I didn't wear any make-up at all.

Rose started in the autumn of 1953.

For the first three weeks at the college I travelled up from Downe in Kent, but it was difficult and tiring and meant that I couldn't go to any of the college lectures. So I talked to my parents about it – they weren't very pleased – and I said I was going to get a room. First of all I got digs on the corner of Gloucester Road with a Christian Scientist landlord. Quite a big corner room with lots of windows. It was thrilling – funny old paintings on the wall. There was a big one in a gold frame, a portrait of an ancestor or something. The portrait I did of Quentin Crisp that I put into the Sketch Club and which got talked about by Basil Taylor needed a frame. The one on the portrait in my room fitted exactly, so I borrowed it. It just suited that painting. I put it back afterwards but it certainly gave something to my picture.

This life painting actually won the RCA Sketch Club prize. Its presentation may have helped, but it was undoubtedly the lively sensitivity and the sense of discovery of objects in space that the distinguished art historian Basil Taylor recognised and applauded.

plate 4. ***Life Painting***, 1954,
oil on canvas,
91.4 x 70.5 cm (36 x 27¾ in),
Royal College of Art Collection

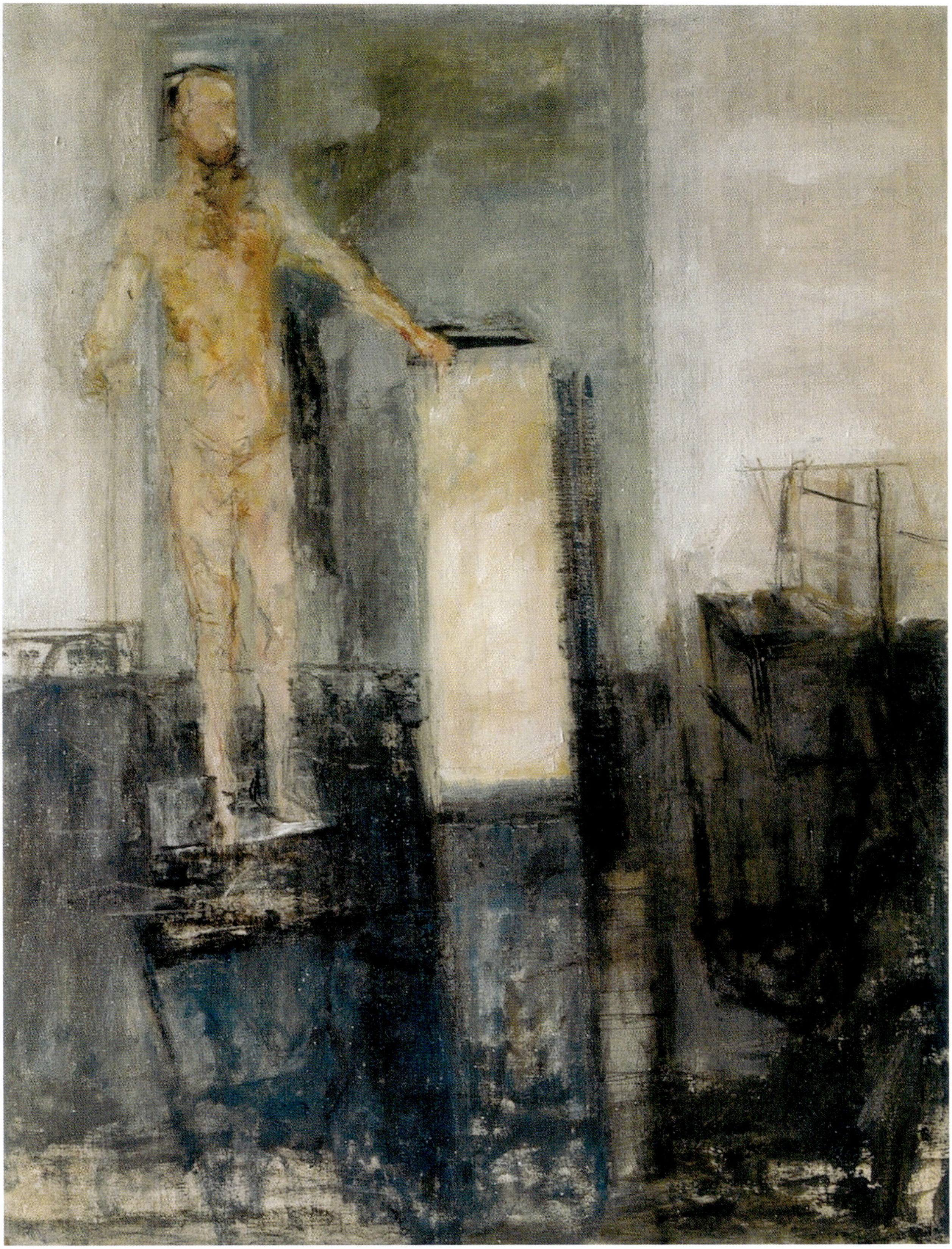

Social life at the college could be daunting, and Rose sought out bases that would be reassuring.

I immediately joined the Christian Union and the Madrigal Society, which took up two evenings a week. I enjoyed both, but the Christian Union was almost like a lost cause for me. I was very wavering by that time. I went rather tentatively to the college hops. That was all rather worrying – which way to go in my first year.

Alan Green was not among Rose's fellow students in that first year as he was still doing National Service, but there were young artists such as Cyril Reason and Gerald Harding, who Rose remembers as 'really intense; he used to get right near the model'. Of the more senior students she says

there was Frank Auerbach of course, and Leon Kossoff was still there then. I remember being in awe of him and was very careful not to life-draw next to him as you'd get literally showered in charcoal. [John] Bratby was there and so was Jean [Cooke, Bratby's first wife]. She became my friend because I loved her paintings. He was very frightening. Because I was friendly with Jean, he accused me of locking her in my room in Gloucester Road. He'd temporarily lost her, she'd probably run away. I told him she hadn't even been round. He was a horrible bully. Sometimes Jean was missing for two or three days because he'd locked her in their flat.

I used to go round with a bunch of students from Sheffield – Brian Fielding, Esmé Ellis and Julia Wolstenholme, who married Frank Auerbach. She was a very talented painter, more talented than anybody else, really. She was also lovely to look at, spirited and intelligent and all the men fell in love with her.

Rozanne Palmer, who Rose had known at Beckenham, was also a good friend.

We used to use the V&A cafe quite a lot, which was next door. There was a door through into the museum and I drew statues from the collections, as I did at the British Museum – the Elgin Marbles. Also at the Natural History Museum, where I drew skeletons.

That first year must have been both exciting and intimidating. Let off the parental leash, Rose was at first too uncertain of herself to sin too liberally. Instead she threw herself into her work and rather neglected herself. She didn't eat properly and worried about boys. Her conscience was in conflict: she wanted to have a fulfilling relationship but she didn't want to be damned as a scarlet woman. The one person who really understood her was her elder brother Robert, and she had long debates with him about her life and hopes. It was probably through this intimate contact with him that she contracted the TB that he was suffering from in a rather advanced form. Already depleted in energy from the unfamiliar demands of student life and her somewhat rackety existence, Rose became very ill, and was forced to leave college and enter a sanatorium.

plate 5. ***Animal Skeleton (Natural History Museum)***, 1954,
ink on paper,
22.9 x 30.5 cm (9 x 12 in)

plate 6. ***Interior***, 1954,
ink on paper,
30.5 x 22.9 cm (12 x 9 in)

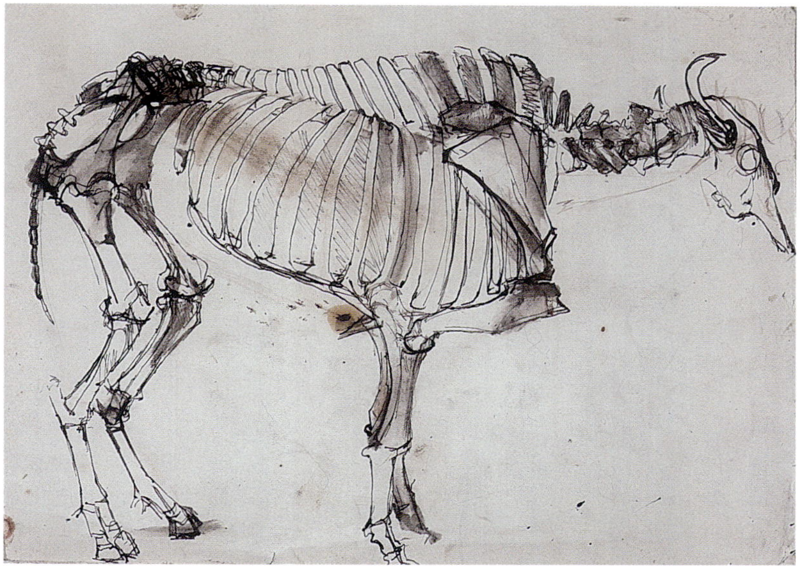

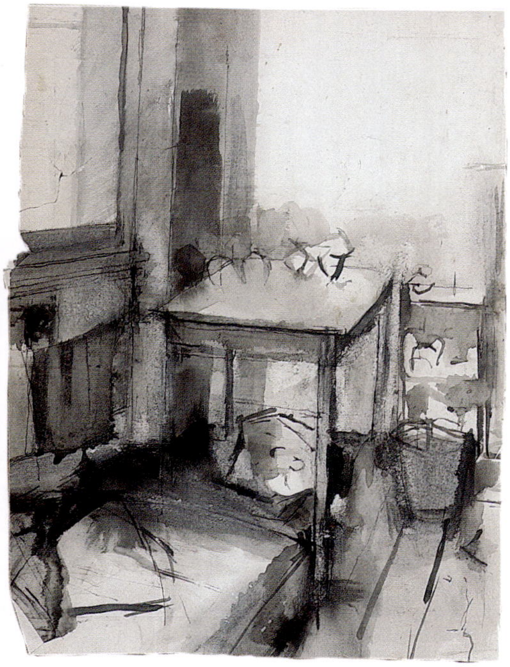

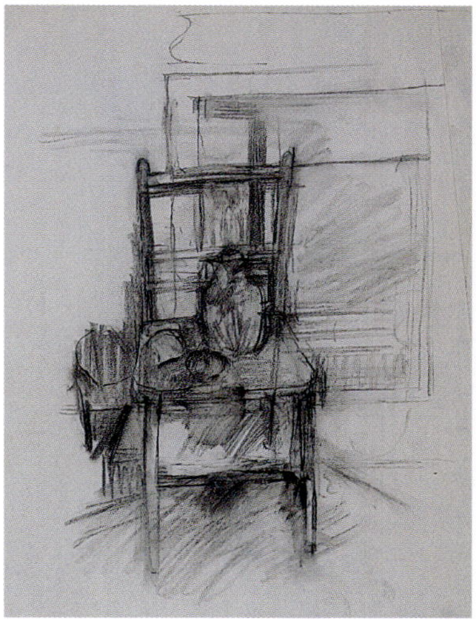

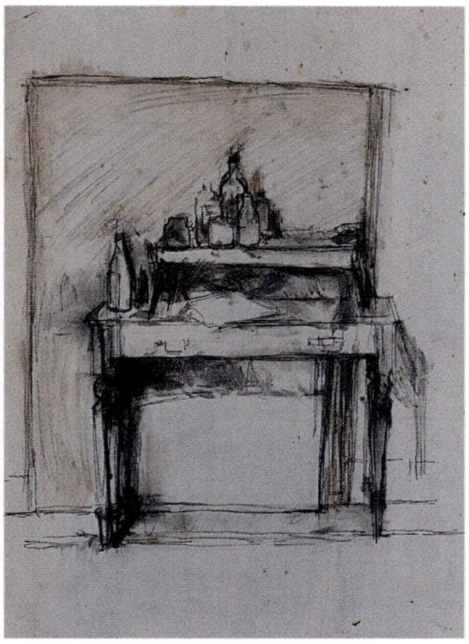

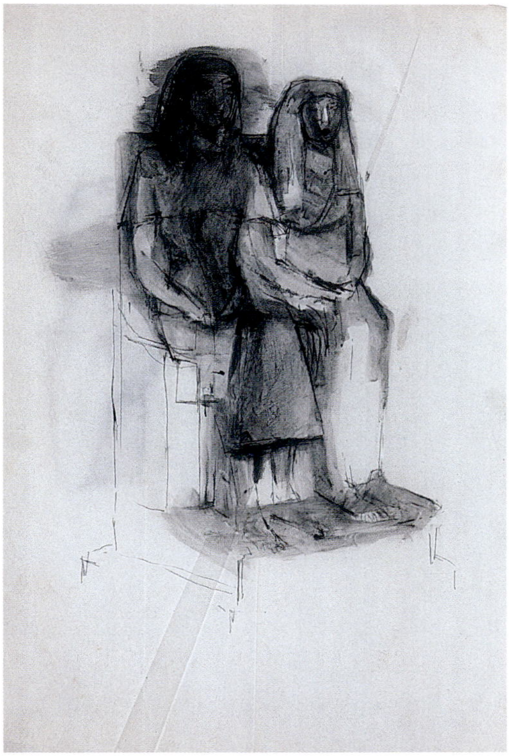

plate 7. ***Still-life on Chair***, 1954,
ink on paper,
43.2 x 33 cm
(17 x 13 in)

plate 8. ***Table-top***, 1954,
ink on paper,
43.2 x 33 cm (17 x 13 in)

plate 9. ***Pharaohs (British Museum)***, 1954,
ink on paper,
43.2 x 33 cm (17 x 13 in)

ILLNESS

HER ILLNESS was quite evidently real - she was coughing blood and in danger of her life – but its origins may have had their roots in the stress she was under. Her old life in the Brethren was under real threat from the new Bohemia of art school and post-war liberation. Rose was in a tremendous muddle. She later explained that her emotions/illness were the equivalent of being unable to cope, almost as if she were inviting death in some strange way. Thankfully, that dire solution was rejected, but a systems breakdown of a different sort did occur. It was as if the mind was saying it couldn't handle all the emotional and mental trauma, so the body responded by providing a complete break or distraction – serious illness. Rose was forced to take a pause and reconsider her priorities. She was run-down physically from her first year in college and in no condition to fight tuberculosis unaided.

As Rose recalls:

In the summer of 1954 I was diagnosed with TB. Roger de Grey [one of the tutors during this period] found me in the college staff room. I was walking along the corridor when I suddenly felt extremely faint, so I went to the nearest room and sat down. He called the college doctor. Roger de Grey wrote a very nice letter to my parents saying they were sorry they hadn't noticed that I'd been ill and when I was better I'd be very welcome to go back. He was kind to me, though Moynihan was more important to me as an artist and teacher. Robin Darwin was the principal then. I didn't have any contact with him but my mother did. She went up to collect my belongings after I'd been taken ill and was very cross because she'd asked for an interview with him and he was very impatient. He didn't want to see anybody's mother and was sitting down to an enormous lunch of lobsters. Also, the Darwin connection with Downe didn't help. She didn't approve of anyone called Darwin.

I was put in the Foot's Cray Ward at the Farnborough Hospital in Kent, and my friend Rozanne went off to spend the summer in the south of France. She told me there was a notice on the college noticeboard saying that anybody who'd been near me or danced with me ought to be X-rayed. That was because I had an active form of TB, and thank goodness I didn't pass it on to anyone.

The sanatorium was near home and my mother came to see me and she said it was God's punishment on me. I was very upset and requested that only my father came to see me in future. The year in the sanatorium was spent resting and reading. I read enormous amounts – lots of Proust and Thomas Mann. The first couple of months I was on complete bed rest, then after that I had a little wheelchair and they organised me to do a Christmas mural for the ward. I really enjoyed that, painting on big sheets of paper in poster colour. I liked the other women there. The things they talked about – what went on with their husbands!

I got to know a boy called John in the men's TB ward who was an architectural student at Regent Street Poly. He was about my age and handsome. We had a film show when the men and the women, all in their dressing gowns, met and started chatting. He and I had the same interests. He'd had a girlfriend so he was a bit experienced, but that relationship had broken down. So he and I decided we'd creep out at night and meet in the Consulting Room. That's when I lost my virginity. It wasn't much fun and rather furtive. When we both got out of hospital we did meet and go to bed properly, but we each got absorbed in our own colleges and drifted apart. He wasn't right for me and I wasn't right for him, probably. But that was my introduction to it all.

I had to be pumped up with a thousand cc's of air every week. My lungs had been healed but they had to be kept at half-mast for three years, so I had to keep going back to this place in Kent. My illness had been very serious and it could have killed me. There was a shadow on one lung and a quite considerable hole in the other. They arrested the tubercle with a new drug and after a year's resting they let me back to college. I fought to get well and back to college and didn't even mind looking slightly pregnant with all that air in me. There was just a scar at the end of three years.

RE-START

IT WAS THE AUTUMN of 1955 by the time Rose returned to college. Her fellow-students were a year ahead and there had been a new intake while she had been coming to terms with the fundamental question of her existence as an artist.

When I came back to college, Rozanne had moved on and I found a new friend called Fabian. It was her first year. She was very beautiful and she also had a good singing voice and we teamed up a bit. We actually dressed up and sang in parts at a college review. I had some fun then, I enjoyed it much more when I came back from the sanatorium.

Rose was now reconciled to her new life and made a healing break with her past. She had also taken the plunge in relationships, and henceforth men were to play an important part in her life.

The students in Rose's second year were very different and the atmosphere had changed. In her first year, Auerbach, Kossoff and Bratby were the dominant influences. In her second, it was somehow less dark – the mood of the art had lightened and the shadow of illness had lifted from her shoulders. John Minton was still there teaching. She remembers him as

totally charming, a lovely man. He was good at Sketch Club criticism. I remember finally going to a college dance. He was coming down the Common Room stairs and I was going up and he said 'Why have you got such a miserable face? Look, cheer up – have a double whisky!' I always remember him saying that. I think he wanted everyone to be swinging.

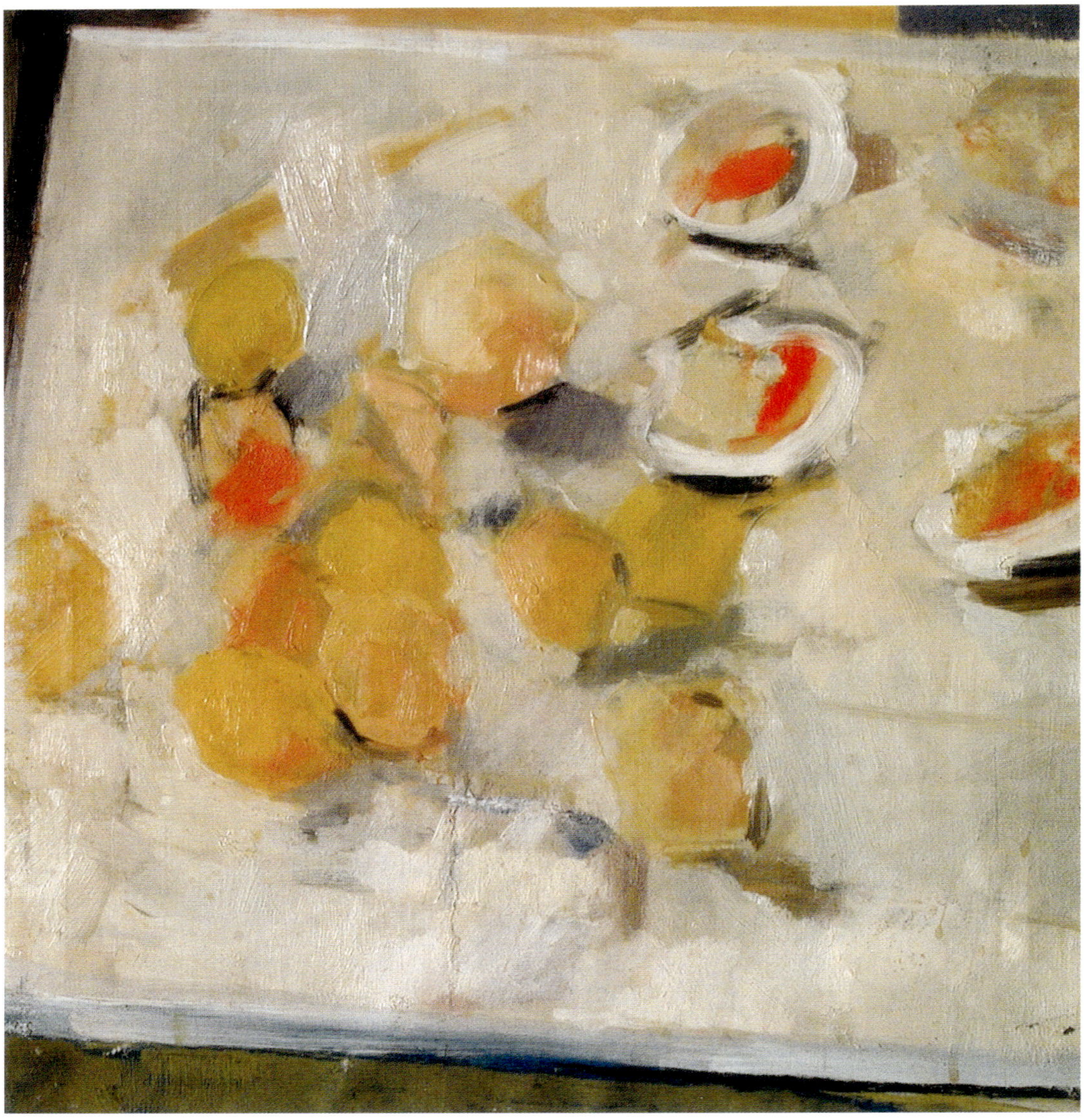

plate 10. ***Still-life***, 1956, oil on canvas, 50.8 x 50.8 cm (20 x 20 in), Royal College of Art Collection

He was a lot lighter than other teachers there. I rather avoided Ruskin Spear because I saw him make a girl cry by telling her to go home and do her knitting. Buhler once painted over one of my paintings in the still-life room, when I was trying rather tentatively to paint the objects on the table. He said 'You must get some direct forms' and he pushed the brush like this and like that. I couldn't go on with it after that because it was not how I worked. [She said nothing at the time, but minded afterwards. 'I feel very sore about my painting now. I am not courageous at all', she wrote in her diary.] But it may have helped me on the next painting to be more direct about composition because you do have to know more or less where to put things.

The tutors came round in groups. Basil Taylor was rather dry I remember. Carel Weight was my tutor when I got back from hospital. He said I was a good colourist. That small still-life that the college kept – that's got subtle colour in it [plate 10]. I think I went back to tonal painting later. I didn't really go in for tonal painting, I was more interested in space, as in that Beckenham Art School still-life. Like Giacometti.

As part of the course work, students were expected to write a thesis, and Rose chose to write about the visionary painters – Blake, Samuel Palmer, Turner. She remembers:

I had to do a transcription of an Old Master. I don't know where it is now, but I chose Piero's *Resurrection*. One picture that has survived is a life painting of Frank Bowling [plate 11], who was a model then. [Bowling is himself a distinguished painter and now a Royal Academician.] He chatted up Paddy Kitchen, who was the college secretary, and married her.

Rose lived in a tiny room on the Bayswater Road for a time before moving to Elm Park Road in Chelsea. She recalls:

I saw an advertisement in a shop window for an attic room to let to a student and it turned out to be Mr and Mrs Clive Gardiner. He was principal of Goldsmiths' at the time. There were lots of his paintings on the wall which were interesting. His work was a bit like the Bloomsbury Group, very influenced by French painters, so his paintings weren't really just academic, they were rather stylised. Clive had done a big mural on the wall as you went upstairs of figures in a sort of Picasso-type way. Quite impressive. His wife Louisa had been at the Slade and still wore long black dresses and painted straight landscapes. It was a painting atmosphere and I stayed for about six months before finding the Fulham Road flat. Their son Stephen, the architect and writer, used to come bustling in sometimes at the weekend with his first wife. I always saw him around afterwards. He was a sophisticated Chelsea presence.

Dino's was the cafe at South Kensington where perhaps we would go and have tea, and if we wanted a drink we went to the Hoop and Toy pub. When I went back to college after my illness I used to go to the Festival Hall with William Green who did the bicycle pictures. [Green was famous for riding a bicycle across the canvas instead of applying paint in more usual ways.] We went to the Festival Hall to hear Mahler and afterwards I was starving. He said he didn't believe in food. But I really liked good-looking people, and he was so limp and weak-faced though he was keen on music. Brian Fielding was very handsome, with a lovely mouth and a kind of Nureyev-type chiselled face. And Tony Messenger was divine-looking! He used to wear drainpipe trousers, a white shirt and a black jacket. He was in the painting school.

Of the other students, Rose comments:

I was rather in awe of Dick Smith, Robin Plummer and Robyn Denny who hung around in a group. Peter Blake was much more approachable. I was still friendly with Alan Green, who I really liked as a person. I did go to that famous American art show at the Tate in 1956 [*Modern Art in the United States*], but I think it got interpreted for me by people like Denny and Smith. I remember seeing Clyfford Still, Gorky, Gottlieb and Philip Guston, though the paintings that affected me most were the early Gustons, which I related to Monets. But American art didn't then influence me directly. It seemed to me that Denny and Smith were really the ones who soaked it up and started doing their versions of it in the big mural room.

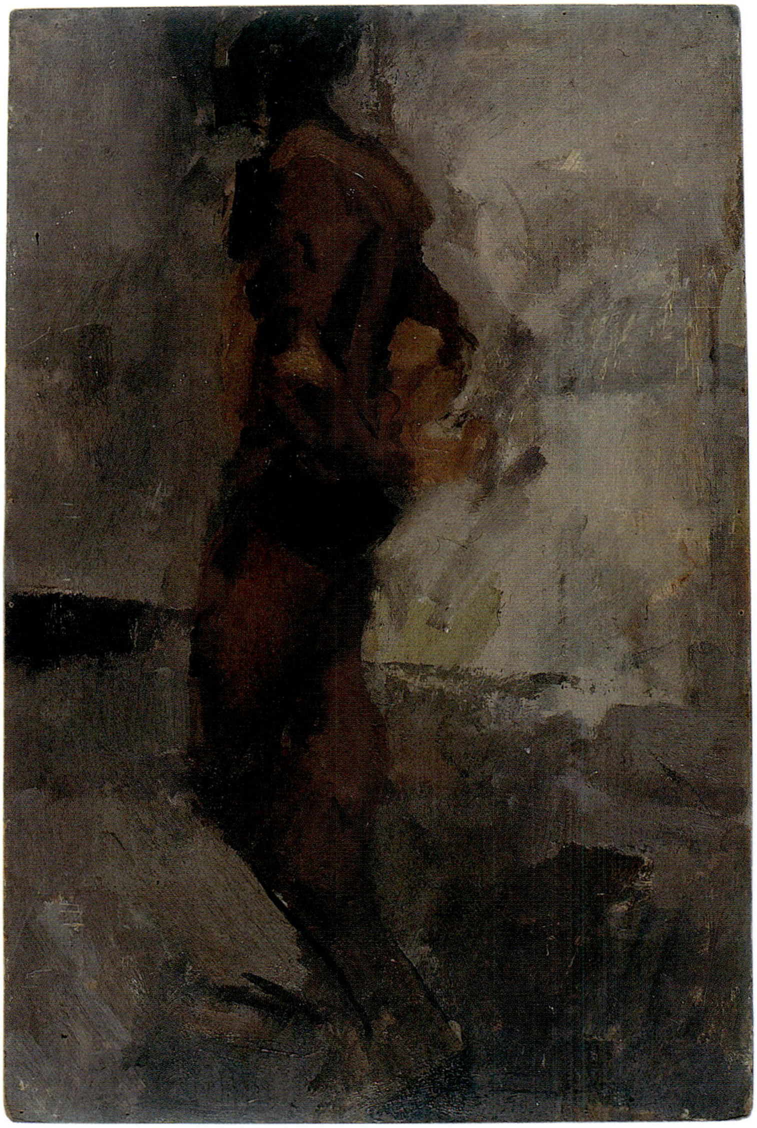

plate 11. ***Standing Male Figure***, 1956,
oil on board,
91.4 x 61 cm (36 x 24 in)

The daily tenor of Rose's life can be best gauged from the diary she kept for 1956. It begins fairly bleakly. 14 January: 'Spent the day in bed – didn't have a penny.' She's painting, at college, seeing Alan Green quite often and sometimes staying with him. As would become typical of the self-analytical tone of her diaries, she criticizes her own mental weakness but records that she is fighting a sense of inadequacy. Loneliness presents its usual forbidding countenance from time to time, but art remains a constant consolation – both her own and the good work of others. On 18 January she saw Frank Auerbach's first solo exhibition at Helen Lessore's Beaux-Arts Gallery. She notes that it 'impressed me more than I expected'.

She writes of pictures she is doing, a still-life and a life painting of a pregnant woman. On 21 February she attended a lecture by Basil Taylor on Stubbs, but passes no comment on it. More important is a memo to herself dated 3 March. 'Brian Fielding. Very nice but hopeless as he is very attached to that girl from the sculpture school. I suppose I must do something about my thoughts, not yet feelings, in this direction.' A couple of days later: 'Crit of life drawing by John Skeaping.' It was a typical student existence, full of ups and downs, although for Rose the added threat of illness was still in the background. But this cloud was lifting. She had been visiting the clinic to have check-ups and X-rays, and there was good news to report. On 8 March she wrote: 'Saw Dr Madigan, he said improvement. Right lung healed.'

On 9 March she records enigmatically: 'Alan came back here. I of course have broken all my vows. I am the dirtiest foulest person. I never keep my vows, yet when I paint I think I have God on my side then.' Art did gradually take the place of her religious feelings, and in effect became a substitute for religion. All the energies she had chanelled into trying to be devout were now re-directed towards being an artist. Rose has commented recently that, going back through her diaries and papers, she found that she was much more serious about painting then than she had remembered.

The injunction to herself to be careful about Brian Fielding, even though repeated a couple of weeks later, evidently did no good. 'A bit unhappy about B', reads one entry, closely followed by 'Brian gone to Sheffield, think about him quite a lot.' Personal happiness is such a huge and engrossing subject to the young, and Rose was no exception. One gets the impression from this diary in particular of a girl who is always trying to keep up emotional appearances – to appear balanced and self-possessed – but really rather terrified of succumbing to loneliness and somehow, in some unspecified way, going under.

Her relationship with painting, as her other all-consuming passion besides men, was equally complex. Sometimes it took her out of herself, at others it brought her even closer to home. On 20 March she writes: 'More interested in a painting. Using myself as model. Bought a big mirror to work from.' Yet a few days later she writes: 'When one is painting one is sad, sometimes very aware, and very unhappy. Yet one can easily forget that state when the painting is looked at and perhaps liked or disliked by others, and one is another person from the one that did the painting. How can one keep the same? It is so difficult.'

During this college period, her mother was still managing her finances for her, giving her an allowance to live on, doling out her grant money to her. Rose decided that she would henceforth take matters into her own hands, and take charge of her grant cheque herself. In the interim, however, she was forced to borrow money from college. She took a job at Shepherds Tavern in Mayfair – which she designates 'very tiring' – to help with her troubled finances. Julia Wolstenholme also worked there with her, and Auerbach used to drop in sometimes for a drink. In May, Rose opened her first bank account. The up-and-down relationship with her mother continued. Her mother sent her £2 when she was broke and didn't have enough cash to buy cigarettes or paint.

Meanwhile, she was still very uncertain about what she felt on the larger issues of existence. On 28 April she notes: 'Am wondering about returning to Christianity. It's almost beyond me to reject as I don't know what else there is.' Later, on 15 May, she writes as if in answer to herself: 'The only thing that matters is that one keeps one's value – and other people theirs, then they can mean something to each other. It's hard because one wants to envelop or be enveloped by certain people one admires.' On this score she chastised herself for not having the courage to stop seeing Brian. But as she says, she wanted to know him, and he remained a major presence at this time in her life.

The entry for 8 May reads: 'Sketch Club criticism. Brian had his painting spoken about. Alan and I did not.' Later that summer, Rose notes that she has been to see a display of paintings by Suzanne Valadon, but she makes no comment about them, positive or negative. For 23–4 August she writes: 'Have had Alan staying with me. Have been trying [to] do some paintings of him', so that friendship was evidently continuing. In the autumn and back at college, Rose records the visit of another, more sympathetic, tutor. 16 October: 'C Weight came round to see my paintings – showed real interest. He is kind, bought me a meal and some goods.' Yet, in spite (or perhaps because) of such encouragement, Rose was severe on her output. Five days later she writes unsparingly: 'Did a small affected landscape.'

Her health was by now much better and she had been taken off most of her medication, only needing regular check-ups to ensure that nothing untoward occurred. The mood of lightness that this news must have conferred is echoed in the diary entry for 26 October: 'Brian and I jived at College dance. It was a sweet, memorable evening, more than I ever hoped for.' It seems that there was a new closeness and understanding between the two, for the next month they were painting together. 19 November: 'Brian posed for me for a painting.' 20 November: 'I posed for Brian today.'

In early December, Rose returned to the family home for Christmas, but she had no intention of stopping work. One entry reads: 'Mrs Bennett posing for me nude. She's good.' A friend and respectable neighbour offering to model without clothes must have seemed a bit fast, even in 1956. And what on earth did Rose's parents think of such goings-on? Actually, the extrovert Mrs Bennett posed in the privacy of her own home and Rose's parents were none the wiser. Later that month Rose records the painting of a landscape, an altogether more demure occupation for a young single lady. Meanwhile, to earn some cash, she worked in the Post Office helping with the Christmas rush.

The habit of keeping a daily diary – or at least some kind of regular record of events – persisted into the new year. In 1957, Rose notes down her London address as '30 Elm Park Road, Chelsea SW3, Telephone No FLA 0661'.

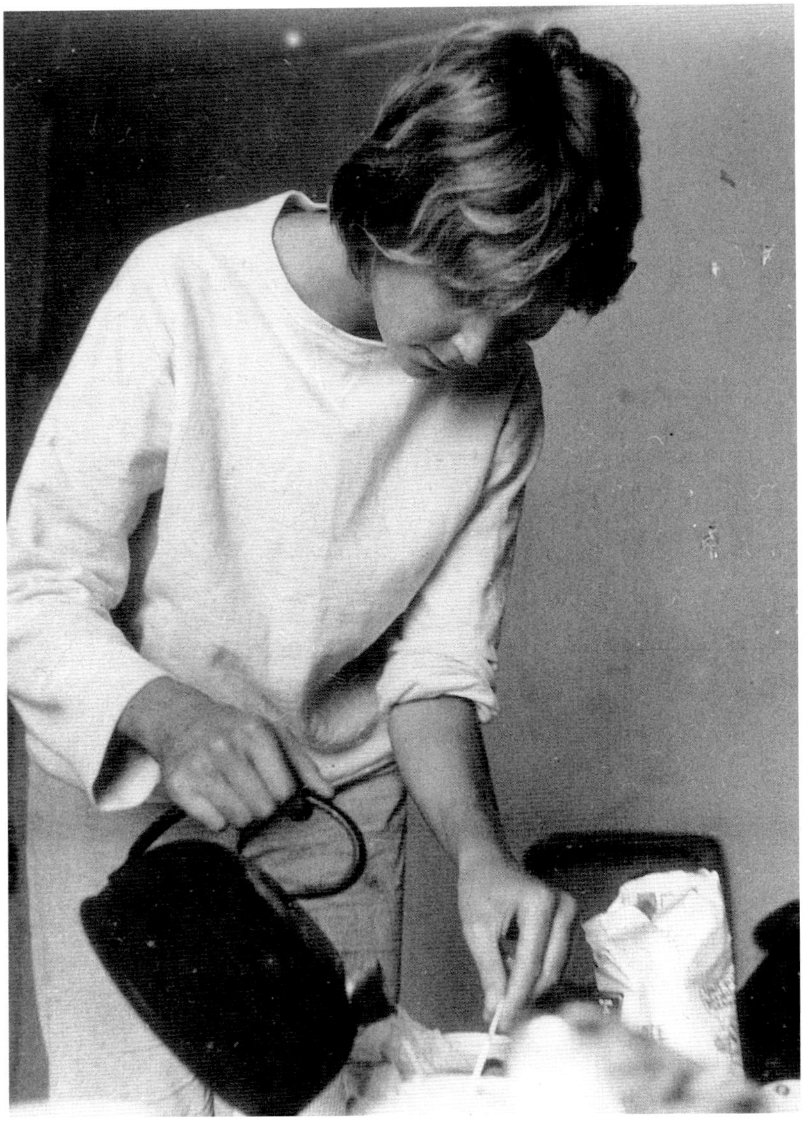

fig 7. Rose at the Royal College of Art, 1957

The year began early back at college, with life painting by 8 January. The next day she records: 'Saw Bratby exhibition with Brian and six young painters. A little disturbing.' The relationship with Brian Fielding was continuing, but not very successfully. It evidently troubled Rose. On 22 January she writes: 'Not looking forward to this week. I don't know if I can feel real enthusiasm for life and painting again – I don't [know] how to act at all in life.'

Subsequent entries alternate 'Wasting time' with 'Drawing'. Then comes a more passionate outburst, on 31 January: 'Very angry with myself.

I have thrown away a lot of kind gestures on other friends' parts for Brian and he doesn't care a damn and I have damaged myself in the process always saving evenings for him and hanging around and the worst of it is that he knows. God! How I hate him at times.'

It has to be said, however, that Rose had certain other irons in the fire, though her dissatisfaction seems to have been general at this time. She writes [1 February]: 'I ... have decided to ignore all my relationships. God help me, I'm in a mess with them.' Painting as ever proved an active distraction. On 4 February she notes: 'Have put 3 paintings in the Young Contemporaries.' Two of these were accepted and she was notified within four days. The student show was evidently organised at the very last minute, for within the week Rose attended the Private View. 'Went to Young Contemporaries opening', she writes. 'My paintings didn't look very good. Whole show rather showy.'

At this point Rose was painting mostly large (by her standards) still-lifes, measuring 3 ft by 4 ft. She later commented that:

> They were influenced by Nicolas de Staël and loosely painted in various greys. That type of still-life has been a recurring interest in all my years of painting. In later years the greys became richer as I learnt more about mixing paint.

Money was a perpetual worry. By the end of February she was working at a cafe in the evenings, washing up, and going to Finch's, a pub in the Fulham Road, for a spot of rest and relaxation. Then on 28 February she writes matter-of-factly: 'In *The Listener* they mentioned my name. First time.' This was surely a momentous occasion for the young student, especially as the writer was Andrew Forge, a respected critic, who made favourable remarks about her work. The laconic entry indicates that Rose not only had other things on her mind but that her pocket diary did not allow the space for lengthy self-examination. A typical entry follows: 6 March: 'Saw Samuel Palmer exhibition. Good.'

Brian was still coming round to see her, and now posing for a portrait. Rose records the films she goes to see – James Dean's *Giant*, Kirk Douglas in *Lust for Life*, and later *Bus Stop* with Marilyn Monroe. Contemporary culture alternated with art of the past. On 23 March: 'Went to National Gallery. Enjoyed this. Liked the German and Flemish paintings.' She admits she is taking risks with sex, and not using any contraception. She continues to play with fire. 'Brian came into Finch's in evening. We went to see my work, he is helpful. I do love him for being so natural.' In April she even visited Fielding and his regular girlfriend, Esmé Ellis, in their native Sheffield over the Easter holidays and went climbing with them.

Back in London, art was still very much at the forefront of her existence and merited a lot of diary space. 15 April: 'Went to Francis Bacon show, also to Tachistes. Liked Bacon paintings very much.' She was also reading Blake and visiting the National Gallery and the Tate. Sometimes art and her personal life hinged together. 25 April: 'Brian won Abbey Minor Prize. Very good.' 31 May: 'All this last month I've been painting Fabian'. Fabian (her surname, but no one called her Valerie) was Rose's best friend, who she described as follows:

She'd come from Bournemouth and was in the Graphic Design School at the college but she changed to painting after her first year. She looked absolutely stunningly beautiful. She had long black hair and a fringe and very large brown eyes and wore very tight arty black clothes. She was shapely and arresting to look at. Her parents were Jewish. She was not very self-confident, and she didn't really want the admiration she was getting.

I loved Fabian and she relied on me as I was much more organised than her. I managed money better and protected her a bit. And we had such fun singing together. She was much more attractive than me so that anyone who came round immediately fell for her. I seem to remember not minding very much as I was very keen on my painting. An involvement takes such a lot. I did paint Fabian in the nude and put the picture in my degree show and she's never forgiven me. All the men were longing to know what she looked like.

I took Fabian home for a weekend to stay with my family. [At this period Rose seems to have had fairly constant rows with her mother.] My mother was a bit suspicious of the tight black trousers and all that kind of thing, and I was pretty grubby as well, but she heard us singing parts from *Samson and Delilah* together. Later she wrote and asked me if Fabian and I would come down and sing 'The Lord is My Shepherd' in parts for her as she was talking at a women's meeting in Pratts Bottom. I was longing to get back in with her – at least to a certain extent – so we went down there and she was very pleased. When my mother was talking in her very evangelical way, she said: 'The Devil still walks

fig 8. Fabian at the Royal College of Art, 1956

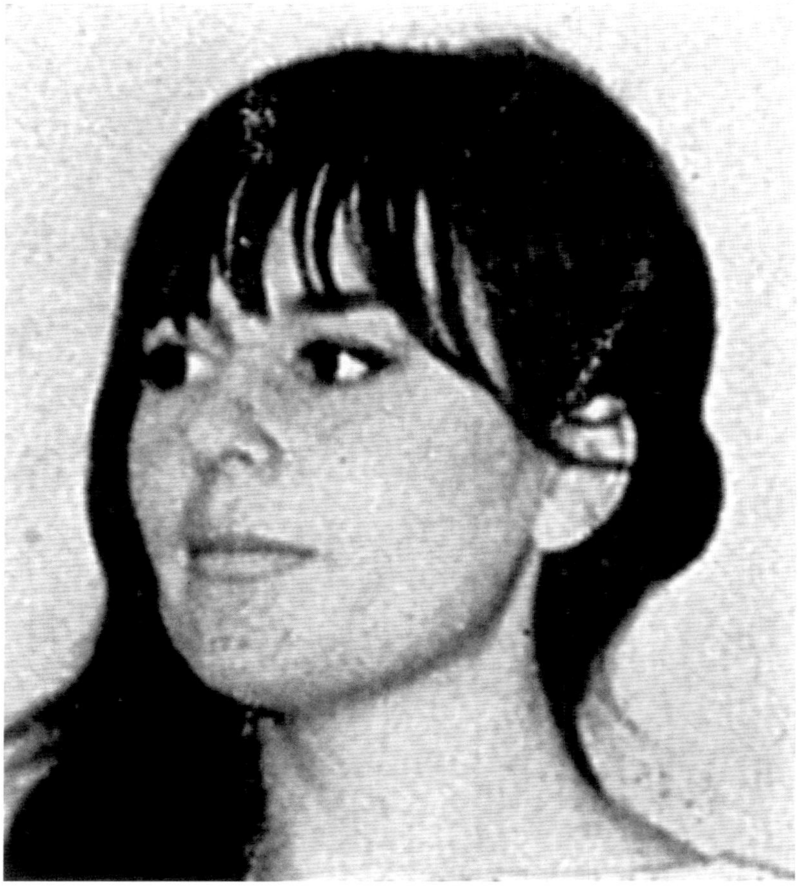

the earth, even in the hearts of the people of Pratts Bottom!', and Fabian got the giggles. I had to keep nudging her. My mother was more extrovert than my father – a show-off really. She did like to be the centre of attention. After that I got on with her a bit better but she still wouldn't come to my Convocation [in July 1957] – my dad came. He was a bit embarrassed about the nudes in my degree show – especially the one of Fabian. But he was proud of me.

Rose did well in her exams, was awarded a first

fig 9. Rose on the roof of her Fulham Road flat in 1958

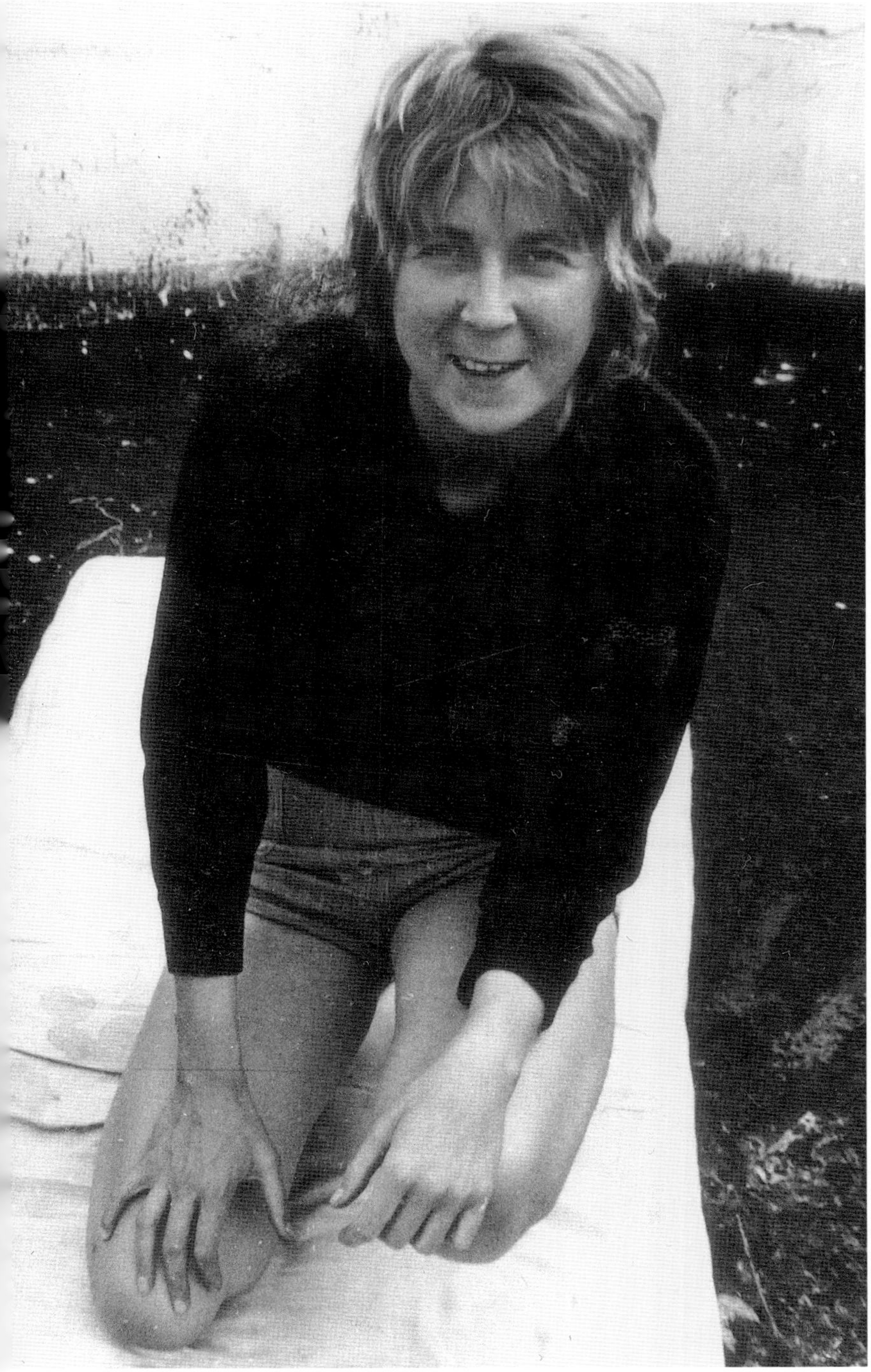

class degree and scooped up the life drawing and painting prizes, justifying her own ambitions and the high hopes of her tutors. Her innate talent had bloomed at the Royal College, and now the longed-for reality of becoming an artist was imminent: her career as a professional painter was about to begin.

Life in the bosom of her family was over, and although her eldest brother, Robert, came to her graduation with his wife, and her father brought her other brother Roger and sister Moira, holidays at home were henceforth restricted to short visits. Rose, no longer a student able to draw a grant, had a living to earn and was applying for teaching posts. She records that she was drinking a fair bit, and that at the end of July she went off to Brighton for a summer break. She found digs, went out to the West Pier, and got herself a job in the bar. But a couple of weeks later she was bored of her escapade and returned to London.

Rose was in need of somewhere to live, when a friend offered her a top floor flat on the corner of Ifield and Fulham Road.

The bottom floor was a laundrette, the next floor was an upholstery firm and the top was completely empty, unfurnished. I saw the landlord and arranged to rent it for 30/- a week. The flat consisted of a tiny middle room with stairs going up where you could get out onto the roof, a big front room with large windows and a cosy back room which made a bedroom. There was a small kitchen which had hardly anything in it except a sink and a cold tap, I had to put a primus stove in, and there was a lavatory half-way down the stairs. No bath – absolutely not –

but there were showers at the college and the public baths in Chelsea and Fulham.

On 21 September she records: 'The studio is a good big light room, but noisy with traffic night and day.' A couple of days later she writes: 'Have been warned about sleeping here.' This was not a warning she took to heart, as Rose moved in, and it was to form her base for the next three years.

All was not well in affairs of the heart. By 9 October she was writing:

I am desperate for some sort of affection and purpose for my existence. I do not know why I wanted to see x as I do not like him but I do pity him. Perhaps I just like anyone who shows a sign of interest in me, or even desire for me physically. I have no self-value. I want to have some. I want to love and live and not be lonely. I want to paint warmly but at present the days are slipping by, cold empty and grey, and no work done. I don't know where to start.

But the effect of having somewhere settled to live and work, somewhere that she really liked, was soon working its magic. Less than a week later she writes: 'Started a still life. Feeling more relaxed and happy in my room.' In November 1957 she got a part-time teaching job at Hornsey, and life seemed more possible.

Back in the late 1950s, love was a constant distraction, though art was the framework and driving impulse of existence. Rose was looking around her with renewed interest, particularly at the work that was being done and acclaimed by others.

The artists who were just coming on the scene then were people like Alan Reynolds, and you'd see a reproduction of his work in *The Listener* or somewhere. He was very much the coming popular man. He and Graham Sutherland were doing those spiky kind of forms based on plant life. At least Victor Pasmore avoided that. He did forms based on nature but much purer and more abstract. And then later on there was David Hockney. He came after me at college, but what a personality! I sometimes went back to his talks when he was still a student and he was just so funny – fluently funny all the time, talking about squashed tomatoes and relating them to his painting. He did those wonderful paintings in the mural room – the pharaoh, the kings.

Checking out the competition was not dispiriting, it was instead a spur to further action. Rose was painting harder than ever, for she had a definite end in view: application for a Rome scholarship.

ROME

ROSE WAS VERY FORTUNATE in that some money had just come her way after the death of her elderly admirer from the days in her parents' store at Downe.

After college, I had £500 which I'd inherited from Mr Bennell, and I lived on that from 1957 to 1958 in my flat in the Fulham Road, and I was teaching life drawing at the London College of Printing. I enjoyed that. It was easy to get jobs if you'd got a first, and I also came out with the life drawing prize. So I just painted for a year – nudes, still-lifes mostly. I painted nudes because the small back bedroom was easy to heat and I had girlfriends who were willing to pose for me. When there wasn't a model available I used the larger lighter front room which served as a studio, for still-life painting. I remember having a Matisse reproduction pinned on the wall and also a Morandi at this time.

Then I submitted for the Abbey Major and got the Abbey Minor, which is a travelling scholarship for six months. (If you get the Major, you live for a year at the British School in Rome, and you're given a studio.) I went to Rome and stayed at the British School where they gave me a small studio instead of travelling around, though I did go up to Venice and to Florence in the early part of 1959 when it was too hot to go round the galleries in Rome. Then I took a job in the city and stayed on. I did try to learn the language.

Rose went off to Rome in the autumn of 1958, and sublet the flat in the Fulham Road that she'd grown so fond of, so there would be somewhere for her to live when she returned from Italy. Robyn Denny heard she wanted to rent the flat and told Sandra Blow about it, whom he knew through exhibiting with her at Gimpel Fils. That was Rose's first meeting with Sandra – when she came to look at the flat. As she recalls:

Sandra came round, with Roger Hilton as her advisor. And the next day she came back again and brought Bryan Wynter. She certainly had the men at her beck-and-call. She was absolutely stunning because she'd just come back from the Venice Biennale. She was brown with short blondish hair and she always looked best in jeans and a T-shirt, which was what she mostly wore in those days. Friendly and good-looking, and unlike Fabian she was confident and knew how to handle her good looks.

I also knew Liz Frink in those years. Fabian was more willing to go round the pubs than I was, perhaps because she didn't really drink and was very out-going and curious at that time about things. I was probably more introverted. I did go to Finch's a bit, and if you ever went there at lunchtime there would be Bill Thompson, Mary John, Elizabeth Frink – a whole group of them having a lunchtime drink. Francis Bacon used to come up from South Kensington sometimes. We also went to The Queen's Elm, but Finch's was nearer.

It was that world that Rose relinquished for a few months when she rented the flat to Sandra and went off to Rome. In a sense, her future direction had already been mapped out when she met Roger Hilton, but of that she had as yet no inkling. Indeed, he had looked so severe – rather like a bank manager, she thought – that

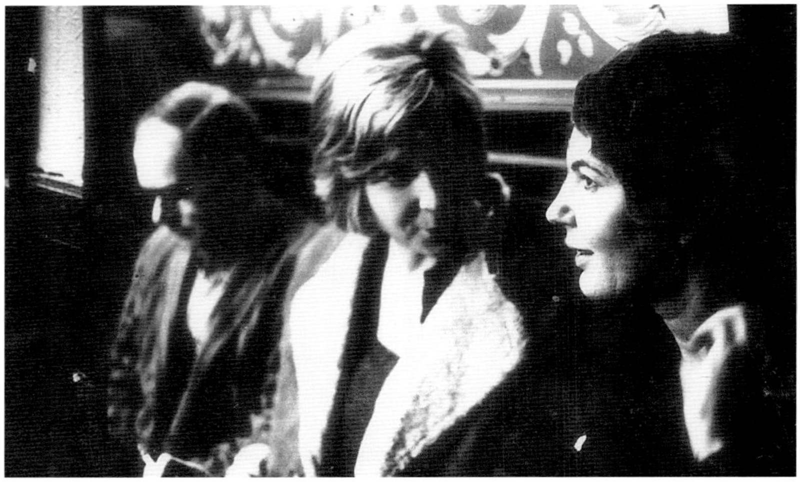

fig 10. In Finch's pub, Fulham Road: Roger, Rose and Sandra, 1959

she'd have been very surprised to learn that their fates were to be so intimately entwined.

Italy was to prove an enjoyable intermission, but not an earth-shattering revelation. Rose liked the country, the people and the art, but could see no immediate way of making paintings out of the experience. She later explained that this was because she was absorbing the great Italian paintings, and because so many new influences were coming at her from all directions. Nor did she find the British School very congenial.

Ward Perkins, an archaeologist, was the Principal of the School, and Derek Hill was the Professor of Painting. He used to come down to see us from his villa up in the hills. He was a society portrait painter who wore a plum-coloured velvet smoking jacket and knew nothing about abstract painting. He was very snobby and painted royalty. I don't think he was any good at all as a professor. Heinz (Henry) Inlander was also living up in the hills at Anticoli, and he used to come down sometimes, a much more interesting painter. There wasn't really any teaching, the idea was that you absorbed the historical paintings of Rome and Florence and had a wonderful studio to work in. I felt uprooted and couldn't really settle to painting, though I did do some drawing.

The trip to Venice was with Robin Plummer and his wife who were also at the British School. He was very keen on food and wanted us to go to a world-famous restaurant in Bologna, which we did and had a great meal, and then went on to Venice. We looked around art galleries and went to evensong in St Mark's. We also went to Florence and to Ravenna to see the mosaics. I loved those women with Picasso profiles.

I loved it out there and didn't want to go back, so when I ran out of money I left the British School and took a job with a well-off family just off the Via Veneto. I was looking after a doctor's children and trying to teach them English while she was at work. That was for another three months and was quite interesting. My knowledge of the language improved, but I did not have any time for culture. It was hard work.

Meanwhile, she continued to soak up the ambience, and look at paintings and architecture. Did she have a boyfriend?

Yes, Mike Chalk, who was at the British School for a year. I liked him but I also had a fling with an Italian boy who came to the school (not a painter), who took me to his aunt's place at Ostia. Once I'd started on that road – and I didn't sleep with anybody until I was in the sanatorium – I realised I had been missing out on something. After that I never looked back!

As Rose confesses slightly ruefully but more than half-amused:

I suppose I didn't have much of a sense of balance about it. It was really art school and the

Royal College that fulfilled a latent desire for drinking and sex and adventure. It was there all right and I thought it probably didn't go with being a Christian, so that went. That's how shallow I was – I wanted all those other things more. I wanted to have fun.

On Rose's return from Rome, tragedy struck, and her beloved brother Robert died of TB. She recalls:

Right at the end of the war Robert had gone over to Germany with the Royal Electrical Mechanical Engineers. He wasn't actually in the war, but Berlin was in a dreadful state then and I think he went a bit wild, which was where he picked up tuberculosis. When he came back he got a job in the City working for Lloyds as an underwriter. He married Eva when he was 21 and then TB gradually took hold. They lived in a big cottage at Penshurst, and she went to work in the City and he stayed at home. I visited him all the time and I probably picked up TB from him because I was in a low state at the Royal College. We were the only two in the family that got it – both my parents lived to a great old age.

Robert fought my battles for me and without him I wouldn't have gone through to the Royal College. We loved each other and were very close. My mother told one of the other members of the family that I wouldn't get seriously involved with anyone else while Bob was alive. I thought that was absolute rubbish, but in a way it happened like that, because the year he died I met Roger. Robert's death left a huge gap in my life emotionally. He read a lot and understood about art. He was totally supportive of me. Even with all my other interests at the Royal College, he was somebody I would always go and see. He died almost as soon as I got back to England from Rome. He'd been that ill and I hadn't realised. Then I met Roger. I didn't get involved with him immediately, but it seemed the right timing. Sometimes I think I wangled it that way but I really don't think we're that much in control. The Fates play a part as to what happens to you and who you meet. Otherwise one would feel too guilty. That's the terrible thought of religion – that you're born a sinner. Really the thing is to work at not feeling guilty.

Rose didn't see her remaining family that much in the years to come, but as she grew older herself, she viewed them in a more tranquil light. In 1958 her parents had moved to Worthing. When they retired they moved to a house at Goring, close to the beach:

[Although] they had retired they still worked, doing stand-ins at post offices to earn enough money to go on little trips occasionally to Italy and so on. They hadn't really travelled much before. My father died first, in 1993. He was 99 and drove the car still. He looked after my mother because she started to have a very weak heart. She died when she was 93, in 1994.

ROGER

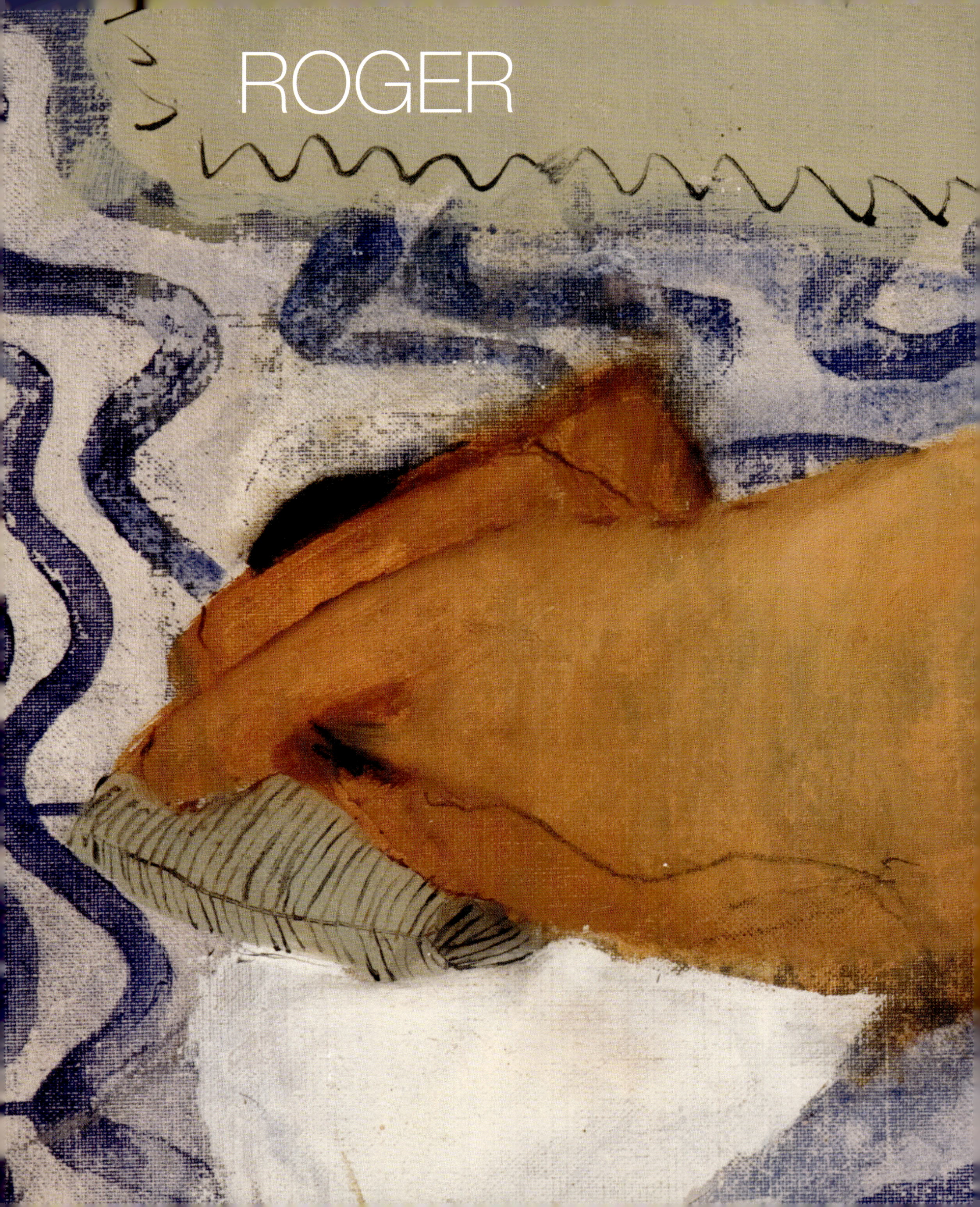

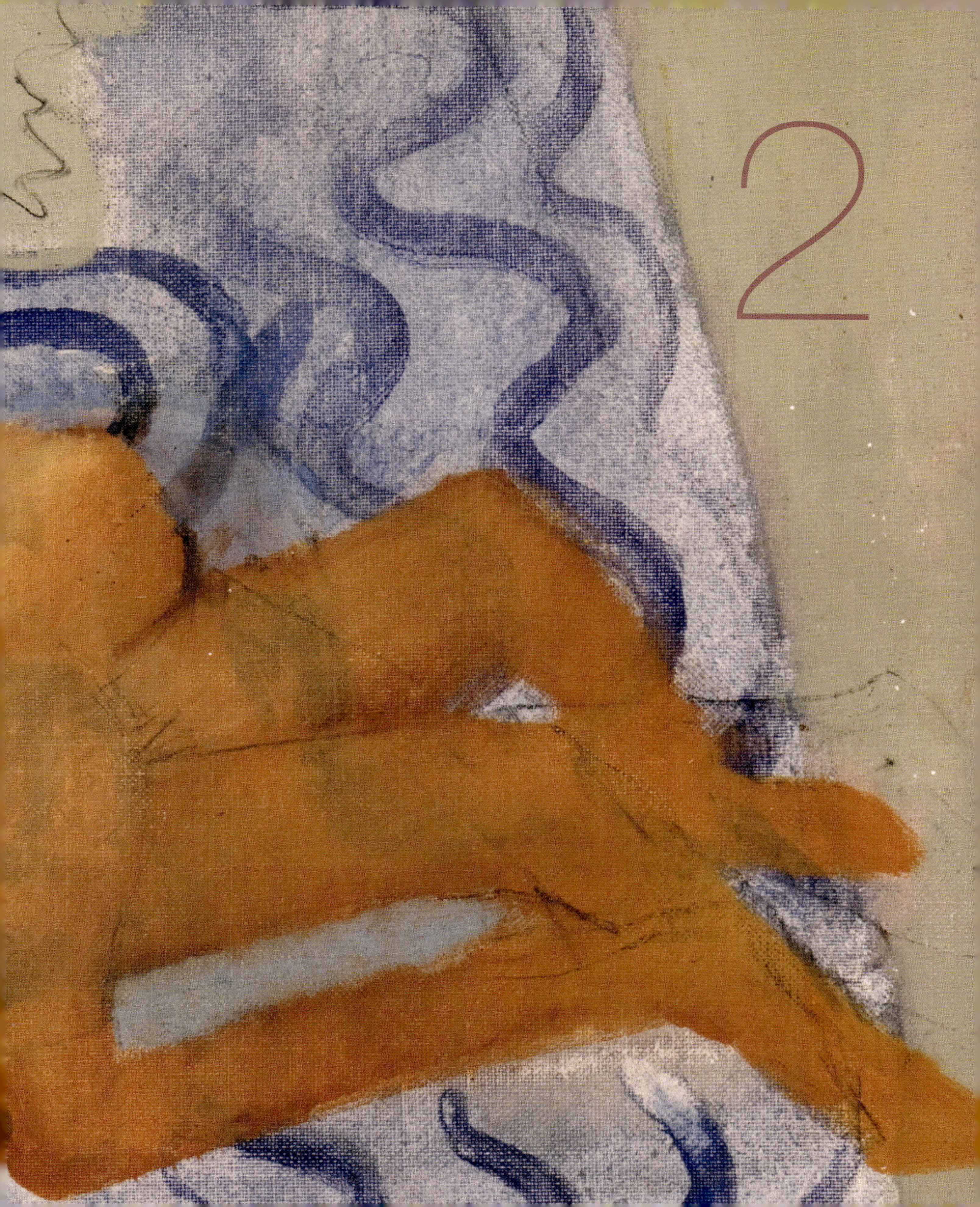

2

MEETING THE MAN

Rose still has the draft of a letter written in 1959 to Mike Chalk, which perhaps she never sent. It mentions a party in Dick Smith and Peter Blake's rooms in Chiswick, and lists some of the guests: Joe Tilson, Robyn Denny, Stuart Brisley, Julia Auerbach, Sandra Blow, Rozanne Palmer. Rose writes: 'It's strange how Rome seems farther away now. In a few weeks you will be back ... perhaps you'll want to start off again quite free. I've written affectionately, I feel that way, but darling I don't expect anything of you'. It was evidently over between them, and Rose was trying to break it to him as gently as possible. Much more revealing was another remark: 'Got lovely and happy and had a confidential chat in a corner with Roger Hilton and he said he had really been Lesbian all his life. He had a bottle of whisky in his pocket and was sadly and profoundly afflicted with melancholia'.

Rose had seen Roger first at the exchange of the flat with Sandra Blow before going to Rome. Fabian was there at the time, and Hilton had jumped to conclusions, telling Sandra that Rose was definitely gay. This was not true, although she was very fond of Fabian. Rose recalls:

When I came back, Sandra wasn't out of my flat, so I stayed with Julia for a month or so. When Sandra found a studio in Glebe Place I moved back in. Roger was still living in his St John's Wood studio and because he'd been calling on Sandra in the flat, he carried on calling. He liked the flat, he liked the set-up. I think he thought there were several girls – which there were very often.

When he started calling on me, I didn't really like him much. He was so difficult. He liked coming to the flat because it was fun. Then he became a permanent fixture and he got rid of all my boyfriends by discouraging them. Friends like Malcolm Morley (who broke my camp bed), Mike Chalk and Roger Mayne who took lots of nude photos when I was sunbathing up on the roof. One time I found Roger [Hilton] hiding in the lavatory until someone had gone. I said 'Oh you did have to wait a long time.' He said, 'I can always wait when I want to.' Then somehow everyone else got sifted out so he took over himself. He must have been quite keen. We were sleeping together by then. He was a lot of fun, Roger.

He was drinking quite a bit and often had a bottle of whisky in his pocket, but we didn't think about alcoholism in those days. In fact we went out for lots of meals. Lots. He loved restaurants. One in the Fulham Road was called Salami's, another was Le Provençal. He always had money on him. There's a photograph of us in Le Provençal, a bit squiffy, me with a nice thick woollen coat on with a fur collar, Roger in stripes with checked trousers [fig.11]. He always wore nice clothes. He looked rather severe really. It was quite an idyllic period once I'd got used to the older man business. Because he *was* 20 years older. It wasn't what I'd expected and I didn't need a father figure. If he hadn't had such charm and such a young spirit – he became ageless – I might have noticed more.

When I met Roger I was already teaching at Sidcup Art School. As I became more and more involved with him, he resented me going off to teach. So he rang up the principal of Sidcup Art

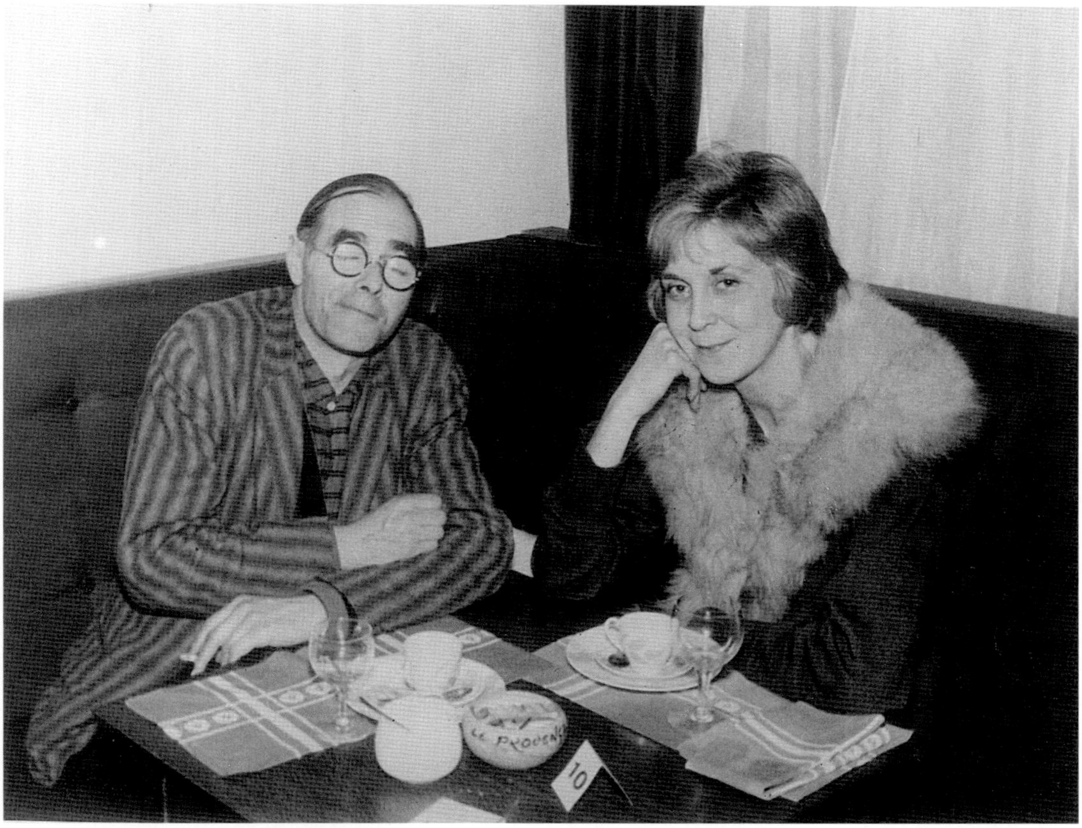

fig 11. Roger and Rose dining at Le Provençal, 1960

School and said 'Why are you employing her – she doesn't know anything about art!' That was just spite. The principal called me into his office and said 'Is this true?' 'Oh,' I said, 'You don't want to take any notice of him, he's just rung you up when he's had a few drinks.' It was so horrible of Roger – he didn't want me to work, he wanted all the attention.

Just before that, when I started teaching, I had to go on a Basic Design course so I could teach at Sidcup. It was no good going there to teach life drawing as the students didn't want to do life drawing. I went to a long summer school at Boxted in Suffolk, which Bridget Riley was also on. I'd already met her briefly at college when she was in her last year and I was in my first. Terry Frost was on the staff, though I didn't know him then, and Harry Thubron. They gave talks about basic shapes and designs, cylinders and squares and things. It didn't make a lot of sense to me, I was a representational painter. So really it was a bit problematic when I started at Sidcup because I wasn't very secure in what I was supposed to be teaching. These were 16-year-olds coming straight from school and I had the misfortune to have Keith Richards in my class. He was good looking and played the guitar all the lunch hour. A cheeky devil! He called me 'Teach' and locked me in the big materials cupboard. The girls were nicest, a bit sympathetic. I suppose I taught for about a year and a half at Sidcup, then I gave it up. There was too much opposition all round.

As Rose became gradually more involved with Roger, so was she drawn into his world. He could be devastatingly funny and quite evidently charmed and intrigued Rose; her later description of this time was that she got 'rather hooked' on him. In the summer of 1959, Hilton disappeared from London down to Cornwall, where he was renting a studio at

Newlyn, overlooking the harbour. Rose followed him down there and they slept in the studio under such masterly paintings as *Large Orange, Newlyn*.

I'd never been affected by an abstract painting so strongly before. It was very alive and slightly spiky. Roger's quality of paint has always been superb. His paintings have a power that hasn't lessened with time. It seemed to me that both physically and in his personality Roger was very like his paintings. I think that deepened his fascination for me.

The Newlyn sojourn confirmed her interest in abstraction, an interest that was to bear fruit in her own work, though not until many years later.

The spikiness could erupt into tongue-lashing, and Hilton was famous for getting into trouble over what he said. He was unsparing and direct to the point of cruelty. Rose recalls:

When I started going to private views with Roger in 1959 or 1960, I did realise that people took a dislike to him, because that's why he was punched by Alloway and then by Frederick Gore. That was at Joe Tilson's party and I was standing by Roger, and he said to Freddy 'You're not half such a good painter as your father'. He was verbally abusive to people. He wasn't to begin with to me, but when we were with other people he started being nasty to me, though not when we were alone together. He liked Keith Vaughan a lot and we went round there. He was a very nice man and while we were in his flat Roger said something sharp to me. Keith said: 'Roger, you've got a very charming lady there and you're lucky to have her, don't speak like that to her.' He told him off, and Roger was quite surprised, and didn't shout at me again until another time. I noticed that John, Roger's brother, was the same with Peggy, and was nasty to her when other people were present.

Sandra Blow, who was a close friend of Hilton's, warned Rose about getting involved with Roger, but it was too late. As Rose remembers:

I got pregnant in 1960 first, when Roger and his first wife Ruth weren't absolutely sure they were going to separate, and I had an abortion, paid for by Roger. I was in love with him but I still wasn't sure I wanted to be with this older man. At first Ruth didn't mind me being with Roger. In actual fact she told me that I was doing 'Dog' (as she and Sydney Graham called him) a lot of good by being with him, as she was having an affair with Sydney. So it was all right until the pregnancy happened and then she wasn't so friendly. Roger himself hadn't yet come to the conclusion that he wasn't going back to Ruth, though he'd been living in his studio by that time for at least a year and a half. Roger was very nice to me over the abortion – I went into a private clinic and he brought flowers and everything.

I decided then it was going to be over between us, and I'd go on with my painting and teaching. But Roger didn't give up, he just went on visiting. And I wasn't really over him in my heart and he wasn't back with Ruth. So we went on seeing each other. And we borrowed

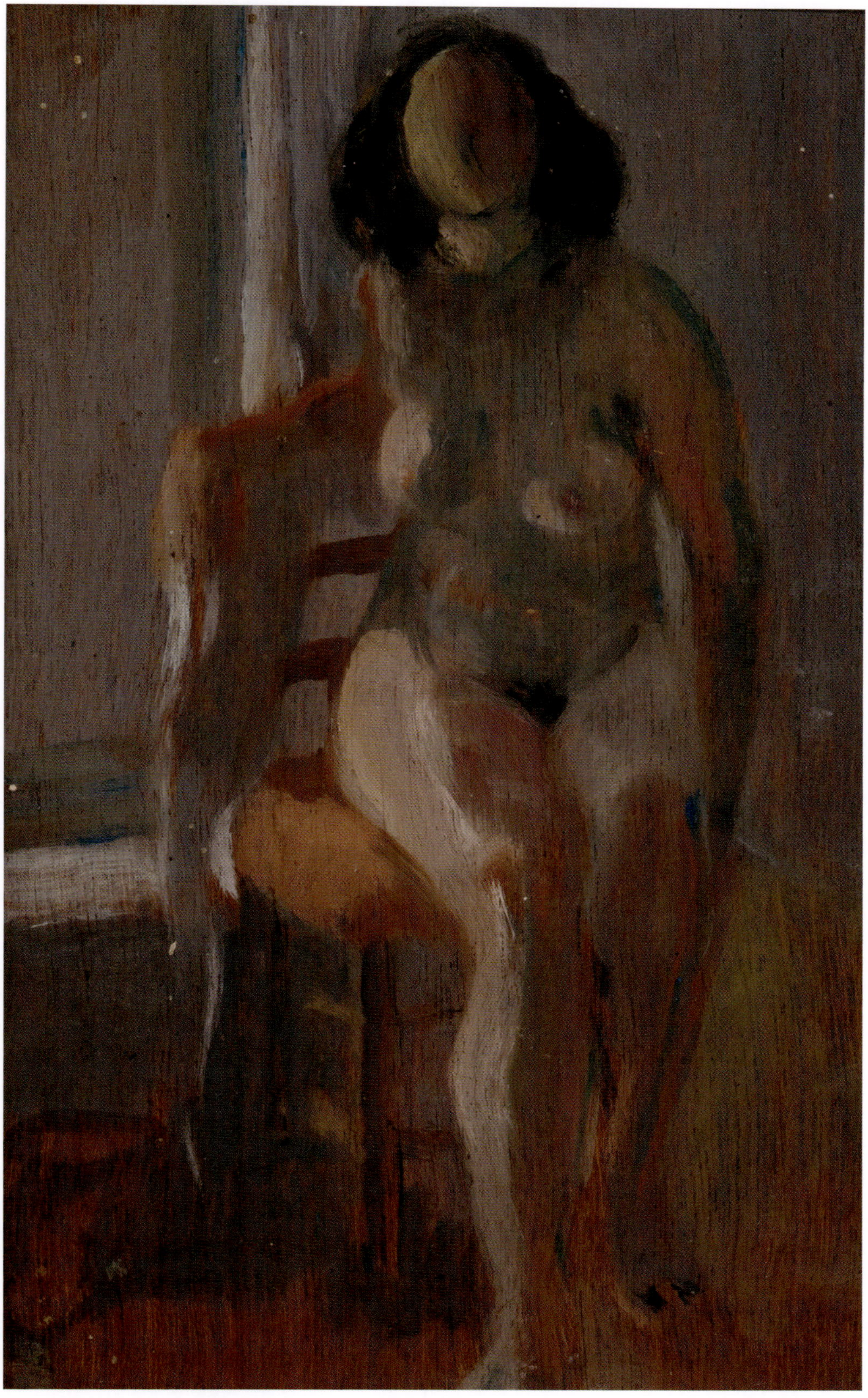

plate 12. ***Nude,*** 1960,
oil on canvas,
25.4 x 10.2 cm (10 x 4 in)

Trevor Bell's studio in St Ives in February 1961 and came away for a whole month, and that's when Bo was conceived. I'd already been visiting down here from 1959, and in 1960 we came to the little cottage at Nancledra that Roger and Ruth owned. I suppose I got broody and stopped using my dutch cap. It wasn't a terribly conscious decision.

Then when I was pregnant with Bo, Roger was sort of pleased but suddenly decided he was in love with Jill Neville. Roger and I went to the Tate and came across Jill going around with Tony Kingsmill, who was very keen on her at the time. He was an interesting man, a painter, the son of Hugh Kingsmill the writer. We said 'Hello', me and Tony. Roger was gazing at Jill Neville. He wasn't like that usually, he wasn't a flirt. I was in love with him and we'd been faithful to each other. I was hurt. He just said she was the most beautiful woman he'd seen. Then he was disappearing round there all the time and I got jealous.

I didn't want to get in that humiliating position of following him around and making scenes, so that's when I called on my friends from the Royal College, Fabian and David Methuen and Anne Martin, and talked it over. We decided that the only way I could keep my sanity, decide on my future, and keep the baby, was to go away. So I went to the Artists' Benevolent Fund, that Carel Weight had a big say in, and explained the situation. I was given money enough to keep myself until the baby was born, which was about six months ahead. I got a ticket to go to Paris and my friends came to see me off at the station. I was rather weepy but it was exciting and made up for

fig 12. Rose in France, 1961

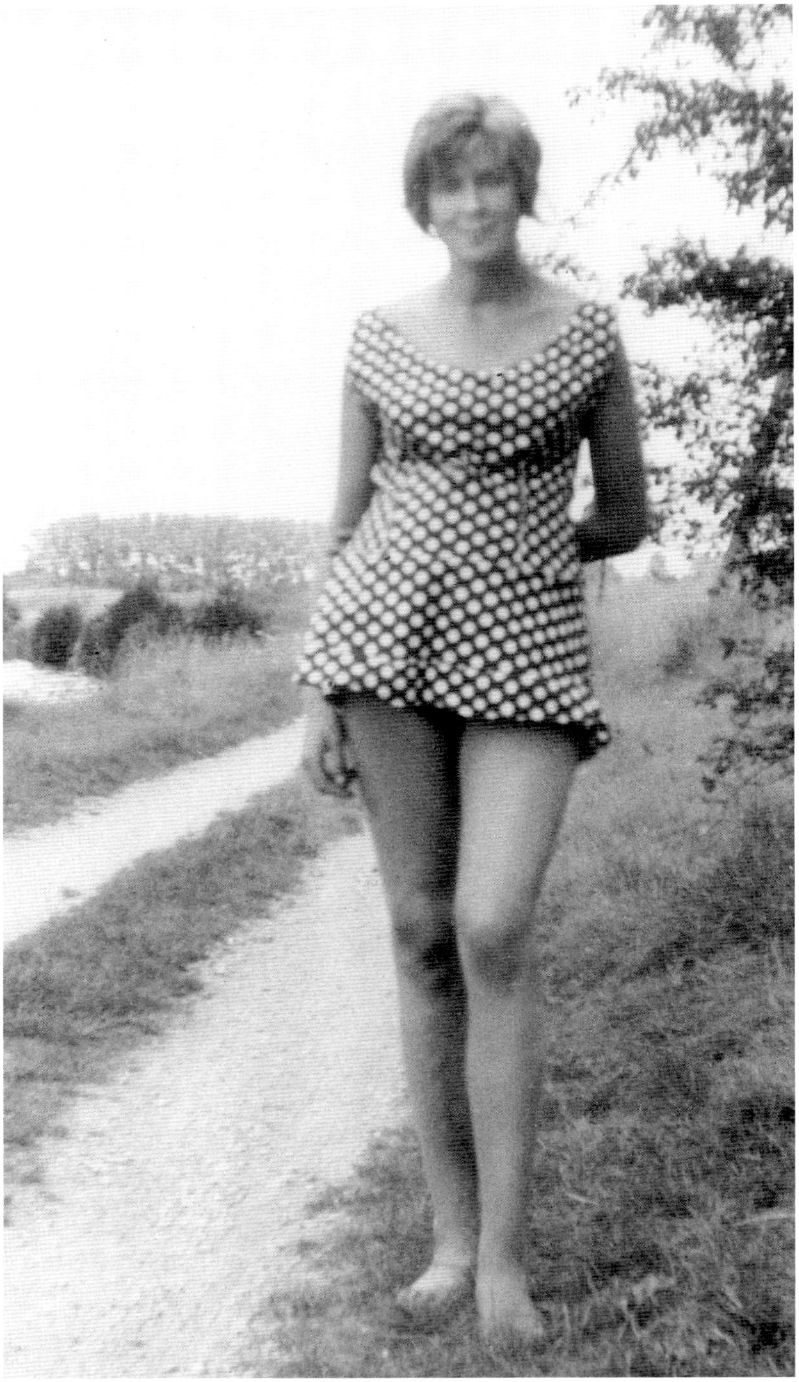

fig 13. Roger with Bo, 1961

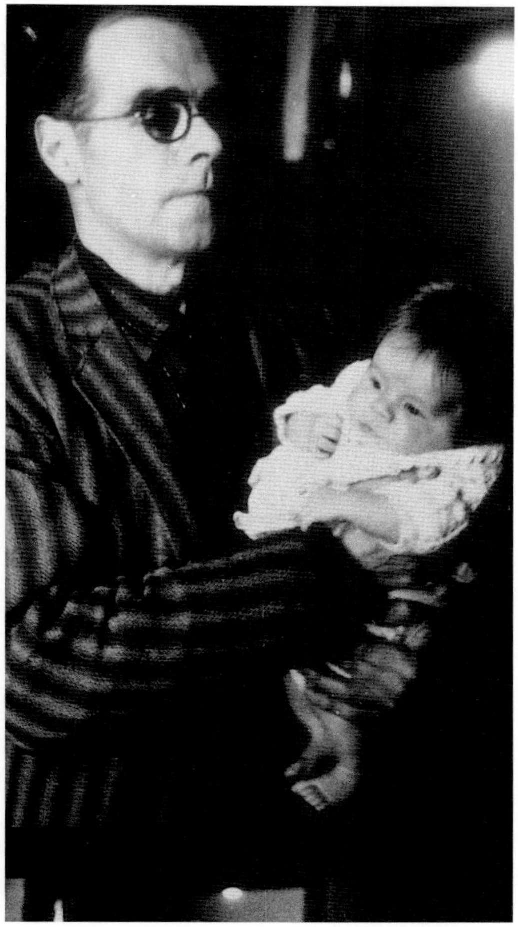

feeling absolutely wretched about Roger's treacherous ways. He hadn't done that before.

I got a room in Paris with a French girl called Maude and a Singhalese law student, Mahen. (He had been a boyfriend of Rozanne's and then Esmé's.) I rented a room in their flat and stayed there a good four months. Maude and I used to go and stay with her family at Auxerre, a hundred miles east of Paris. She was pregnant by Mahen, and we lazed about really. I also got to know Edwin John, Caspar's brother, who inherited all the Gwen John pictures because he was her favourite nephew, and his daughter Sara. I came back to England once to have a check-up and I bumped into Roger in the doctor's surgery (which must have taken a bit of arranging, with Sandra probably). I was looking very brown and pregnant, and I made sure I disappeared back to Paris quite quickly. I had rather a nice time over there. Is there something wrong with me that I can throw myself into the present so easily?

The idea of coming back from Paris and bringing up a baby on my own didn't fill me with anxiety. I still wanted to get on and do what I wanted to do. By the time I came back to have the baby, and was booked into the Princess Beatrice Hospital at the top of Ifield Road, it had all blown over between Roger and Jill in a terrible way. I don't think she was particularly attracted to him and I felt hurt for his sake, because she said she'd sleep with him if he gave her a painting. And then she said: 'Hurry up'. He didn't deserve that, did he? It doesn't reflect well on her. So Roger and I arranged to meet through Sandra. It was definitely resolved with Ruth by that time and he said: 'Don't think you're going to have this baby on your own, it's mine too', and he went out and found the flat in Cathcart Road. And he visited me all the time in the Princess Beatrice and brought Joe Tilson in, he was really boasting about his baby. It was really rather nice as I hadn't been expecting it to turn out like that. I was getting what I most wanted, but I can quite honestly say I was prepared to go it on my own. People were beginning to have babies without being married then.

CATHCART ROAD

All of my 1960s were spent with Roger. My whole attention was really taken up with living in Cathcart Road, going to private views with Roger, or going over to Paris with him. So I didn't even have the whole influence of The Beatles properly, let alone Mary Quant or Biba, because I was wrapped up in Roger's influence and his whole atmosphere really, which was a good one for me, I found. And the fulfilment of having children. Without an exaggeration it was a very happy time in my life. That it had worked out that I was actually going to *be* with Roger was something I didn't expect. He wasn't boring, ever, but he was trouble. If you've got to be with someone on a desert island – or in our case, in the deepest countryside in France, which we did twice for three months – he was the kind of person you'd want to be with. He was a universe in himself.

For Rose, art had finally replaced religion. She says,

I was given the gift of art, so I didn't feel too guilty about not being a missionary or a social worker. That was OK. And there was a lot of truth in someone like Roger – more than in some of the people I met in the chapel. That's how I felt about it, and that's why I felt absolutely certain about being with him. Those first years, in Cathcart Road, were some of the happiest of my life. Roger went off to his studio every day in St John's Wood. It only got so tricky later, which is why I wrote in all those diaries, when we were in Cornwall and he was off with Sydney all the time. It got unmanageable then for me with two small children.

But while they lived in London, and there was a regular routine to their lives, their relationship blossomed. Rose describes their home:

The flat in Cathcart Road had a big living room with two long windows down it. It was first floor and had a balcony, which was really lovely. It had a smaller room attached, a bathroom and a kitchen. All big rooms with high ceilings, quite elegant really. Upstairs on the mezzanine there was a little glass conservatory, maybe 12 ft by 10 ft, where I secretly stored all my painting stuff. It didn't seem to belong to anybody. So when Roger went to his studio, and the baby was asleep, I did a few paintings in there. As usual, if I could continue even for a couple of hours to express through paint what concerned me in daily life, I felt more grounded.

Rose made paintings of Roger from memory and of Bo as a baby (plate 13). Roger had become the chief focus of Rose's life, but Roger equalled art. As she says, it wasn't like having a relationship with an ordinary person. Roger was one of England's leading avant-garde painters, a radical abstractionist who also carried on a love affair with the human figure and kept bringing it back into his art. Living with him meant being at the heart of a highly original creative process, in effect being part of it. Although Roger did not sit drawing Rose, her presence figures in hundreds of drawings he made over the years with her, and in many of his finest paintings. If Rose chose to put her own work on the back-burner for a while (though she did carry on painting when she could), art had not ceased to be her lodestar and

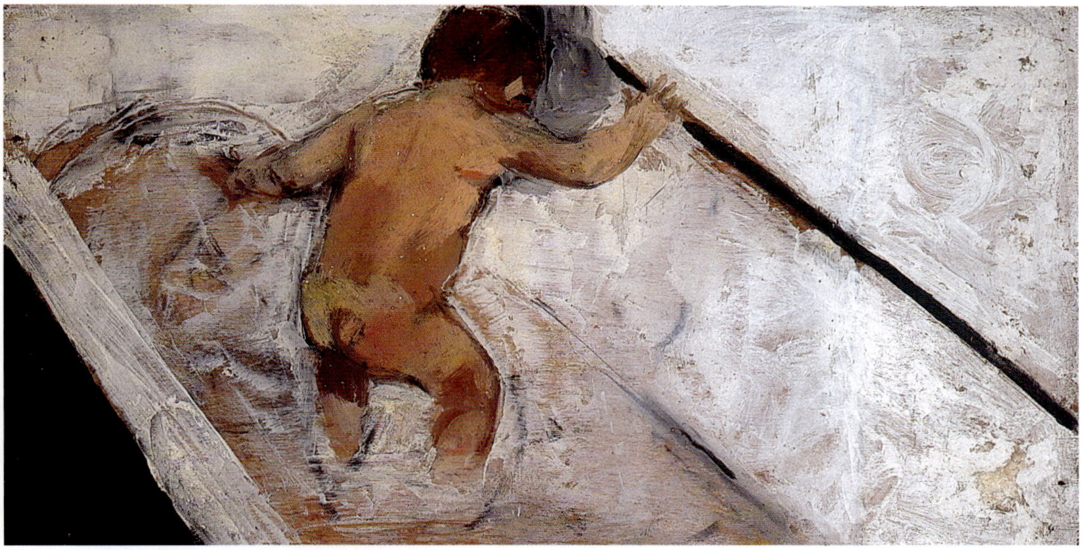

plate 13. ***Bo in the Bath*****,**
1963,
oil on board,
22.9 x 43.2 cm (9 x 17 in)

driving force. It just took a different form.

One of the reasons Roger took Rose to Paris, she says, was in order to train her in the type of food he liked.

I went to a girls' technical school and I did art, needlework and cookery as well as the academic subjects, so it was strong on the practical side. But according to my diary, nearly all my cookery exams were failures. My younger sister reminds me that I was always escaping at home, I was never very good on the domestic front. Yet I didn't mind the idea of cooking for Roger because I wanted to please him. When he first visited me in the flat on the Fulham Road, I didn't have a proper kitchen and I cooked on a two-legged primus stove. Roger was horrified but fascinated. So he took me to Paris and I'd never had meals like it. I'd never had an avocado pear or oysters. I remember in one restaurant he said: 'Now we'll go and speak to the chef so that he can explain how he does things'. I said I couldn't understand the chef's French but Roger translated and I learnt country recipes: how to do stuffed cabbage, haricot beans and lamb, and ox tongue. It was all very good – not terribly expensive food – and I learnt how to cook those dishes. Roger did like his evening meal.

I didn't fall instantly in love with Roger, but he persisted. And when Bo was born and Roger said 'Well, it seems to be working', I really threw myself into it. Food was one way of pleasing him. It was a happy time. Roger would get up. He had his bottle of whisky on his table and his pastels and charcoal, and he drew for an hour or more. I don't think he drank in the morning then – the whisky was for the evening. He had coffee and tea. Often we had breakfast and I cooked bacon and tomato. We had a great big old pram and I used to walk down to the North End Road and get lots of vegetables. It was a nice fulfilling time. Roger went over to his studio in St John's Wood and came back early evening and I would make a meal. He'd go over to the local pub, The Hollywood, for a drink and come back for the meal. So we had a routine.

It was the lack of a similar structure to their life together in Cornwall that was to cause such havoc in later years.

CORNWALL

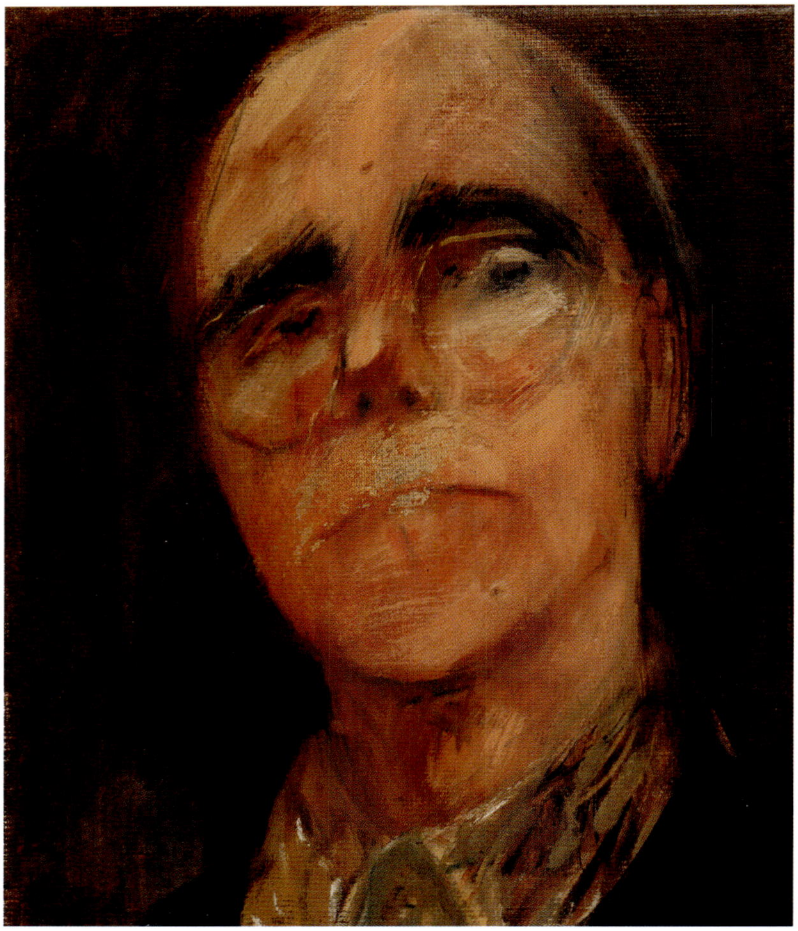

plate 14. ***Roger Hilton***, 1965, oil on canvas, 30.5 x 25.4 cm (12 x 10 in)

ROSE REITERATES HOW CONTENTED were those first years with Roger, living together in London with their young son.

I couldn't believe how happy I was. Roger was there with me and wanted me to be with him. It started to go wrong when we moved to Cornwall. It was the difficulty of Roger and Sydney drinking really. When Roger introduced me to Cornwall and we went to pubs in St Just, which were full of miners singing hymns in parts, I loved it. I thought it was amazing, and of course I'd been brought up to that at chapel. People were all going to chapel in those days. And the humour! The Cornish are quite different from the English. The wild Celts. They'd come out of chapel and shout the rudest things across the road. I didn't know anybody down there but I felt this was where the artists were and I was going to feel OK. I went to the little chapel in Botallack when it was still up and running and took the boys to Sunday School there.

A word here about W.S. [Sydney] Graham (1918–86). A Scottish poet born in Greenock, Graham was early associated with the neo-romantics, and rather too closely with the distinctly word-drunk Dylan Thomas. His later work moved away from these roots towards a greater exploration of language and meaning, aiming for what he himself called 'intellect sung in a garment of innocence'. He was not particularly successful in his own lifetime and settled in Cornwall in 1954 partly because it was cheap, though posthumously his poetry has enjoyed something of a revival. Graham was a roistering boozer and he and Roger Hilton took to each other when first they met through Patrick Heron in 1956. They became great friends and sparring partners, and great enemies too. Hilton was always generous with what money he had, and would rarely fail to buy the whisky. One of the main attractions of moving to Cornwall for the Hiltons was the presence of Graham at Gurnard's Head. Rose rather liked Sydney and his long-suffering wife, Nessie Dunsmuir, but grew to fear his effect on Roger.

Was coming down to Cornwall a mistake?

I didn't have enough experience to know. When Roger was left some money by his mother he was just as keen to go and live in Newcastle or Norwich, where we went together to look at places. He wasn't absolutely stuck on coming to Cornwall. But I think he found after looking

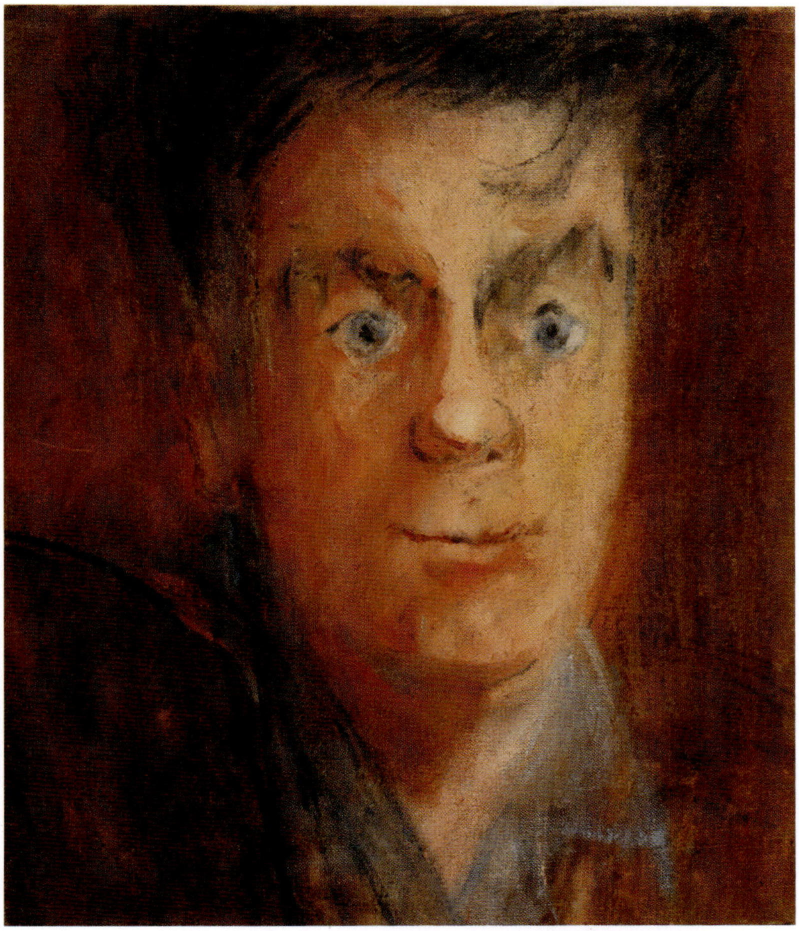

plate 15. *Sydney Graham,*
1968,
oil on canvas,
30.5 x 25.4 cm (12 x 10 in)

around that nothing came up to Cornwall – or whether it was the draw of Sydney really being down here, I don't know.

There were also the other members of the art community: Heron and Terry Frost, Peter Lanyon and Bryan Wynter. This might have been an attraction, but Hilton had never been very keen to join groups, he was too much of an irascible individualist. According to Rose, Roger did not really want to become a St Ives artist. He didn't want to live in St Ives and be a part of that scene.

The house in which Roger and Rose settled in 1965 was on the wind-swept cliff of Botallack Moor, in the middle of fields down a bumpy track. To begin with, they didn't mind the isolation, but things weren't helped by Roger losing his driving licence. They had to take taxis to get anywhere, or rely on the fabulously infrequent bus. Roger's studio was a room in the house, which meant that the routine of getting up, drawing for an hour, then taking a taxi to the St John's Wood studio, was lost. Without that structure, the days could easily descend into a maelstrom of waste and formlessness. And the temptation to go on a binge with Sydney Graham was often impossible to resist. Rose later admitted that the move to Cornwall was a mistake.

Roger's mood-swings became more pronounced the more he drank. Rose was frequently the butt of his hostility, particularly if there was an audience, with instances such as being told to go to the kitchen, 'where she belonged'. How much can his drinking be attributed to the traumatic experiences of the war? (Hilton was a Commando who saw active service before a lengthy imprisonment in Poland.)

If he was a bit bipolar, which he might have been, perhaps the experience of adventure was something he enjoyed. The action of it and the risk. But now I've been influenced by people who say alcoholics are alcoholics for no reason at all. I thought I only began to drink when I met Roger, but I see from re-reading these old diaries that I actually used to drink quite a bit when I was a student.

After a break of many years, including all the early ones with Roger, when Rose was no doubt too contented to take up her pen in self-analysis, she began a diary for 1966 on 22 April: 'We have lived in Botallack since December last. At first very isolated except for

Sydney and Nessie who we saw on an average once a week. I wonder what Roger's and Sydney's relationship really is. I mean whether it is equal in affection and esteem. I am interested in Sydney and Nessie, but not thank God emotionally. It's strange that I want to write in my diary again after a lapse of years. This time with less feelings of guilt and dishonesty, probably because during these years I have become more brazen in some respects. And realize that the act we put on is more part of us that we realize.'

There was evidently a new interest in Rose's life, a distraction from the ties and demands of domesticity. On 24 April she writes: 'I realize that I love J but I am older (veins in leg) but maybe there is a way of loving, detached, that enables one to give and not be furtive, controlled and generous. I love R too, probably basically more than I realize. He has stopped drinking whisky, is very quiet and agreeable, it is my feeling restless all the time that is making any disagreements we have. It is such a sudden switch from complete disorder, rows, fights, love and chaos which had for me a certain vitality, although I many many times wished for a more ordinary existence with R. Just as I was toughening and looking elsewhere to express my emotion, everything has changed. So this person J may not be part of my life, but at least I can value him as a person.' She goes on, 'I am becoming more ordered in the house but am evading any creative work I think just out of laziness. Even though I probably could not attempt much painting at present with Fergus so young. [The Hiltons' second son was born in August 1965.] I could within my domestic limit do wash drawings, watercolours and small stuff with a greater effort and hope. Not this negative despairing attitude'.

All was not well in the house of Hilton. On 14 May Rose writes despairingly: 'Am I sorting myself out, I wonder? R hasn't touched me for a fortnight. I find this very mangy sex ration very difficult to take. Hate the thought of DIY sex – anti-social loss of self-respect'. The alternative, of course, was to take a lover. In her diary, Rose discussed the pros and cons, as she would continue to do for the remaining years with her husband. It was a problem she never resolved, and to which she could only apply temporary and largely unsatisfactory solutions. Her various infidelities undoubtedly helped to keep her sane, but they also absorbed a great deal of the nervous energy that might have fed into her own work in a more ordered existence. But she could only deal with things in the way she did, and life (as ever) was far from perfect.

Back in the diary she writes: 'I've stopped feeling guilty about Roger, he really does ask for unfaithfulness, probably wants it. Anyway 7 years together and we have been pretty much attracted to each other up till now. Don't let this ignoring of you eat out your self-confidence or cause you to act unwisely. Wait – <u>try control</u>.' It was not easy, however. Her relationship with J deteriorated and Rose grew jealous when he turned his attention elsewhere. She implores her diary, as if it were her father-confessor: 'Help me to be strong. To see people in a straightforward light. Made terrible scene with R when I arrived home. Lonely, unsure of myself ... I still ardently believe sex is a social loving activity. Have I any qualities at all with such small breasts? HELP [the last word underlined twice].'

Then came a bolt from the blue. On 2 November, Rose notes: 'Roger in Exeter Prison on remand for 3 weeks following quite an unusual week.' She proceeds to describe the frenetic events that led up to this disaster: 'On Sunday night feeling restless we went calling on people – no response – ending in Commercial [Hotel]. Livened ourselves up with some stiff drinks and started the singing. I really enjoyed singing the old hymns and knew the words of old Salvation Army hymns from childhood that I haven't sung or heard sung for years. Good strong masculine musical voices for the best part. Took whisky back. Monday went with R and children to Sydney's. Unpleasant evening with quarrels and fights, very terrible for children. I left at 11pm with children. Tuesday morning went back after Bo had gone to school. Dear Bo. Met Roger and Sydney in the road near Gulval, bought whisky, went back. Enjoyable morning. Roger and I returning with Fergus, slept in afternoon. Roger met John and Peggy, took them to Sydney's. Paul [Roger's nephew] arrived here. All met for supper here. Wednesday spent with relations. Interesting and rewarding if argumentative time. Evening spent at Karl [Weschke]'s. Thursday, John and Peggy left, Paul staying. In evening, three of us went to party for Bristol and Falmouth students at Paul Feiler's studio at Kerris. Home very late, exhausted, cried and frustrated. Worried Roger all night. Friday R supposed to teach came home midday drunk and exhausted. In the evening Sydney and Nessie came over. R went to bed. I took S&N&P on to Ander Gunn's until 1pm. Saturday R supposed to teach again but rainy weather and students not working much. In the evening we, Roger, Paul and I, set out to go to Newlyn Art Gallery to see students and their work. Went to Sydney's instead. Drank a lot. I became very aggressive and unpleasant. After several attempts to go home, R P & I finally left at 12 pm and were stopped by police on the way home. Roger driving. Roger taken to police station. Stayed there the night. Paul and I worried at home. R returned midday Sunday on bail due to appear at Court Monday. Monday, Paul, Roger and I went to court. R remanded to Exeter for 3 weeks.

Now he has been there one week. I at Botallack alone with the children. In some ways I feel deeply relaxed as it has been a long time of struggle for us both and hardly a separation. I want to regain some independence spiritually during this time. Unpleasant for Roger but it looks as if he is heading for the "cure" in Bodmin. Dear Roger, perhaps it is necessary too for him to have a period of isolation'.

Hilton made several attempts to control his drinking in these years, giving up and undergoing various treatments both chemical and psychological. It seems that he genuinely wanted to stop boozing, or at least to keep it within manageable limits (perhaps the more difficult task). But every effort at reform was a failure in the end and he returned to alcohol with renewed appetite. He didn't try to hide the fact that he was an alcoholic, nor did he use it as an excuse. He lived with it. But it was becoming increasingly clear that his self-imposed regime of a bottle of whisky a day and 500 cigarettes a week was exacting a terrible toll on his health.

Roger's mood-swings made him even more

plate 16. *The Mirror*, 1968, oil on canvas, 71.1 x 30.5 cm (28 x 12 in)

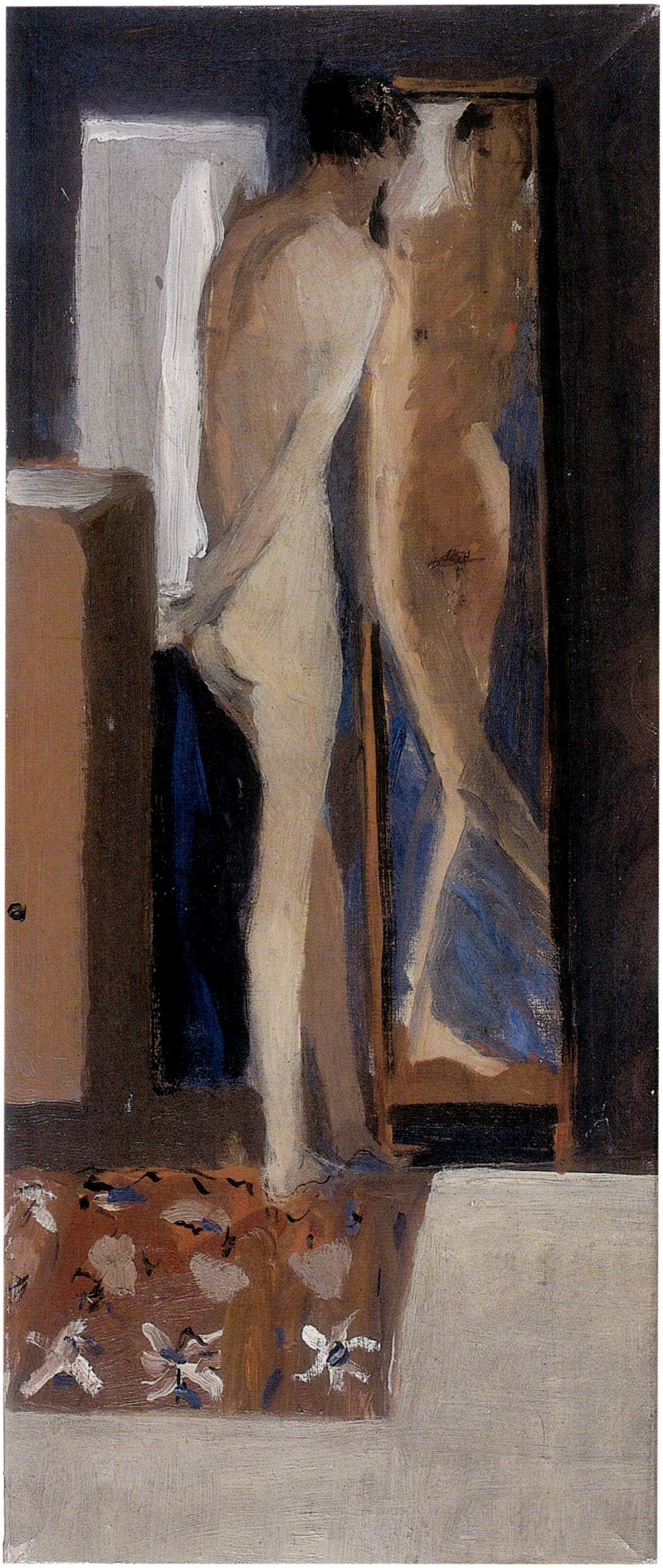

unpredictable than ever, and he must have been difficult to live with. Rose coped by having other interests: bringing up her children, painting when she could, and the occasional clandestine love affair. At the beginning of 1967 she wrote in her diary: 'Everything going smoothly but tediously. Have desire to paint again. Sometimes disgusted with myself at wanting so much time but I am doing the cooking, housework and children. It doesn't satisfy me completely.' Later, in the summer, she was able to record: 'Whilst waiting for Fergie to go to sleep write that during the last 6 months I have been painting quite a lot.' As she recalled later: 'I painted in the garden and the house relying on my Bonnard influences for inspiration.'

There was a certain furtiveness to her life, a habit of secrecy, as Roger had decreed that there should be only one painter in the house and it was to be him. So not only did any extra-curricular love interests have to be kept hidden, but also the act of painting. In April 1968 Rose wrote in her diary: 'Haven't written for ages. Sold a painting [of Sancreed Church] to John Miller, quite bucked by that. Going to London soon. Hope Roger keeps well. Drinking a lot these days, but perhaps with the good weather his health will improve. I am not in love, everything else is good. Children nice. Very affectionately deep love for Roger but perhaps would like the excitement of a new involvement if it was someone I cared about.'

Rose was determined to be practical. In June she wrote: 'I must face certain fears that affect my relationship with Roger that have nothing to do with him. Fear of inability to manage my life and the children alone. Finance. All this I must know that I can face. Work or poverty I must face if necessary with spirit, knowing the worst, having considered myself prepared for it if necessary. I then will be more balanced in crises. Emotional ones I mean, and I must work on the "existence of my conscience". How much I must feel guilt about in fairness, how much selfishness is absolutely justified. (Responsible for one's own decisions and strength to stand by them with one's head up.)'

Towards the end of the following month she wrote: 'Perhaps I have invented someone to love like this F ... because I need so very much to be in love. I wonder if he realizes I have feeling for him. I suppose it is desire, although I cannot bring myself to make any advances, even to touch him on the shoulder or a casual gesture like that.' Three months later she was able to note: 'I am over the F thing now.'

It had been a strange and stressful year. At the end of November Rose wrote: 'Roger home after 2 months of being in the Priory. Very depressed at having to live together again. I love him but it is difficult to live with him and keep painting and keep my centre ... I would like more support. I would like to be loved by the people I love, especially R.' That was the end of the attempted cures. Rose remembers that life became increasingly chaotic from 1969 onwards, and that Roger went upstairs to his studio less and less frequently.

For Rose, 1969 began with an adventure. As she writes ruefully on 1 January: 'Yes but what a disaster. Two nights but left feeling I was done a favour. Ultimately this has not been good for my morale, but it has swept a bitterness about other people's sex lives away. I suppose I have a bad reputation now ... Roger drinking at present. Perhaps we are going to have difficulty in accepting each other as people. Also money will be short.'

On 11 March, after a lengthy analysis of a failed affair, she writes: 'I am painting in the mornings, small paintings [mostly done from drawings of her sons], not throwing myself into the whole process like I sometimes do, but still pulling off the occasional thing ... Perhaps I will keep the diary as a friend at present and record my actions and feelings for a sort of helpmate purpose.' The affair was known to Roger, and it seems that at some point he stole Rose's diary to find out what she was confiding in it. A long description of her lover's qualities have the scrawled comment in Roger's hand: 'Balls! He is very shallow. Damned attractive.'

There are a number of entries in different inks, obviously made at different times, and there even seem to be pages torn out of this exercise book, which is serving as a diary. The tone of the entries is such that perhaps Rose wrote some of them knowing (or hoping) Roger would find the book and read it. 'I love Roger so much, and I feel so guilty', she writes. 'I can't tell him how much I feel and how sorry I am to have hurt him. The affair ... is over.' Then further down the page, in green ink: 'R, dear tortured Roger, what are we to do?' Roger's comment is incisive. In his characteristic italic fountain pen he writes: 'Shit off!'

Later Rose writes: 'Roger loves me, hates me too.' This is annotated by Roger with 'Lie'. Rose continues: 'I love him very much and I am nervous of hurting even killing him in one of our terrible sudden fights.' This fear is annotated by

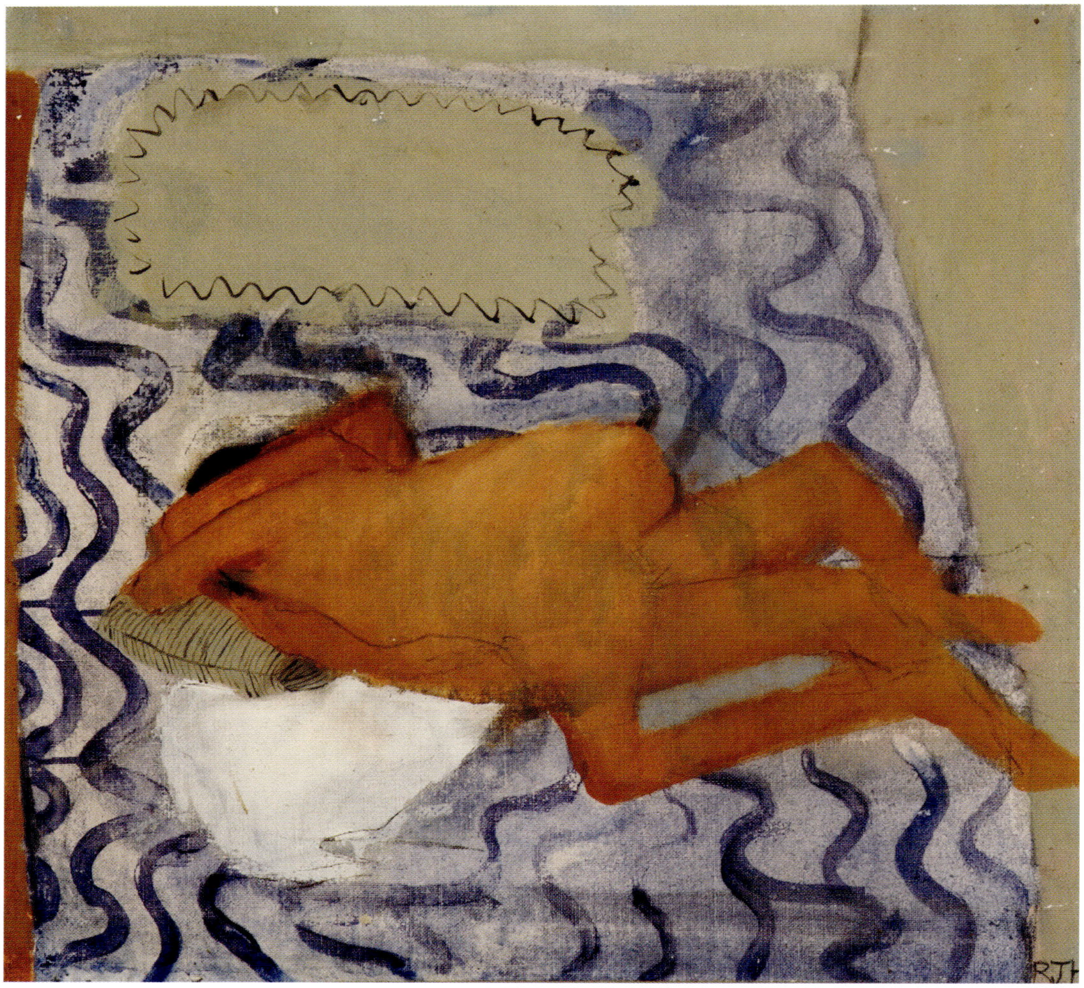

plate 17. ***Locked in Love***, 1970, oil on canvas, 50.8 x 50.8 cm (20 x 20 in)

Roger: 'Shit to you'. The strange dialogue continues. 'I don't think I can ever sleep with x again', writes Rose. This is annotated with a cross by Roger, and the succinct comment 'Balls'. Rose pursues her thought: 'I am affected by him very much but again I must remind myself that now is a very good time to fight the entanglement as I have other interests and R means a lot to me.' 'Thanks' annotates Roger. 'More than any human being on earth', writes Rose. 'But I don't know what to do about sex.' 'Nor do I', writes Roger. 'What have you done all your life? Can't you just go on doing it? ie masturbating?' Then he writes: 'NB You are fairly and squarely off your rocker.'

That squall evidently blew itself out, but life did not suddenly become easier. On 5 April 1970, Rose made a list for herself:

Must paint.
Make new friends.
Be sophisticated and as glamorous as possible.
My new spring image.
See how it goes girl.
If he rings say Piss off.
Be Firm.
See how it goes.
I want to congratulate myself on something.
Try it for one month. Then two etc. be firm.

It was good advice, but so much easier to write in a diary than act upon.

ROGER'S LAST YEARS

On an undated scrap of paper is Rose's touching 'Christmas Greeting to Roger', written at some point in these troubled years when the threat of his absence loomed over the family. (There were, for instance, three separate spells in the Alcohol Unit of Bodmin St Lawrence Hospital.)

Your whisky
You're frisky
You're light
And you're tight
Those bandages and creams
Get mixed up with my dreams
Those glares and those stares
Produce my nightmares
But when you go away
I'm paralytic, pathetic, blue, through –
What shall I do?
Don't you know that I love you?

A diary continued to act as a lifeline for Rose, an essential means of letting off steam. Some of the diaries have little drawings in them, either on the actual dated pages or on loose sheets slipped in. A figure, or a house in a landscape with trees. This became a feature of later diaries and was partly a sort of inspired doodling while she thought out what she was going to write, and partly a jotting down of visual ideas that would not necessarily make it into paintings. Rose's painting was like a river that is forced to go underground from time to time, but emerges again into the open with undiminished vigour. Living with Roger in the late 1960s must have been particularly difficult because he was producing so little art himself and must have been feeling its lack. This changed only at the end of 1972 when Roger, by now bed-bound through the debilitating effects of alcohol, appropriated a set of poster-paints given to one of his sons for Christmas.

Thus began the long and remarkable sequence of gouaches he made virtually every day until his death. These are perhaps Hilton's best-known work, packed with colour and vitality (in contrast to the state of their maker), full of visual wit, invention and humour, a truly extraordinary and celebratory outpouring of creativity made in the face of death. The courage of these works is tremendous, though so lightly worn. But just because Roger was making great art didn't mean that he became any more bearable to be with. And the year leading up to this late release into gouache was perhaps the worst of all. A detailed diary survives for 1972, and much of it makes sorry reading.

Among a list of things to do in 1972, compiled at the beginning of the diary, after gardening and yoga, Rose has written 'Try to have patience with Roger', and then even later 'Do some painting'. The act of painting was evidently not a high priority that year. Much of Rose's energy was taken up with dealing with the daily grind.

The year does not get off to a good start. 1 January: 'Roger and I venomously wished each other dead for 1972, but as the day proceeded some of the old warmth came creeping back. I have been reading and resting' – Rose was suffering an exhausting bronchial cold – 'not having left the house for a week has made me feel restless and depressed, but I have made some resolutions which I shall enjoy breaking.' Two days later she writes: 'Having thoughts about '72 in general. What about Roger? Will he ever be stronger?' Four days later: 'Frightful rows with Roger. Weakly got drunk and went to bed after insulting him to high heaven. Woke through the night with ghastly headache. I hope the diary gets more topical or at least more scintillating.'

However sorely provoked, Rose's love for Roger kept breaking through. The very next day she wrote: 'I think it was this evening that I caught a look on Roger's face that made me feel desperately sorry for him. It was in the pub and he had the look of a child who must keep looking around and be amused and amusing, even although underneath he was sad and perhaps unsure of himself. This temporarily changed my attitude towards him, and instead of being hostile, I try to remember this change of heart, in fact all the things that made me like him anyway.'

In pursuit of this change of heart, Rose asks about his early life and encourages him to tell her about it. 'Roger has had an interesting history. He talked a little today of his first days in Paris, strolling in to the Academie, painting for an hour or two, then going to a magnificent restaurant, which I gather was not very expensive, then eating imaginatively, returning leisurely back and talking to the most interesting amongst the students. He said he did about 2–3 paintings a week, and then Bissière would give a criticism on Saturday mornings, taking people's work individually and saying which out of their presentations was best and why, the why of course being very important.'

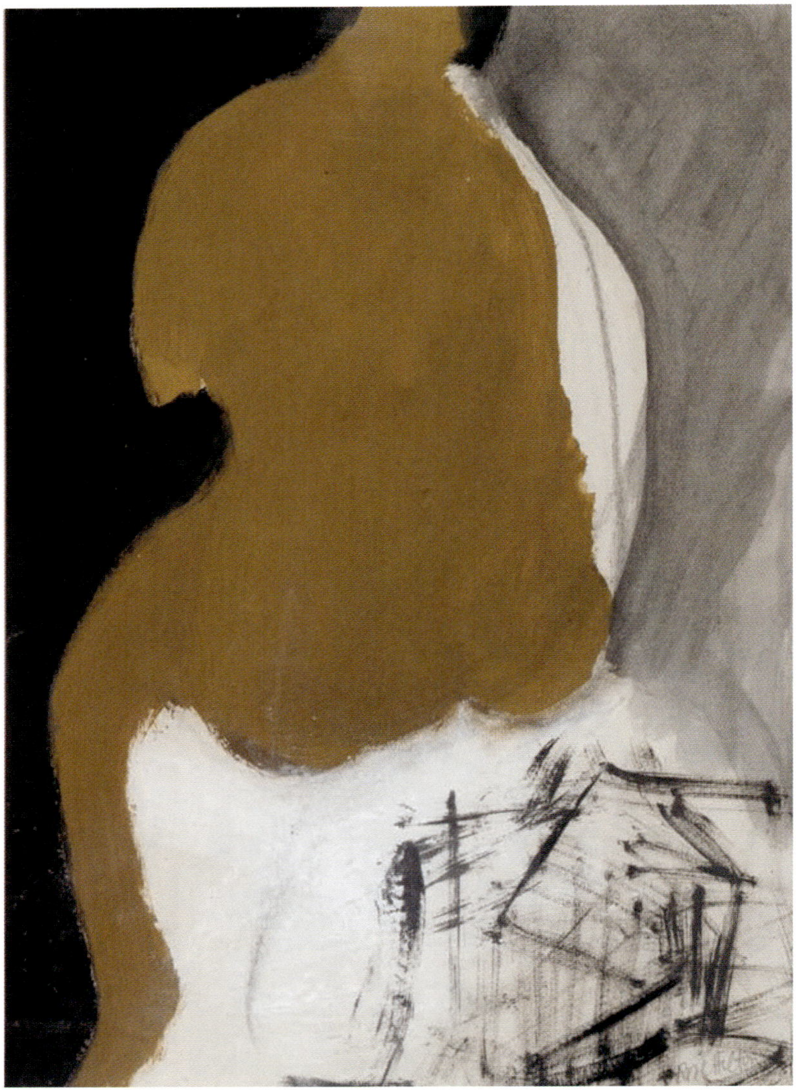

plate 18. ***From the Ingres Series***, 1972,
oil and charcoal on paper
36.2 x 26.7 cm
(14½ x 10½ in)

There followed an affectionate period between them, though Rose was able to do very little of her own work. 'Roger much the same', she writes in mid-January, 'drinking anything up to a bottle a day. He has taken all his small paintings from his studio, all the early ones that is, and put them against his bedroom wall.

Some of them are very good, genuine little exercises that are also paintings. Will he ever paint again, or lessen his drink to draw more because his drawings are still as good.'

Rose is unsparing of herself as well. She writes: 'I seem to be putting off the moment to settle seriously into painting ... I am in a very low inner state, perhaps it is just being 40 and not yet wanting to enter this new period in my life.' The next day she writes: 'I think about Sydney and Nessie quite a lot. I would like to see them. Roger and Sydney don't seem to be keen on seeing each other at present. I must keep going. Like this: try and get clothes together and look very smart. Get good work out. Have an outer confidence whatever the inner conflicts and personal self-hate.'

Later in January, the Hiltons invited Patrick and Delia Heron to supper, then took them to the Count House, the local bar/restaurant, afterwards. Rose comments: 'Quite a lively evening, Patrick being a good talker. R became sloshed pretty soon so he returned home.' Now she is getting back to her own work: 'Painting a little every day. It doesn't look very good to me, still very old-fashioned but I'm feeling better and more occupied doing something every day. It also makes my interest in other people's paintings greater. Roger's have such quality.'

As Rose recalled:

Roger was aware at this time that I was painting often when I had spare time. He asked to see what I had done. After looking carefully at the works one by one he said quite lightly: 'If you must paint in this "old-fashioned" way I can help you to produce better work.' I gathered he meant 'old-fashioned' to mean direct copying of nature or very figurative painting. He then talked to me about treating the canvas as a whole, and changing the colour when you changed the tone. I had more help from Roger about painting than from all my art school and college years. Despite his reluctance to impart information to me about my work, he opened up a path for the future.

The mood of appraisal continues.

25 JANUARY: 'I wish Roger could cut down on the whisky. I do notice that it makes him a) forget more b) repeat himself c) weakens him physically, but he is a remarkable person who must ring every drop out of people, and living.'

27 JANUARY: 'Life is very very bleak at present. Perhaps it is all just a mood but I do feel very bitter and frustrated ... it isn't Roger's fault. It is more something to do with myself and not feeling any good. Also being 40 isn't pleasant so far.'

28 JANUARY: 'I am trying to continue painting but the results are not too good ... I don't want to consider R's death, although it is inevitable sometime, but maybe if I go on painting whatever they are like I can sell a few and what with Truro money [from her job teaching art in Adult Education] I can live at the cottage for a while.'

29 JANUARY: 'In the afternoon Roger and I and Fabian went to see Sydney and Nessie. We all

met in the pub at Madron. Sydney was *full* of emotional annoyance and hurt against Roger and a little against me. I think they have hit a low time. But Roger's virulent tongue cannot be tolerated any more, not even for a bottle of whisky ... After all even a poet needs the right sort of sustenance.

'I feel the same way about Roger myself sometimes, that is why morally I ought to leave him. I could love him at a distance, the courageous qualities in him that is.'

31 JANUARY: 'I have a ghastly hangover as I became very depressed yesterday with Roger's a) continual talk about dying, b) his nagging and vicious tongue concerning the house and its appearance or my lack of housewifeliness'.

At the beginning of February, Rose showed Roger her paintings. 'He didn't like many, just one small landscape. He said that I have got to be more myself, unmistakably Phipps. I do copy photos and get stimulation from looking at other people's paintings but I understand what he means by saying be myself, that the paintings are all over the place at present.' Rose comments: 'I was trying to understand a different approach. It wasn't until the red painting of Roger [plate 19] that I made my first satisfactory painting of colour being used positively.'

Now, although Roger didn't actively encourage Rose to continue painting, he didn't try any longer to stop her. A few days later she writes: 'Things have cleared up a bit. I have about 3 or 4 small paintings on the go, so I am feeling happier and occupied but I don't know

plate 19. ***Roger Reading***, 1973, oil on canvas, 45.7 x 45.7 cm (18 x 18 in)

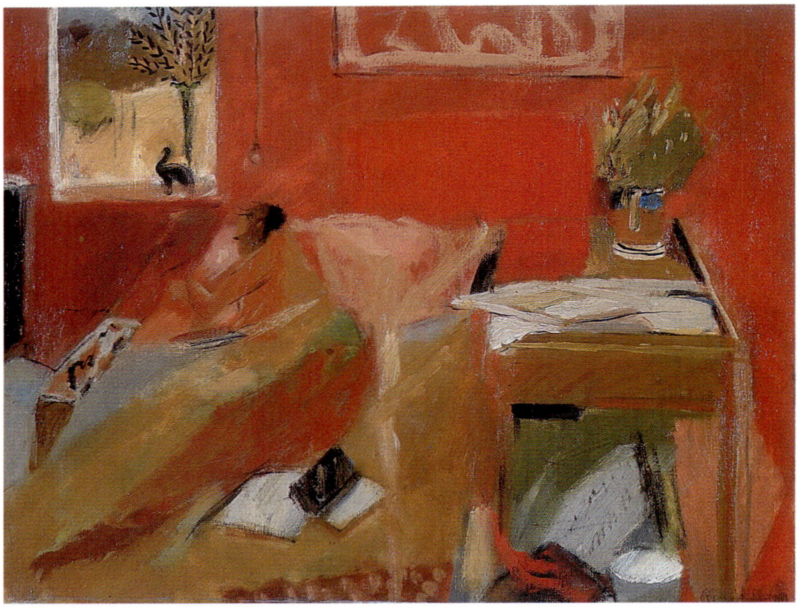

plate 20. ***Roger***, 1973, oil on board, 25.4 x 30.5 cm (10 x 12 in)

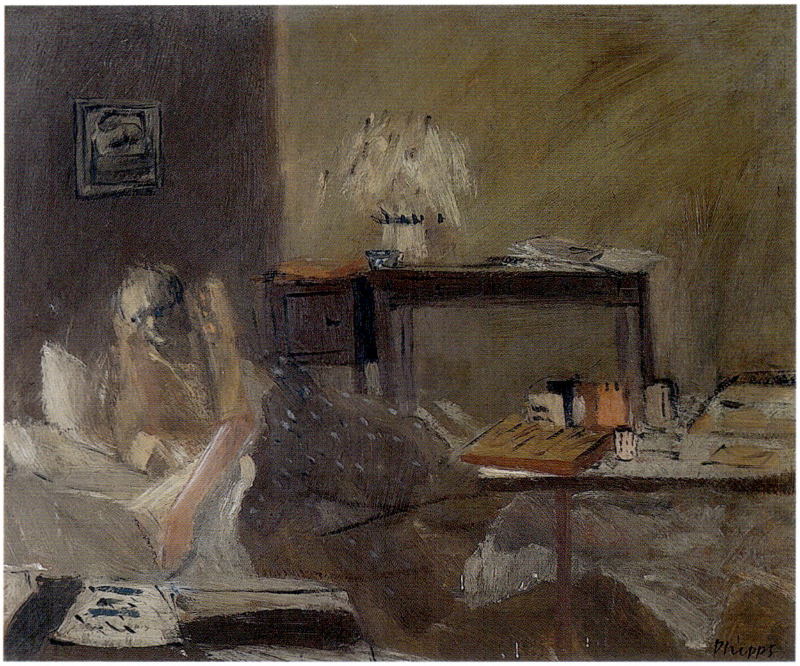

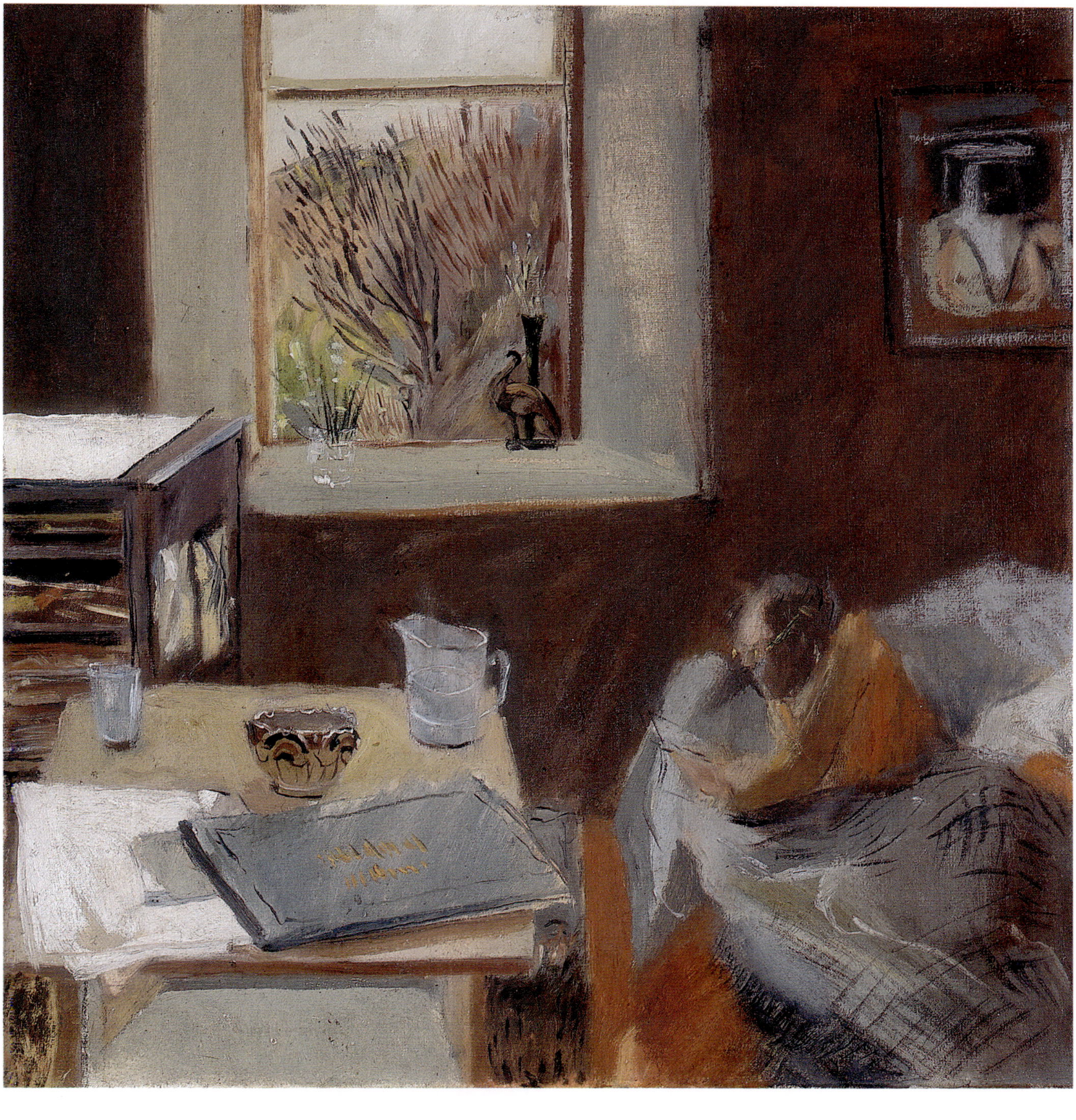

plate 21. ***Roger's Room***,
1973,
oil on canvas
50.8 x 61 cm (20 x 24 in)

whether I'm really achieving anything. I think that painting is not just concerned with talent, it is making something on a board or canvas. So this is not always pushing nice paint around. It may not necessarily be that the painter has to be romantic, unpleasant, bohemian or mad, but he or she must have a brain, unless of course they happen to be an instinctive painter, a natural, a primitive. Milton Avery uses big areas of paint in a way that has an emotional effect on the viewer although he is keeping a certain degree of story-telling in his paintings. These painters who have pushed the representational painting around very cleverly, so that it has quite another effect on the viewer, interest me. Real abstract art, to me, has to do with space ...'

Rose notes that Roger is worrying about money. 'It is so sad to see him like this and yet [he] seems intelligent and concerned about world interests. The real signs of deterioration show in his tiredness, physically, morally and mentally. I wish I could help more'.

On 10 February, returning very tired after teaching at Truro, Rose drank too much and had an argument with Roger over him not letting her be friends with Fabian, who had recently moved to Botallack. Rose hit him and gave him a black eye. 'A real beaut as Bo calls it. The children don't like this at all. They don't like to see him hurt, neither do they like to see their mother capable of violence.' Later that week she reveals that she feels 'guilty over Roger's black eye. He is becoming addicted to bed, and says he doesn't feel strong. His heart is weak, he says.' He still managed to stagger out to the pub from time to time, to break the tedium, but Rose found more and more oppressive the responsibility of keeping him out of the doldrums. A few days later she notes with relief: 'Reg Watkiss taking an interest in producing prints of Roger's drawings. He is extraordinarily kind. And my God! We need some kindness now.'

The two things that concern her most are art and Roger. On 18 February she writes: 'I know that I have a "nostalgic" love for painting to catch the moment of a domestic scene, but I respect ideas that I think men use if they are inventive, which Roger is, Christ knows, at what cost.' The following day it was his absence as an active lover that she lamented. 'This morning badly missed having a man in bed – in fact, I longed for one. I then imagined one. It seems to work, as I can come to a climax but it isn't like holding and fighting, loving a man.'

Then on 26 February: 'There's an unspeakable blank here. Roger the bastard pinched the diary and read it. Not that I wouldn't have given it to him anyway, but to sneak it!' And two days later, the malaise continues: 'Roger and I on unspeakable terms. He went off to Sydney's yesterday and then to the Count House. He spent all yesterday lunchtime in the pub with the Gunns and their crowd. I am paranoid about what he might be saying concerning me. I really think he isn't saying anything, just working hard at getting himself loved, mainly by flattering to women and insults to men, to stir them up.'

The Hiltons' friendship with W.S. Graham fluctuated almost as much as the emotional weather between Rose and Roger. On 11 May Rose observes: 'Sydney still keeps up his "sending to Coventry" with Roger and me.

Roger not really strong, still drinking and not really liking it any more. I am having a very uneventful life of depressions and lifting myself out of them, only to fall back again. I am hoping by returning to my diary to get a stock of myself and at least stop making an ass of myself.' But it was not so easy to put into practice, and there's a long blank here until October. Then this: 'Well if I can keep R alive, myself healthy, the children happy with the modicum of discipline I might keep the balance. Will I manage not to drink, to keep busy? It depends.'

In 1973, the gouaches made by the bed-ridden Hilton really began to pour forth. As Rose comments practically:

> He did them for something to do, as well as creating art. He did edit them. I'd pin them up round the wall and then he'd decide which were weak. He had a huge wastepaper basket and he chucked a lot of his stuff into that. Once a boyfriend of Sandra Blow's came and stayed here for six weeks to drive Roger around. He was a real crook. He used to take Roger's gouaches out of the bin and iron them. He nicked a Henry Moore from a gallery in the end and had to go to prison.

Rose noted on 23 January: 'Roger is strong in his spirit but getting weaker in his body. This nags at my happiness constantly. As I, although to a certain degree tied to the house, am able to live quite fully with him as his spirit, and his understanding of people, especially women, is considerably great.' The following month Rose records: 'Have many conversations with Roger. He hates Andy Warhol from the bottom of his soul. R doing a great many gay and vital gouaches. He hardly ever gets out of bed. I miss a man ... My love for R is deep and I cannot judge yet how great my dependence on him is. Today I have framed up some of his gouaches and hung them in the long room.' She alternates between hope that Roger is looking a little better and despair at her own condition: 'I feel completely sold out at present.'

Pictures come to her in dreams. In May she recounts: 'I dreamt of some paintings that I thought beautiful. They were landscape and slightly going into abstract. The colours were sort of raw sienna and rich Indian reds with a break of a cadmium, say, orange, different blues for skies, all tonal. [does sketch] perhaps this one all in yellow, browns reds [another sketch] another in blues [sketch] another in mixed blues and earth colours. I thought someone else had done them. I was very envious and then when I woke I remembered the paintings so vividly that I would like to have them in reality and perhaps will try and paint them.'

To liven herself up, Rose indulged in dalliance. 25 June: 'Am having a little affair ... What do I make of him? I first thought him attractive, then too soft and pink and white, now, in the summer, I think him gentle, sensuous, non-violent (which I miss, I like a pinch of steel in a man). God hope I never get hooked on him ... Roger working on his paintings all the time. Am I being unfair to him? I don't think so. He doesn't want a miserable woman around.'

Two days later she writes: 'This week has been utter misery. Not that I love the man, I don't. It is the frustration of not being able to talk to him, move the relationship, so to speak. Do women even in Women's Lib day and age suffer this self-disgust after giving themselves? It is not self-disgust from myself by how it is reflected back off the man. It is what I think he thinks of me that I cannot tolerate. I have got to believe in my impressions of what people think rightly or wrongly though they be, or else I am out on a limb. Because of my inner disgust I have been an utter misery to live with. Roger and I had the most fearful row. He wants to divorce me so he says but he has no grounds. I never tell him anything relating to my affairs which are after all only a small part of my total life. Something to keep the balance.'

Something to keep the balance – this was evidently what Rose needed more than anything in the dynamic of her difficult relationship with Roger. He could and did say the most hurtful things. His violence was verbal, not physical, but it still hurt. Rose comments:

Roger wasn't a hitter – he got hit. He did bash me once but I bashed him back and we didn't do it any more. This was after too much to drink. We were having a row. Our rows were usually if he came back very drunk from Sydney's or he was flirting heavily with someone else maybe. I tried not to be the jealous wife. He used to say to people sometimes 'Will you marry me?' But if I left him alone with them he was terrified and would not flirt; only when he felt safe. It could be very irritating.

That particular row happened when we'd both been drinking and I tripped over, being somewhat unsteady on my feet. And he kicked me in the ribs. I leapt up and hit him with a bottle, about half-full of his whisky. I didn't break the bottle and it didn't knock him out or anything, but it did make a gash on his head. So we both went into Penzance Hospital. I had a fractured rib and it was very painful. He was very nice to me after that, but it was about six weeks when I couldn't laugh or cough without pain. After that he thought twice about hitting me. I wasn't a battered wife – except verbally.

It was definitely abuse. Towards the end of his life if I was late shopping – couldn't help it – he would shout in rage for about 10 minutes so that I was really worried about his health. I was pinned to the house then, and that's when it became very stressful, and I pushed off to America for a time in the winter of 1973. That was when Roger kept saying as I was rushing to try to get the Christmas ready: 'You're so grey and uninteresting I don't know how I put up with you'. I thought: 'That's it – I'm just doing my best.'

Rose was so upset she rushed down to the Hiltons' new local, the Count House, to pour out her woes. The Count House (now National Trust offices) is a substantial building on the cliffs at Botallack, which existed in Roger's day as a restaurant and bar. Rose describes the set-up:

It was run by John and Charlotte, a very nice married couple in their late 20s or early 30s, and a gay man called Richard Warhol who was a cousin of Andy Warhol. He used to wear silvery suits and call himself Richard Warholic so people wouldn't bother him. They were quite something for Botallack. Roger found all this very attractive and before he took to his bed, when I'd been teaching at Truro I'd often find

fig 14. Rose and Dudley Sutton, 2003

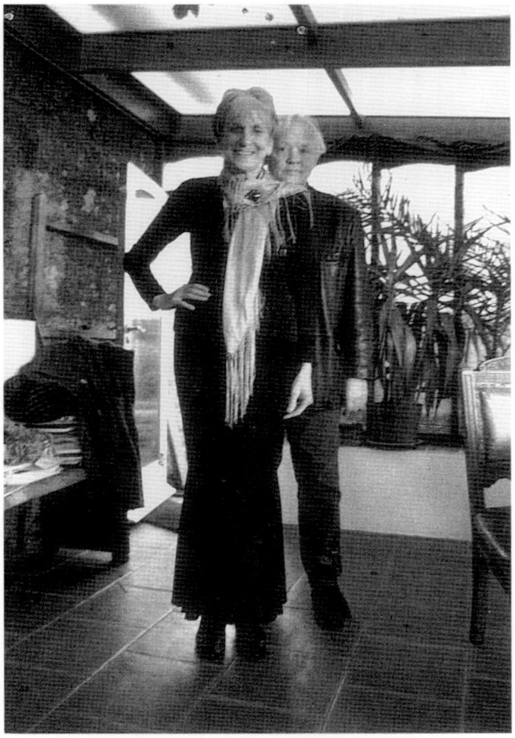

him down there after he'd put the children to bed, having a meal.

Richard Warholic suggested he contacted his aunt about her summer house in the Everglades, and I was lent it for three weeks that winter. I was at the end of my tether. I was doing my absolute best to see that the boys had their meals and I was getting all Roger's paint, rushing here and there and him shouting at me, and to avoid a tragedy the thing was to remove myself. I was desperate. I must have been – it was over Christmas when I went.

By 17 December the ticket to Florida was booked and Rose was writing in her diary: 'Roger as dear as ever, but unhappy about being left unless of course, some fascinating woman is to be found, to distract him and keep him from missing the family. He does like the "family hearth". A paradox really for such a drinker and mental womaniser. Dudley [Sutton, the actor, a new and lasting friend] would be good for Roger over Christmas.' Rose arranged for people to come in and be with Roger, and the boys went to stay with their best friends. She flew out on 23 December and kept an excited diary of the trip, imagining Roger shaking his fist at the plane as it flew over Botallack. Her arrival at a long low house in an orange grove in West Palm Beach was magical. 'I couldn't wish for anything better', she writes.

She suffers a reaction of homesickness (she is living on her own), but realises how much she needs the time and space to sort out her life. On 1 January she writes: 'Roger wrote me a letter saying on the envelope he was dying! Caused consternation with the PO. I passed it off as a joke, what a joke. Death. Oh Roger.' Nevertheless she writes back to his demand to come home: 'No, I'm living'. The instinct for self-preservation is strong.

She writes: 'I needed to become unstuck, to be oiled by the juices of separation, love and the right kind of appreciation of my dear family from my perspective ... for months, years I've tried to hold things together, to pretend it's all right ... it isn't all right and yet it is, in this whole world of uncertainty. Just wait. The INEVITABLE lies ahead anyway. Which means immediately Roger's going sometime, but he, what he is, will never go.'

A week later Rose met a bunch of ex-Hell's Angels and rather surprisingly fell in with them and their charismatic leader, Snake. She writes a long psychedelic description of dawn in the Everglades and praises their essential maleness as hunter-gatherers. Snake carved a cross for her with their initials on it. The whole encounter bordered on the mystical, and it was evidently an enormous morale boost for Rose, who was able to return to England and all its problems, renewed and reinvigorated.

After that Roger was very very nice to me when I came back. If I had stayed at home I'd have had a breakdown or something, but I came back suntanned and rested. I was feeling absolutely wonderful. When I got back to England there was a train strike and I couldn't get down to Cornwall so I went round to Sandra's. I phoned Roger and said I was on my way. 'Come home immediately', he said, 'take a taxi. Get down here at once.' I went in a minicab and it cost £50 for the journey and £50 for the driver to get back. It was nice to be wanted and not to be grey and uninteresting.

However longed-for and much-needed, the Florida sojourn was only a temporary respite in the tragic course of events. Rose's diary for 1974 doesn't begin until 7 May when she writes: 'I suppose I ought to pull myself out of the lethargy I have sunk into. On the surface it seems OK but all the time I am worried about not doing enough painting, gardening, talking to Roger. Very beautiful weather. Roger continues in bed, but eating more, and seeming stronger, despite his matchstick legs.'

Some 10 days later she is writing: 'I am so lazy. Roger lays – very exhausted and declining

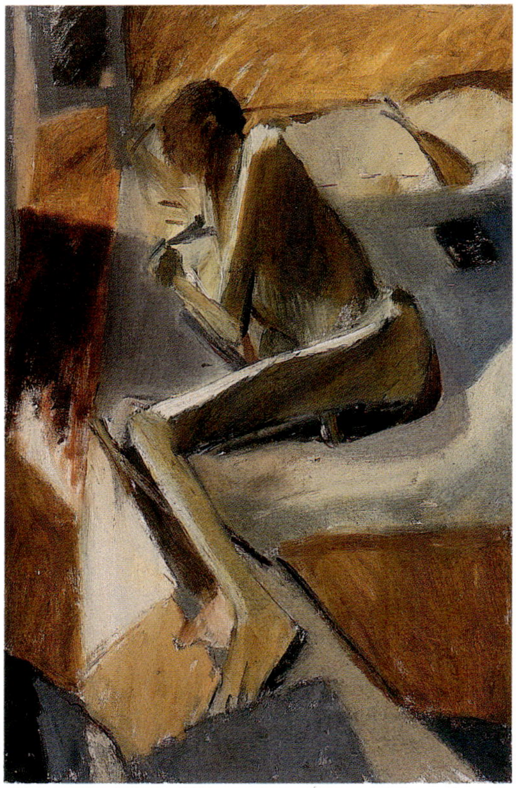

plate 22. ***Figure in Browns***, 1974, oil on canvas, 91.4 x 61 cm (36 x 24 in)

in health, I ought to be filled with energy and ideas to get him better. Instead I tend to mope. Inwardly feel frustrated. I know I could paint when he sleeps but I just can't start. The fact that I am worrying and writing about it is a good sign. Perhaps it won't be long before I start. I know what I want to do. Interiors and life pictures.'

After that, there is nothing else written all year. Rose recalls:

At this time my world was limited to home and family and visiting friends. I painted interiors of the house and people who were in my life, even Sydney Graham. There is no doubt I would have looked at other painters in reproduction who would have used these subjects, as a guide for my own work.

She made a few paintings she now regards as

fig 15. David Brown and Rose in Edinburgh, 1974

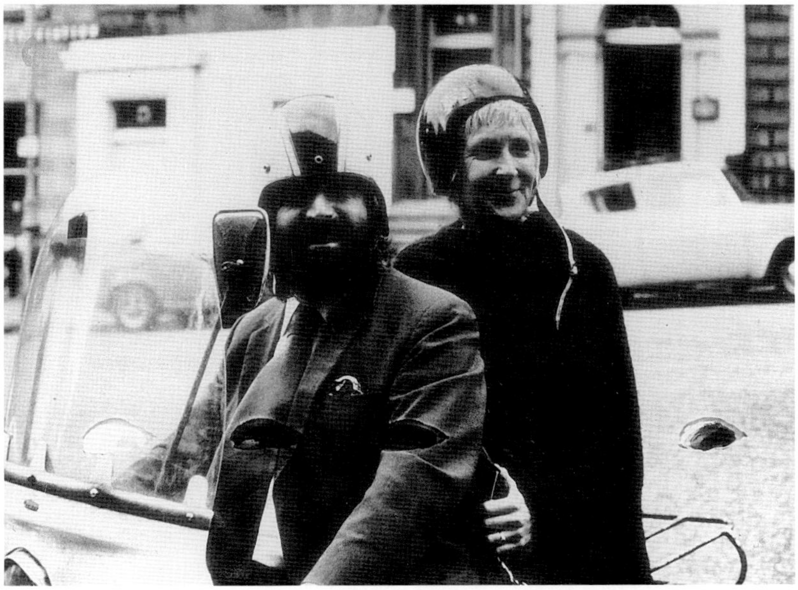

fig 16. Bo and Fergus, 1974

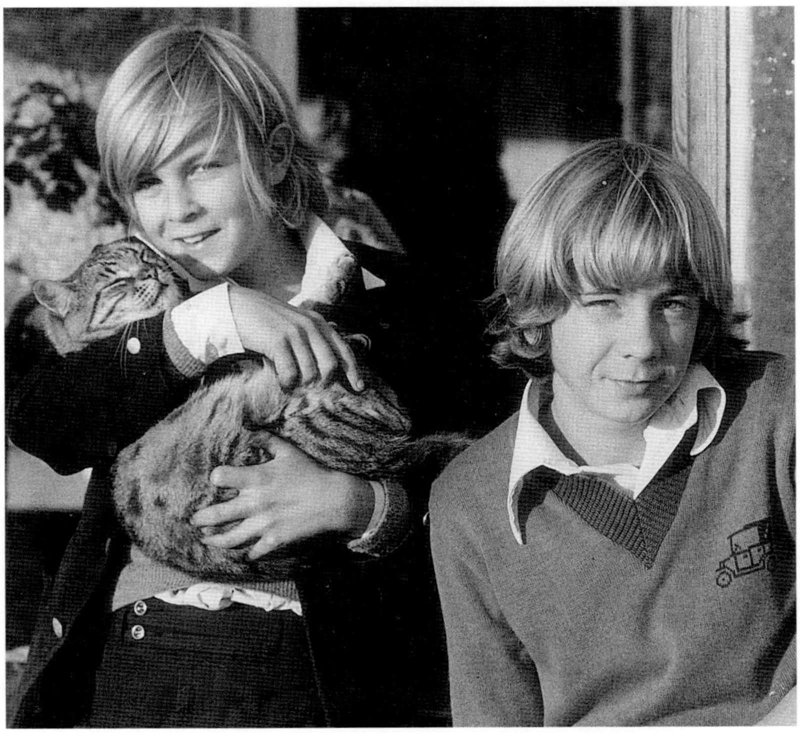

derivative or otherwise unsuccessful. It was altogether a difficult and unhappy period.

As 1975 dawned, it was evident that Roger was nearing the end. Rose's diary records in painful detail his deterioration, and her attempts to distract herself with her painting. 30 January: 'Roger still in bed, was iller than usual yesterday. I got up in the night to see if he was OK. We talked for an hour. He was better, we talked about my painting. He said not to paint so many nudes, put all the collection of small bits that he reckons I do so well together in one painting. I wonder if I could. Not today anyway when I don't feel courageous. It is awful. I either just copy nude photographs, making up a few variations on the colour, or else don't do anything and feel guilty about intense waste of time.

...

I am painting these little nudes. I don't know why. I think they will sell, that is a good enough reason. We have no money at present. Income Tax being £1200 this year. Roger says he won't pay it but I intend to pay £100 monthly somehow.

...

I am not writing much about Roger. He is about 7 stone now, still painting in bed. We get on very well some days. I have recently done several paintings of him whilst he has read Kilvert's *Diary* to me. I have enjoyed these days immensely.'

February 8:

'I have been painting a lot over the last 2 months. The results are all over the place in impact, half academic, half me being loose yet

plate 23. ***Roger***, 1974,
bodycolour on cream paper,
24.8 x 28.6 cm (9¾ x 11¼ in),
British Museum Collection

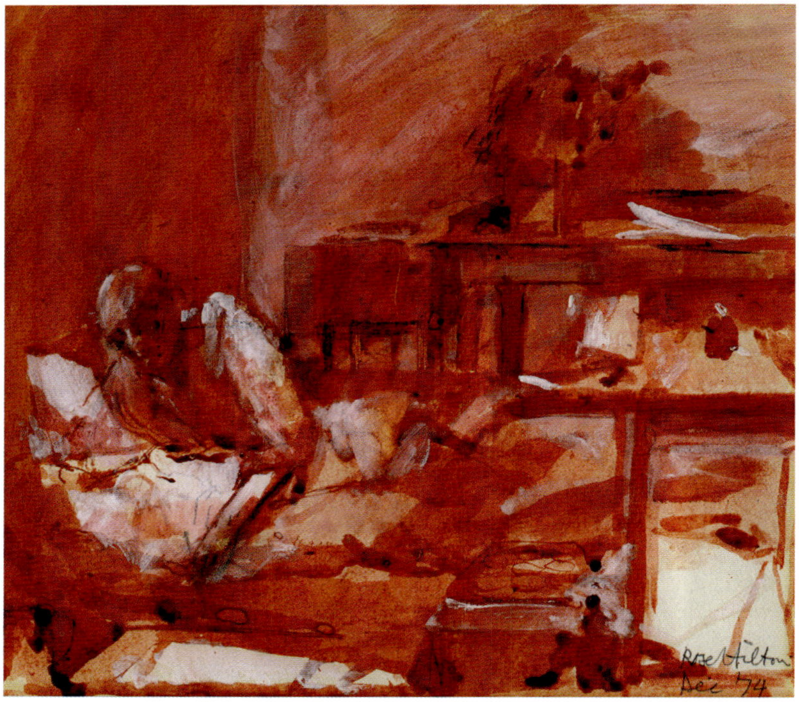

sensitive with paint. I want to paint in a theme. I have been trying to do a series of people in their environments. I thought of having an Instamatic and lots of canvas and working more in a series.

1) look for material – do a series of just patterns
2) room and people series

That's for a start.
Roger still working in bed.
We have quarrelled a lot this week but finally made it all up.'

March 4:
'I have to write it sometime. On February 23rd Roger died. I have put it down now.

I went to London on the 18th February early in the morning. David Brown was down here. He had come down to write notes on R. He is doing a book about him.

Roger didn't really want me to go away. I took some of his work up to Waddingtons for a show that David had arranged for him to have in Plymouth ... Leslie Waddington was not there and so I asked Janet to discuss with him buying in a painting of Roger's to pay off our income tax.

I returned home on Thursday night, arriving at Penzance on Friday morning. Got home quickly. Roger was being sick. I thought he was annoyed at me for leaving him – I was rather ratty with him. I cleaned up the sick. He said he had been sick all night. David rang the doctor but could not get through to him. I said that Roger had these sickness attacks from time to time and I immediately set off for Penzance again to buy him a bedpan and a bottle as he said he felt too weak to use his pail. I was worried, but not unduly so. In the evening Natalie and Adrian Frost came over, rather late, to supper. I was already drinking quite a bit of wine. It was just before my period and I felt very tense. They both had a chat with Roger and then we ate, and sang songs. Roger asked Adrian to ask me to go in to him which I did and he told me he was very tired and not well and not to let anybody in that night. About 2 hours later, it was I suppose about 2 am, I called in to see him. When I saw him lying there moaning with his eyes looking very unnatural I panicked and shouted to David who came in and asked him to phone for the doctor who came out. The doctor said R had suffered a small, he said small, stroke and found he was paralysed down his left side. When David went to bed I laid by Roger and fell asleep, awaking about 5.30 when he was still unconscious and muttering. I went up to David and cried and he came down and we made tea and sat in R's room. Later in the day D went over to Terry's. I stayed with Roger. Dr Bartlett came about 11 and didn't give me much hope. The nurse came at 12 and gave me quite a bit of hope. She returned two hours later with a cup to give him drinks with. All this time the children were unaware that he was particularly ill. I told them on Saturday evening. Bo was heartbroken. I said he may get better. Fergus chose to believe that he would.

On Saturday night Terry and Kath came round. It was a surprise visit as they had already been there in the afternoon. In the afternoon visit Roger had summoned up a very straight look for Terry.

Most of his unconsciousness took the form of being partly conscious with something frightening happening to his left side every quarter of an hour or so. A flicker across his forehead and his eyes would then turn to the left and roll about. Dear dear Roger, it makes me cry when I think of those hours spent with him. People keep telling me that I mustn't live in the past, but I am hardly over Roger yet. I miss being needed by him. The way I resented so much all the minutes being accounted for, and now I have nothing to be back for. I do not feel desolate, I shall always be able to amuse myself, but I shall miss loving, being loved and quarrelling with one person, very much.

Well, to get back to events. Terry and Kath came back over with some beer. This was Saturday 22nd. We were all quite jolly really, although it was a false gaiety, everyone aware that Roger was very sick indeed. The doctor had given him an injection which had sent him to sleep. Looking in on him every so often, he seemed to be sleeping peacefully but with a temperature slowly increasing. I went into Roger's room after Terry and Kath had gone, got into bed by him, after arranging with David to awake him at 3 am. Slept by Roger. Awoke around 3.30 and woke David. I found that I could not sleep in my own bed and so while he sat with Roger I tidied the long room just for something to do. About 4 we both sat in his room drinking tea. Roger's breathing was getting very heavy. I think pneumonia had set in. About 6 I went up the lane saw Simon Gargety getting the cows in. Spoke to him. He said: "Well if Roger is dying you had better get back to him". I went home. It was obvious that he was dying. I told the children … I rang my parents at about this time to tell them R was dying and how desolate I was feeling. David came out and said "It is the end" and I went in to see Roger foaming at the mouth, wiped it away and kissed him. His heart was just faintly beating. It stopped. I closed his eyelids.

That is all. It was a foggy morning. 23rd Feb 8.15 awful. I told the children, they just stayed in their rooms crying. David Brown was stalwart. He subsequently broke down so I have heard.'

27 February
'We buried Roger.'

4 April:
'Remembered how Roger crawled on all fours two weeks before his death to the garden door. The sun was shining. He wanted to see the crocuses.'

AFTER ROGER

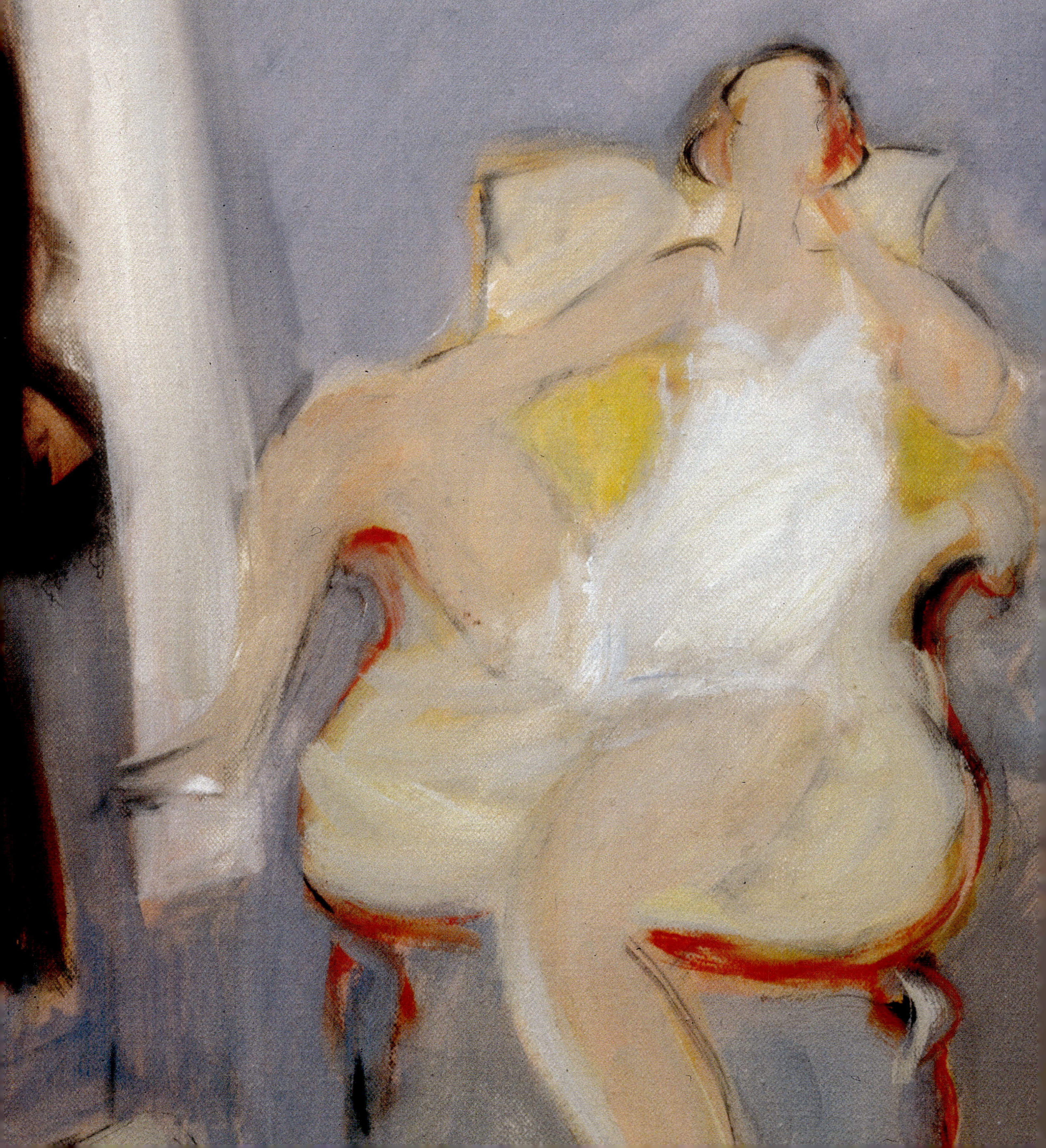

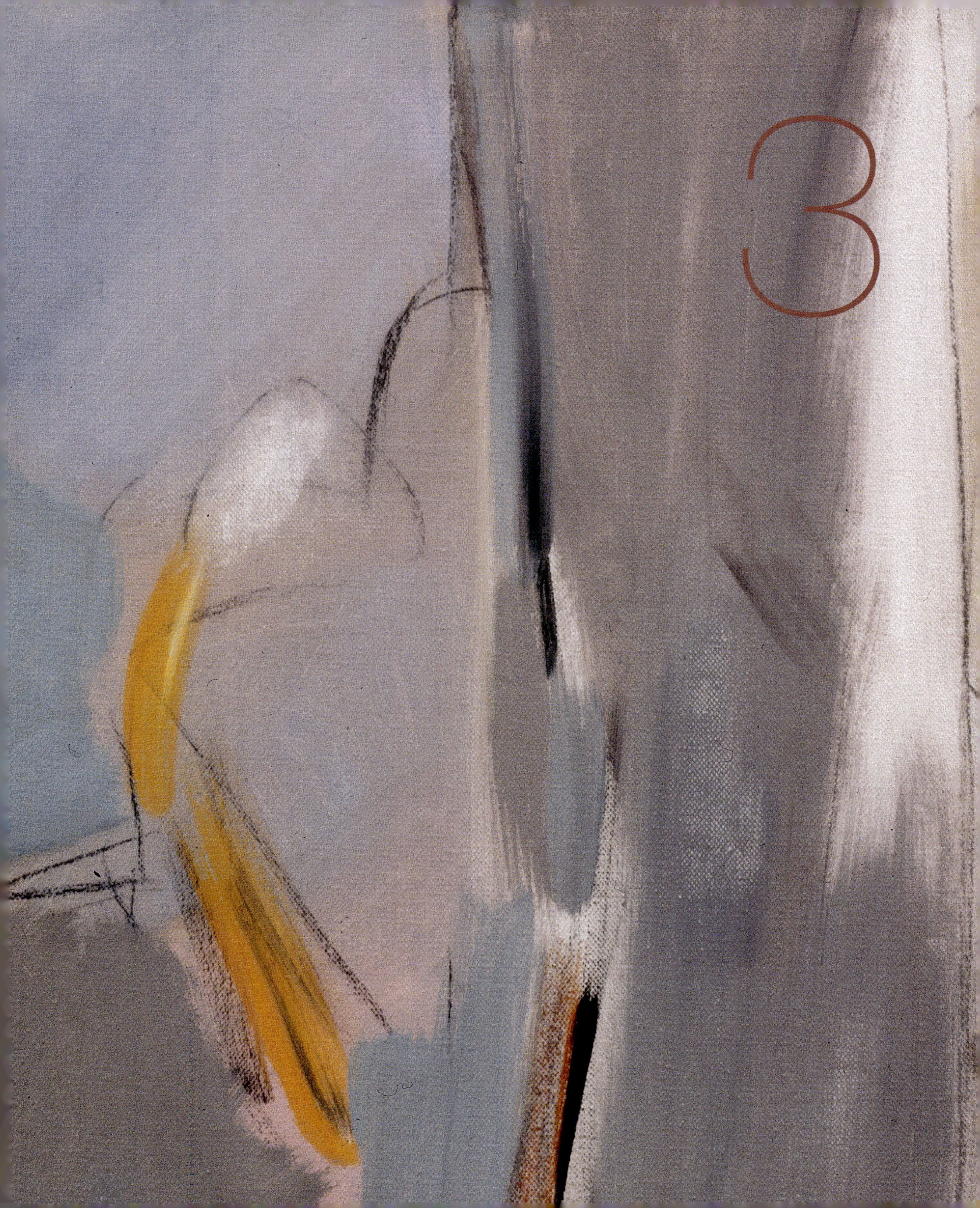
3

LIFE HAD BEEN SO DISRUPTED by Roger's death and all its implications, that for months Rose had not the heart to keep a consecutive diary, and confined her writing to occasional dated comments in a sketchbook. On 11 April 1976 she wrote: 'I miss Roger. It was hell some of the time but there was a bond of being together, of belonging, being part of each other.' Talking recently about the bereavement, Rose singled out one source of consolation.

> After Roger died, I found a book in an Oxfam shop that really helped me. It's called *The Way of All Women*, and it's by a student of Jung called Esther Harding. There's a chapter called 'The Ghostly Lover' and it's all about the animus and the anima and understanding why they behave as they do. I still turn to it at times.

Art was one way of getting through the days. Rose was trying to be organised about painting, having a model, making sure she got up early and put in about four hours in the studio every day, but this routine went out the window that August and she spent the days on the beach. However, by the end of September 1976 all her good intentions were back in place. She notes in her diary: 'I am reading *Vuillard* by John Russell. It is a fascinating book. Also I am painting small pictures under the good influence of this book. I hope to get a studio in St Ives but I do not know yet. I want to go forward in painting. It is difficult ... It has been stimulating to me to work at Pendeen with a model ... Sydney and Nessie came over to supper on Tuesday, the first relaxed meeting since Roger died. I want to see more of them.'

And then a sharp downturn. 5 October: 'Difficult few days ... senseless drinking to obliterate insecure emotional feelings. I am painting this week on paintings started but not finished.'

Rose recalls her work of this time:

> The more I was absorbing a different approach, triggered by my talks with Roger, the more painters like Vuillard and Matisse interested me. The way Vuillard would use a low-key palette, black becoming an essential colour (for instance in the ladies' dresses) for the composition. Or the way Matisse would choose a palette of, say, reds and paint a whole room with this colour dominating it. It was this kind of thing that was suddenly becoming alive to me.

Rose's diary for 1977 continues in the same sketchbook and she predicts it will be 'mostly about the long continual haul from Roger's death.' By March she has organised other distractions that will also contribute to the family finances. 'Two days teaching at Falmouth. Very stimulating. I've got lots of material to go ahead now.' But the shadows are still long. A few days later she writes: 'Dreamed very intensely of Roger. His dying was very much longer: we communicated. The sense that we are all mortal was strong, even in this way it was, to me, good to get into contact with him. I have been numb about Roger for so long. In my life in general there is 75% of the time a great sense of unreality. The boys are the quarter that is real. My life seemed completely involved when R was alive. I did not think it was just a dream. Often it was hell and good, difficult or relaxing. My painting now is more of a struggle. I am getting more involved with this.'

A lot of her diary entries are taken up with her art. On 11 March she writes: 'I am working a lot now. Becoming more calculating in what might unwittingly upset my flow of work ... Anyone can do art, can train. Few people have imagination. I am not sure whether I have much. Even if I have not, I would like to go on tearing the shreds away of rigidness to be able to appreciate the work of people that do have it.'

In Cornwall, the summer for Rose is a time of friends visiting, swimming and eating outside, and often painting drops down the list of priorities.

On 7 September she writes: 'I am very disgusted with myself. For one thing I have not painted for 3 months. I have made myself available to two men both of whom turned me down. I am 46 now and behaving very immaturely ... I went over to St Ives and called on Norman and Margaret Levine. Margaret is very ill indeed. Norman has a good effect on me. A steadying influence. I can't find anywhere to place my emotions. Sex is not so difficult because if the worst happens and one cannot find anyone to go to bed with there is always DIY, which is a rather limp much condensed sexual experience. And always accompanying guilt.

...

I have to start the long slog uphill, going inwards. No socialising – was it Norman Levine who said you are just going to one party too many? I wanted him to have a good image of me, but I think he thinks I am superficial, on the trot from middle age. I wish I could be honest with him ... I think I must go to my studio, set up something to paint and get into it.

And not worry about any relationship.

I am not a good person.

My life with Roger was very involved.

I sometimes let him down.'

Later that month, she writes peremptorily: 'All this schoolgirl reporting must stop.' Yet she also notes: 'Spiritual life depends on honesty.' In October, Rose speculates that a rival might explain her promiscuous behaviour to her friends 'saying that it is all a result of Roger's continual slanging of me in public. Well he did treat me badly but it is a Hilton trait I have noticed and only let's say a third of the complete relationship which contained affection, need and my great luck to have his companionship and conversation.'

The diaries become sporadic, often only a glorified notebook with an important event or emotion noted down. In April 1978, Rose has friends to stay, goes out to the Gurnard's Head one lunchtime and bumps into Terry Frost. 'I had an encouraging talk ... he said to go on working whatever happened.' In July she records that she has started to paint again. Things are quieter at home, the boys are growing up and don't rely so much on their mother. 'This phase of my life is very full, because for a time without Fergus being here, I am able to act as a more complete individual, however extreme this is. Sometimes dissolute, sometimes kind, sometimes selfish. But myself, and not all mothering.' Her entry for 1 January 1979 is fairly typical: 'Now is resolution time. Usual cut down on smoking. More exercise – a walk or jog a day. A painting routine.' On 12 May, 'This is a boring old book but it is therapeutic for me. This week I fell in love with the Vicar!'

That summer, Dudley Sutton was acting in a film with Michael Caine called *The Island*, which was being shot on location in the West Indies. Dudley, who had become a much-loved family friend, sent air tickets for Rose and the boys to fly out to Antigua and stay for a holiday while he was filming. It was something in return for always coming down to stay with the Hiltons in Cornwall, but it was also a very generous gesture. The family spent six weeks there in beautiful weather and had a marvellous holiday. Rose returned feeling healthy and confident.

plate 24. ***Evening Landscape, Cornwall***, 1986, oil on canvas, 35.6 x 45.7 cm (14 x 18 in)

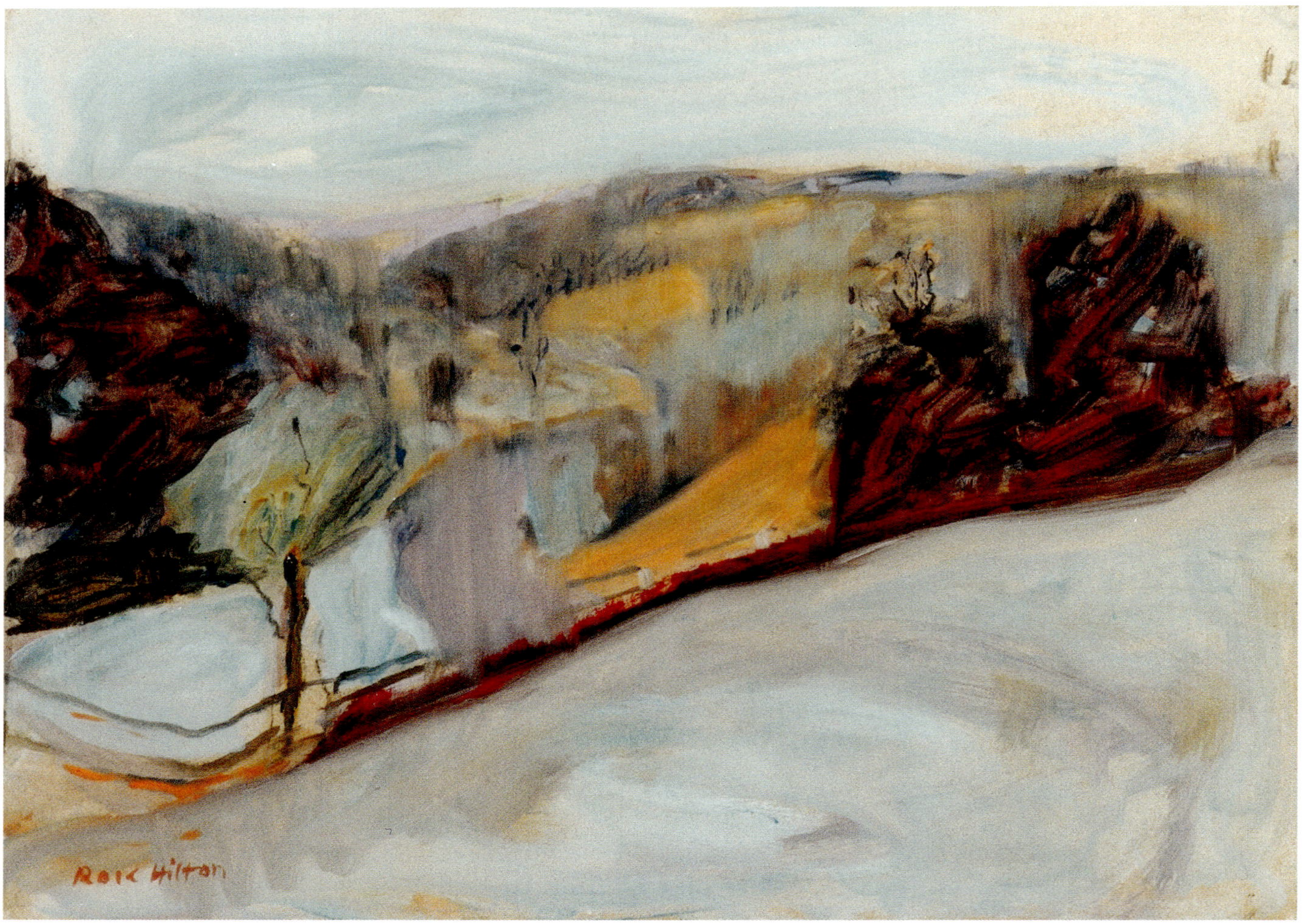

THE 1980s

THERE WAS ALWAYS something about the men she chose which kept Rose from any lasting commitment. Undoubtedly she was constantly comparing them to Roger and finding them lacking, but she also held back on account of her painting. She was beginning to make some progress in her work, and she did not want a relationship that competed too strongly for her time and energy. There was an on–off relationship with Ander Gunn, the photographer, but as Rose recalls: 'He was working up in Leeds so I only saw him occasionally.' Nevertheless she must have been drawn to him, for she calls him in one of her diaries 'the beautiful but elusive Ander'. The yearning for companionship and physical intimacy did not suddenly evaporate. As Rose says: 'It seems to me that I've always longed for somebody. A bit like the religious thing. But I didn't really want them because I wanted to paint.'

Did the other artists in Cornwall have much influence on Rose?

Bob Bourne did [plate 27]. Roger used to call in on him and talk to him about his art. When Roger died and Bob became my best friend, in return for giving him a good meal and a bath every Sunday we'd talk about painting all the time and go on walks. It was through Bob that I got very interested in painting again. He really talked about composition and dividing up the canvas and that gave me an extra push to

plate 25. ***Study for 'The Singing Lesson'***, 1986, coloured chalks on paper, 15.2 x 14 cm (6 x 5½ in)

plate 26. ***Seated Nude***, 1986, coloured chalks on paper, 41.9 x 30.5 cm (16½ x 12 in)

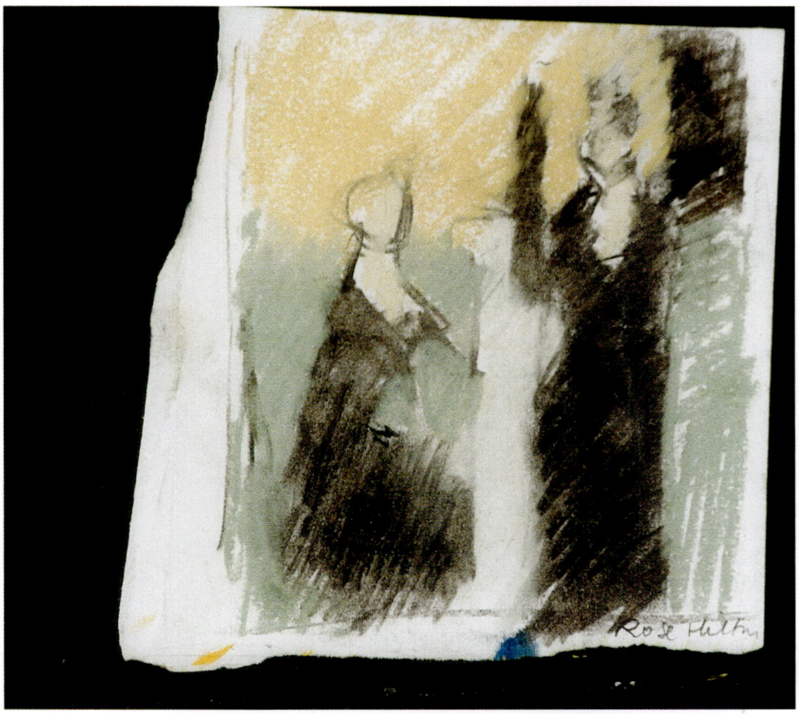

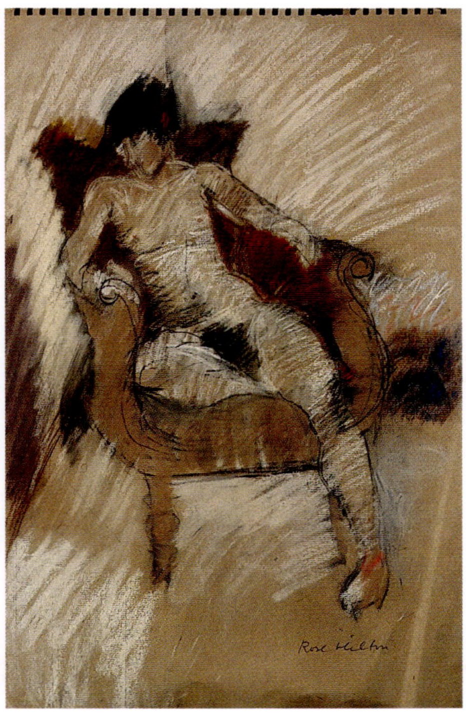

plate 27. ***Bob Bourne***,
1980,
oil on canvas,
25.4 x 30.5 cm (10 x 12 in)

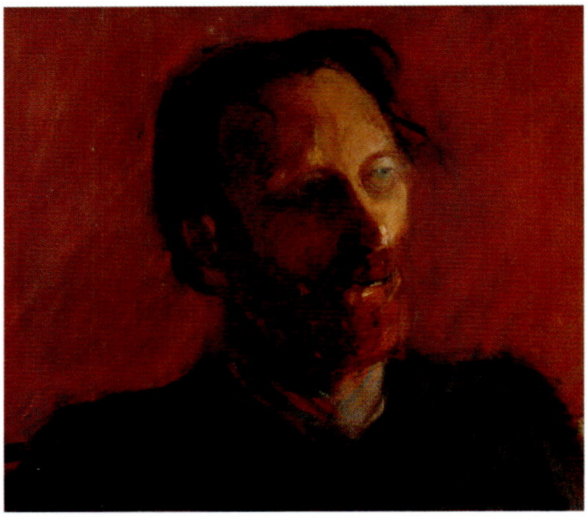

explore rather than just paint a portrait. This was relating it to a much bigger cause, not just drawing the model. Bob talked to me a lot about shapes and composition and said that Roger had helped him with all that, to simplify things. So he gave me back what Roger had taught him and we looked at each other's work all the time. He influenced me a lot, though he was a different kind of artist. He had no facility like I had, though that often got in my way. I'm glad for his influence and I've always acknowledged it. And he kept my interest up. This was the late 70s and into the 80s.

Patrick Heron was awfully kind, and wrote me a reference for a studio above the Penwith Gallery soon after Roger died, just to get me out every day while the children were at school. I had that for about two years, but it was really too far to travel to St Ives. I only went about three days a week, though it was a kind of discipline.

I didn't see Terry very much. Sydney and Nessie continued to be friends, though I couldn't go over and booze a lot in the daytime with them. I did once and met the boys after school and drove into a parked Landrover. So I made a decision that I wasn't going to drink at lunchtimes and I didn't. That was probably about three years after Roger died. We had big parties here instead – perhaps about three a year. We had an Easter Bonnet party and everybody made fantastic hats. So they had a bit of style. The editor of *The Cornishman* came with a whole tray of drinks stuck on his head. All the characters came. The boys were in their teens and twenties and they loved these parties. So I have been rather sociable. That was all through the 80s.

In July 1981 Rose notes: 'Last year I thought I was selling Botallack Moor but the sale fell through. Bo and Fergus and I went to live in Penzance, in New Street. We let this house in Botallack. The stay in Penzance was good for us all ... There have been happy days of solitude – golden sunlight. I have been living alone here in Botallack this summer as Fergus is staying with friends.

I am painting for an exhibition in Taunton. It won't be very spectacular. One or two good paintings. I haven't had a serious relationship since Roger. The one with Ander never got going in physical fact, but a lot of unhappy longings for me and I am relieved to have got out of it at last. The other men in my life are dear friends like Dudley, David Brown [plate 29] and sometimes a confrontation with other people's husbands, glimpses of relating that could, but never will be, except fragmentary exchanges that help them in their marriage, help me in my aloneness.

plate 28. ***Reflective Nude***,
1987,
oil on canvas,
73.7 x 73.7 cm (29 x 29 in)

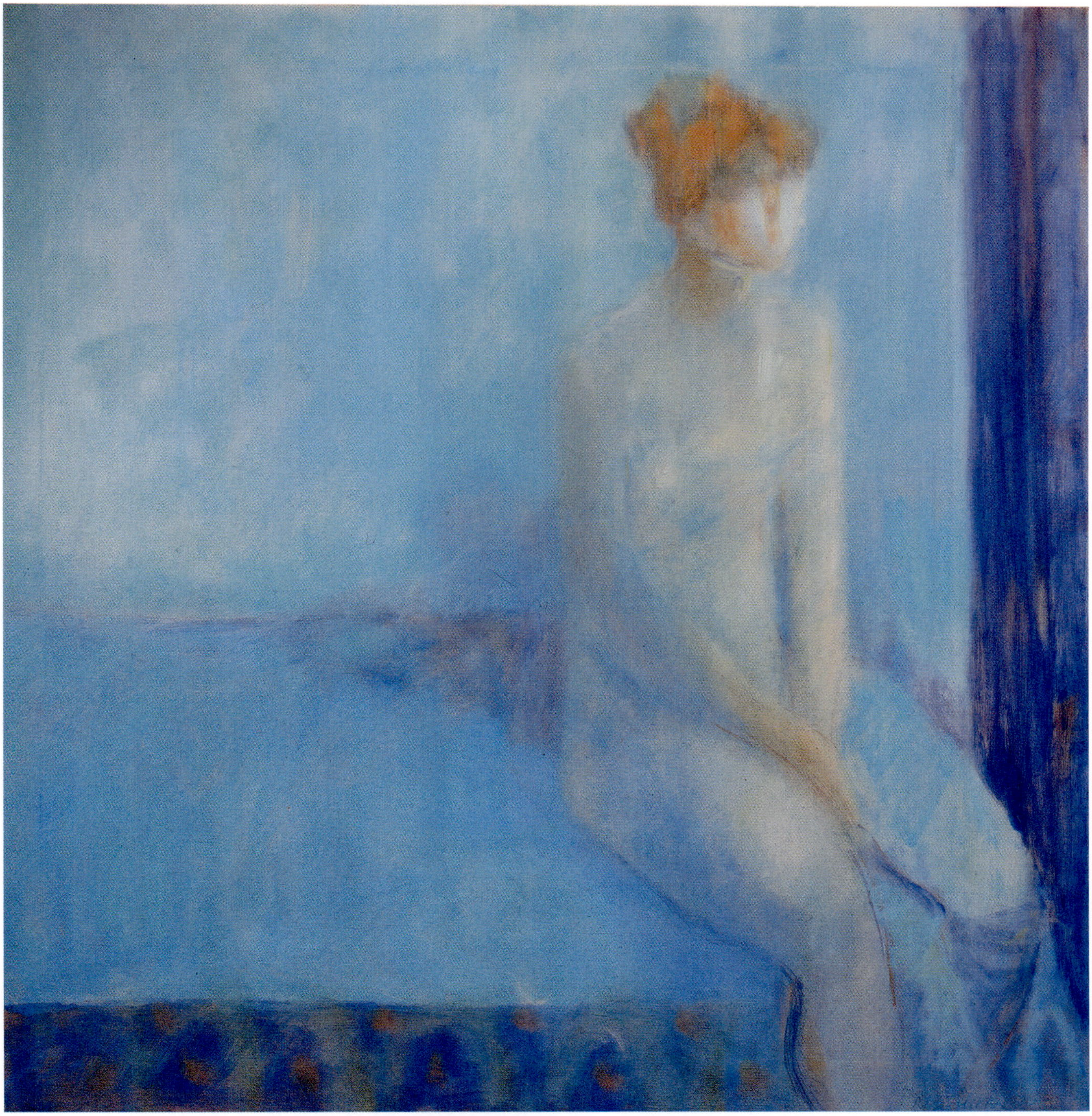

plate 29. ***David Brown***, 1966, pencil on paper, 25.4 x 20.3 cm (10 x 8 in)

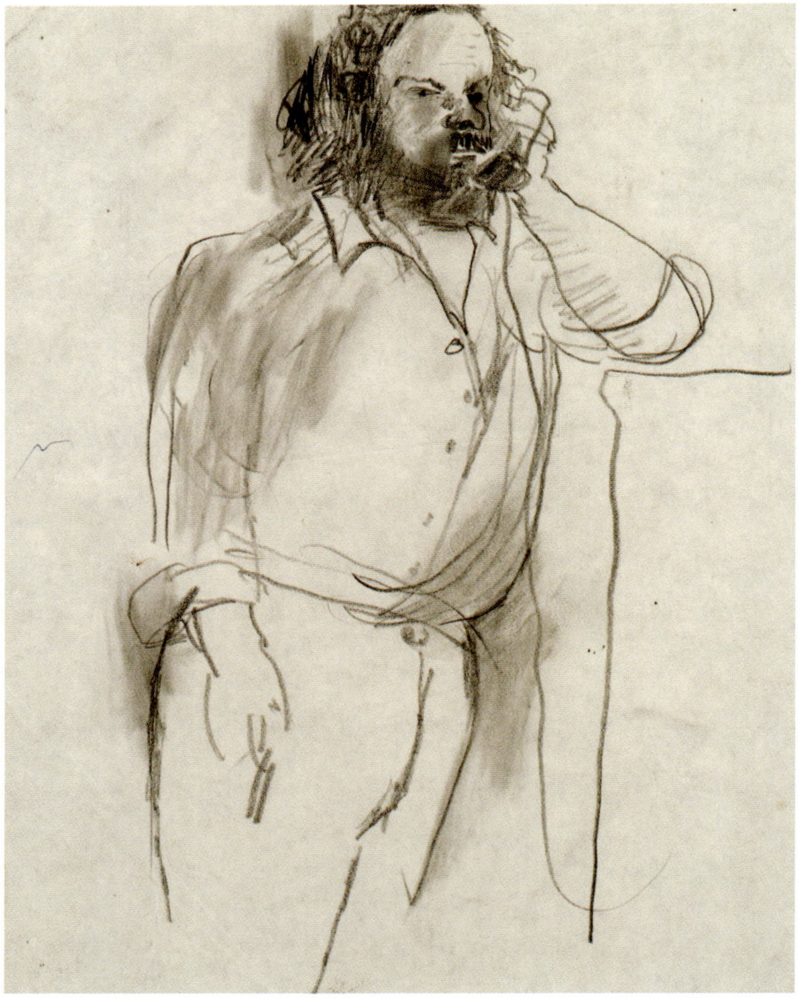

Occasional moments of depression recur, but Rose surmounts them. Does she actually need a relationship? She debates it very frankly with herself. 'What do I want out of it? Not a fuck particularly. More a valuation of myself as I am at present.'

Two months later she writes: 'Back at Botallack the horses are coming to live in the field, we are preparing to keep chickens. Bob Needham has bought the field for 5 thou – we are getting out of debt and preparing to stay on.'

In January 1982 she did embark on an affair with a larger-than-life Don Juan, called Raoul.

> I decided that if I had anybody it was going to have to be light and fun. Before I really understood myself a bit more I tended to go for alcoholics. There was my great big handsome Dutch sea captain. I didn't want any more art problems for a while. He certainly drank a lot. The boys loved him and I had fun with him. But I realized I was going to endanger my relationship with my children if I went on drinking. Bob Bourne was a more steadying influence on me.

Yet the charms of Raoul were certainly seductive, and Rose wrote: 'He has opened up a warm channel in me, going out towards other people. He has shown me more affection than anyone I have ever known. That is I have been ready to accept his affection as I like his temperament. It will be interesting to see what happens. The good way of experiencing an interchange of personality is an affair which is somewhat of a fight too ... I have learned a lot from him. How to be truly what you are which required self-discipline, strong will and an ability for introspection. I must start with my own work. Maybe do some landscape.'

By the end of March she records: 'Now I am working in a studio in Penzance. I have had it a month or more. Very valuable to me.' Painting and love, rarely do the two go equably hand in hand, but there is certainly movement on both fronts in Rose's life. On 4 July she writes: 'Serene month. I have toyed with the idea of sharing my life. I am unable to make a decision. Eric L has been a very dear companion these last two months'. Needless to say, nothing was resolved, and the year ended with a riotous party. Rose records its salient points in her diary.

31 December:
The most crowded stampede of a
New Year's Party
THICK WITH PEOPLE HERE!
One must learn to love the human race
Petty thieving
Damaged furniture
Fights
A few lovings it seems.

The 1983 diary for 12 January reads: 'Very important quote from Matisse writing in 1948: "I have always tried to hide my own efforts and wished my works to have the lightness and joyousness of a springtime which never lets anyone suspect the labours it has cost. So I am afraid that the young, seeing in my work only that apparent facility and negligence in the drawing, will use this as an excuse for dispensing with certain efforts which I believe necessary".'

Rose's admiration for Matisse was a constant encouragement and inspiration, and later that year, in the summer, she flew to Russia for two weeks on a Saga tour especially to visit the Hermitage and see the Matisses and the other French paintings in the State Collection.

But at home her own life wasn't so easy to regulate, especially when there were the distractions of people to meet and pubs to drink in. On 14 January she writes: 'Finally after a week back from London, trying to think creatively, ha. Did two lousy pastels. Not too happy in myself. Drinking fast and too much when I drink ...' In an attempt to reintroduce some discipline into her life, Rose started doing yoga again.

On 21 March she notes: 'The constant theme of my thought is how I have lacked a courage to act for myself. It usually is how it will look in other peoples' eyes. I want to act out of deep instinct, like drawing a line. Making acts of faith, believing I am right because I think like that.' A couple of weeks later she continues: 'Full of jealousies, nagging doubts ... If I get my internal life straight by prayers, routine, painting, I will cope.' And a day or two after: 'Love is positive. It is the only way of true renewal, breaking down and going on again. I need Faith. I have glimmerings. Pouring all this out now so as to encourage myself to try harder. Rise early. Obey the inner voice. Roger says that somewhere re: art. It can apply to one's life.'

According to the diary, June was a time of particular self-searching. She writes: 'I am seeking like mad for stability. Now not so much coming from another person, but trying to feel right in myself.' And again: 'Painting is expressing. It is more important to relate to the areas of one's personality that are intuitive. These are useless in everyday life where practical solutions are demanded. Introspection is valuable. It's difficult to know oneself, separate the areas, use with confidence and trust (Roger did) the true responses to objects, life figure, landscape or interior. It is difficult as he said to speak about your inner workings but it is most important to respect them, use them, spend

plate 30. ***Sara Sarong***,
1994,
oil on canvas,
83.8 x 71.1 cm (33 x 28 in)

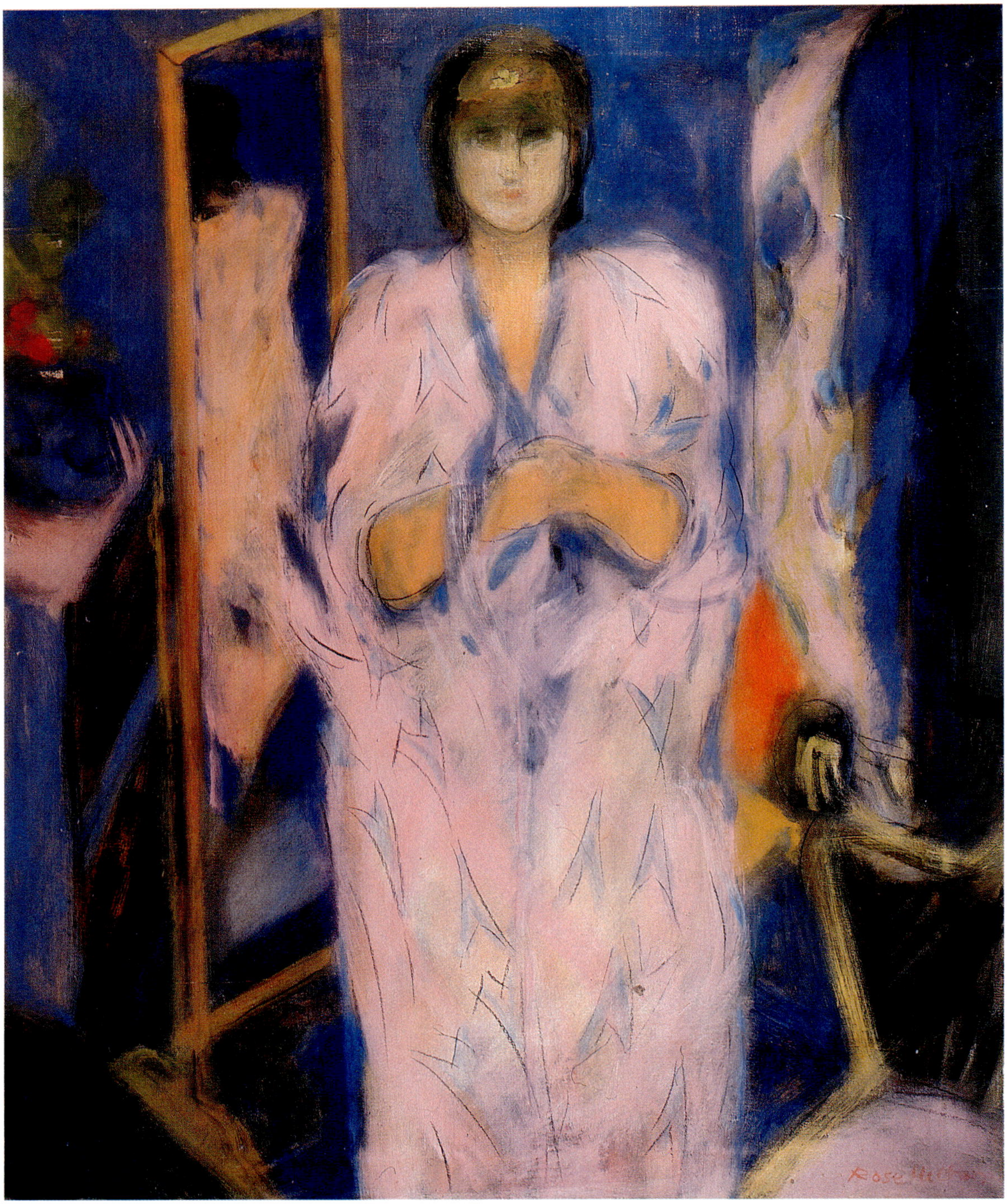

time strengthening them, combating doubts.'

Money was still a problem, but she continued to paint. She comments:

> As Roger once said you don't need all that much money if you really want to paint. He didn't believe in huge studios. Some artists do and have all the equipment, but he made all those gouaches from very little. It's in you to do it or it isn't.

Other artists continued to inspire her. On 25 January 1984 she writes in her diary: 'Went to see Raoul Dufy show at the Hayward. It was very good. The paintings meant a lot to me as I have been struggling with the portraits of Sara [a very beautiful half-Indian woman who often posed, [plate 30] and have now managed to finish them.'

On 16 February, a momentous decision was taken. Rose records: 'Talk with Janet Leach. Very good. Decided to call [myself] Hilton.' Up until this point, Rose had been signing her work Phipps and exhibiting under this name, but Janet Leach, second and surviving wife of Bernard Leach, who had personal experience of the value of a famous name, advised her otherwise. Later Rose had certain reservations, noting in September 1995: 'I may have made a mistake in not keeping to Phipps as there are so many Hiltons in the Art Game. I don't doubt my own talent. It isn't huge but it is there. I think I am intelligent and have a sort of endurance.'

Work progresses, but there are moments of despair. 27 February 1984: 'In a stupid attempt to "get on" with my painting, I attacked one of the big still lifes and slopped grey paint all over it, ruining its fresh quality. I don't know whether I can redeem it. Must get back to routine and energetic painting with big canvases.' A week later she records: 'Worked on small painting from drawing. Going to have a go at the Royal Academy.' Two months later she is able to write: 'Had painting *Locked in Love* [plate 17] accepted by RA.' Less than a month later a buyer appears. 'A good sense of well-being brought about by hearing that Lord Gowrie (Minister of Arts) bought my picture in the Royal Academy ... I am conscious that my painting now is rather achieved in a vacuum but I have very good conditions and hope to pull off some more to have a show.'

On 4 June she writes: 'Reading Anthony Powell's [memoir] *To Keep the Ball Rolling*. I like his writing although he irritates me by packaging people, writers possibly more talented than himself – Orwell, Greene. By packaging they are somewhat diminished. I find David Brown does this about Roger. It is a subtle thing. I find some powerful presence, or rather personality, putting their version of a complex man does limit the fantasies one has, rightly, about Roger, other writers etc.'

Lord Gowrie had for many years been an admirer and collector of Roger Hilton's work, so when he bought Rose's painting at the Academy, he was naturally intrigued to meet her. This took place at Plymouth on 13 June. 'Had an animated conversation about Roger's work in which he mentioned that his first wife had met R at a private view where R had put his hand through a hole in a Henry Moore sculpture and pinched her bum. Didn't know that.'

Another important event occurred that

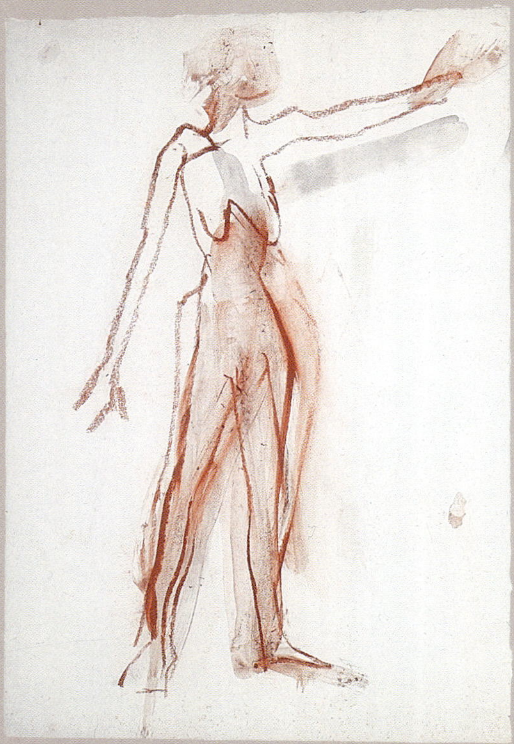

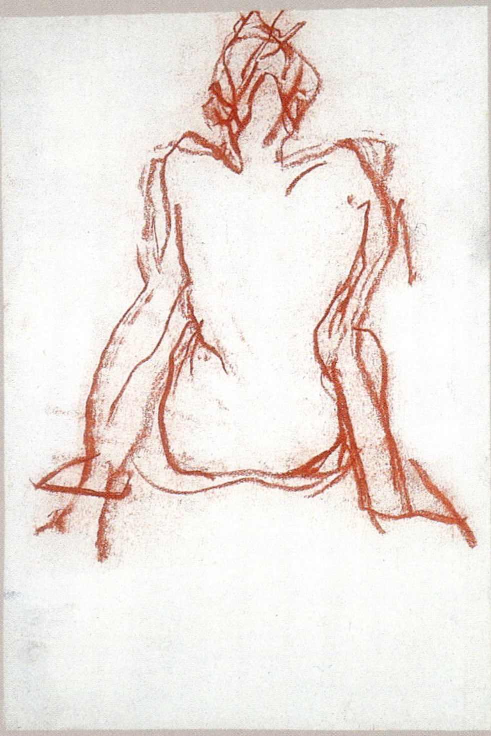

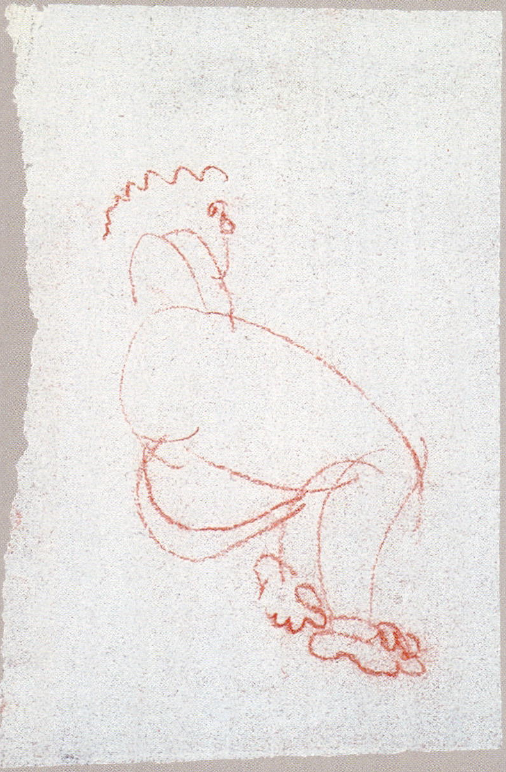

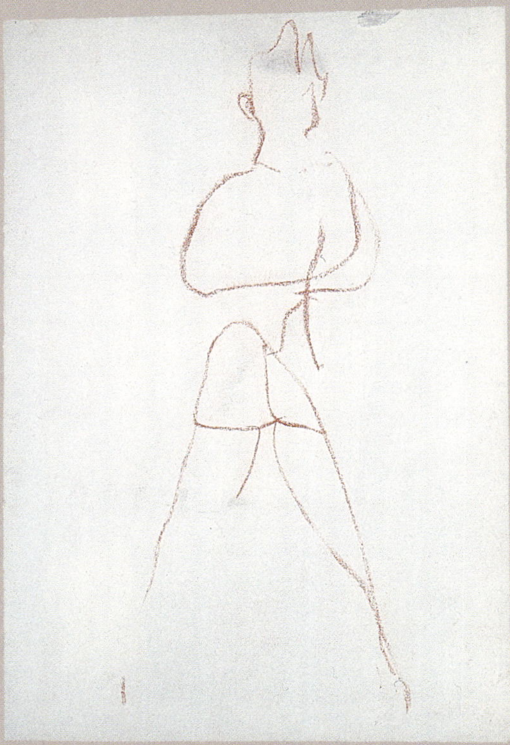

autumn of 1984 when Rose enrolled in Cecil Collins' drawing class at the Central School of Art. She met him first on 30 October: 'Drew all day in his class. A spectacular experience. Have sadly neglected my diary out of a lurking fundamental depression.' The next day she records, evidently retrospectively: 'In London for a few weeks. Utterly stimulating, depression lifting.' On 13 November she writes: 'Went to Cecil Collins' class at the Central. I gather what he is about is his approach to drawing. He likes to get the essence of a person to show through, to waken their perceptions. I can't go on copying from photos if I go deeper into his philosophy, but fear being left in a mess with my painting.'

A week later she had a further talk with Collins who stressed the need for discipline to let creativity through. Rose writes: 'He believes in communal work, anything but self-praise for doing Art. He did say, which thrilled me, that if we could have you for another 5 years you would come through. I don't know whether I can get through another term. I want to desperately. I don't feel I have had enough of him to make it stick.' In fact Rose did attend more of Collins' classes and derived a lot of confidence from his teaching, which had the effect of freeing up her drawing from an over-dependence on an academic approach ultimately derived from Augustus John.

plate 31. ***Four figure drawings done in Cecil Collins' class***, 1984, red chalk and wash on paper, each 27.9 x 20.3 cm (11 x 8 in)

LAUNCHING HER CAREER

FOR YEARS AFTER Roger died it continued to be difficult for Rose to make ends meet. She recalls:

Leslie Waddington wasn't very interested in promoting Roger's work, though marvellously he still paid me a retainer. Enough to keep us going but not really enough to live on. Roger wasn't really in demand and his work wasn't selling. In 1983, Michael Harrison and Andrew Wilton came and looked at Roger's work and took some for an exhibition called *Alive to it All*. They hung about 20 of his pictures at the Serpentine, which looked very good. Then Julian Spalding came and he was going to buy a picture of Roger's for the Graves Art Gallery in Sheffield but then decided he couldn't. I was really looking forward to having some money because I didn't have any. I'd borrowed £5,000 from the bank in order to manage and I took any odd teaching job on offer. I did some at Bristol and some at Falmouth too. But we were short of money. And I didn't join David Messum until 1989.

Above all I wanted to get on with my painting. I stretched all my own canvases and painted on the cheapest primed cotton possible. I don't like painting over old pictures though occasionally I have reversed the canvas, though you have to size it a lot. I also painted on wood and board. I started showing at the Newlyn and Penwith annual exhibitions.

Then in 1987 I was asked to have a one-man show at the Newlyn Art Gallery, on the top floor, which is a lovely gallery. Janet Bennett worked at the Newlyn. I'd been painting for 10 years and I'd collected quite a lot together. Although I continued to paint still-lifes, most

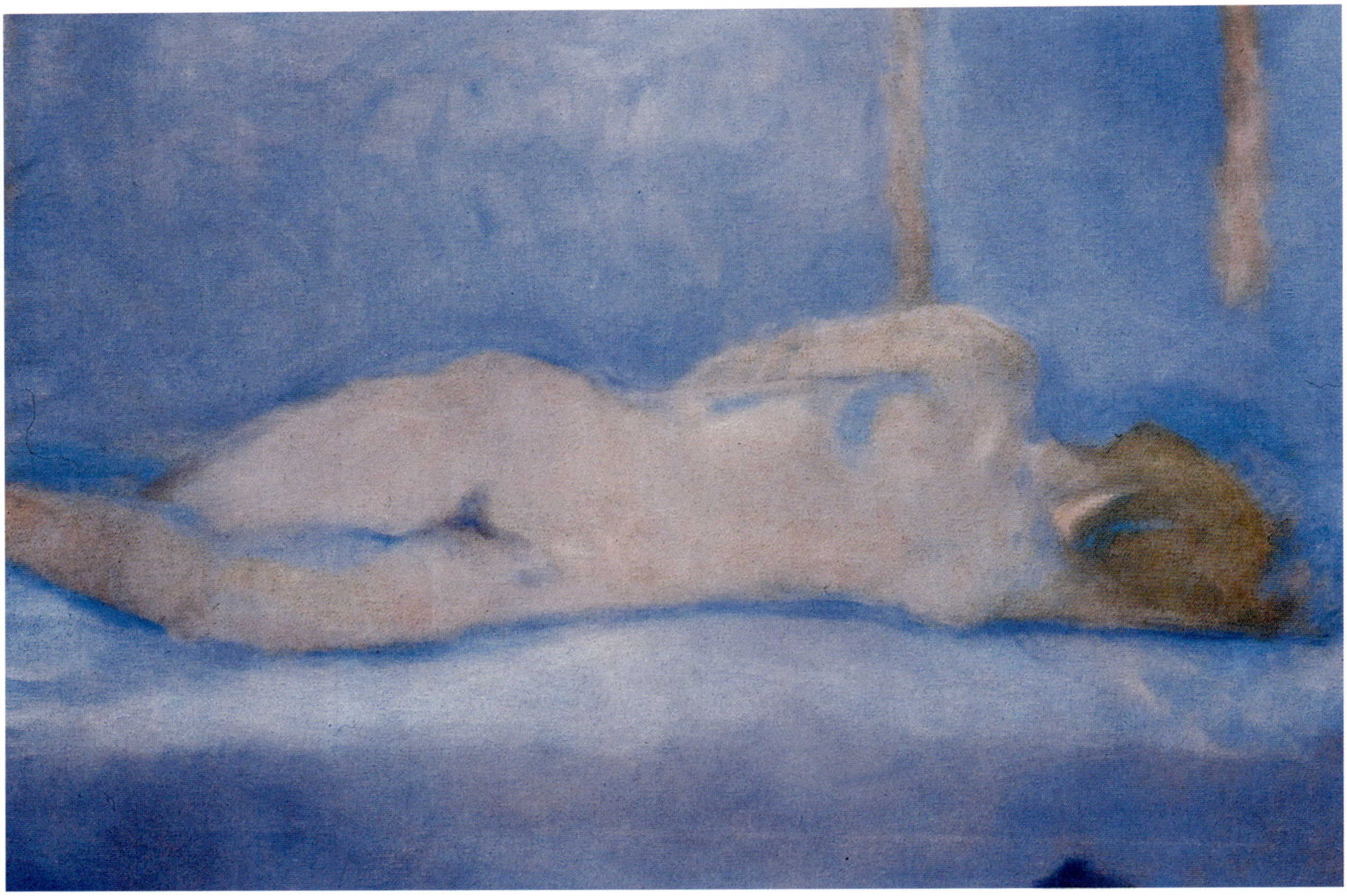

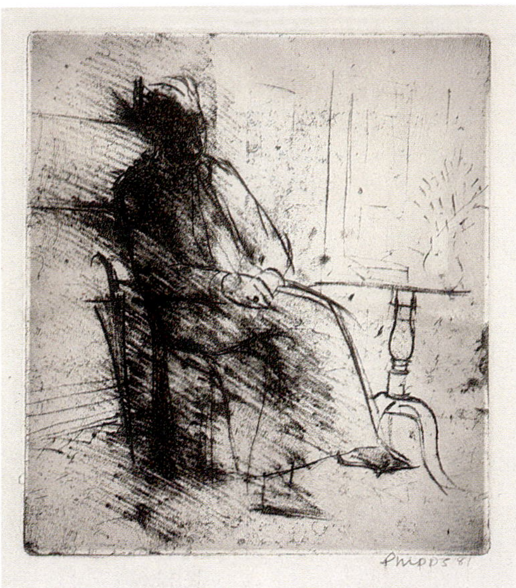

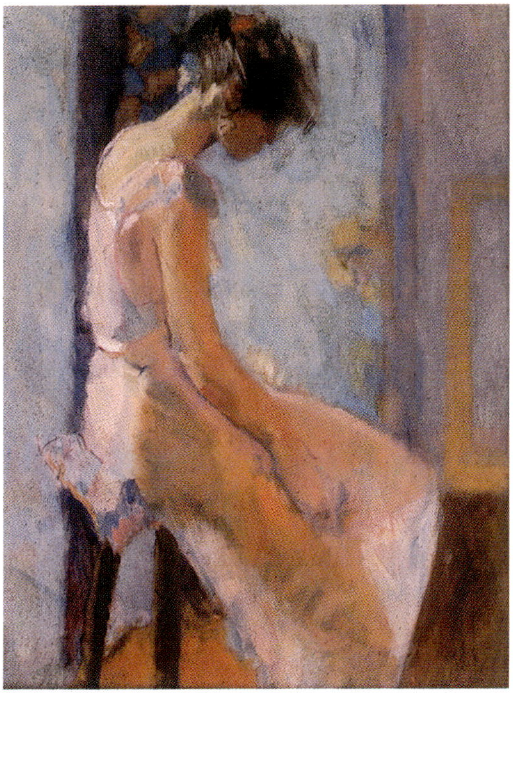

plate 32. ***Figure***, 1986,
oil on canvas,
50.8 x 76.2 cm (20 x 30 in)

plate 33. ***Evening*** or ***Seated Girl***, 1987,
oil on canvas,
50.8 x 45.7 cm (20 x 18 in)

plate 34. ***Mrs Johnstone***, 1981,
etching,
22.86 x 20.3 cm (9 x 8 in)

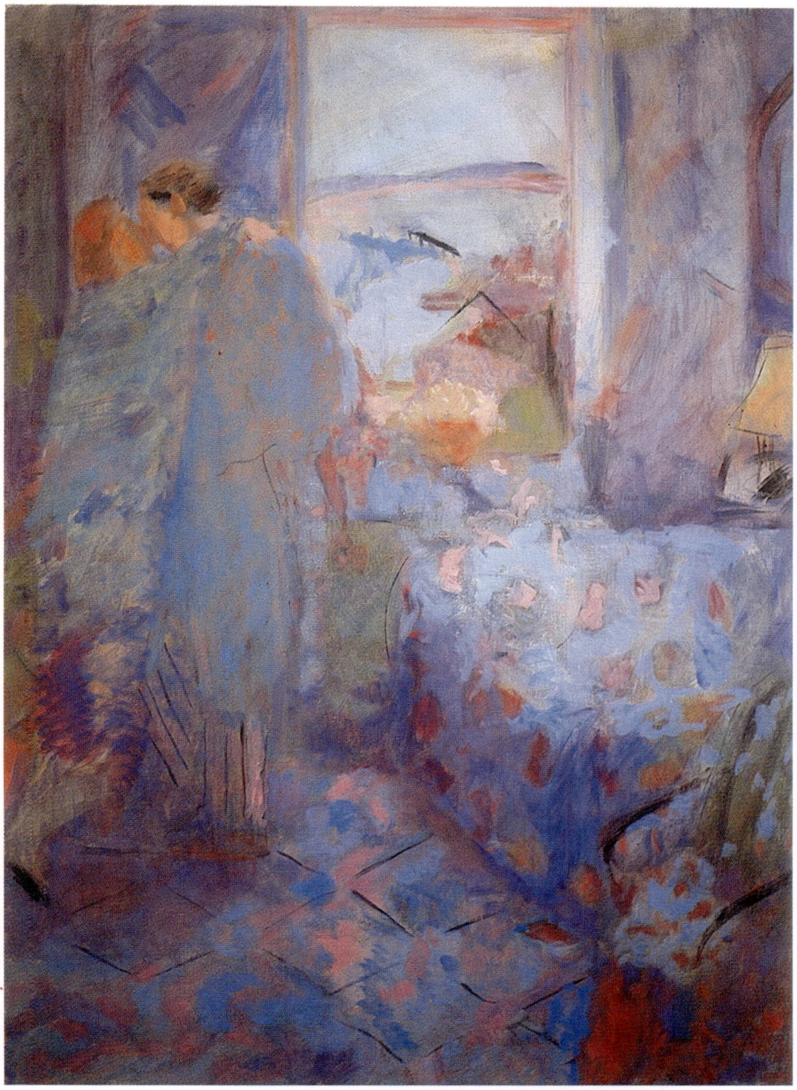

plate 35. ***The Honeymoon***, 1987, oil on canvas, 91.4 x 111.8 cm (36 x 44 in)

were pictures of friends posing for me. I dressed them up in all sorts of costumes and put them in interiors. They were mostly decorative in essence, but the figures were far more related to their background than before.

I think Janet bought a painting. I shared the show – but not the room – with Michael Upton and David Kemp, who had the rooms downstairs. Cornwall County Council bought a big one and so did Plymouth Museum and I had rather a wonderful time. David Messum saw the show – he was down looking at John Miller's work. And then he asked me to show at his gallery. All that gave me confidence. It was a big step to show at the Newlyn.

After that I arranged to have a show in Oxford, in 1988, rather pretty paintings which sold well. And then I also had a show with Michael Parkin. Meanwhile David Messum said he'd like to take me on permanently, and in a way he seemed a better proposition. I felt safe there and I just wanted to get on with my painting.

But there were other concerns on the horizon. In 1988, Rose's younger son, Fergus, suffered a mental breakdown. The problems attendant on his condition and anxiety over his welfare absorbed a great deal of Rose's immediate time and energy. In 1989 he was diagnosed as schizophrenic, and he has lived in care ever since, though pursuing a remarkably creative life as a poet and painter. In the midst of these worries, Rose struggled to maintain her life as an artist, and keep a routine going in the studio. She needed to produce a fairly constant stream of paintings in order to make a living and satisfy expectant clients. Rose was making a name for herself.

Exhibitions of great art were a periodic boost and inspiration. In February 1988 she went to the Miró show at the Whitechapel and found it 'most stimulating.' In March she visited the Royal Academy to see the Italian show. 'The Modiglianis marvellous, the Morandis stupendous', she notes in her diary. But it was difficult to maintain the momentum. On 1 April she writes: 'Not painting at present but still very interested in the time when I will be. Have found a new direction.'

In May, another close relative was rushed

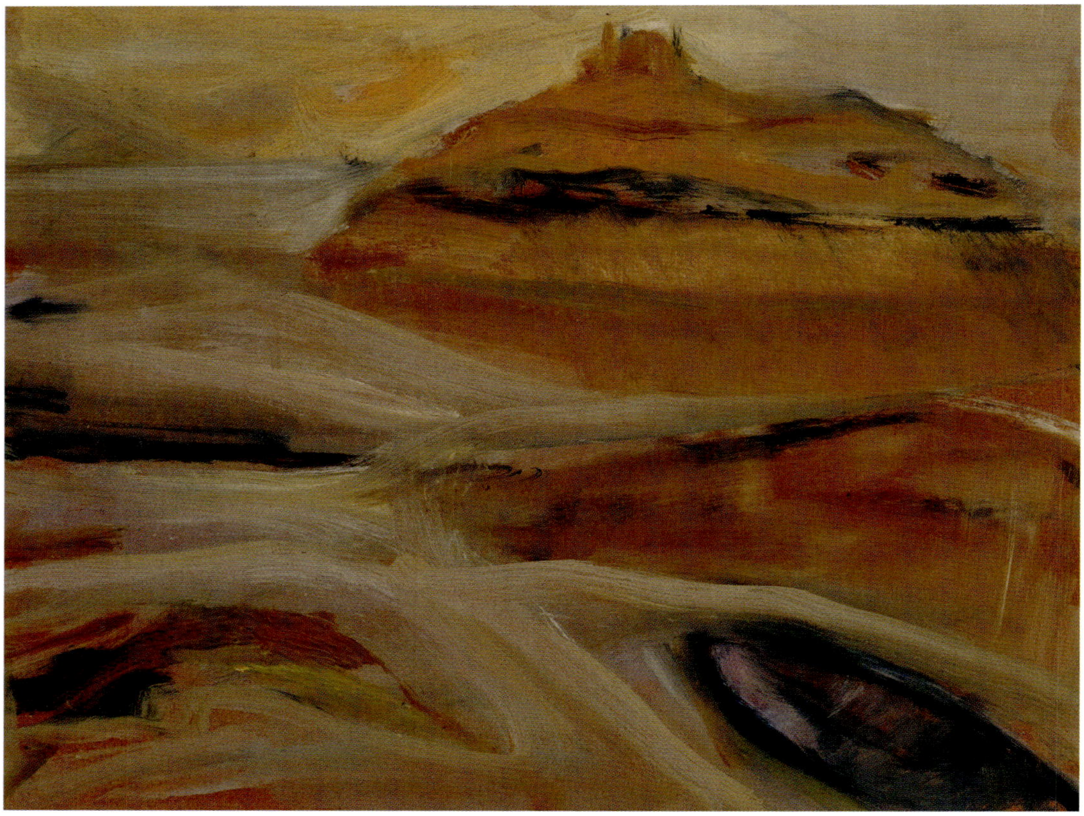

plate 36. ***St Michael's Mount***, 1988,
oil on board,
22.9 x 30.5 cm (9 x 12 in)

into care. 'Today mother had a heart attack. I was staying with Mum & Dad to help clear up. Dad & I put her into hospital, she is recovering. She was very frightened and childlike in her panic. I think she needs this extra time to calm herself. She has worked physically too hard, mentally is not prepared for death. Went to visit. Feeling very fond of her. The pepper and salt sparkle and crackle and naughtiness all come from her. Dad thoroughly good, perhaps too passive.'

The days of real conflict with her parents are over for Rose and she can now appreciate them. But not all is sweetness and light. On 24 September she notes: 'Row with Mum. Very upsetting for both of us. Over religion as usual. We made it up in the evening over lots of tears.'

Painting continued and Rose was painting a model who would feature a lot in years to come. 27 June: 'Val came today. I painted a simpering picture.' The sharp criticism is very healthy, and the following day Rose is able to report: 'Altered picture'. Rose painted a lot from the figure, employing a number of girls to come and pose casually as well as more professional models. Cornwall is still a poor area of England, and there are always girls who need the extra income, although the Tate in St Ives has made quite a difference. At this point, Rose's existence was a quiet one. Occasionally she would go to London for an exhibition (Ivon Hitchens was an autumn inspiration) or go out painting locally with her older son, Bo, an accomplished realist in the Ken Howard tradition. On 27 October she writes in her diary: 'Life in Botallack is nearly all to do with painting or reading'. At the beginning of December, it's time to make Christmas cards again. This year Rose: 'painted up cards ... originally starting with a lino cut.'

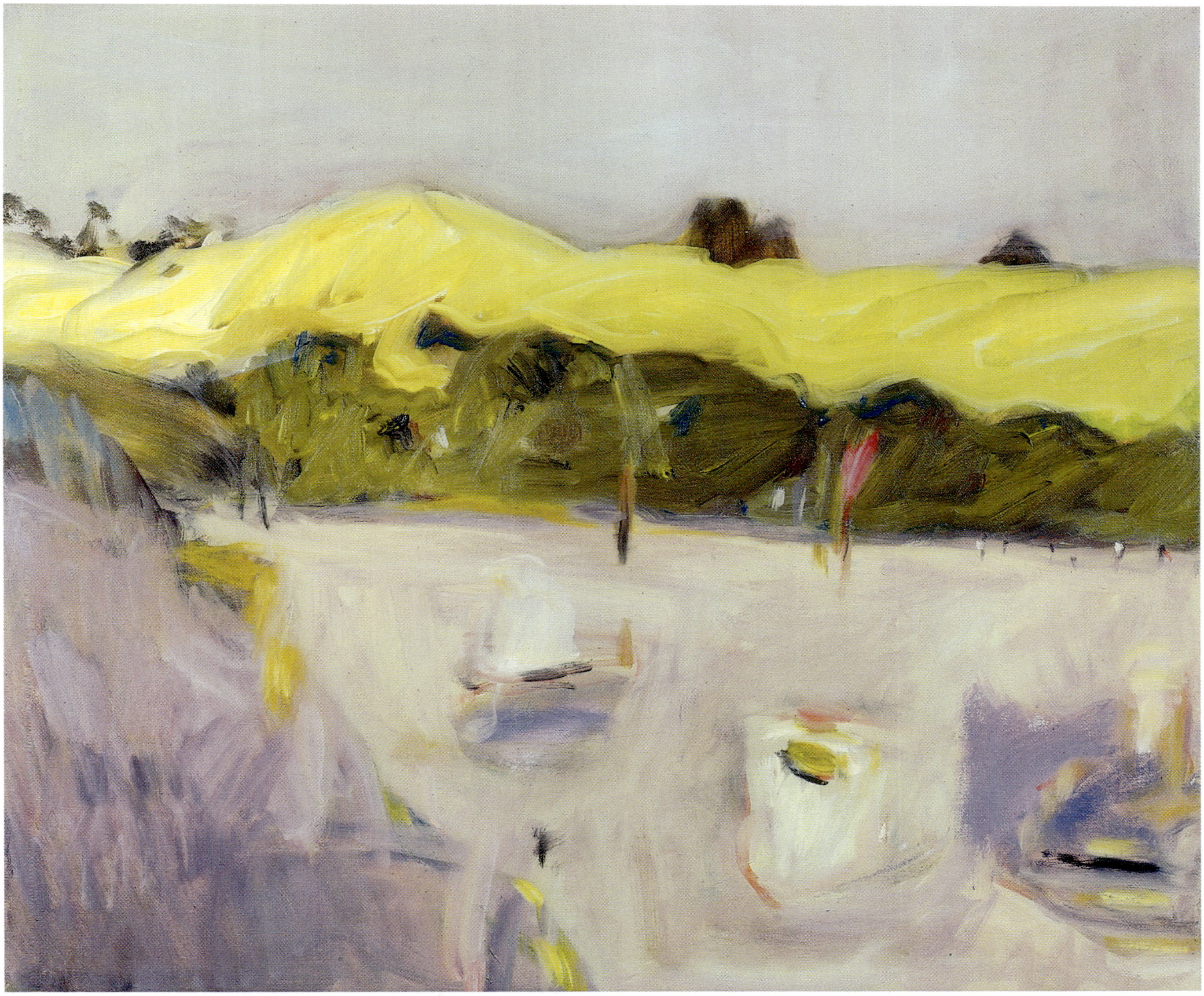

plate 37. *Hayle Sands*,
1989,
oil on canvas,
48.26 x 58.42 cm (19 x 23 in)

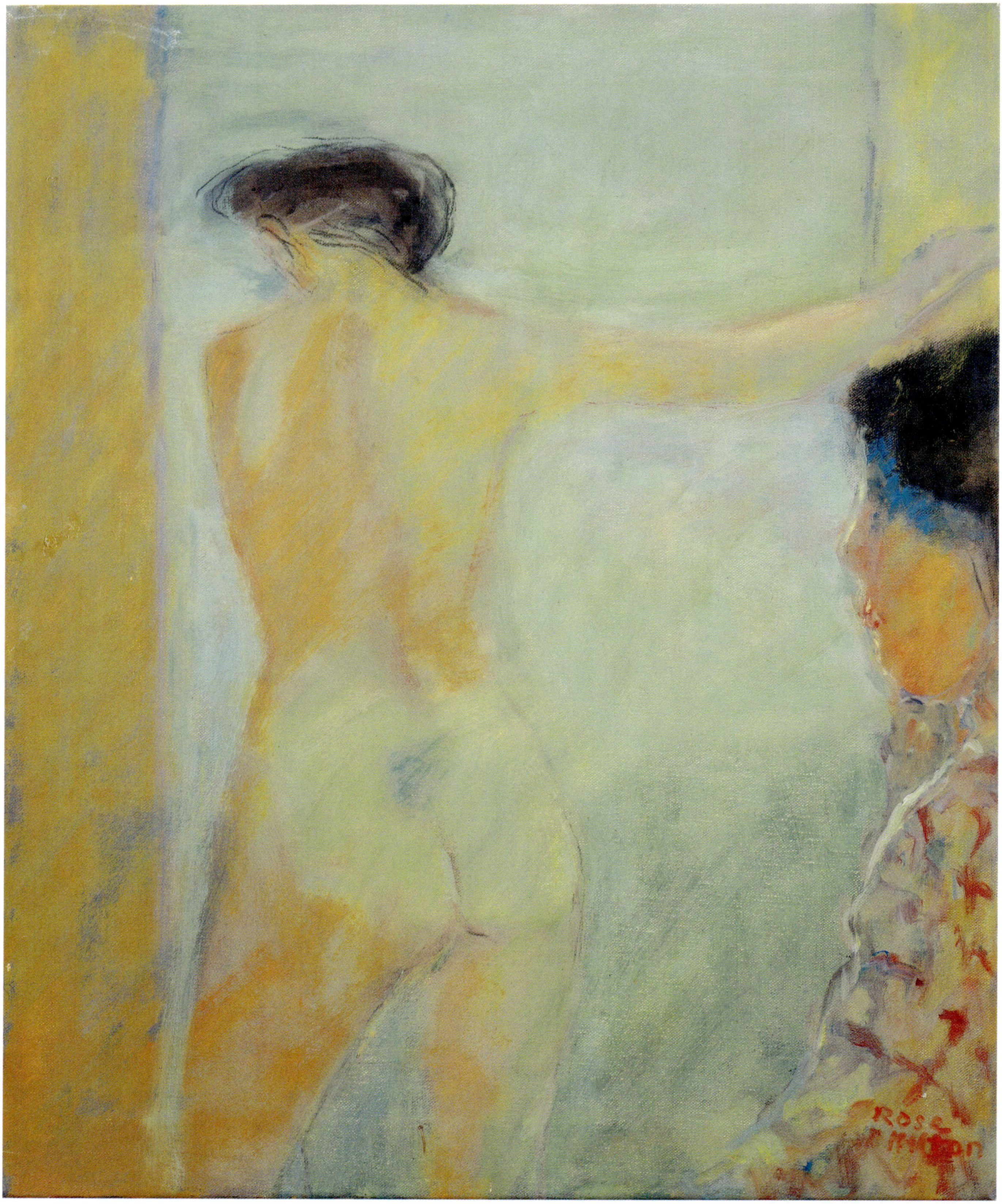
ROSE HILTON

plate 38. ***Figure at the Window***, 1987
oil on canvas,
61 x 50.8 cm (24 x 20 in)

plate 39. ***Penwith Landscape***, 1989,
oil on canvas,
91.4 x 91.4 cm (36 x 36 in)

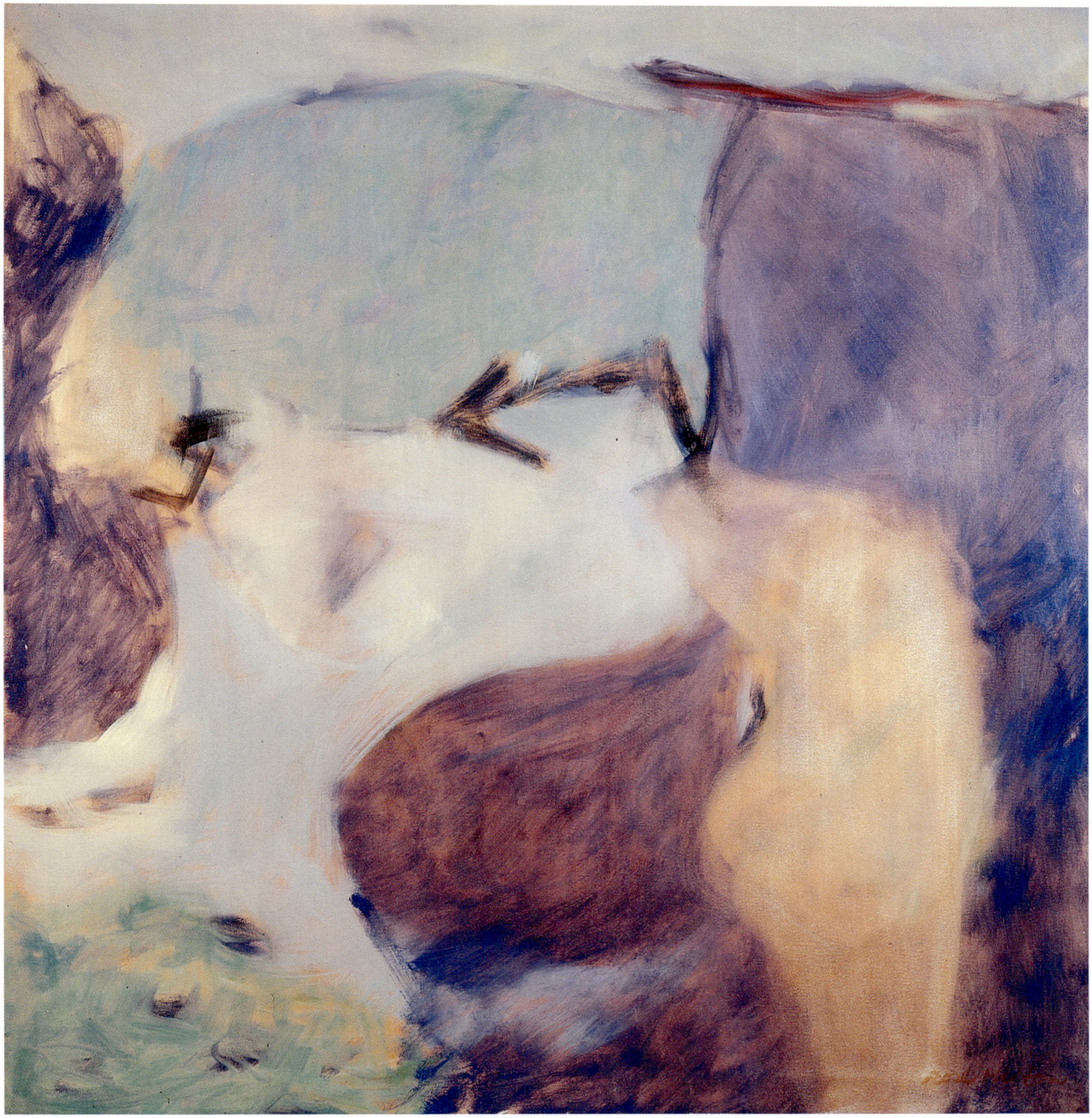

plate 40. ***By the Window***, 1988, oil on the back of an envelope, 30.5 x 25.4 cm (12 x 10 in)

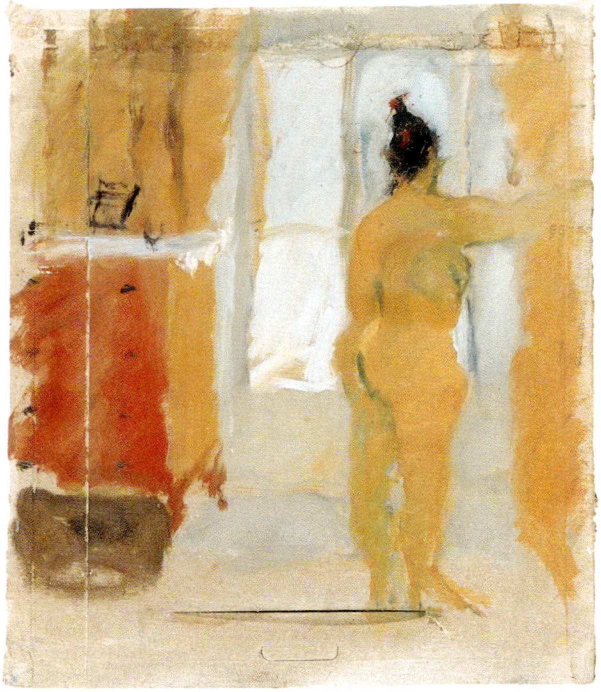

plate 42. ***Studio Nude II***, 1988, oil on card, 25.4 x 20.3 cm (10 x 8 in)

plate 41. ***In the Bedroom***, 1988, oil on artist's board, 25.4 x 30.5 cm (10 x 12 in)

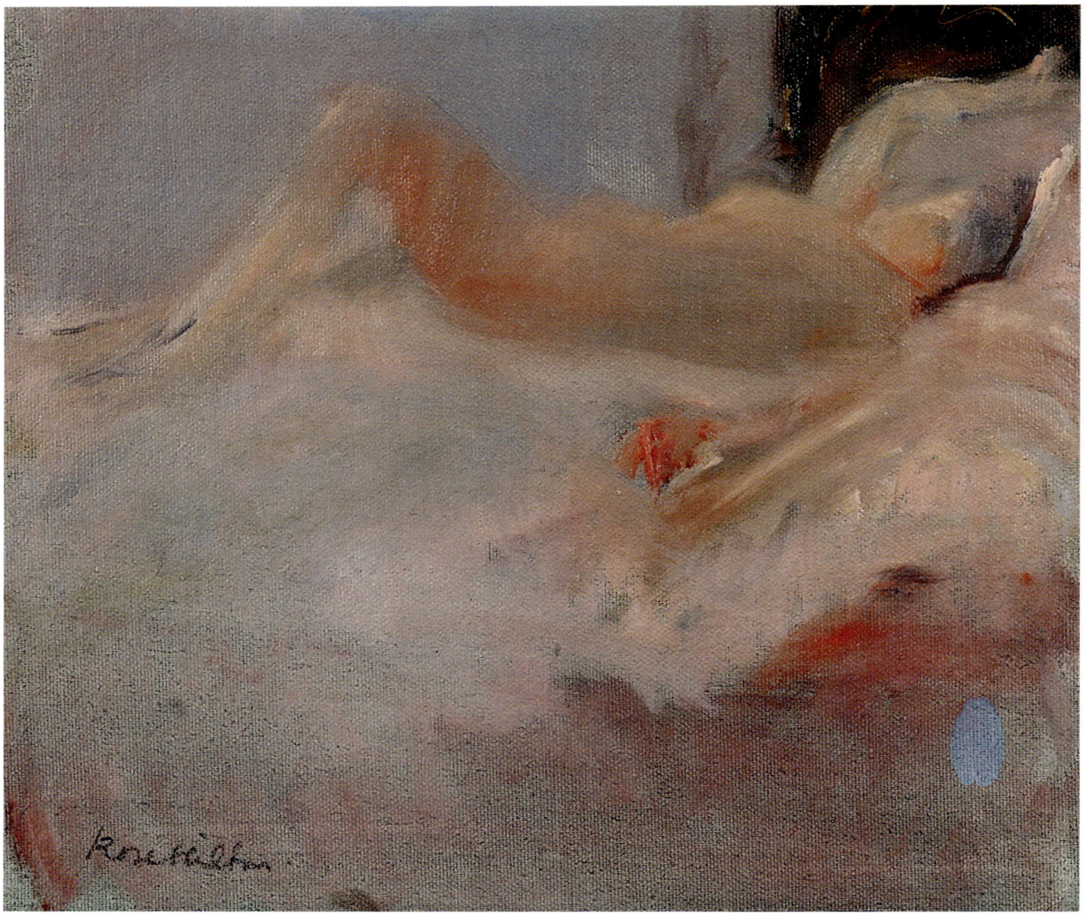

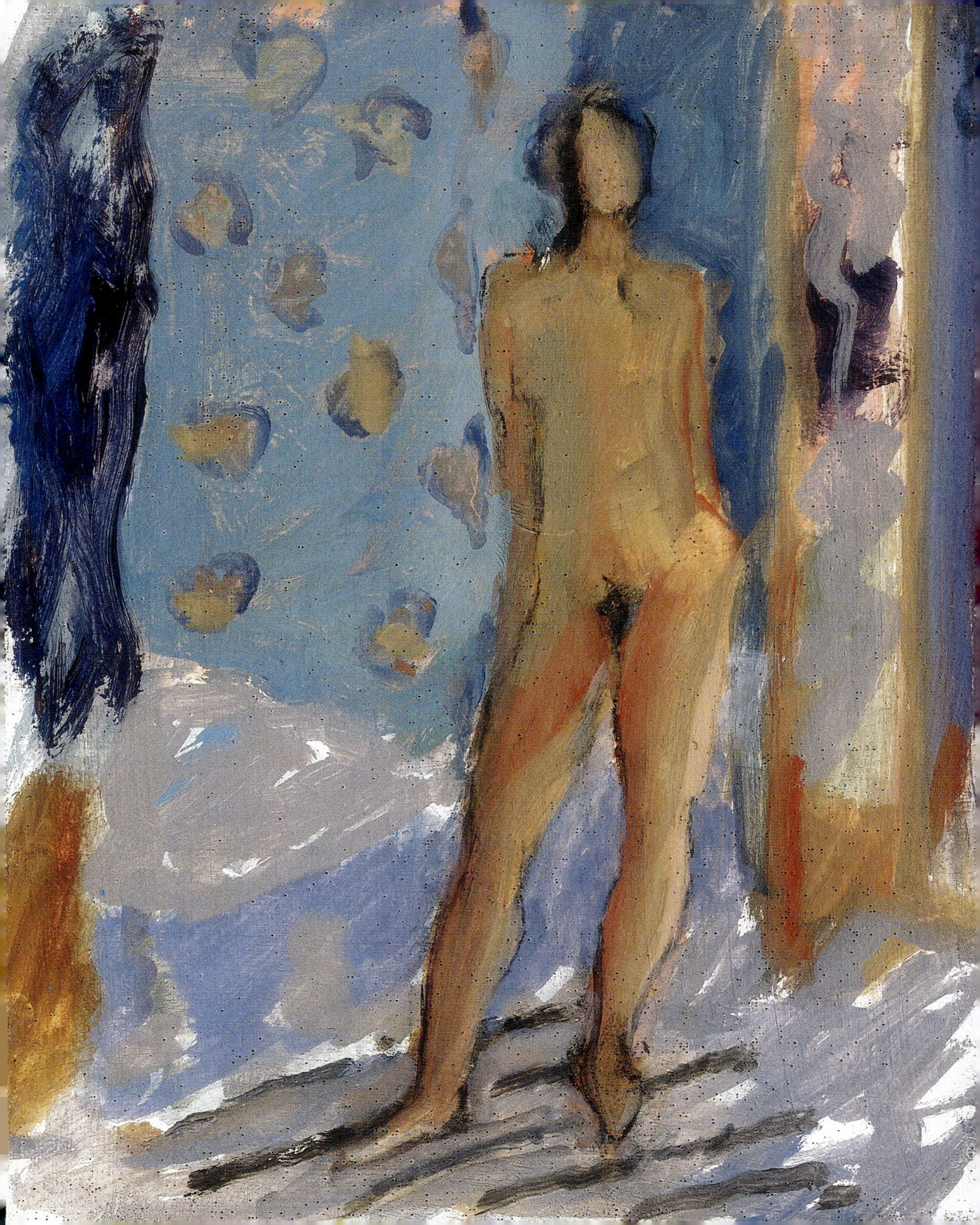

1990s

LIFE DEVELOPED ITS RHYTHMS: painting, visiting Fergus, seeing friends. Her work was growing in assurance and scope but it didn't come any easier. Rose's diary for 1995 records the usual trials and tribulations in the studio, the various inspirations from friends and great art. On 14 January she writes: 'Today I completely ruined the painting I had worked on all the week, a panic trying to make it more interesting. Always a mistake. Trying to abstract the shapes. This is not so bad but the colours I used in playing safe just didn't work.' Perhaps as an antidote she bought herself a Milton Avery catalogue. On 25 January: 'Bob Bourne and I had lunch together and chatted about our lives. I showed him my paintings after lunch. He was critical but constructive about them.' The next day she was in London: 'I went to the Barbican and saw *Impressionism in Britain* which I enjoyed, especially Conder and v. especially Matthew Smith.' This trip was to be a feast of art. The day after: 'I went to RA and saw the Poussin exhibition which overwhelmed with its energy.'

Friends were supportive. 29 January 'John [Miller] came about 2 and we looked at pictures. He was helpful, saying which ones were all right [this is pre-David Messum's visit], which ones were not, which ones had something minor wrong with them. It more or less tallied with my idea of them. He is intelligent, charming voice, a little garrulous, sentimental sometimes, solid and trustworthy.' Then in February Rose notes that Sandra Blow had moved back to Cornwall permanently, after many years of living in London. The two old friends enjoyed a reunion. Rose notes: 'Sandra has marvellous sense of humour, I must see more of her if I can.'

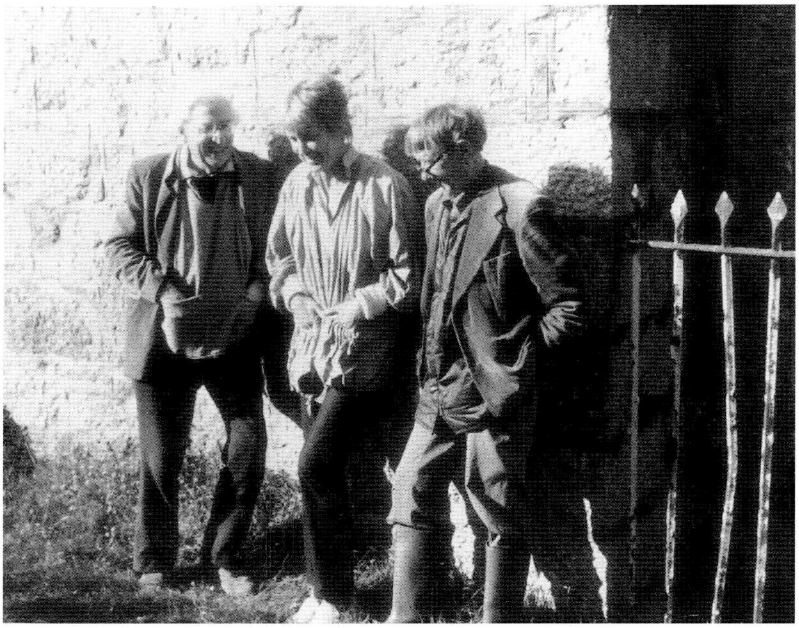

fig 17. Denis Mitchell, Rose and John Wells in 1990 outside the Newlyn studio Mitchell and Wells then shared, now occupied by Rose

Other painters were still providing Rose with the confidence to make her own pictures. It's almost as if she needed the reassurance of their example. On 24 March she writes: 'Went over to John Miller's where I saw a reproduction of a Morandi landscape. Beautiful subtle colours. I am glad I saw this as it stayed in my mind and was useful in selecting a painting for the Newlyn.' Two months later she notes: 'Did Winifred Nicholson type of small still-life. Her shapes I borrowed, but different image of flowers on table. The painting came off rather well and I hope to include it in my show. I feel a bit of a cheat, but it will look good with the other abstract still lifes.' Rose recalls: 'I was making a lot of interiors with still-life objects and flowers at this time, usually in the square format which I discovered suited my feeling for all-over composition.'

There's nothing like a diary for encouraging self-analysis. On 1 June she writes: 'I have a compliant nature like my father's. I want to work on making it more decisive, not such lazy agreeing.' On the other hand, Rose was constantly reproving herself for being competitive with friends such as Mary Stork. And when it came to men, she still compared them to 'Roger who I found madly attractive, thin, charming, good lover'. On 17 June she goes to Lyme Regis for a Roger Hilton show and notes, rather self-deprecatingly: 'People made a lot of fuss over me. Of course I'm beginning to expect that kind of attention.' Only a few days later her own work was in the spotlight, in a new show at Messum's in London. She writes with heartening honesty: 'I liked the paintings a lot but thought that one or two, perhaps 6 or 7 lacked edge. They could have done with some darks in them. It was therapeutic to see them all together.'

At this time Rose was still questioning herself over religious commitment, but she decided to re-approach the local church, where she took Communion in June. She writes: 'this was an emotional experience for me. I hope I did the right thing for myself'. Meanwhile, other friends could be exacting. Bob Bourne came to supper on 6 July. 'He was also cross with me. He said my work had too much white in with the colours and also he thought I was working too much, too many paintings and not enough looking hard at them is what he said. I found this very depressing.' Perhaps in response, she decided to take herself off to Prague for a course of soul-searching and strengthening with a lively bunch of younger people. On 27 July she notes: 'I feel rather fragile in my personality. Desperately want to gain the moral strength that Ida etc want to pass on to us but I find it difficult to "Speak my own truth" which was my particular affirmation. [Ida Kelakova was a charismatic singing teacher who ran workshops called "Singing with Body and Soul", which Rose attended on and off for five years, initially in Cornwall, then in Wales and Slovakia.] I pray I will keep doing it. That was what so attracted me to Roger. He spoke his truth and didn't care whether he was liked or not'.

The pattern of Rose's life features sporadic bouts of hectic socialising, which seem paradoxically to feed her work. Or perhaps the calm and serenity of her pictures are an antidote or escape from all the people. Yet it has to be said that Rose loves nothing better than giving a party or going to someone else's. In the 1990s, she saw a good deal of Mollie Parkin. Rose recalls: 'Just before Roger died, Mollie and Patrick Hughes came to live in Cornwall and that's when I first met her. Mollie was dynamic. When she arrived all the women perked up, and tried to look their best because of her amazing outfits.' In September 1995, Mollie and Rose visited the British Museum to see Japanese prints. 'Utamaro's prints wonderful!' notes Rose. 'Erotic, sensitive, patterned, inspirational.'

The restlessness that makes Rose such a dedicated traveller surfaced occasionally in other departments of life. On 6 October she notes: 'Felt like putting house on market and moving to Devon.' On 28 October she writes: 'Drove to St Ives to see Sandra who has done some quite amazing abstract pictures the best she's done down here. Why don't I love her as much as I feel I ought to? She does inspire me but I feel she is never happy or content emotionally in her relationship with men'. Perhaps this was a little too close to home and the way Rose herself felt? Or perhaps it was the not so simple competitiveness of two mature artists. (Of Sandra and Roger, Rose once commented: 'I felt I didn't have a place in their painting relationship.') Certainly as friends of long-standing they remained fond of each other though they did not spend a great deal of time together.

Art was the abiding preoccupation of Rose's life. On 4 November she writes: 'Painted all day. Felt terrible as painting got worse. Suddenly it became something with a life of its own and after 5 or 6 hours I left it as it is. It is more in the direction I want to go.' On 13 November: 'I did a good still life at last. Val posed in the morning. I rubbed out what I did of her but went on to do a good one. I am feeling tremendous energy for painting a definite painting not a little nude but a statement which is either going to be in the form of a still life or a landscape.'

On the personal front, she is able to report on 19 November: 'Lonely, but content. No agony.' The next day, she turns her attention to her spiritual state. She notes: 'Still going through belief crisis, always wondering whether there is a God'. A few days later, and she has been reading Alan Bennett's diaries about the actor Kenneth More who left a large part of his character under-developed because he wanted to be liked. She writes: 'I feel like this as a person. Although I feel that Roger developed a tract of my character during my

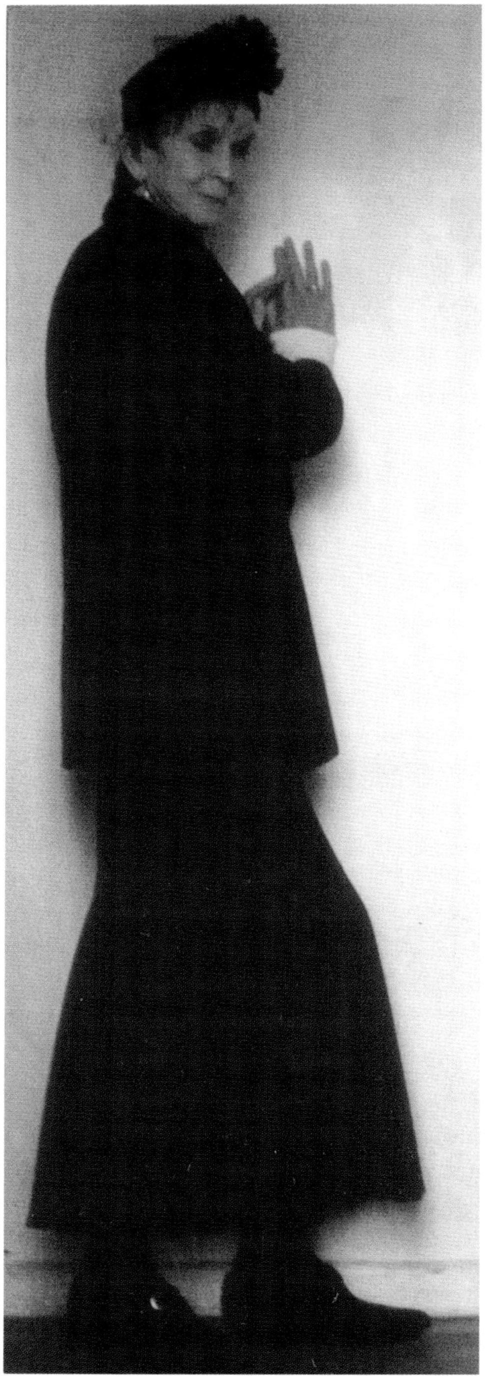

fig 18. Rose in 1997

thirties and I became at times quite horrible although more fully alive.'

In November, Rose travelled up to Edinburgh for David Brown's 70th birthday party. She writes: 'David very happy and much better – still irritating and self-absorbed – we have an affection for each other.' The next day she was off again. 'Caught the morning train to Glasgow. This was exciting for me. I still feel the same sense of freedom and excitement as when I first left home and used to travel from Bromley South to Victoria and the unknown.' She visited the Burrell Collection, and particularly loved the pastels by Vuillard, Degas, Monet and some small paintings by Boudin. The travelling back to Cornwall did not phase her. She writes: 'I love these long journeys and never get bored. I used to, now I like to doze off and just day-dream and so don't mind the length of travelling.'

fig 19. Rose in 1998

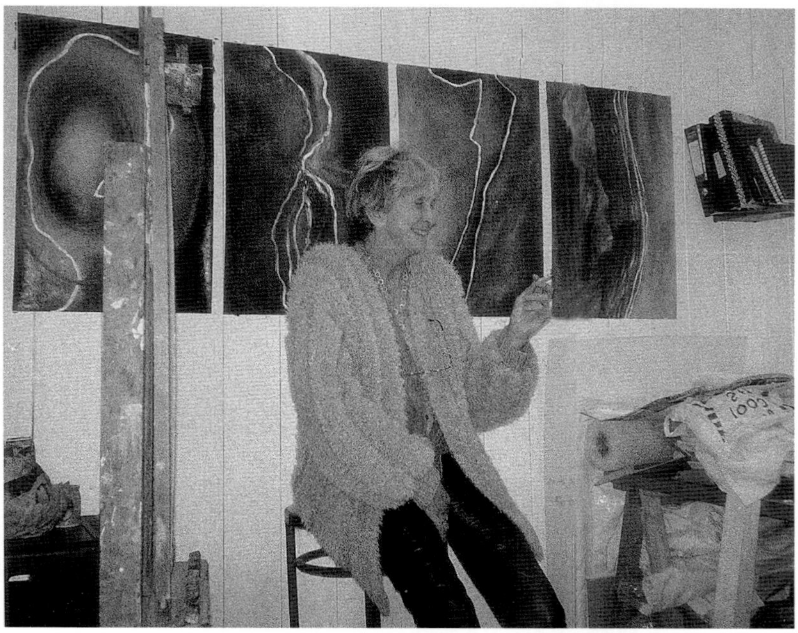

As the year ended, the self-doubts re-emerged and jostled for attention. December fields such comments as: 'Create your own realities. Am I doing this in my work?' (3 December); 'I feel in my personality quite limited, and often mean-spirited. I pray to understand more, to love more and not to shut down on ideas' (5 December); 'I have got to the end of this year having recorded it all, sometimes more scrappily than others. I feel at a low ebb emotionally and wish I could be with someone but it would have to be nourishing and right for both or it would be hell' (27 December). As New Year's Eve arrived, Rose debated whether to go out and, if so, where and with whom. Afterwards she writes: 'In the end I stayed in and had a great drink with myself – a continual love-hate affair.'

In 1998, Rose resumed her diary. On 1 January she writes: 'A gap of two or three years, but I need to write again to sort out feelings choices decisions.' She also needed to write down her thoughts about art. One of the most interesting from the beginning of the year is this, from 12 January: 'In all the paintings I like there is canvas showing. Masterly knowing what to do, which must mean a lot of drawing first.' She travelled to America, took tea with David Hockney ('David charming, witty and generous') and then visited the Guggenheim in New York. She records on 19 January: 'Fantastic show of Helen Frankenthaler which I came on unexpectedly. I think she will be quite an influence.' Four days later, she re-visited the Frankenthaler exhibition: 'Realized that the pictures that I love so much were done in 1957–9. I like them better than her later ones. Still feel I could be influenced by them.'

On 25 February she writes: 'I seem to be in demand and selling paintings very easily. It is partly a reflective glory from Roger's show being at the Tate. [A small display of drawings.] I haven't quite got going with my painting again yet.' But that period of readjustment after travel was soon over and Rose settled back into a rhythm of painting and entertaining friends. In June she joined the Pendeen church choir, which she enjoys very much and from which she derives emotional strength. All of which contributed to her peace of mind to enable her to paint for her next Messum's show in October. She reviews this critically: 'The impression was of light and colour. And depth in some of them. I noticed a lack of decision which could have been there. It was slight but there in some. It needs more aggression I would say, my work that is, to confirm my ability and push it further.'

Later she notes: 'I sold very well indeed. This ought to make me feel good but it has stopped me working as I feel I can do those pleasant paintings and if I go on I want to reach more unconscious parts or at least more abrasive parts of the spirit. There doesn't seem much point in being a painter unless one expresses something which cannot be said in words'.

But the financial gains were put to good use, and Rose enlarged the conservatory. A small conservatory had been added in Roger's lifetime, and the accommodation had been extended by the purchase of a caravan. This fell to bits in the late 1980s, when Rose bought another, which eventually fell apart too. A chalet/studio was built in the garden and later another, less elaborate one, just for printing. The property was becoming really quite well set up.

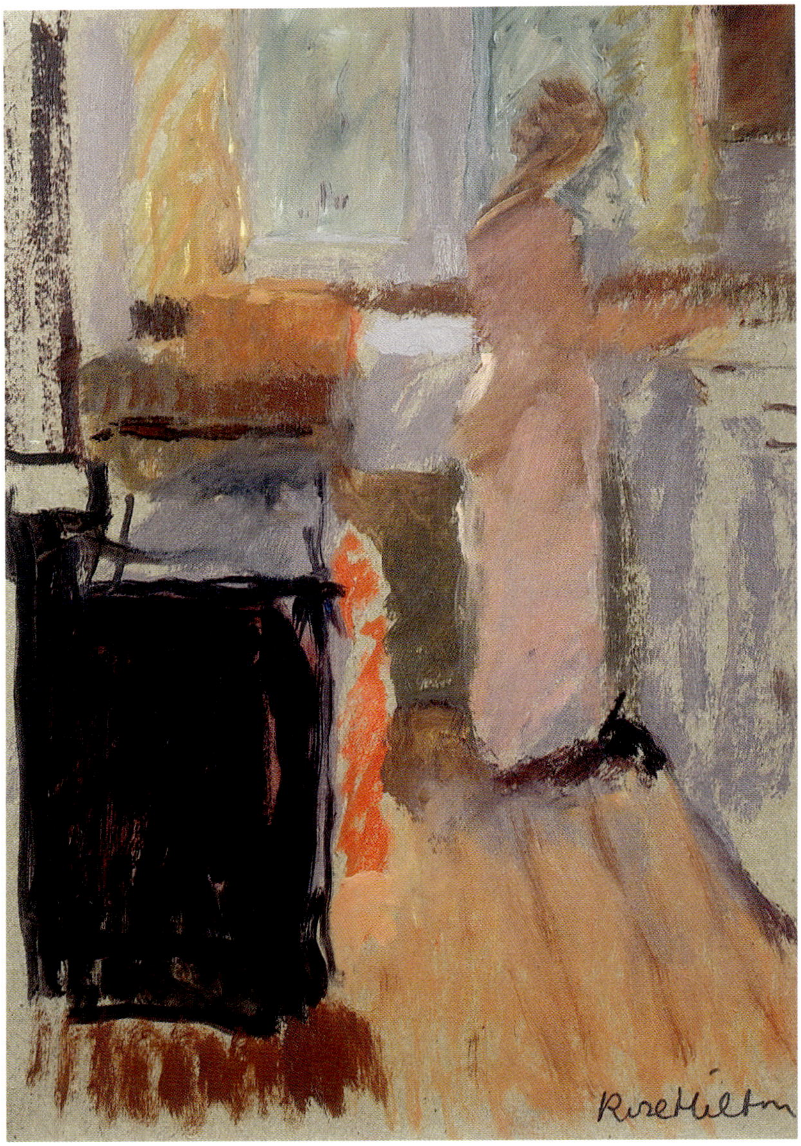

plate 43. ***Dudley's Kitchen***, 1990,
oil on card,
35.6 x 25.4 cm (14 x 10 in)

plate 44. ***The Lovers***,
1990,
oil on canvas,
76.2 x 50.8 cm (30 x 20 in)

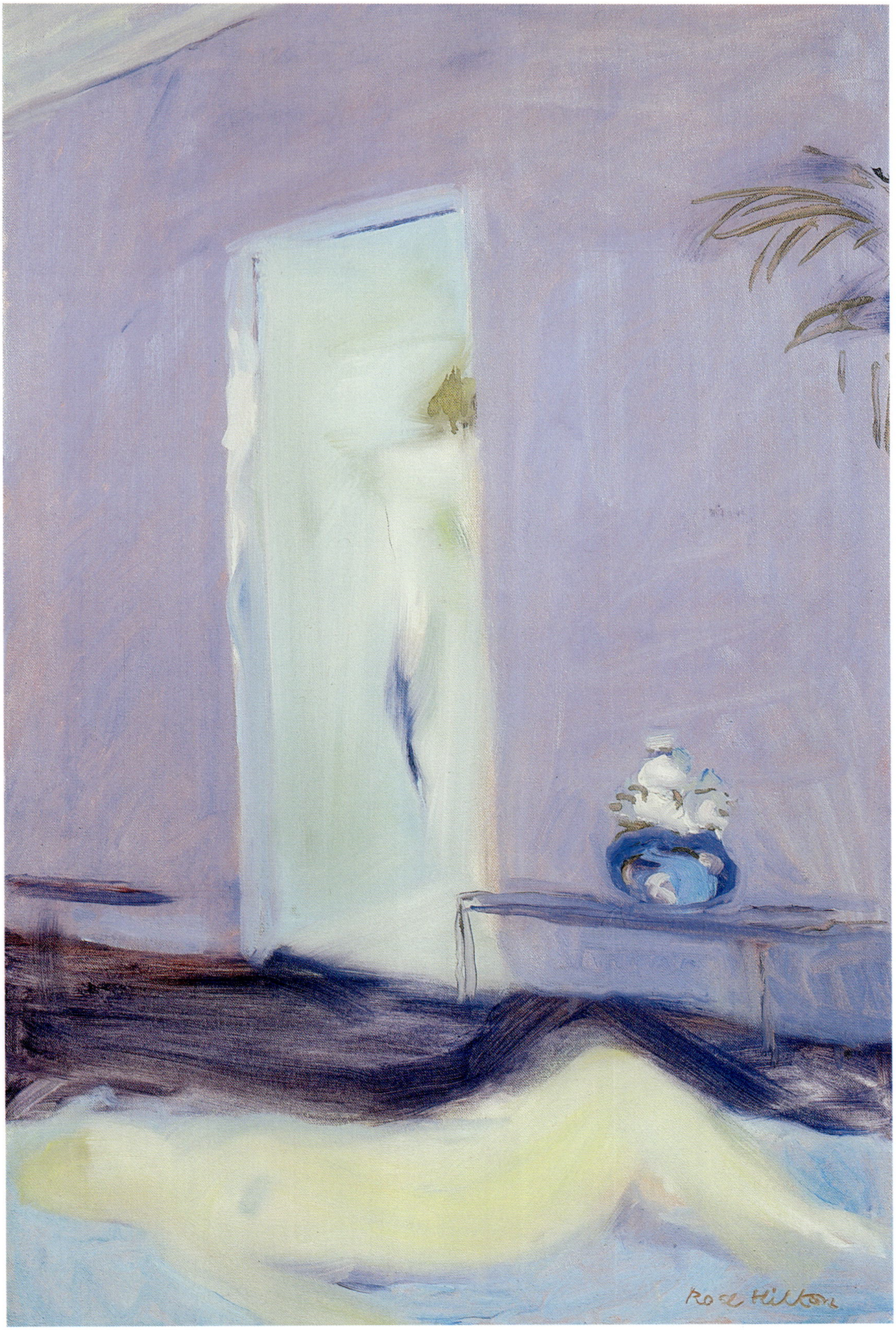

plate 45. ***The Brisons***,
1990,
oil on canvas,
35.6 x 45.7 cm (14 x 18 in)

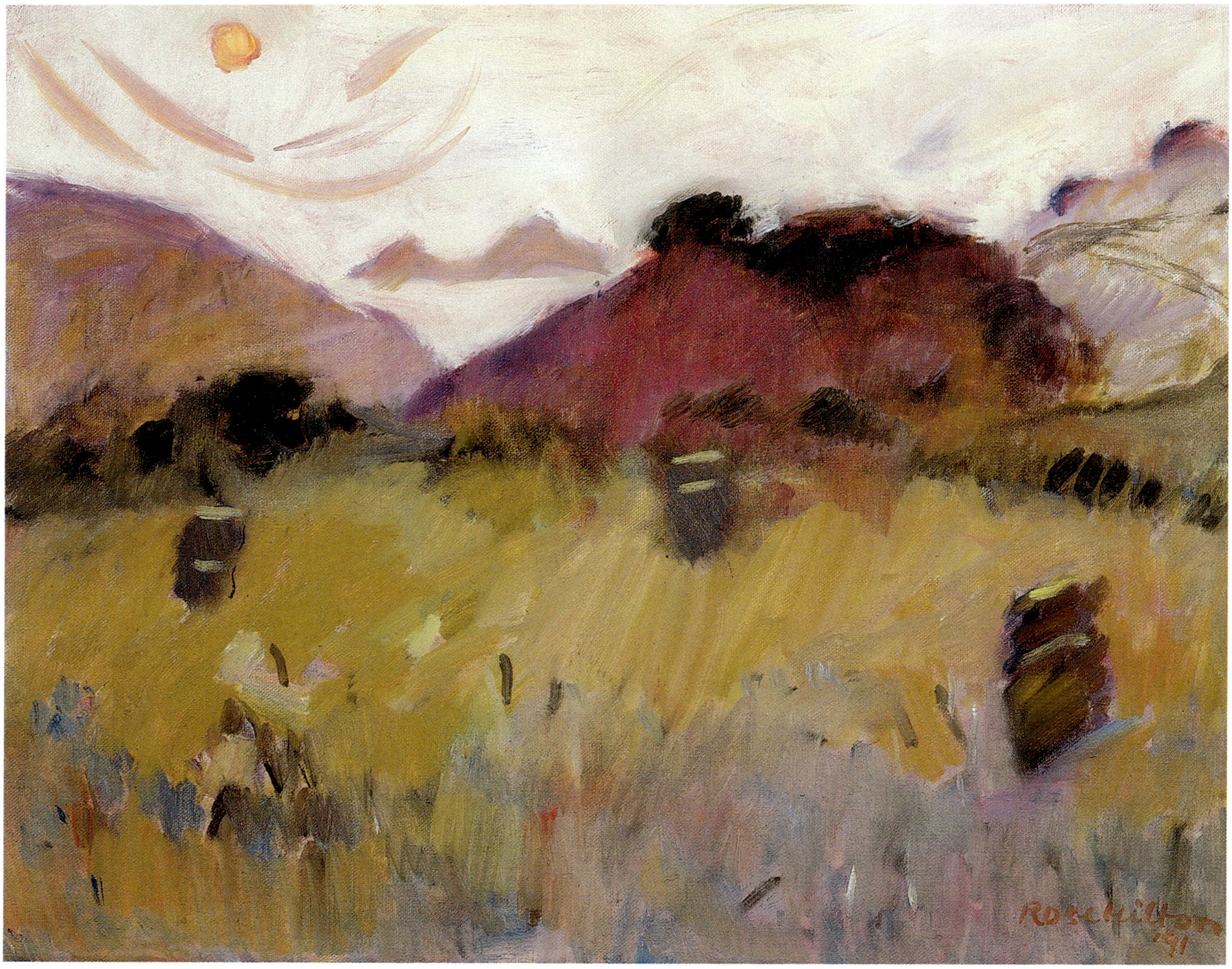

plate 46. ***Café Interior***,
1990,
oil on canvas,
119.4 x 83.8 cm
(47 x 33 in)

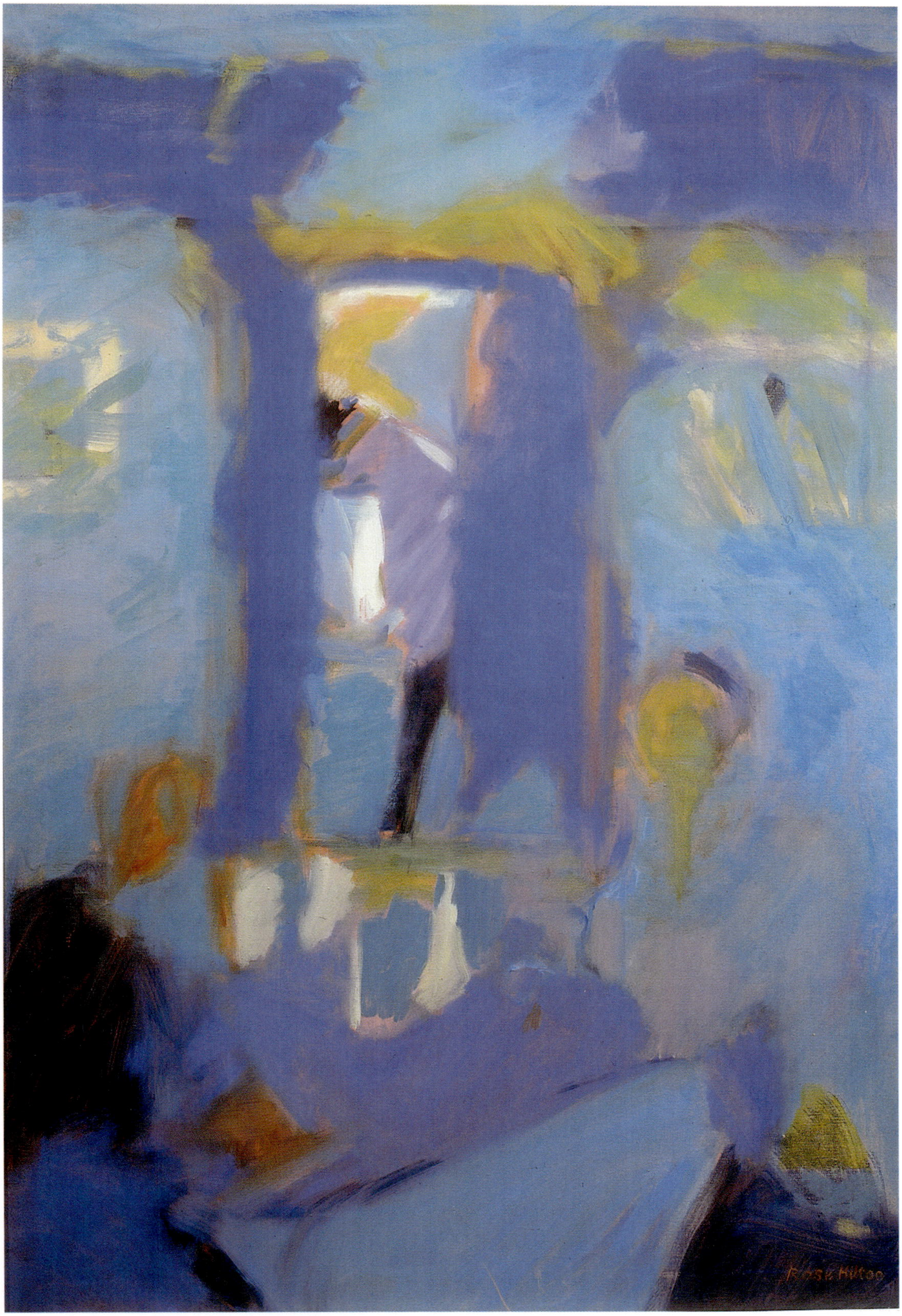

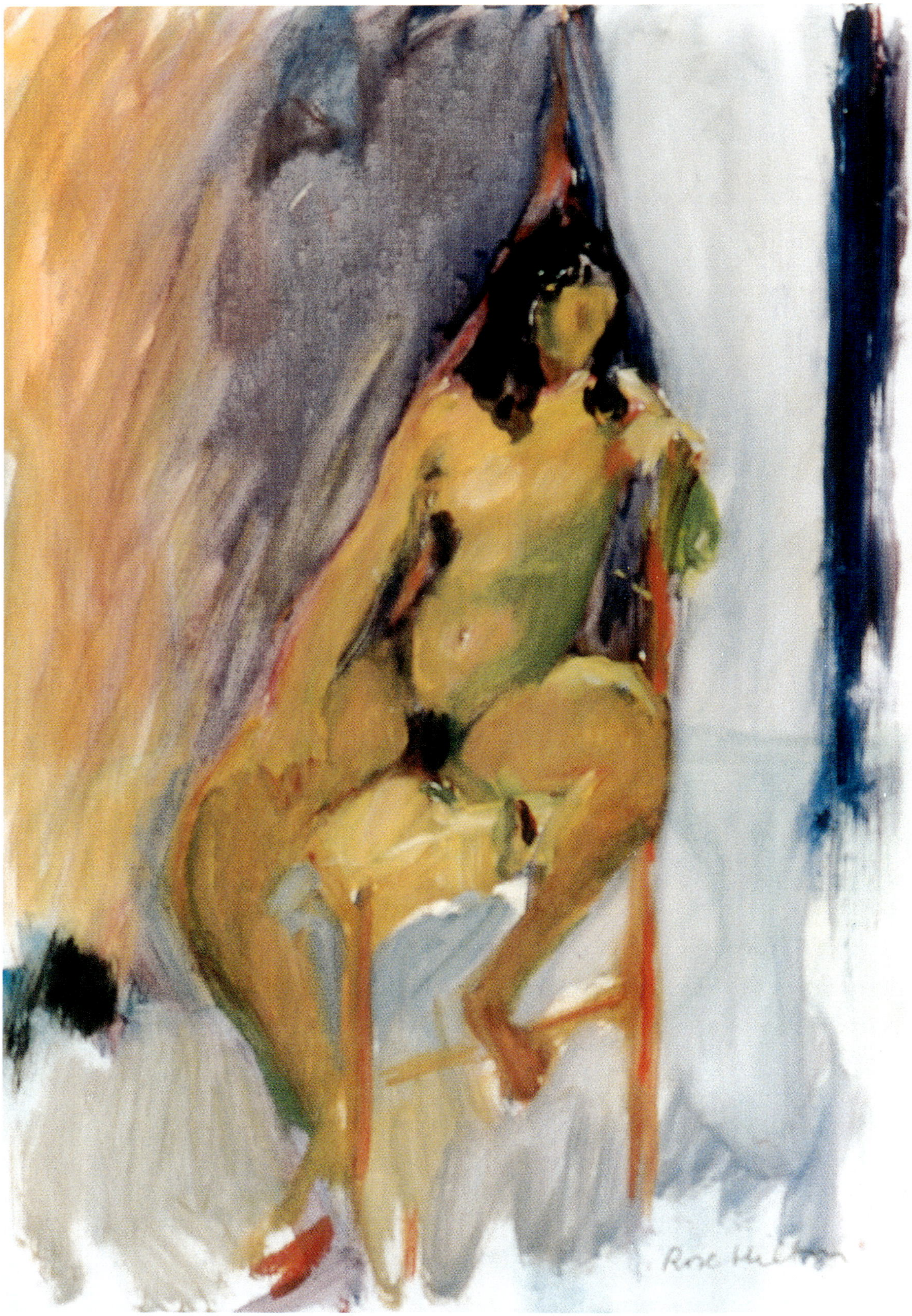

plate 47. ***Seated Nude***, 1990,
oil sketch on canvas paper,
35.6 x 25.4 cm
(14 x 10 in)

plate 48. ***Godrevy, Cornwall***, 1990,
oil on canvas laid down on board,
20.3 x 25.4 cm (8 x 10 in)

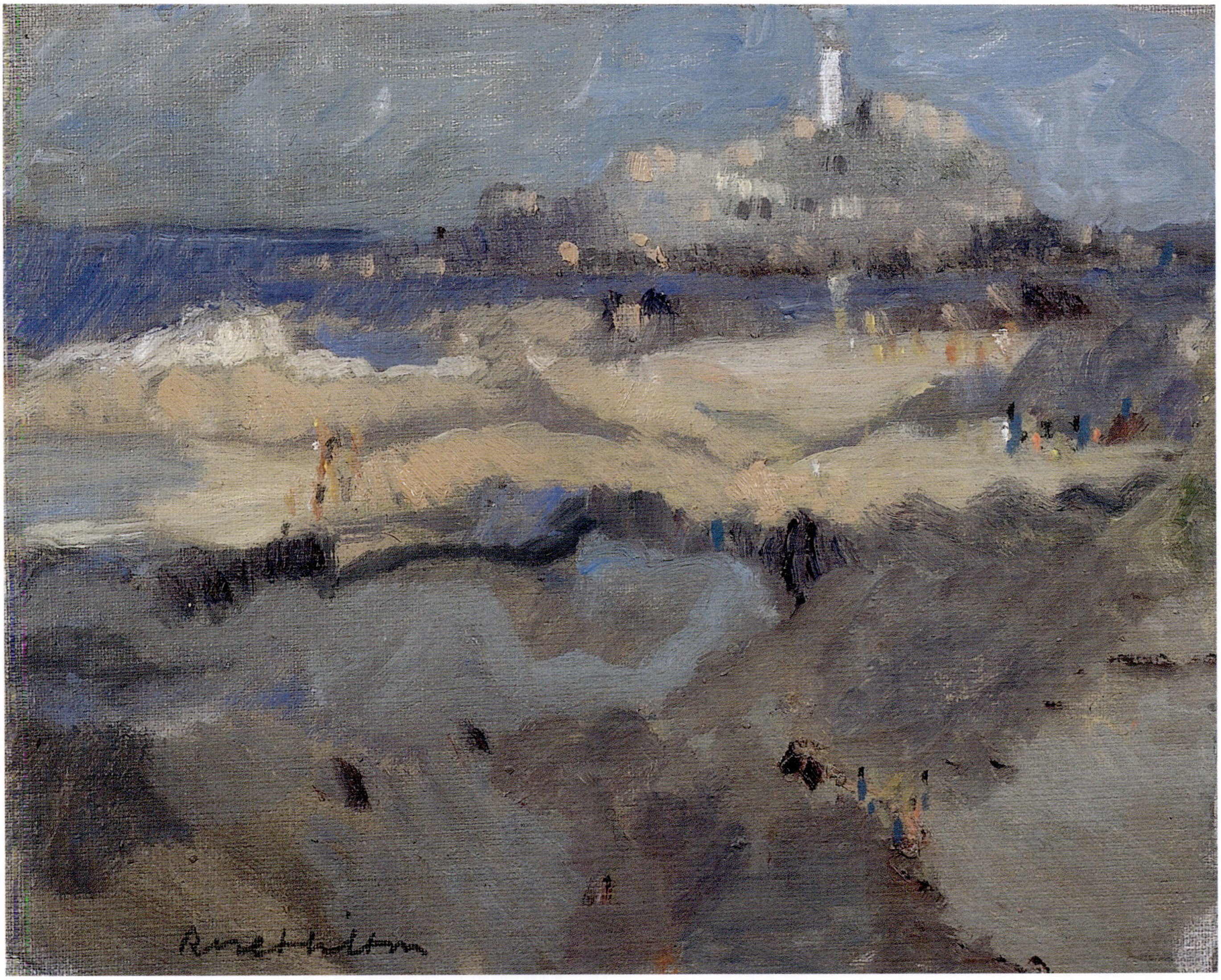

plate 49. ***On the Terrace***, 1990,
oil on canvas,
76.2 x 76.2 cm (30 x 30 in)

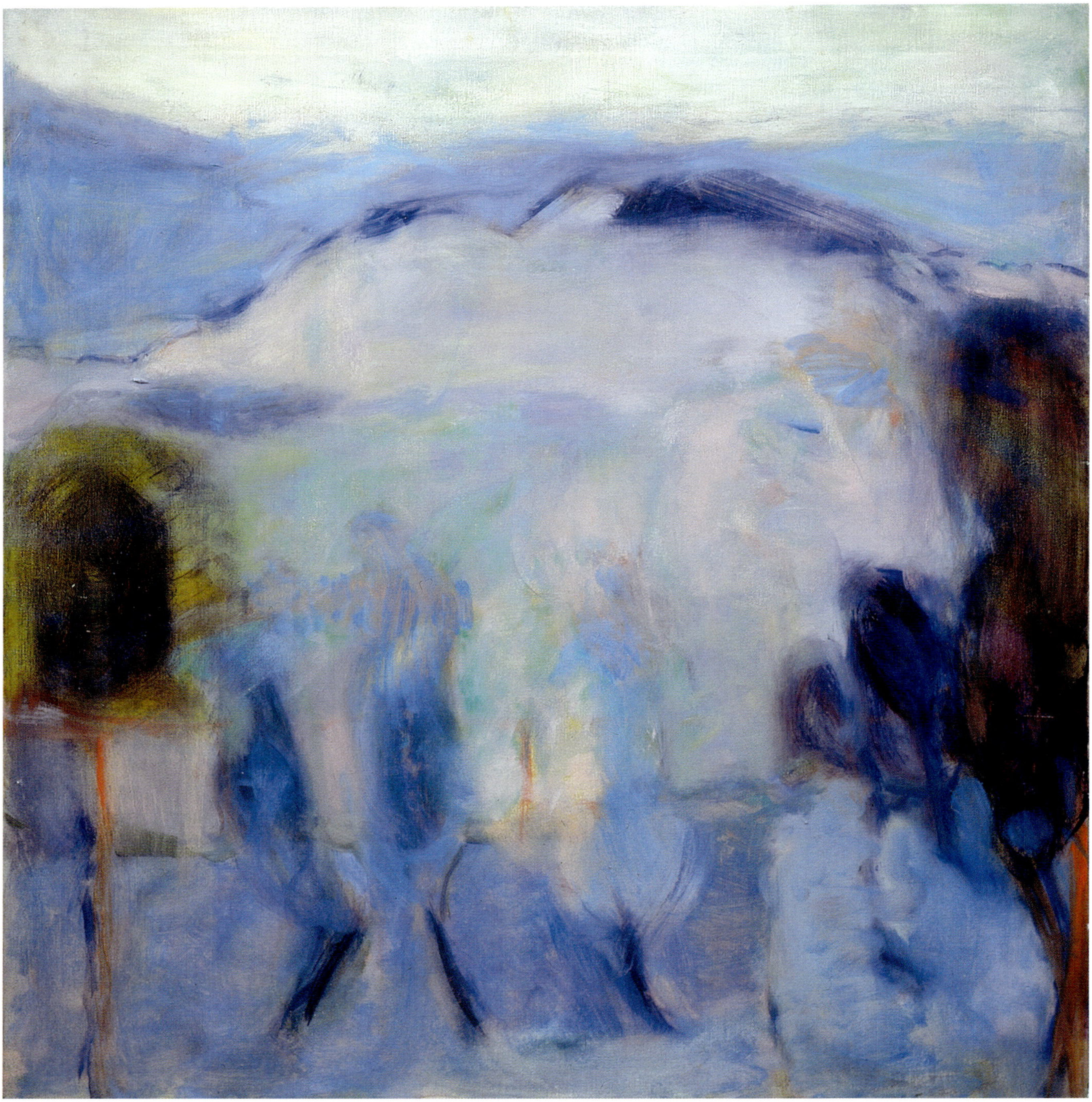

plate 50. ***Boskenna Nude***, 1993,
oil on canvas,
61 x 50.8 cm (24 x 20 in)

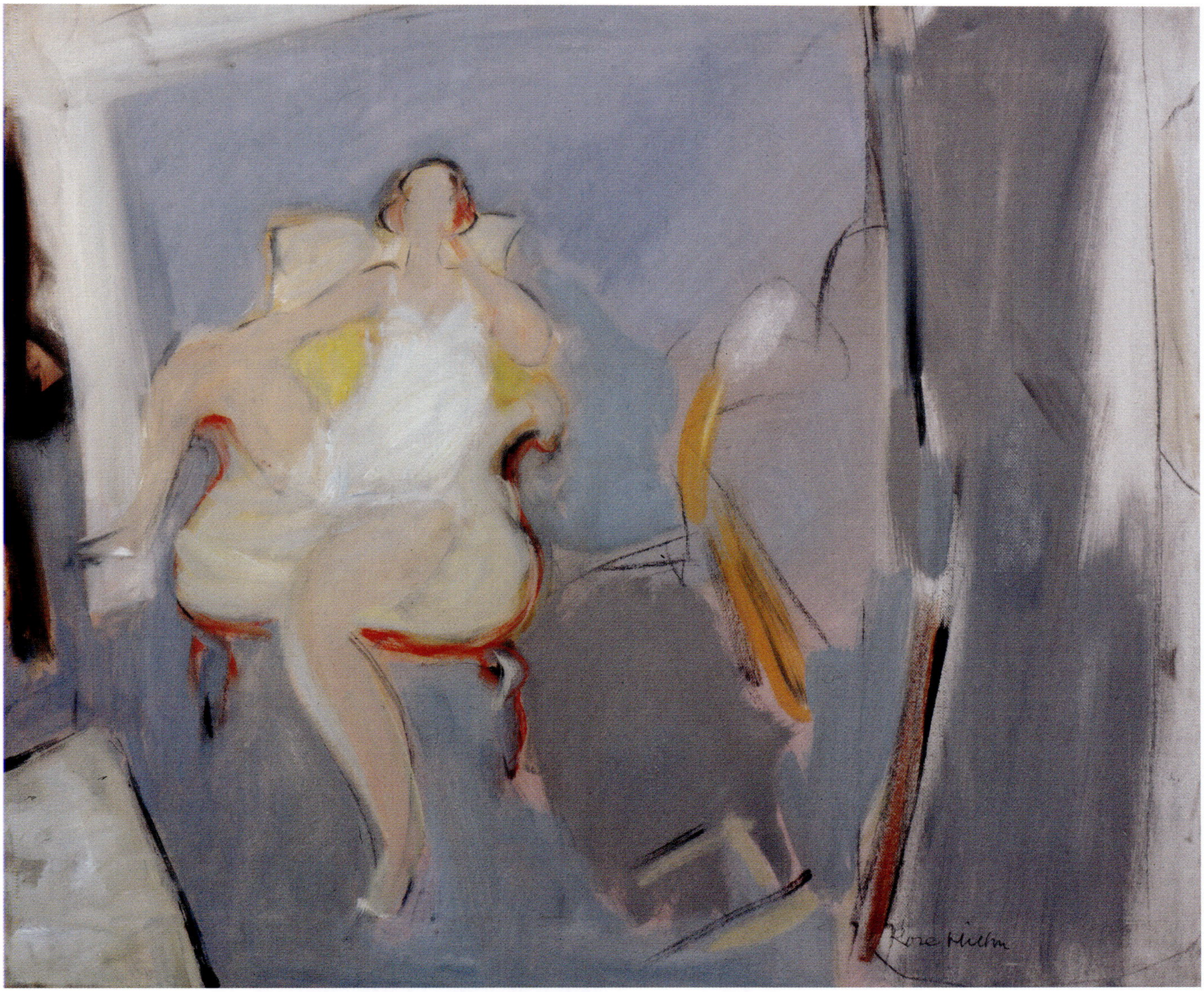

plate 51. ***Still Life No. 1***,
1991,
oil on canvas,
71.1 x 61 cm (28 x 24 in)

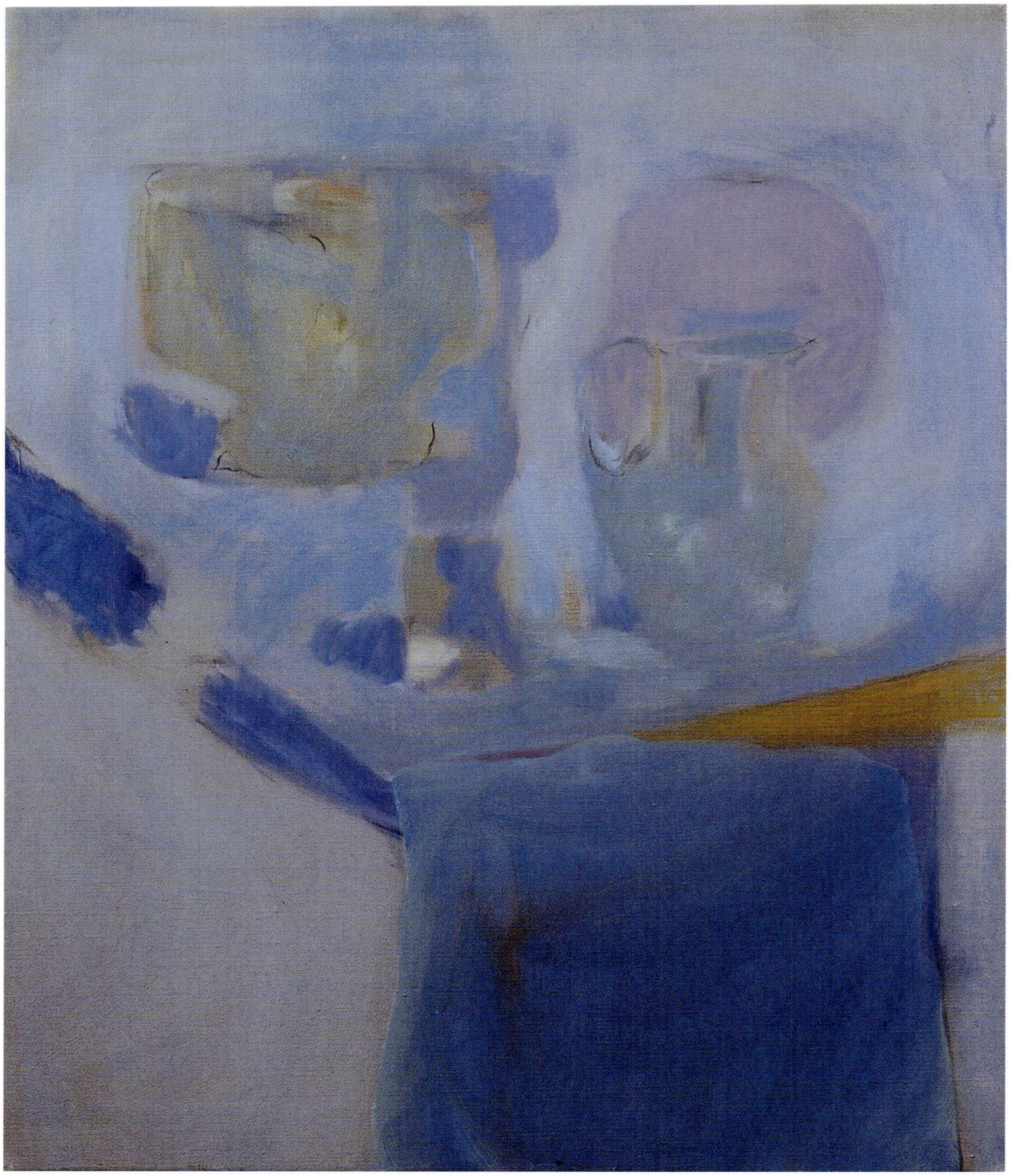

plate 52. ***Mousehole Harbour***, 1990,
oil on canvas,
76.2 x 76.2 cm (30 x 30 in)

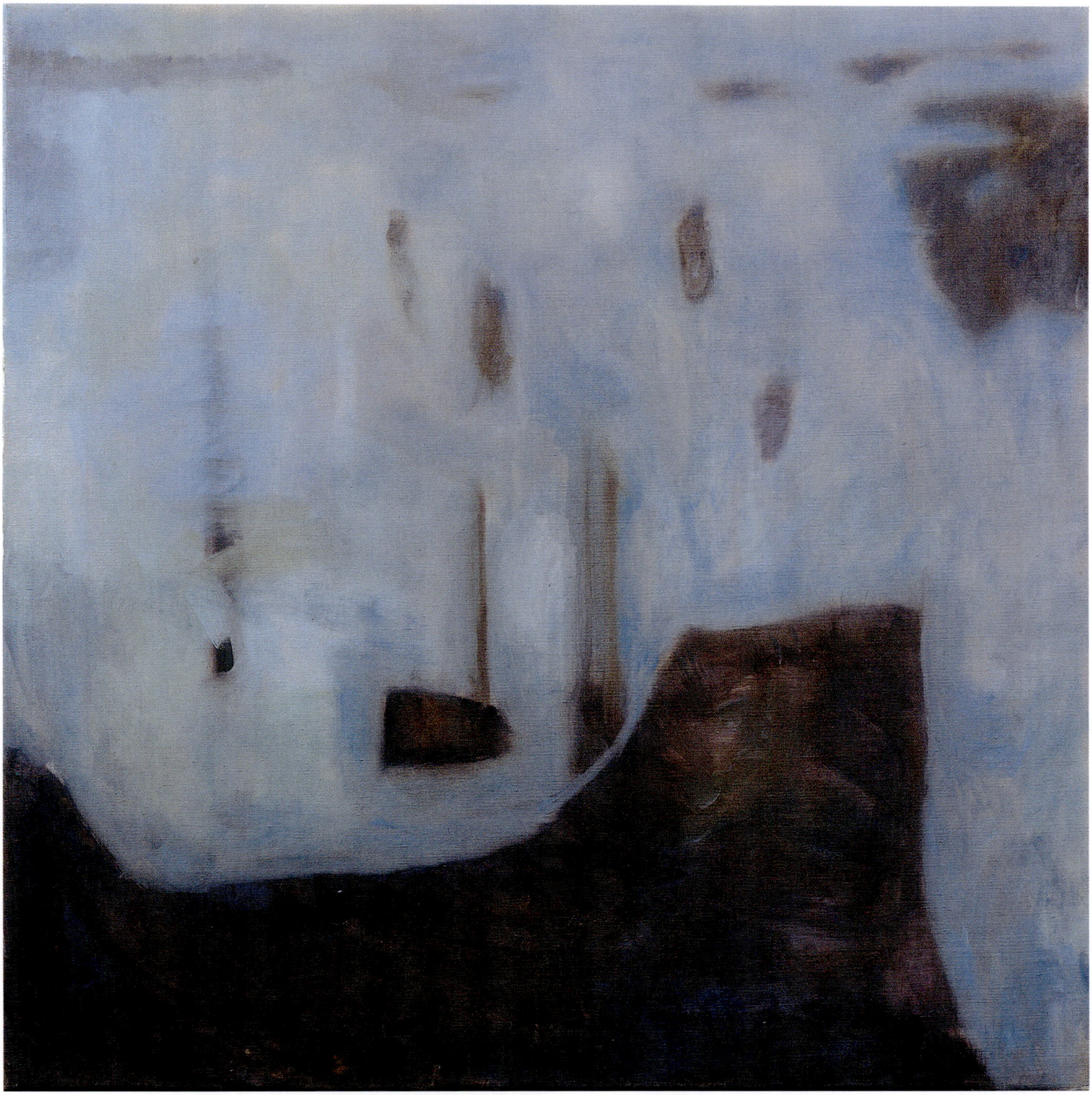

plate 53. ***Figure in a Landscape***, 1993, linocut, 35.6 x 45.7 cm (14 x 18 in)

plate 54. ***Nancharo House, St Just***, 1992, oil on canvas, 35.6 x 50.8 cm (14 x 20 in)

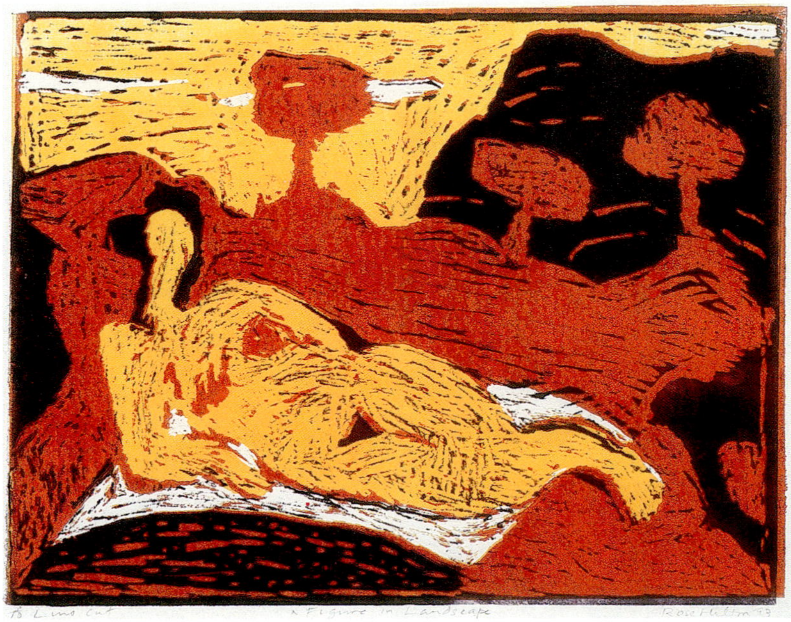

plate 55. ***Nude Figure II***, 1991, oil on canvas, 61 x 50.8 cm (24 x 20 in)

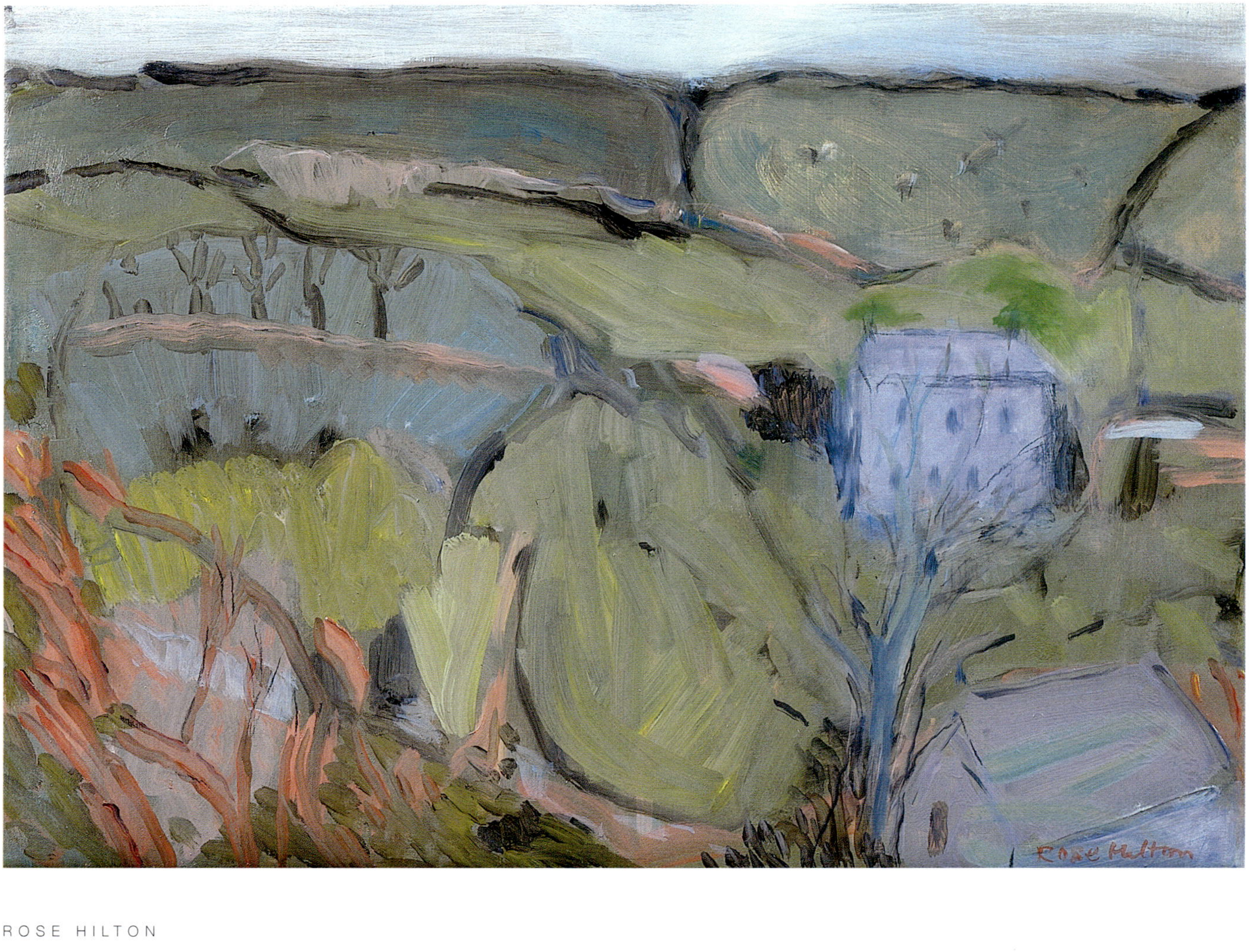

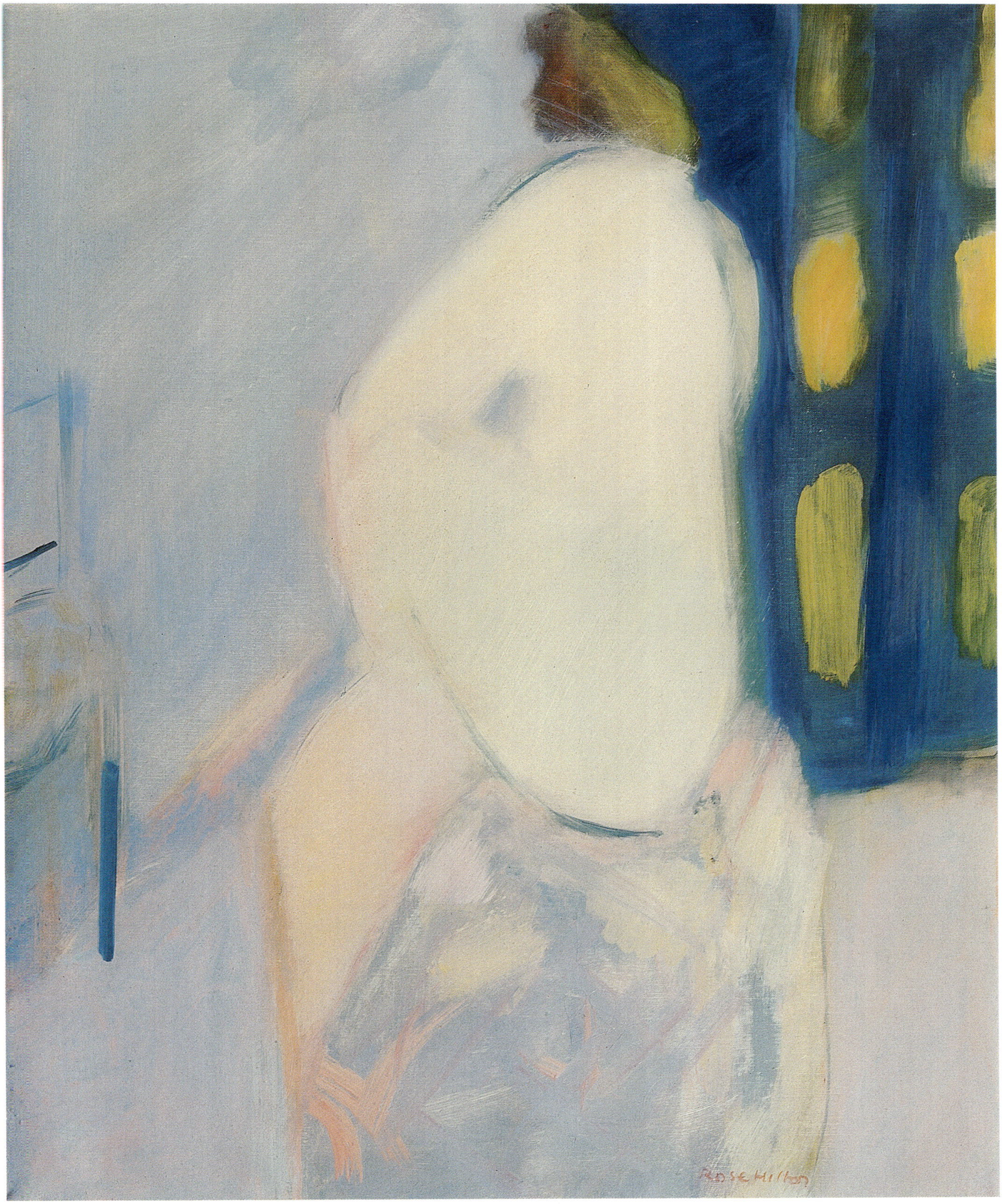

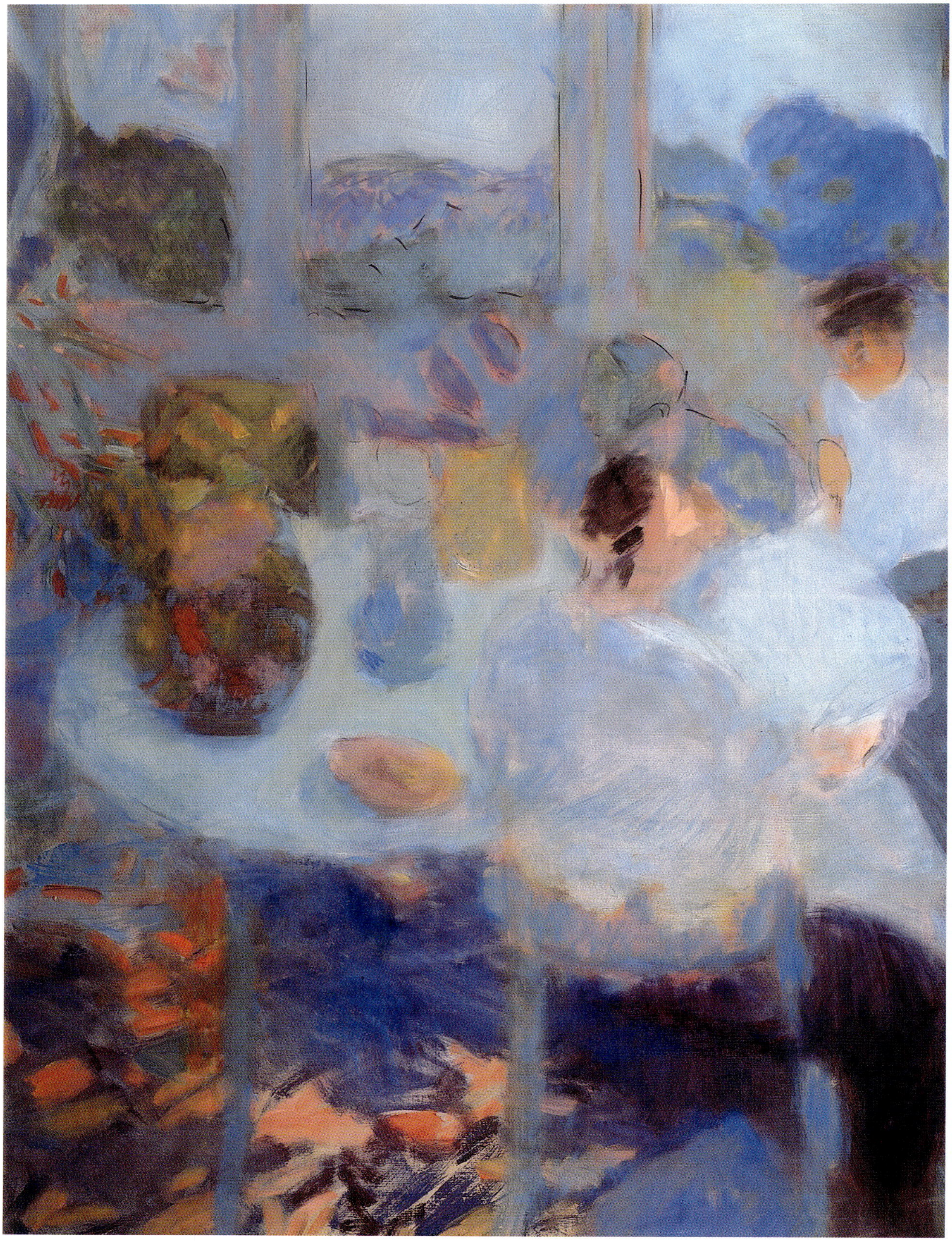

plate 56. ***The Breakfast Table***, 1992, oil on canvas, 121.9 x 91.4 cm (48 x 36 in)

plate 57. ***Golden Still Life***, 1990, oil on canvas, 91.4 x 121.9 cm (36 x 48 in)

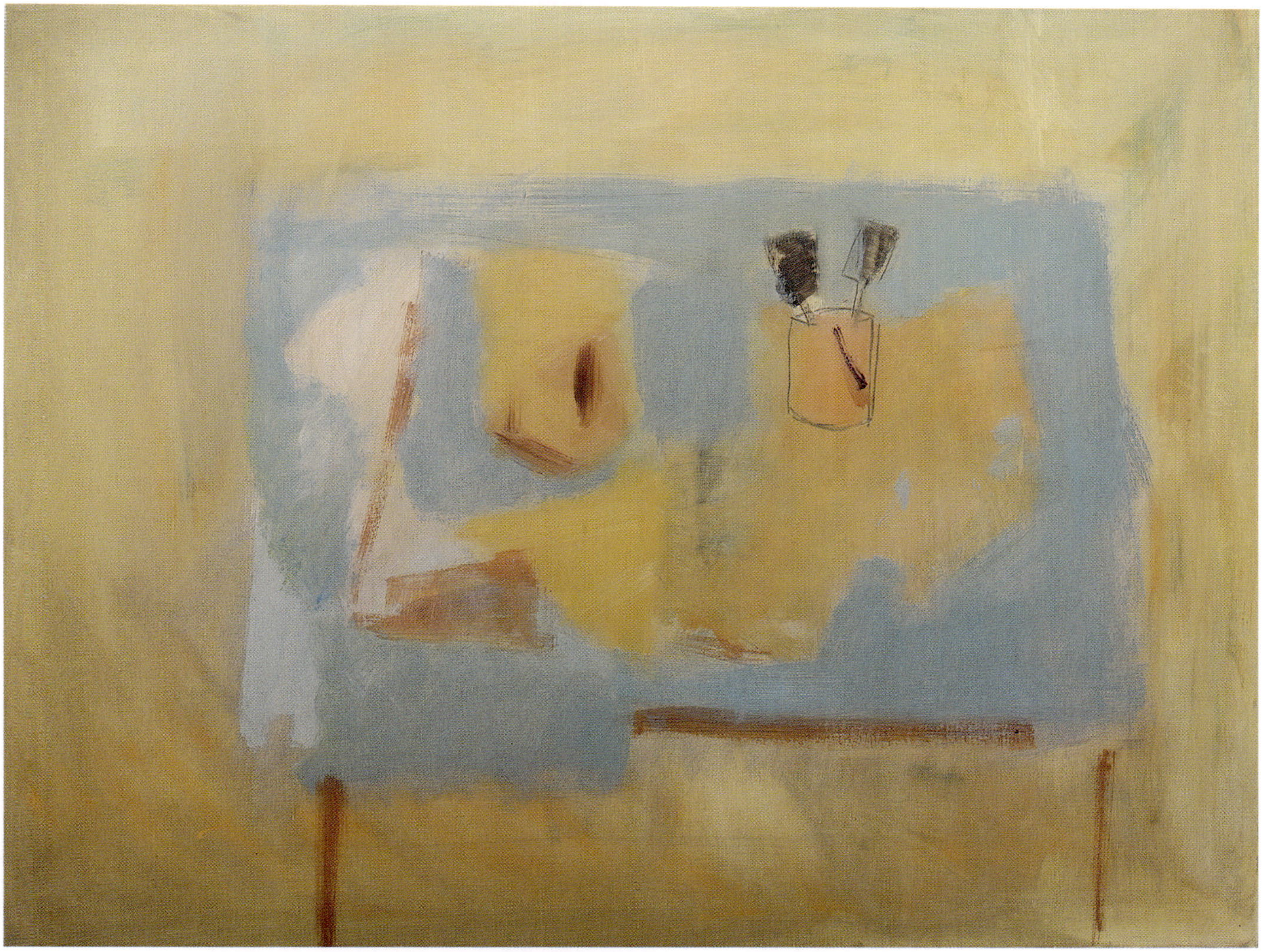

plate 58. ***Children in the Park***, 1993,
oil on canvas,
45.7 x 61 cm (18 x 24 in)

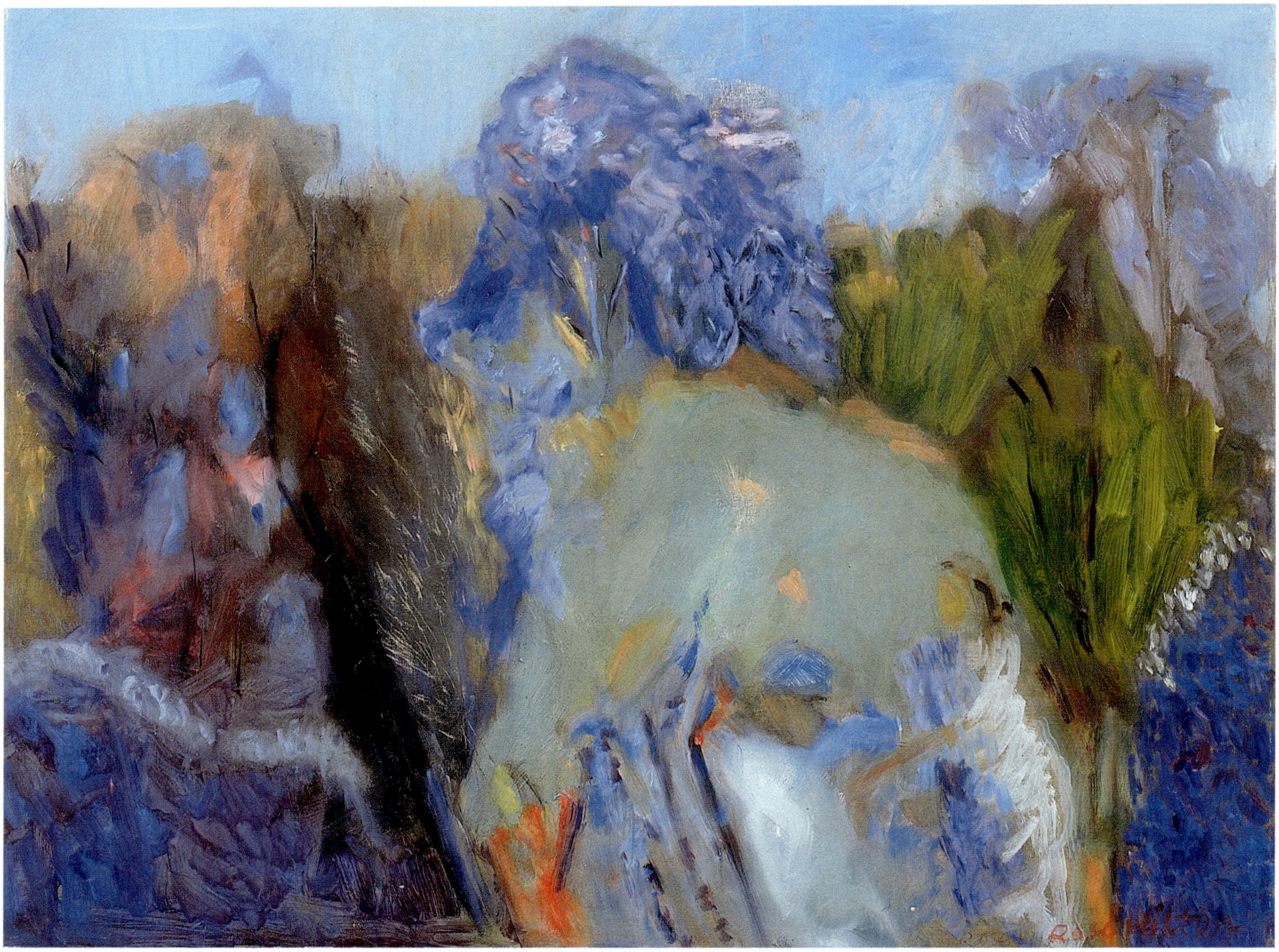

plate 59. ***Summer Forms***,
1994,
oil on canvas,
121.9 x 152.4 cm (48 x 60 in)

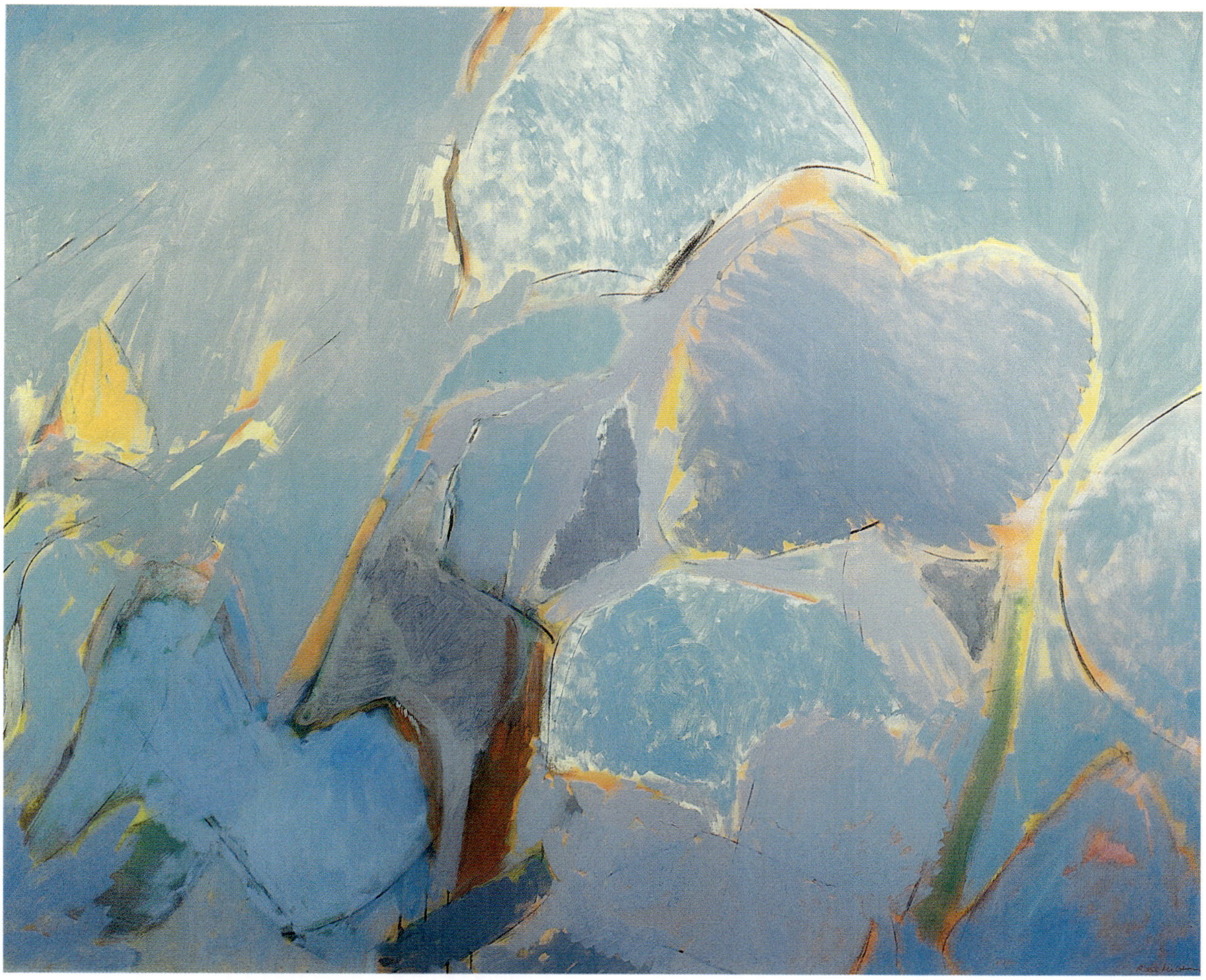

plate 60. ***Landscape on the Avon***, 1994,
oil on canvas
61 x 76.2 cm (24 x 30 in)

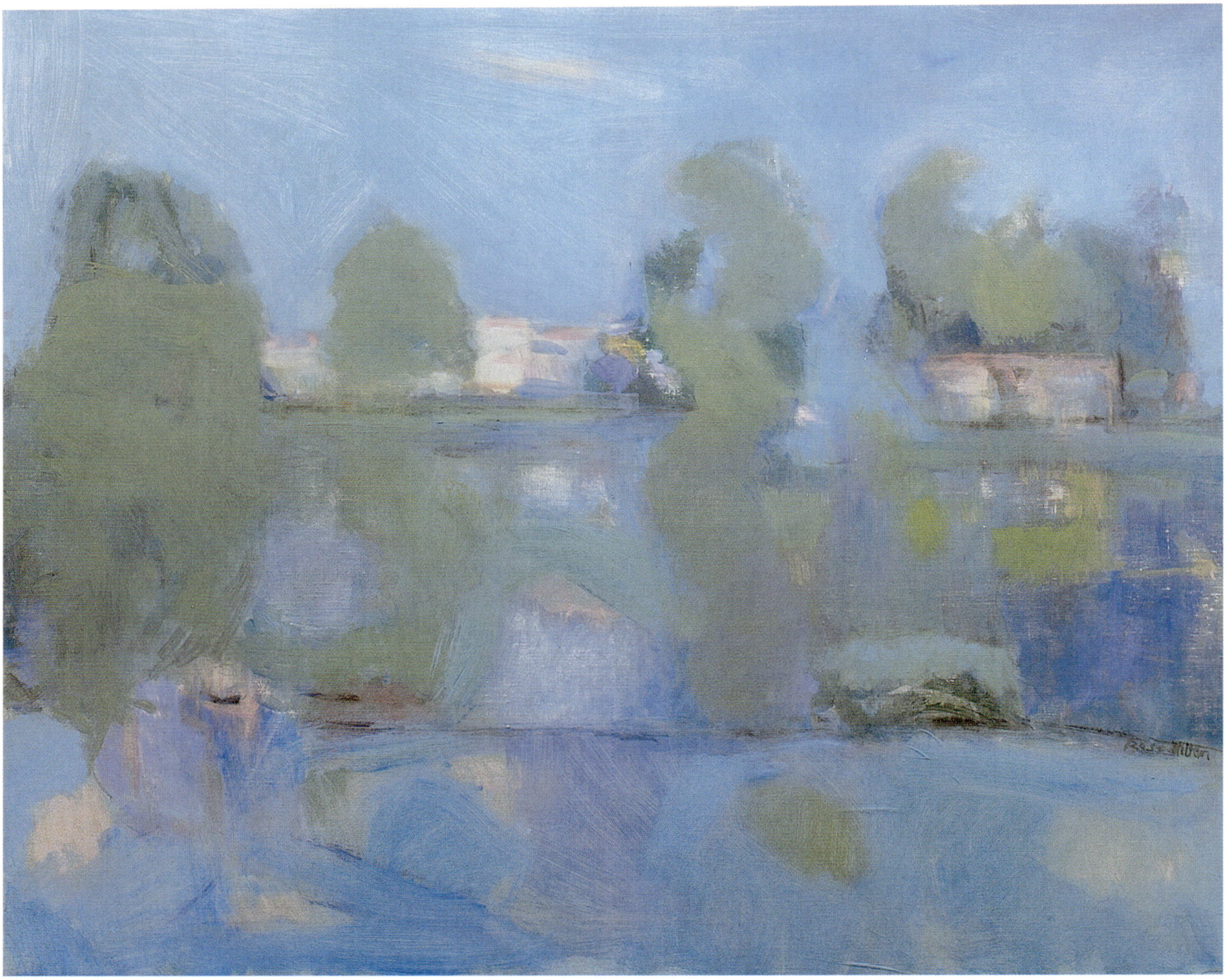

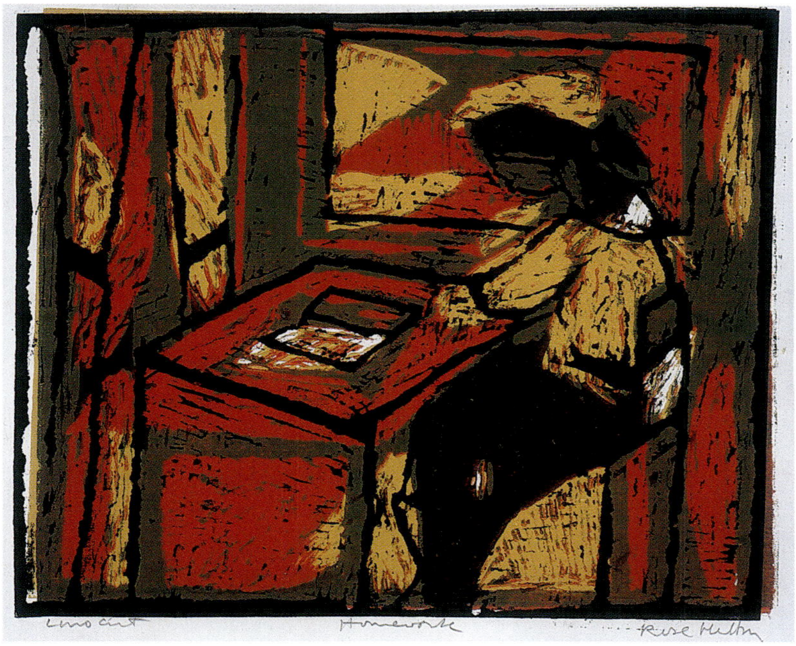

plate 61. ***Homework***, 1995,
linocut,
25.4 x 30.5 cm (10 x 12 in)

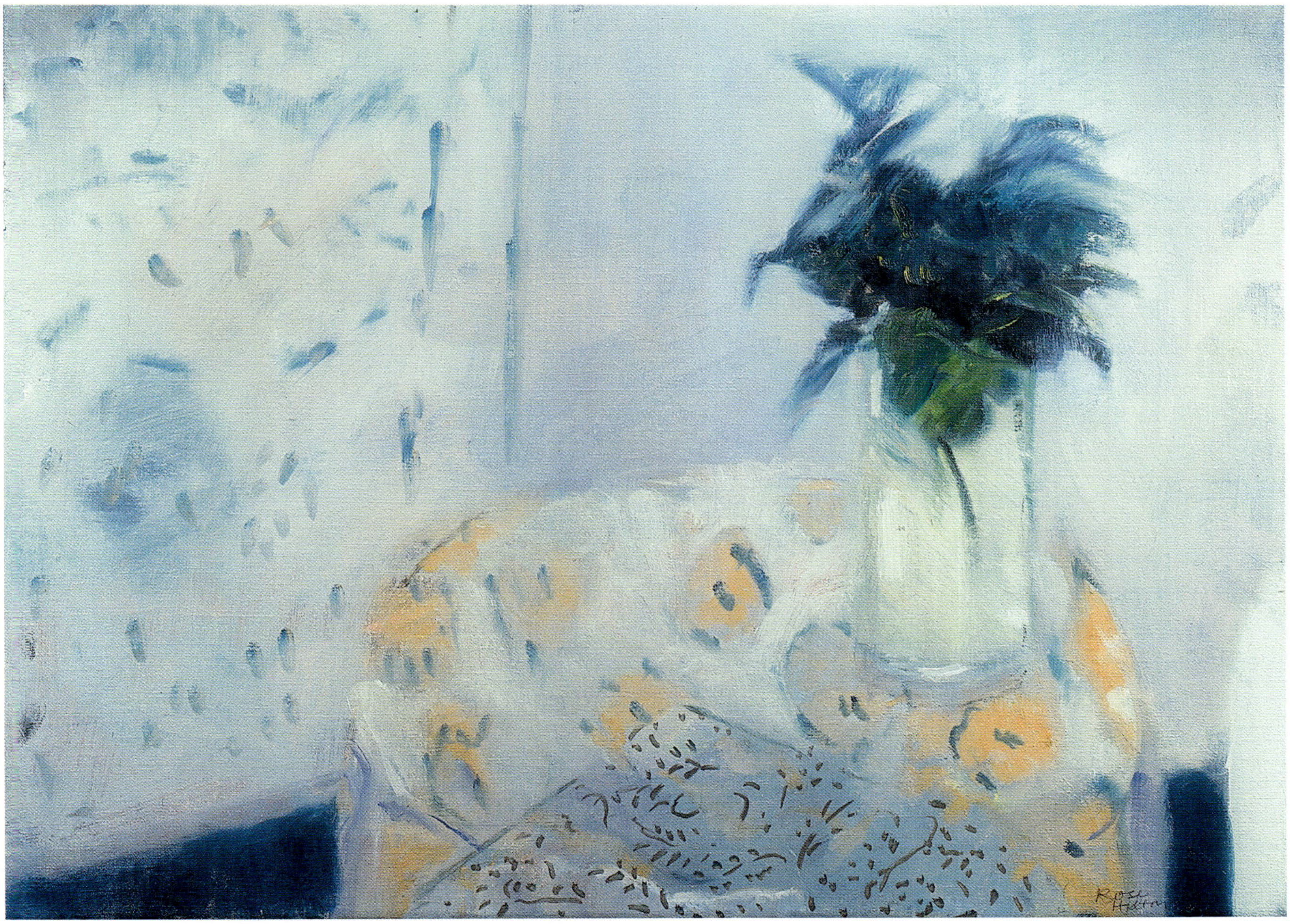

plate 62. ***Winter Leaves***,
1996,
oil on canvas,
45.1 x 64.8 cm
($17^{3}/_{4}$ x $25^{1}/_{2}$ in)

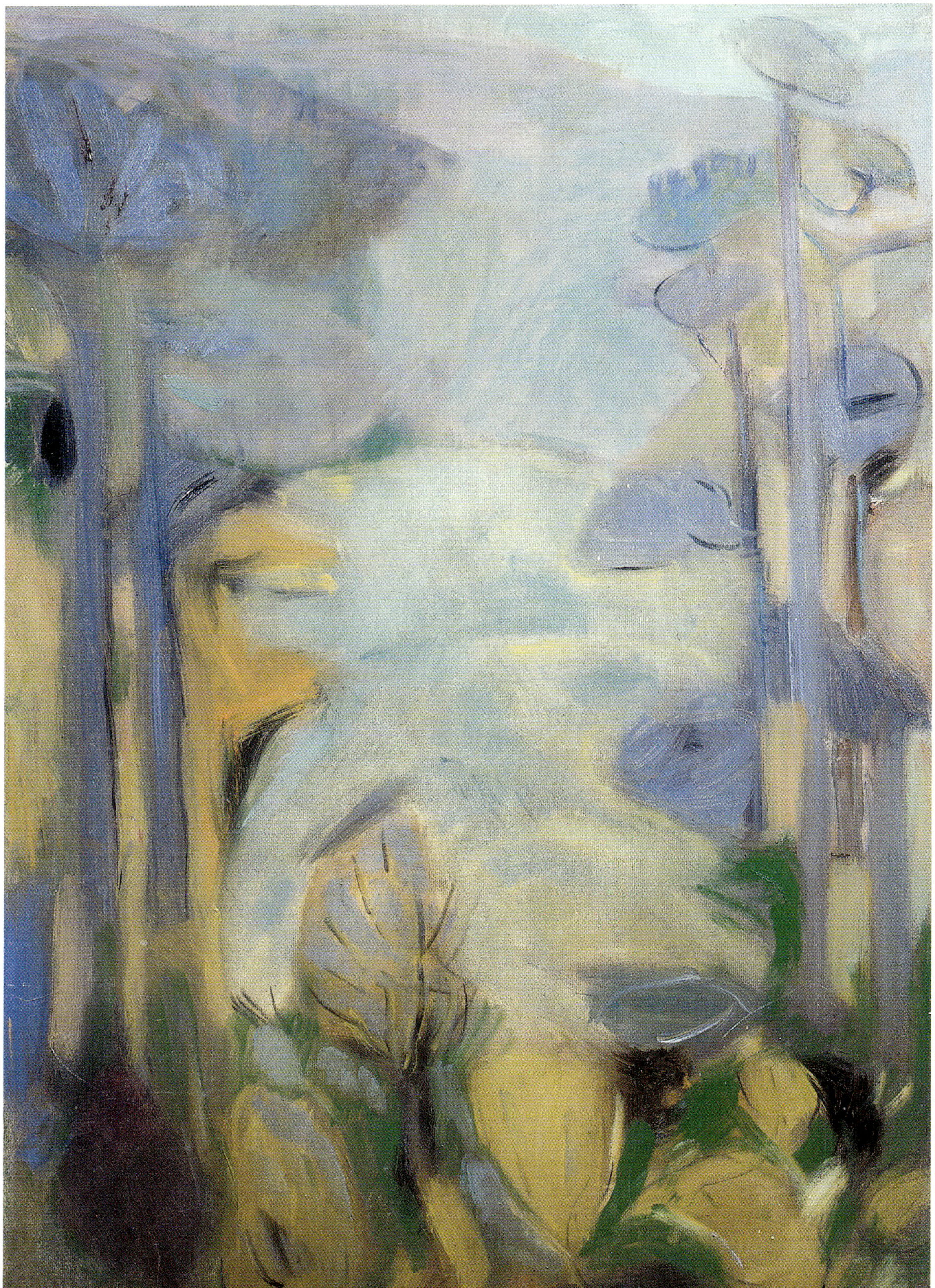

plate 63. ***St Just-in-Roseland***, 1996,
oil on board,
71.1 x 50.8 cm (28 x 20 in)

plate 64. ***Favourite Things***,
1997,
oil on canvas,
91.4 x 121.9 cm (36 x 48 in)

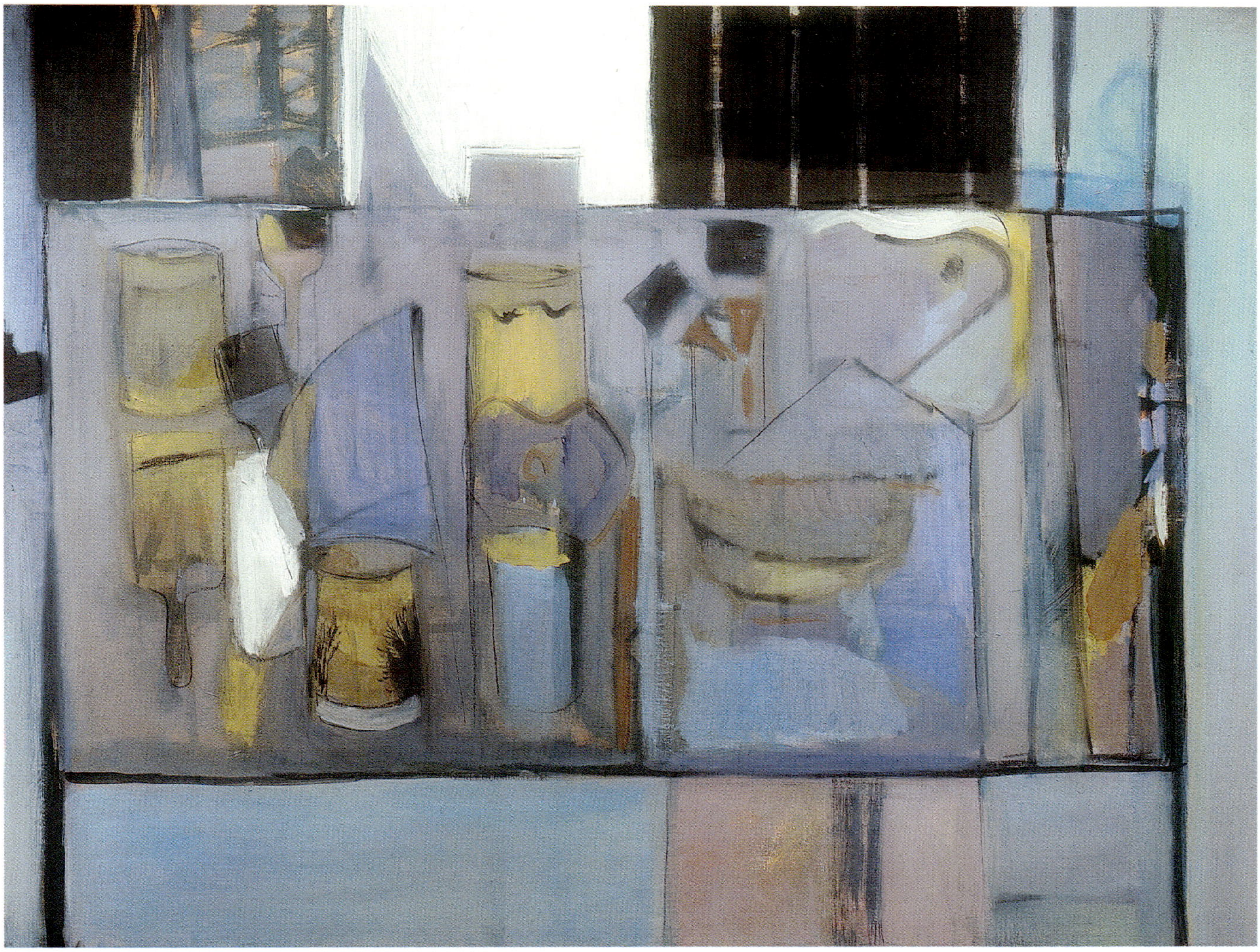

plate 65. ***Studio Still Life***, 1995,
oil on canvas,
75.6 x 77.5 cm (29¾ x 30½ in)

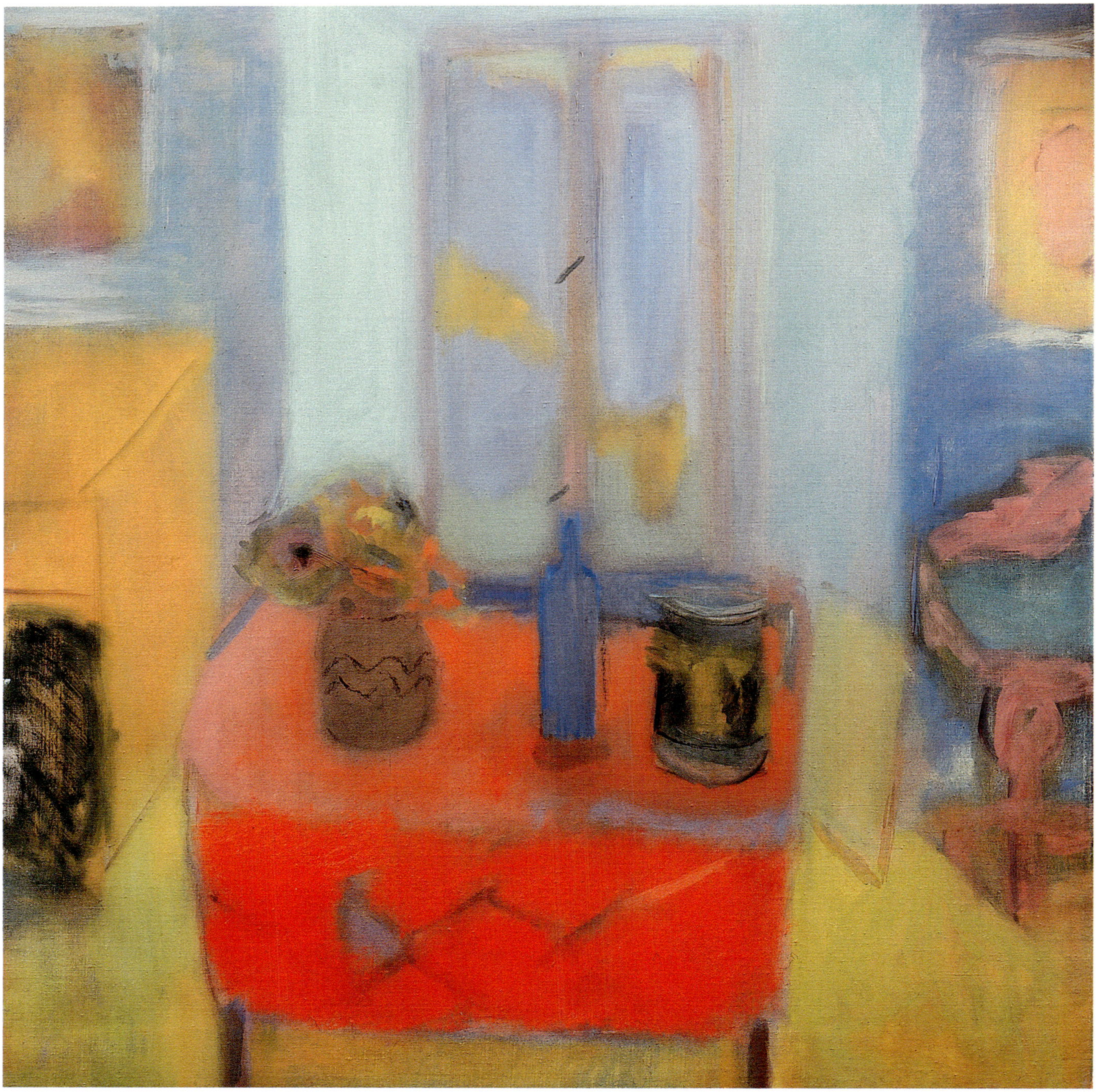

plate 66. ***White Table***,
1996,
oil on canvas,
76.2 x 121.9 cm (30 x 48 in)

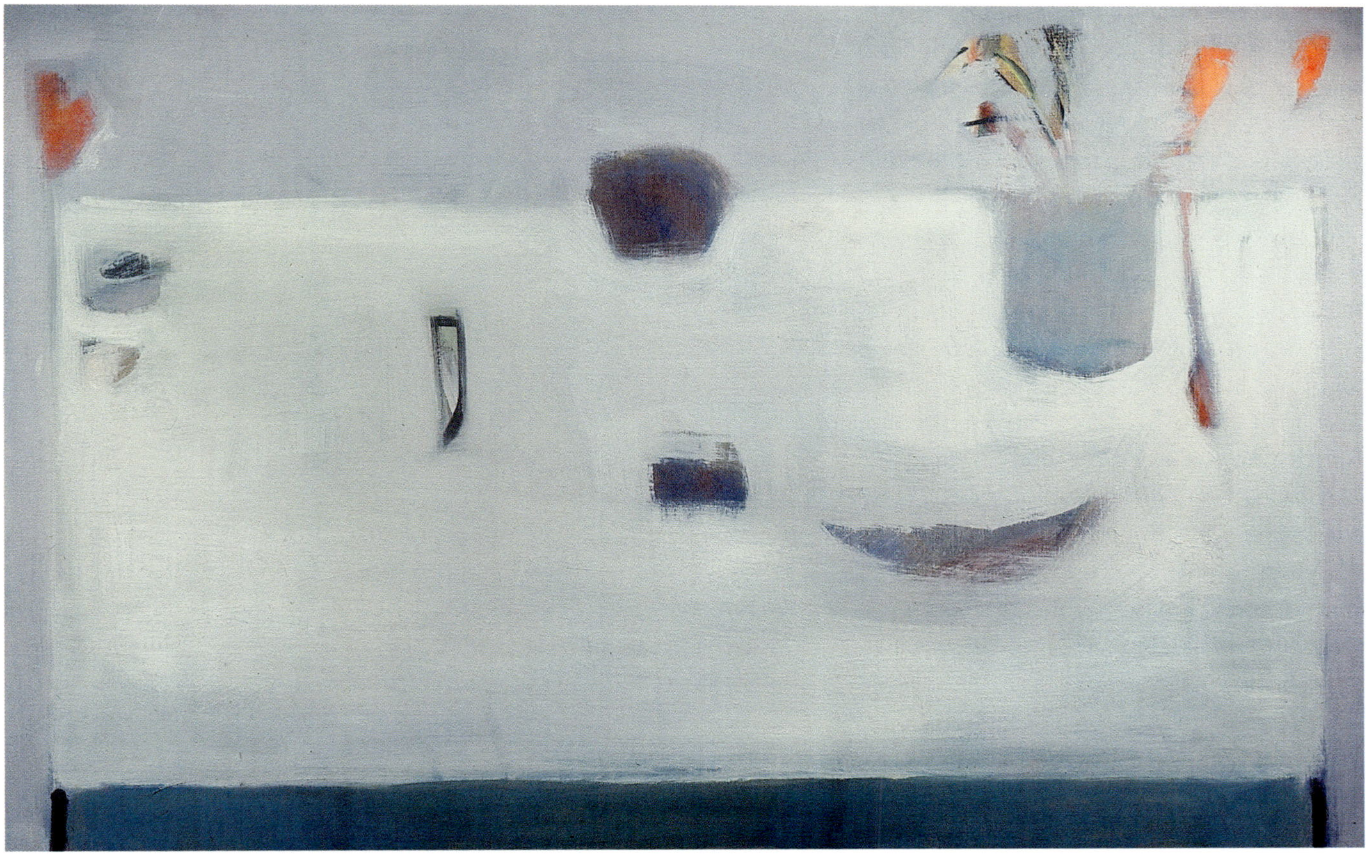

plate 67. *Mousehole*, 1992,
oil on canvas,
90.2 x 123.2 cm (35½ x 48½ in)

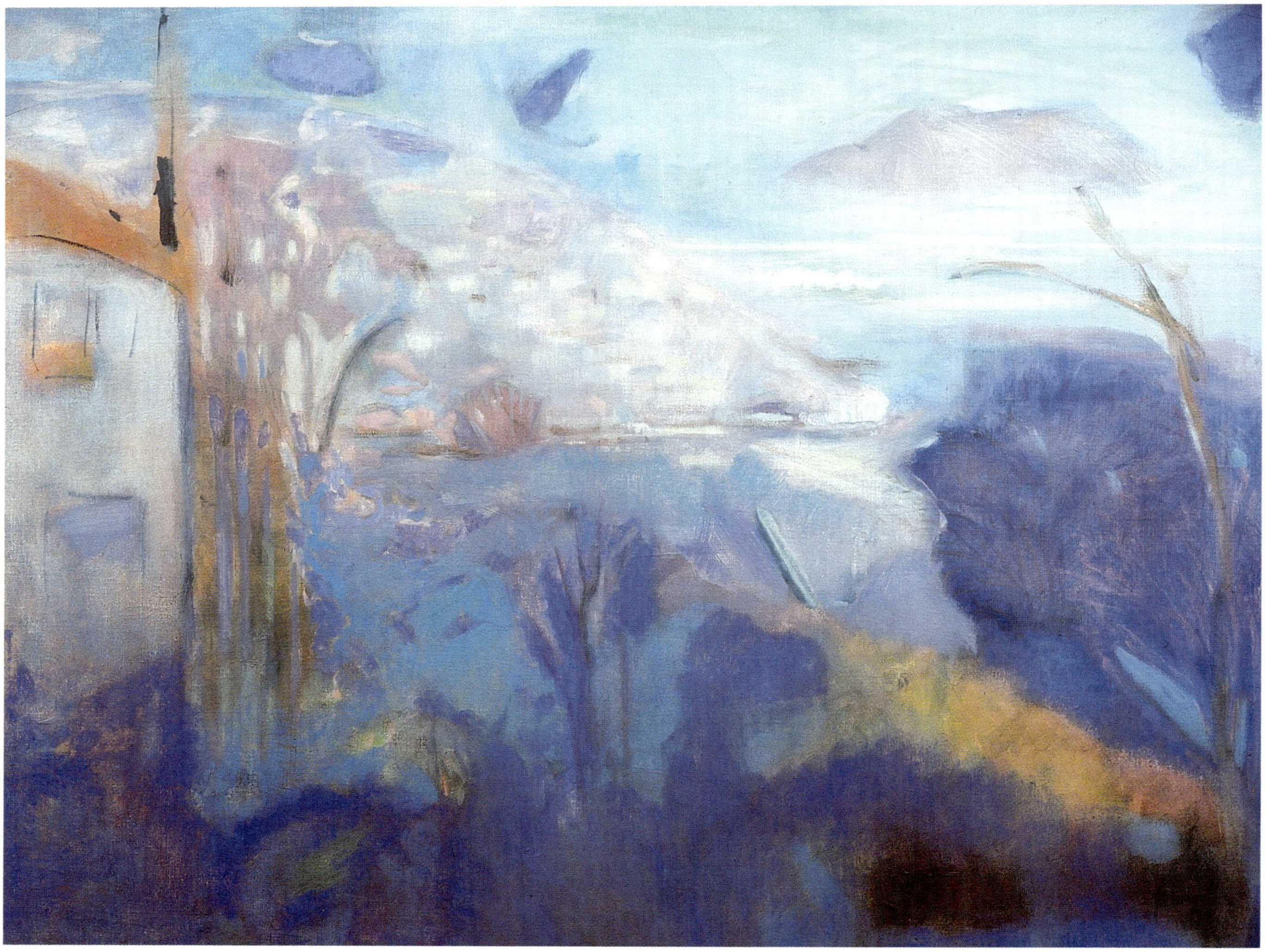

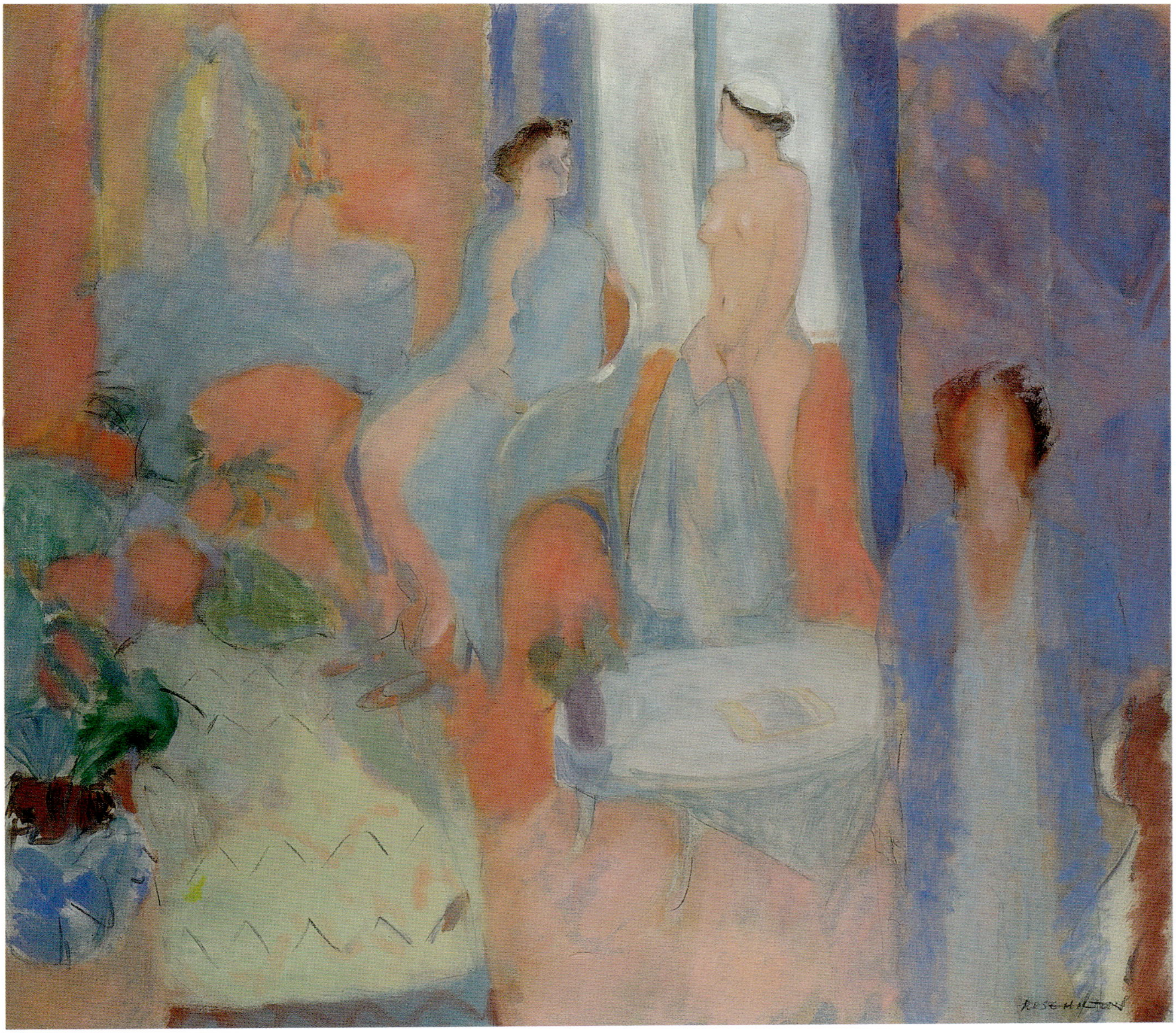

plate 68. ***The Sisters***, 1997,
oil on canvas,
106.7 x 121.9 cm (42 x 48 in)

plate 69. ***Reclining Figure***,
1997,
oil on canvas,
35.6 x 45.7 cm (14 x 18 in)

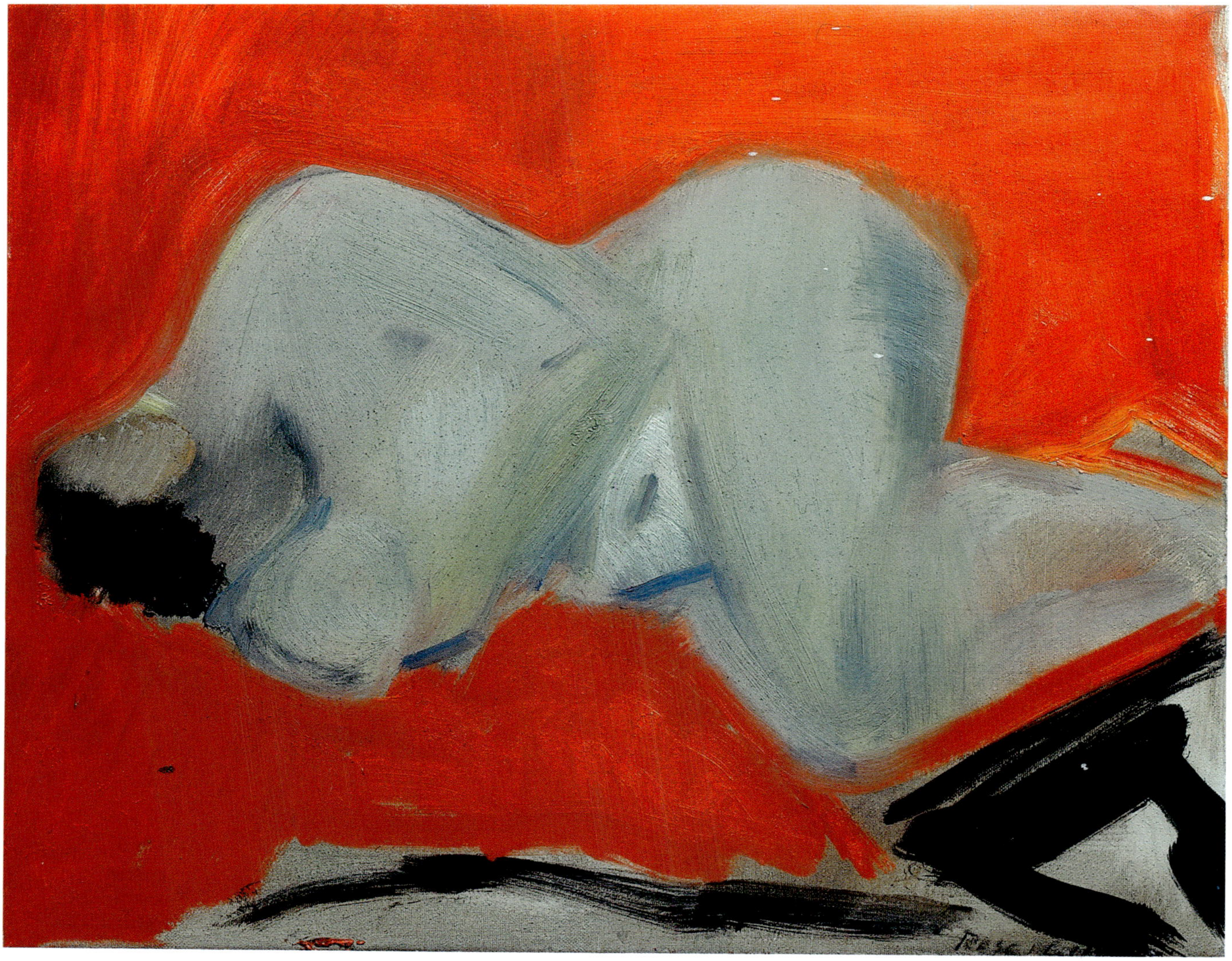

plate 70. ***Orange Still Life***,
1996,
oil on canvas,
50.8 x 61 cm (20 x 24 in)

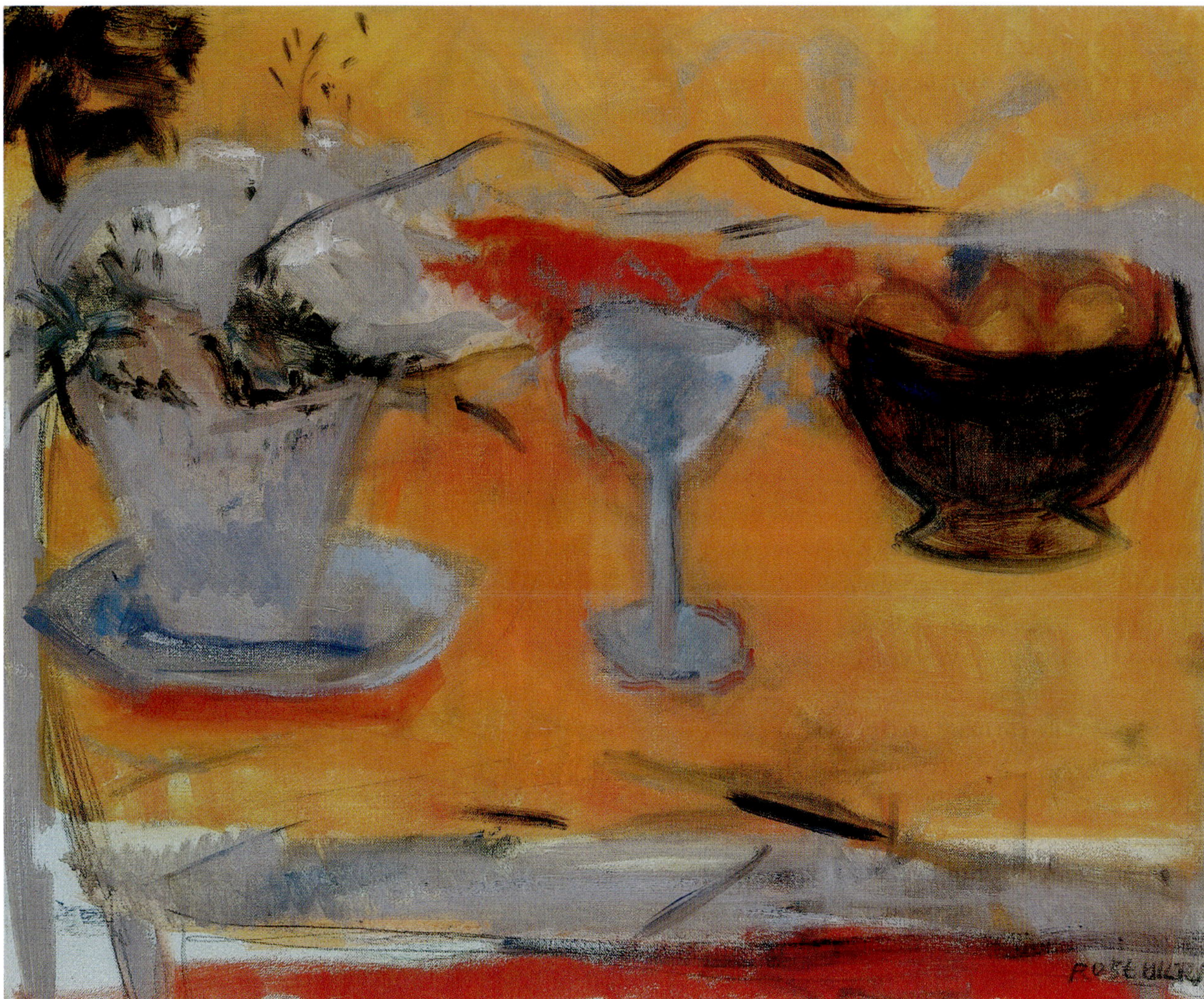

plate 71. *The Goldfish Bowl*,
1993,
oil on canvas,
91.4 x 121.9 cm (36 x 48 in)

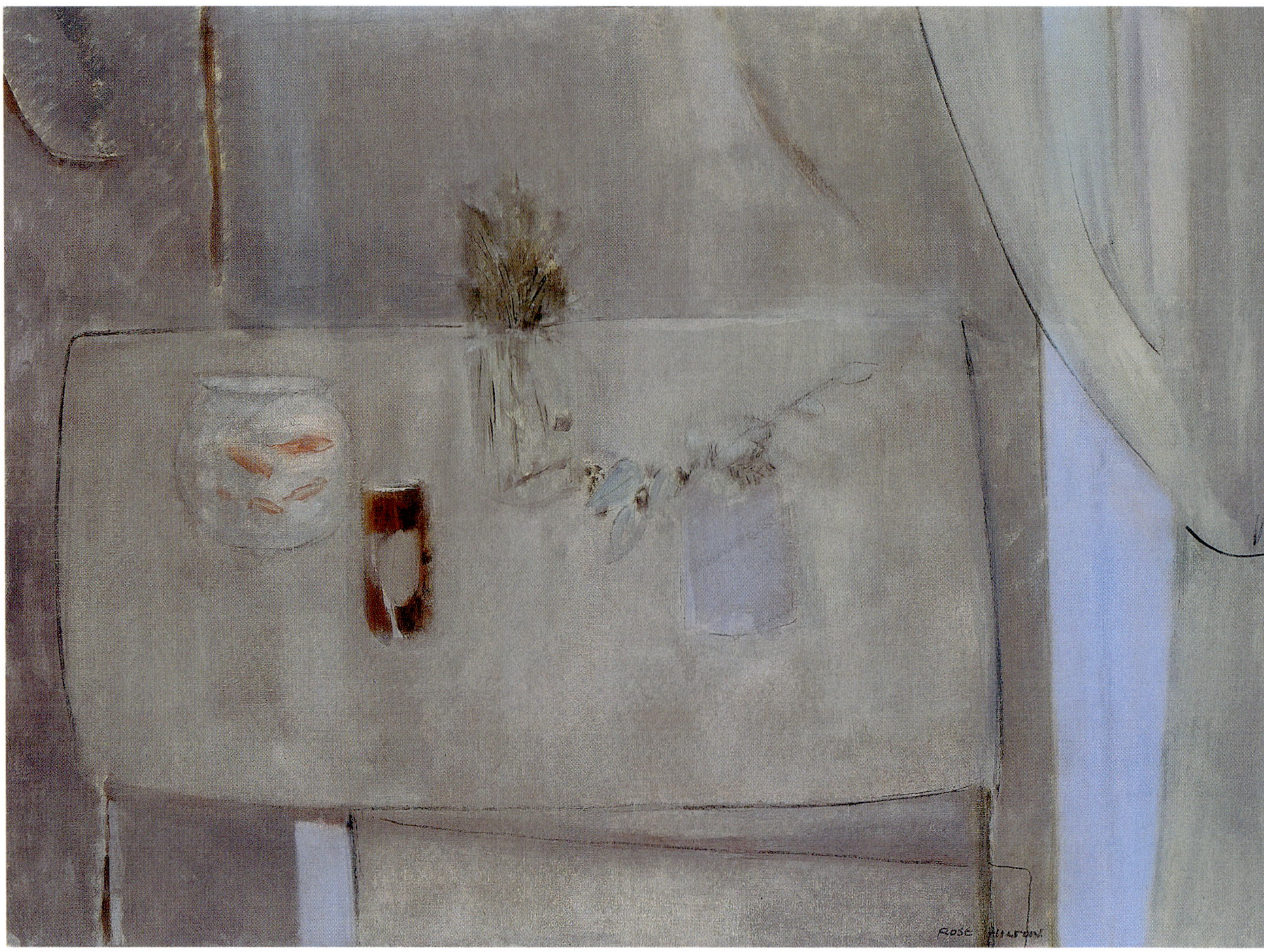

plate 72. ***Serenity***, 1997,
oil on canvas,
76.2 x 76.2 cm (30 x 30 in)

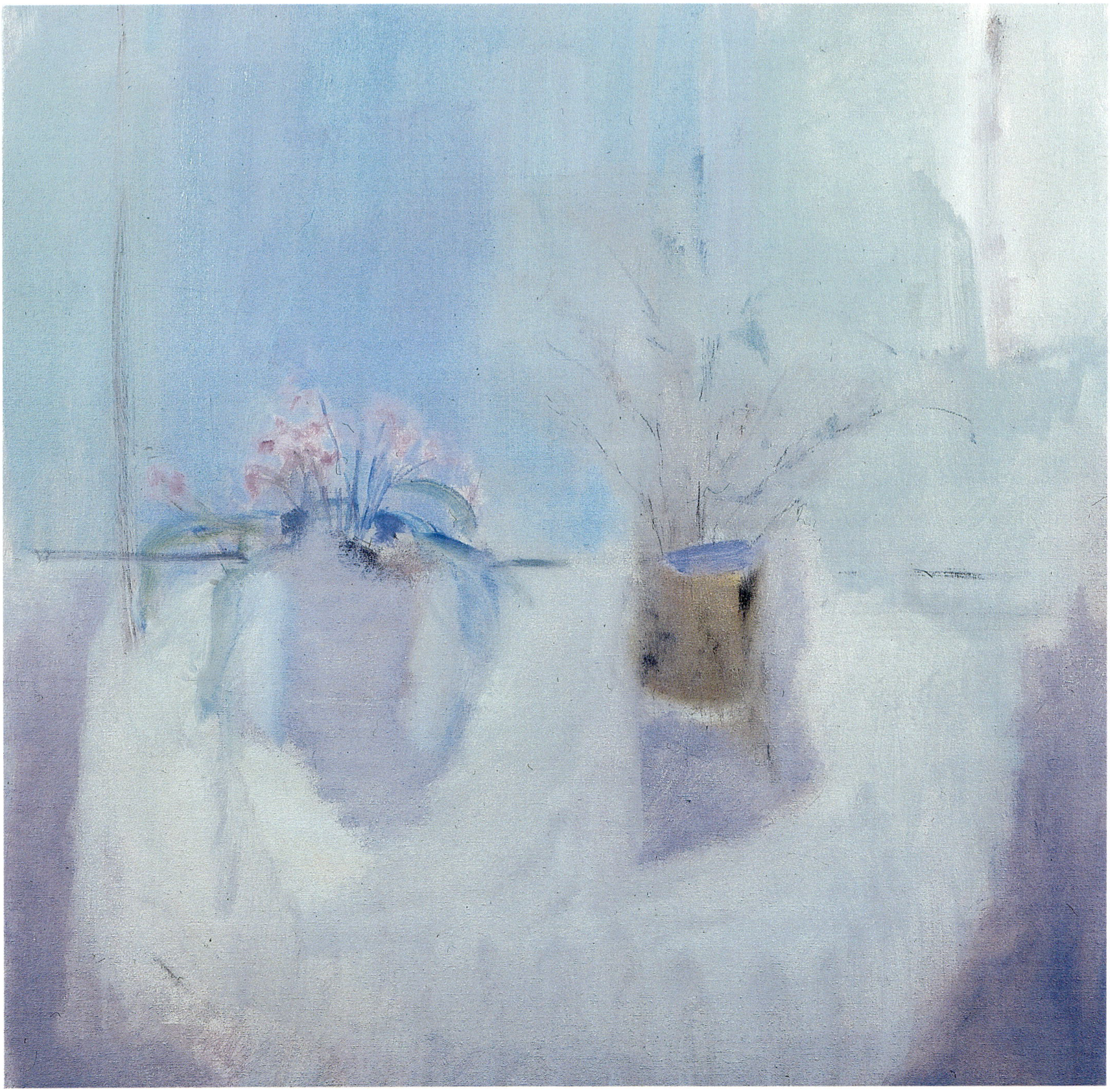

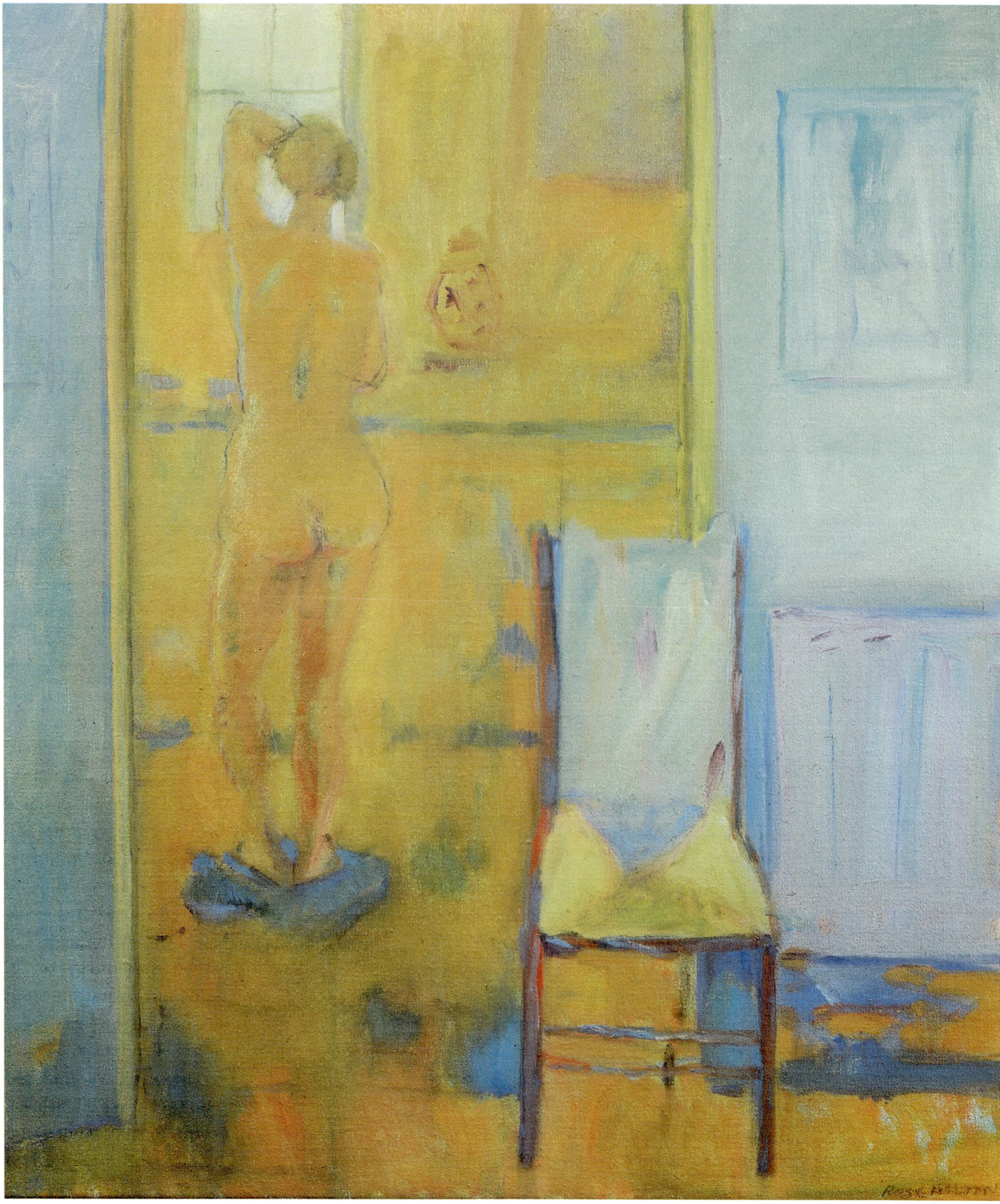

plate 73. ***Undressing in the Kitchen***, 1996, oil on canvas, 61 x 50.8 cm (24 x 20 in)

plate 74. ***Summer Morning***, 1997, oil on canvas, 106.7 x 121.9 cm (42 x 48 in)

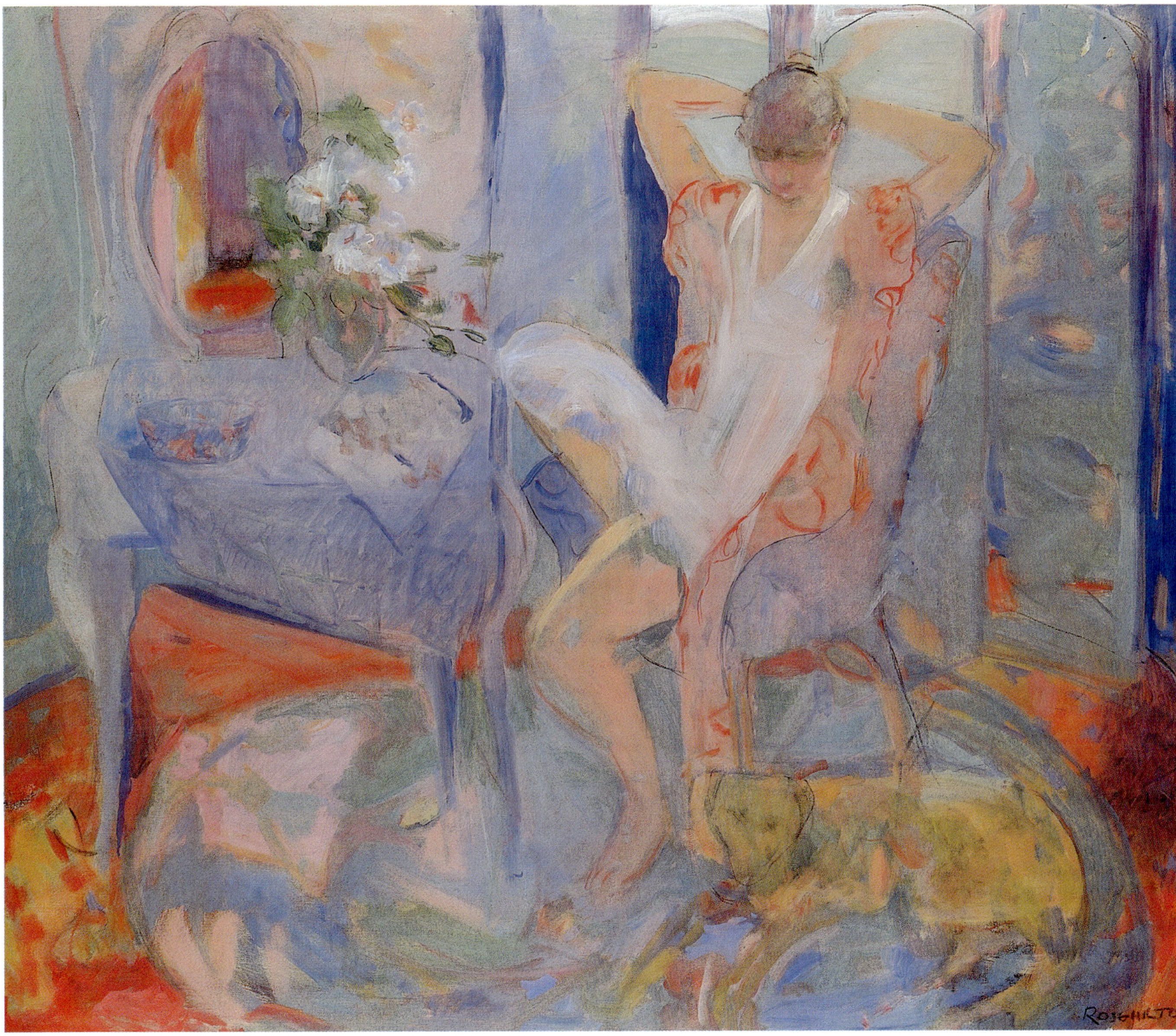

plate 75. ***Lillies***, 1995,
oil on canvas,
50.8 x 61 cm (20 x 24 in)

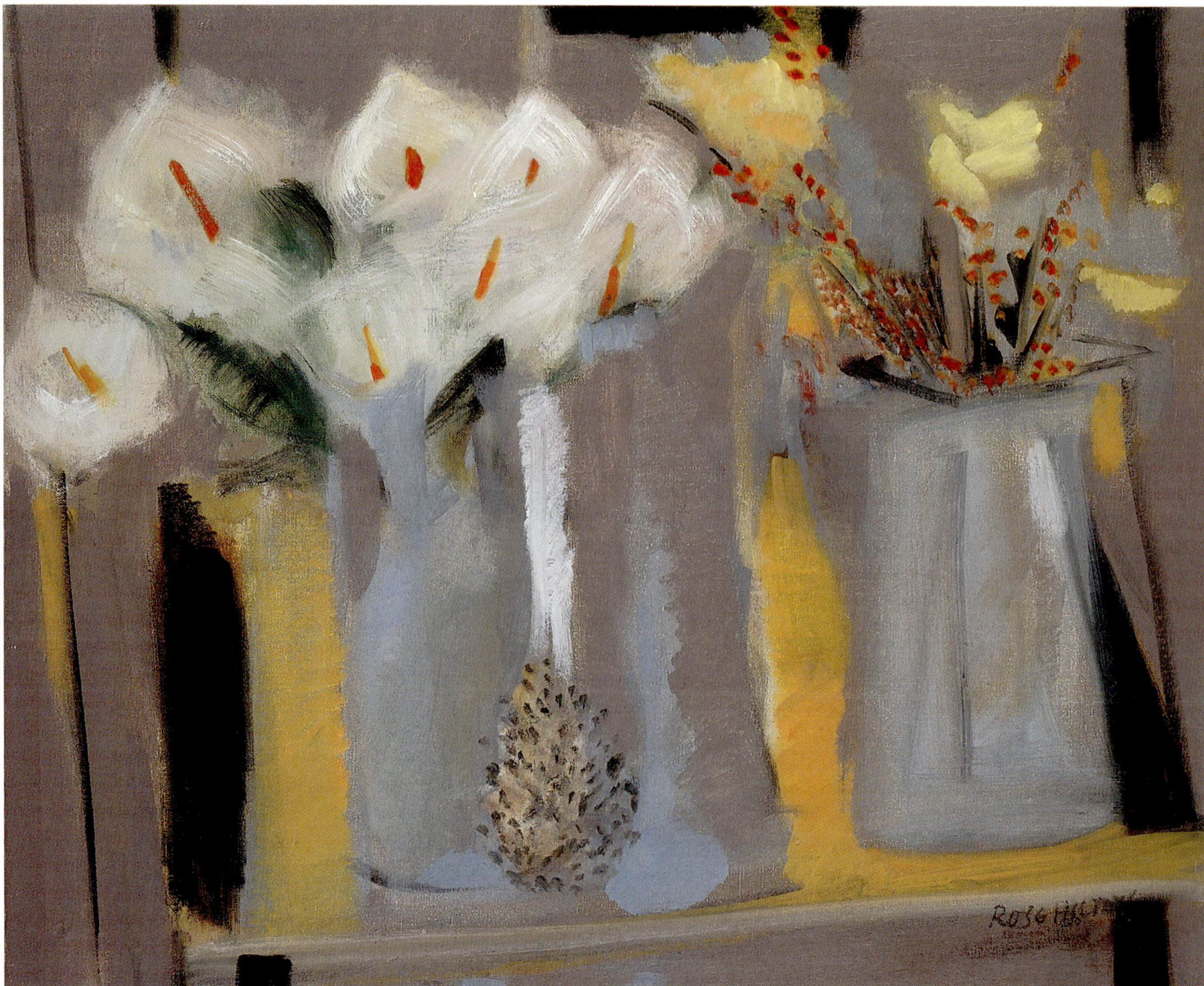

plate 76. ***Winter Hills, St Austell***, 1996, oil on canvas, 50.8 x 61 cm (20 x 24 in)

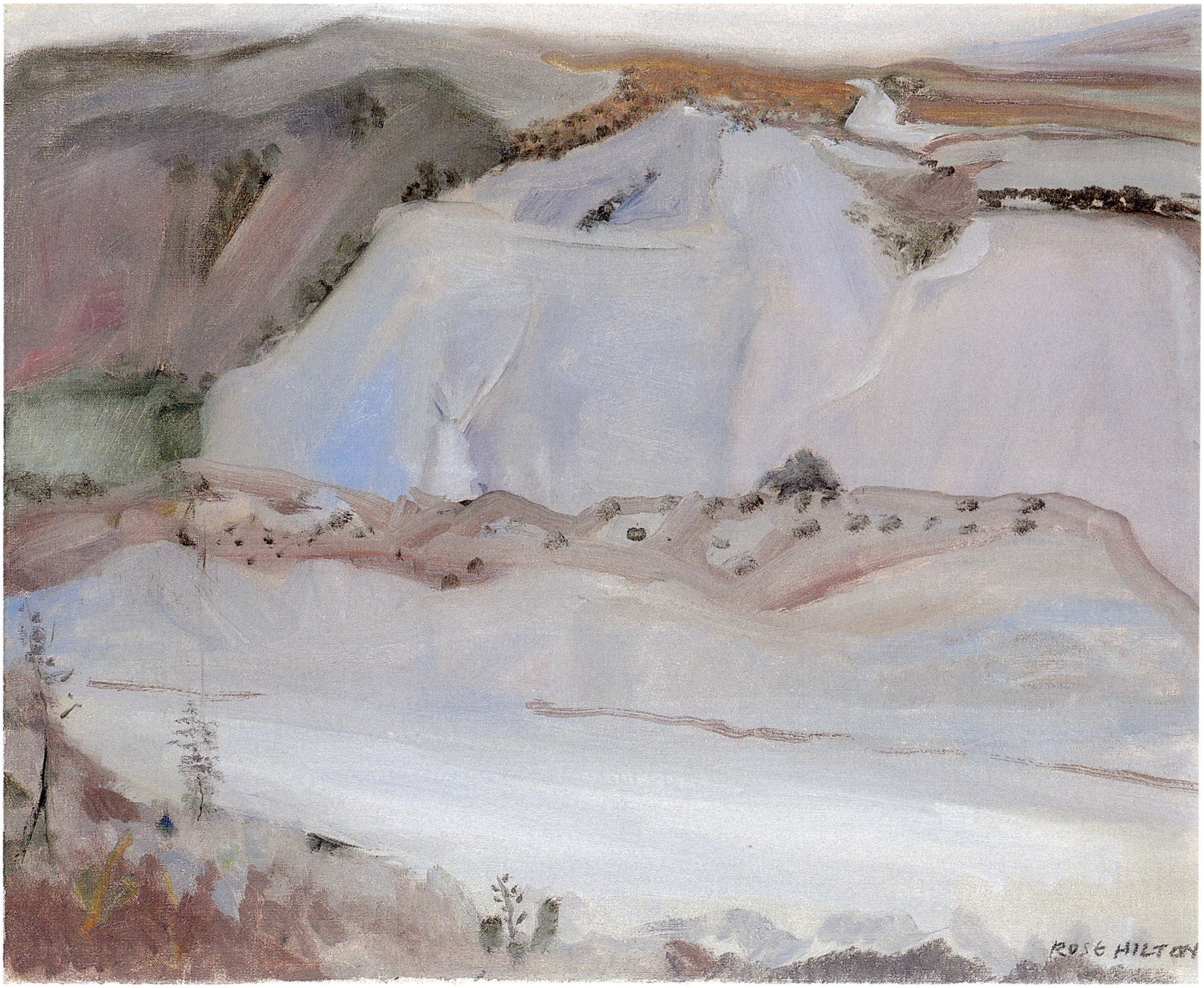

plate 77. ***Claypits Series 1 (St Austell)***, 1996, oil on canvas, 76.2 x 76.2 cm (30 x 30 in)

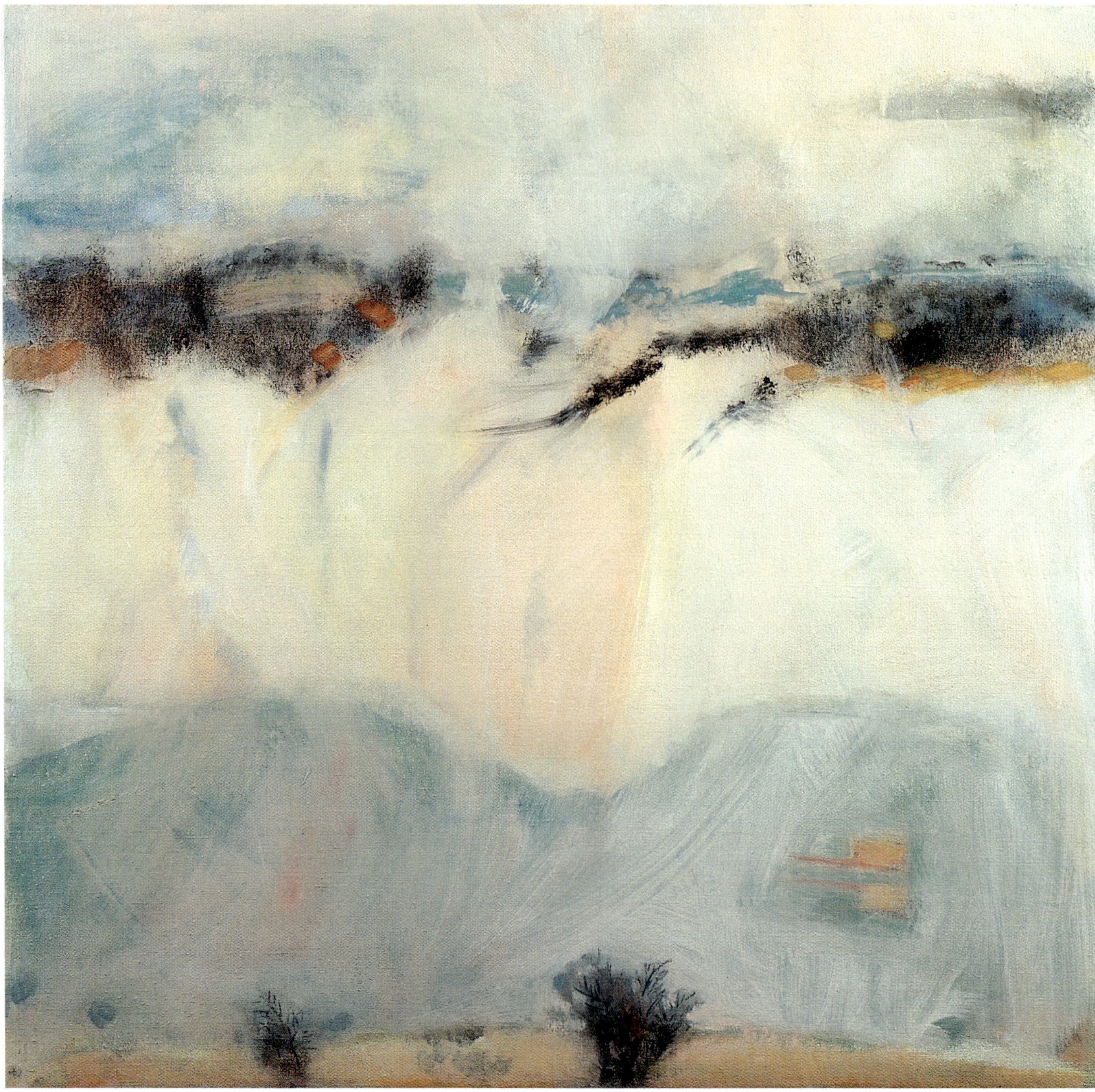

plate 78. ***Summer Place***,
1995,
oil on canvas,
73.6 x 92.7 cm (29 x 36½ in)

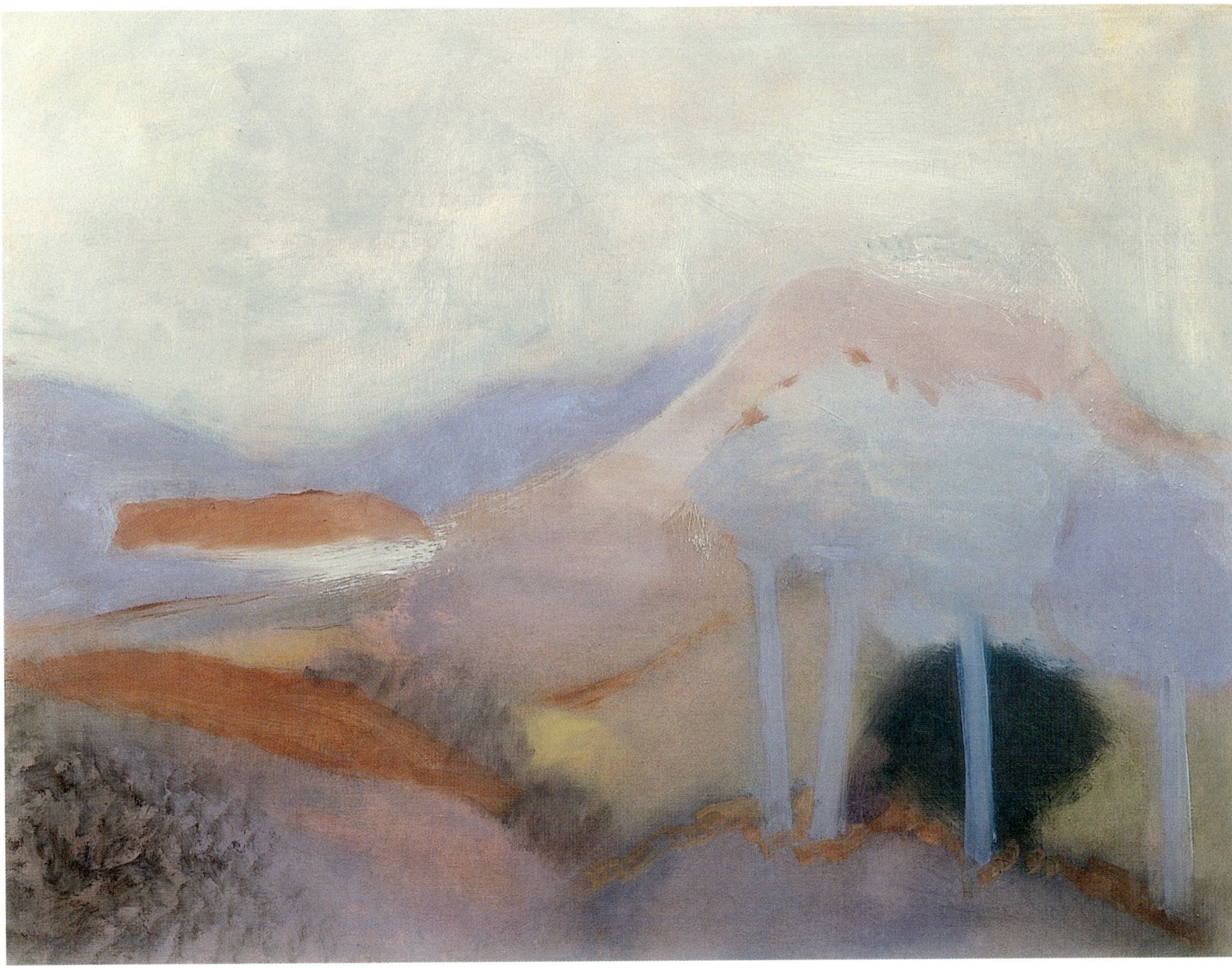

plate 79. *The Road to St Ives*, 1995,
oil on canvas,
91.4 x 121.9 cm (36 x 48 in)

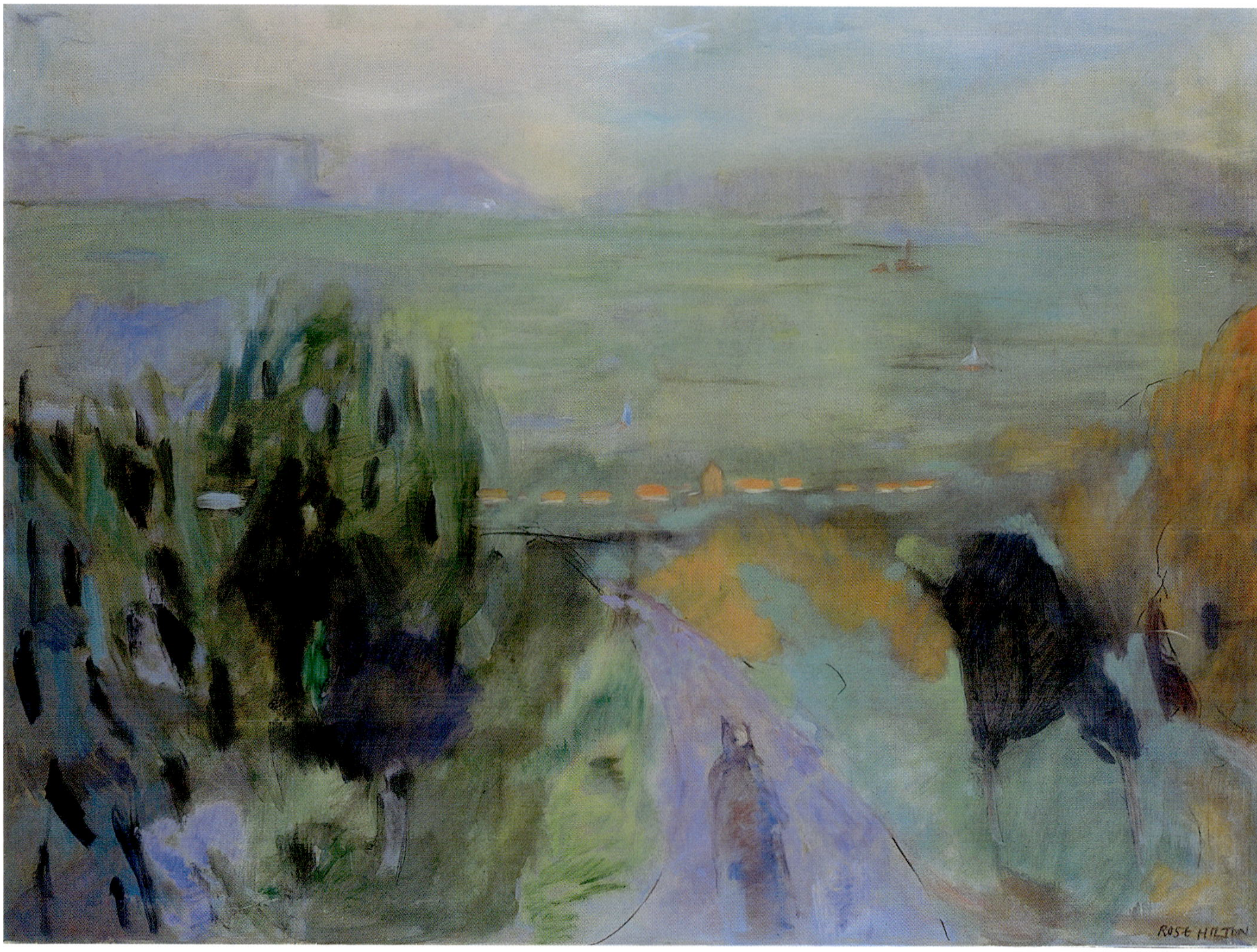

plate 80. ***Study for Steven*****, 1997,**
oil on canvas,
74.9 x 38.1 cm (29½ x 15 in)

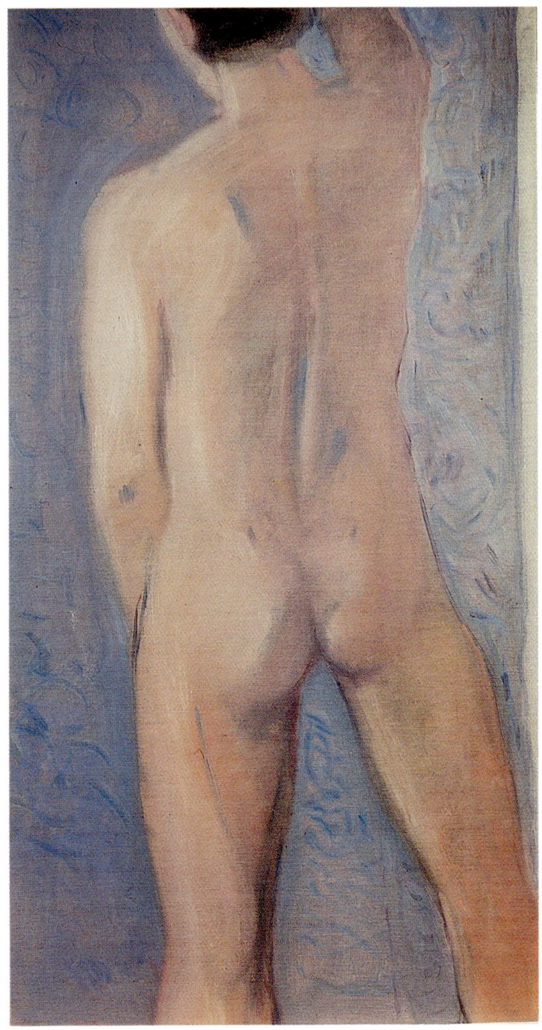

plate 81. ***Red Room***,
1999,
oil on canvas,
76.2 x 76.2 cm (30 x 30 in)

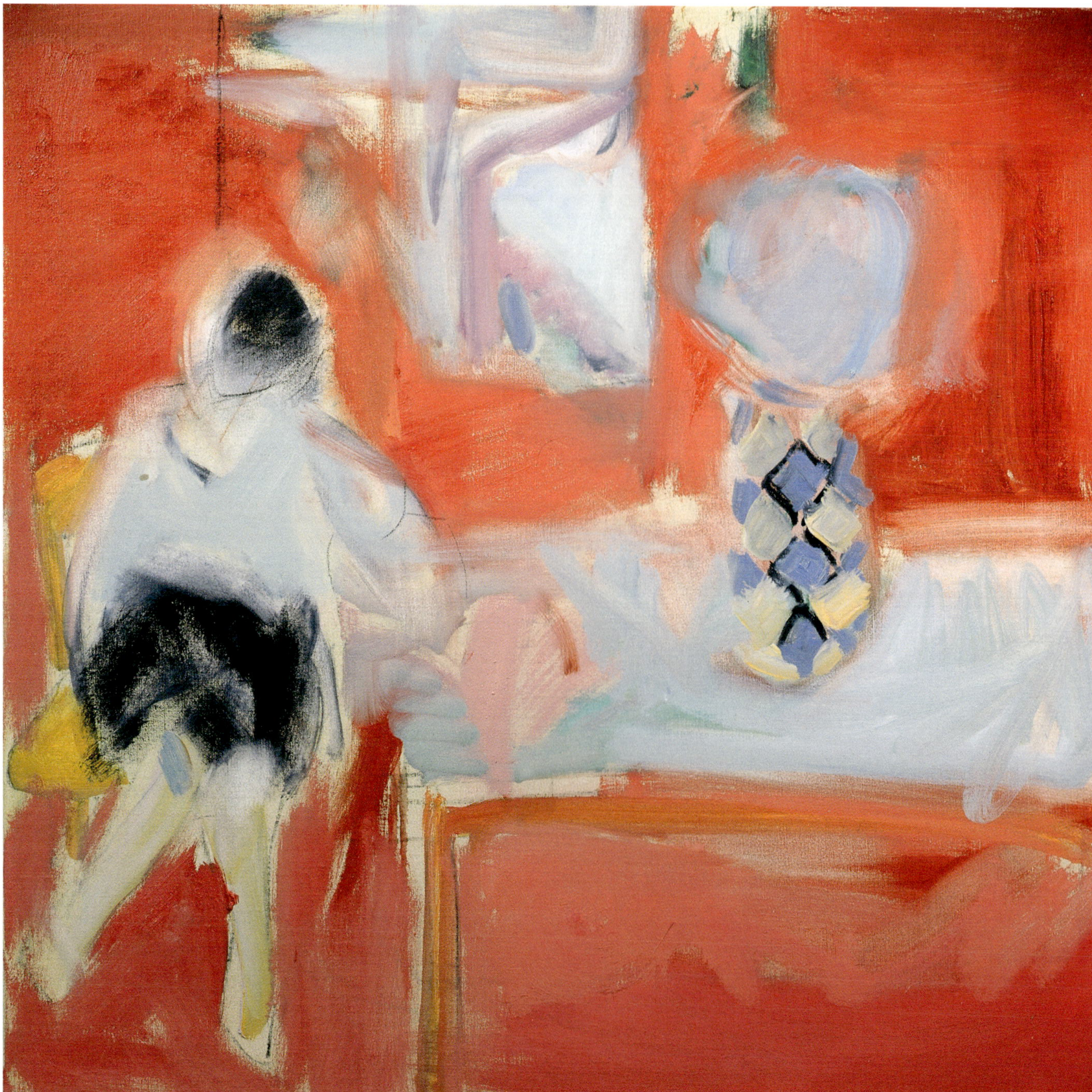

plate 82. ***Salcombe Landscape***, 1999,
oil on canvas,
121.9 x 121.9 cm (48 x 48 in)

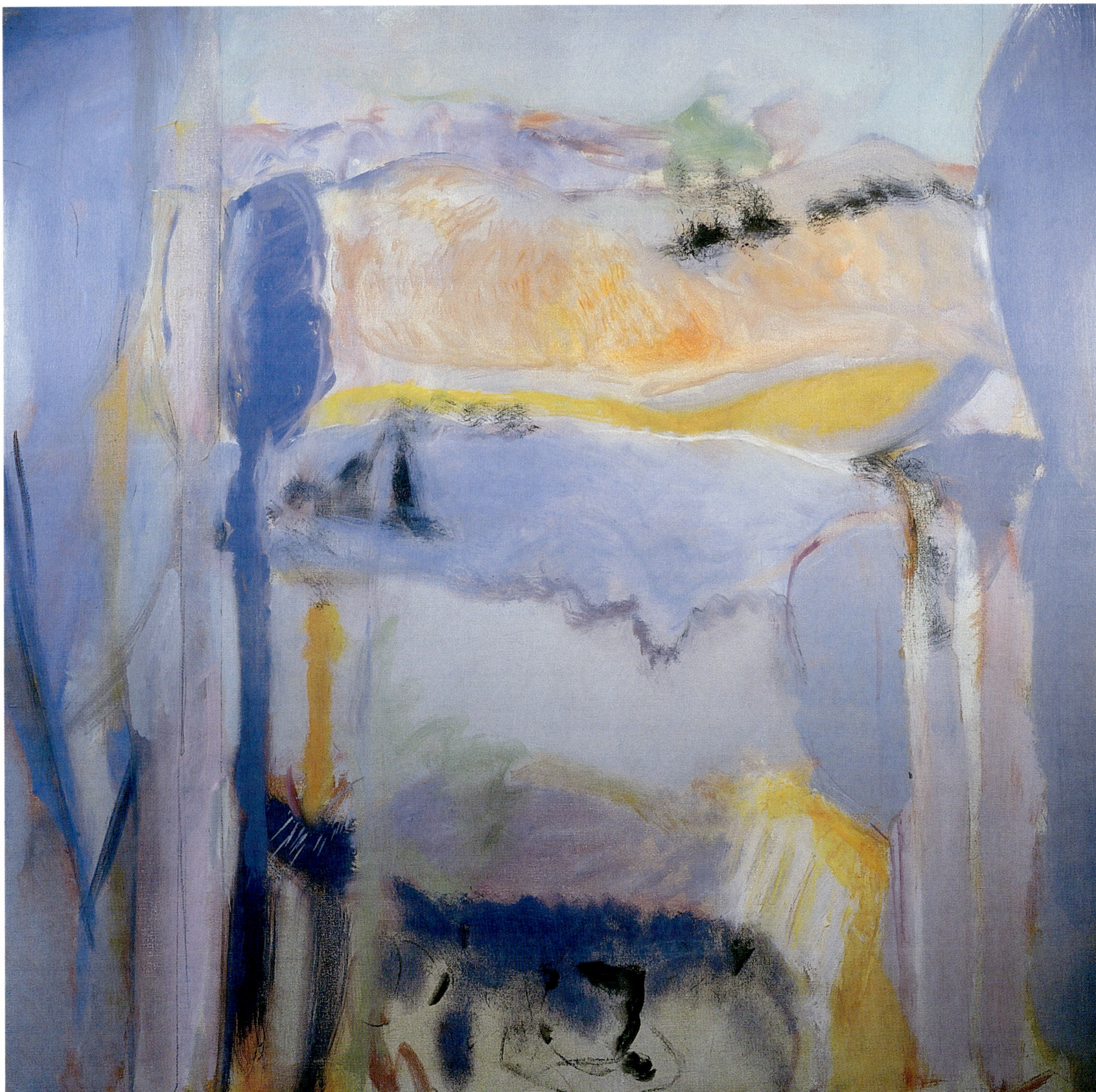

plate 83. ***Yellow Interior***,
1999,
oil on canvas,
91.4 x 121.9 cm (36 x 48 in)

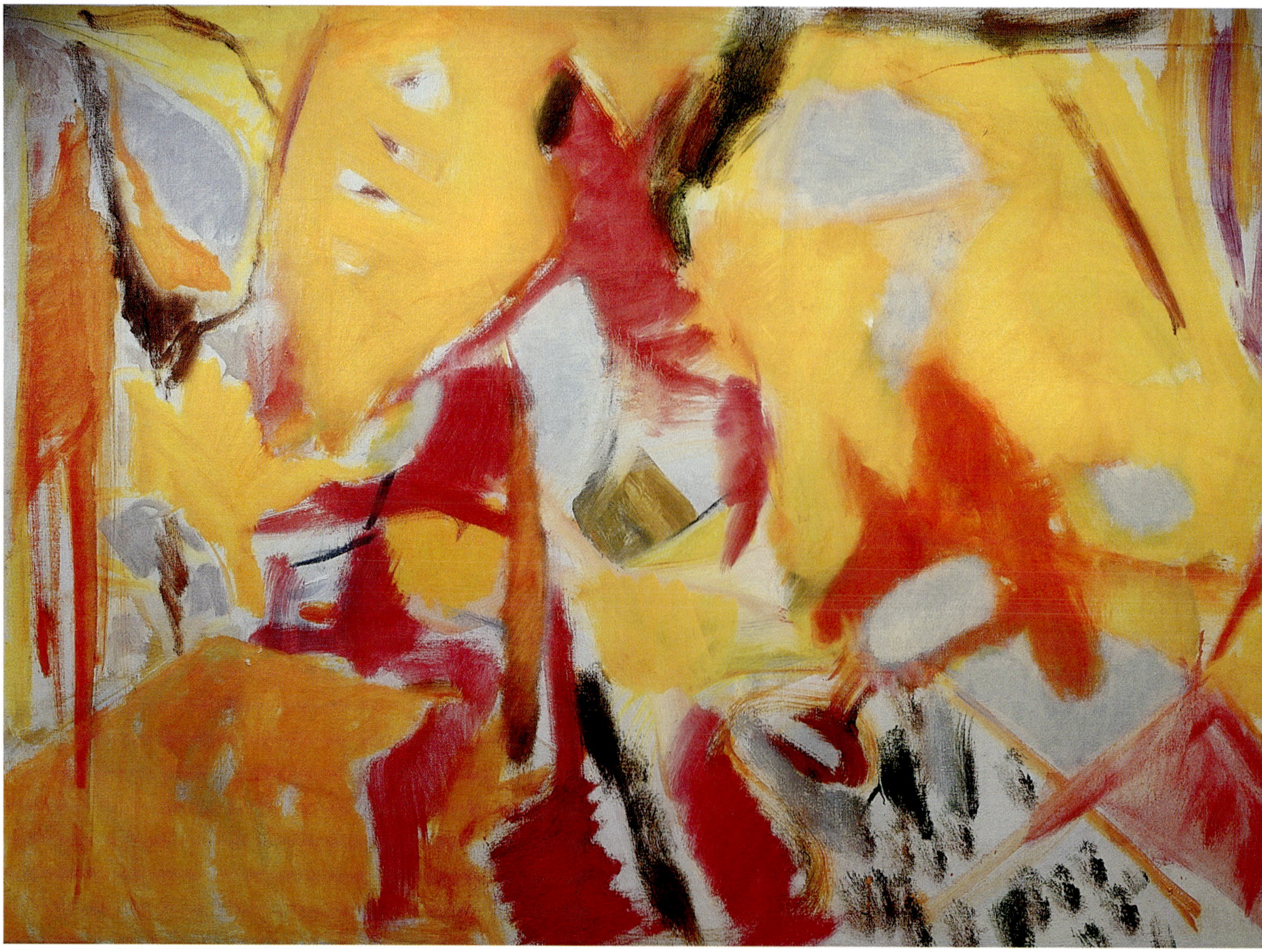

plate 84. ***Summer in the Conservatory***, 1999,
oil on canvas,
76.2 x 101.6 cm (30 x 40 in)

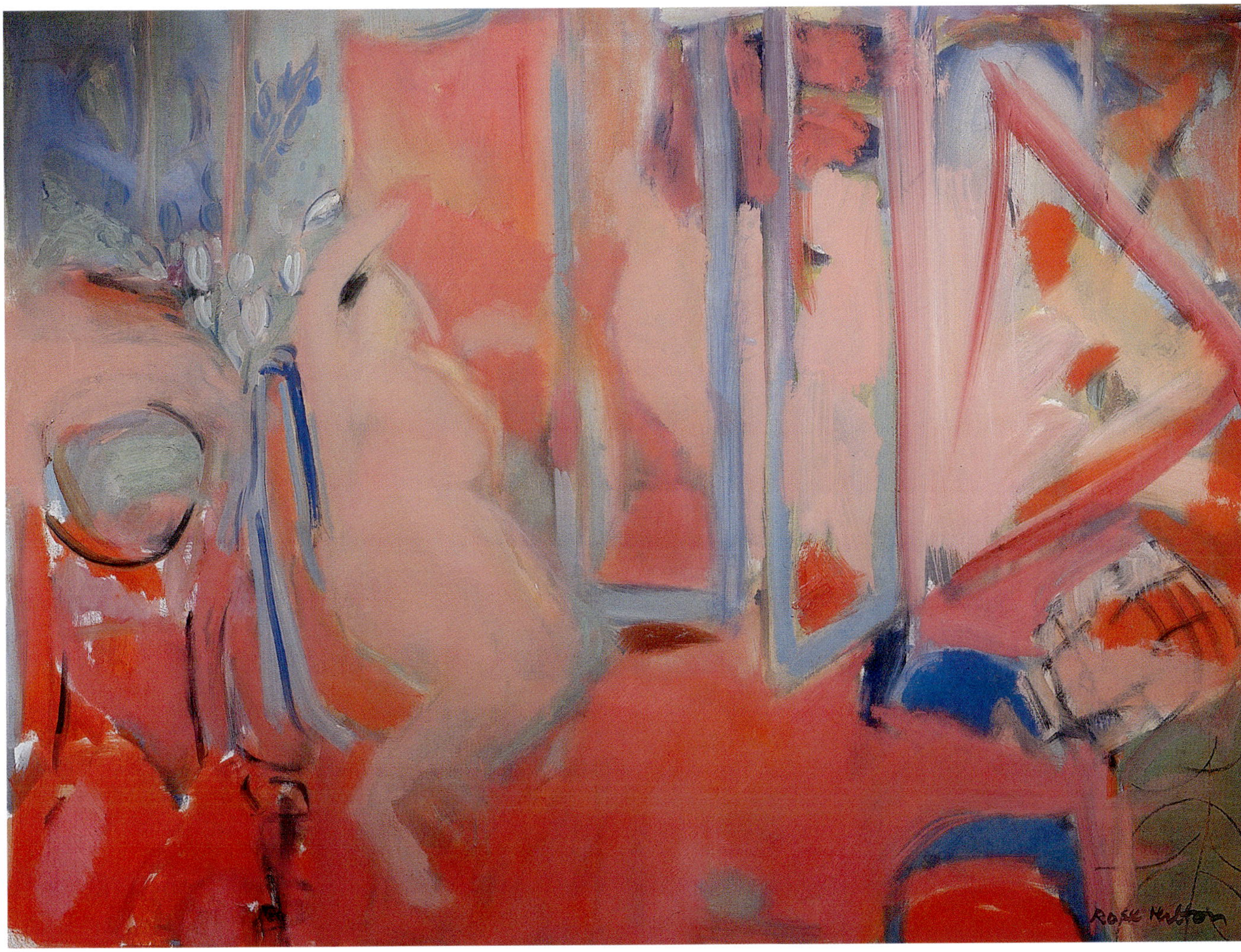

plate 85. ***Autumn Still-life***,
1998,
oil on canvas,
76.2 x 76.2 cm (30 x 30 in)

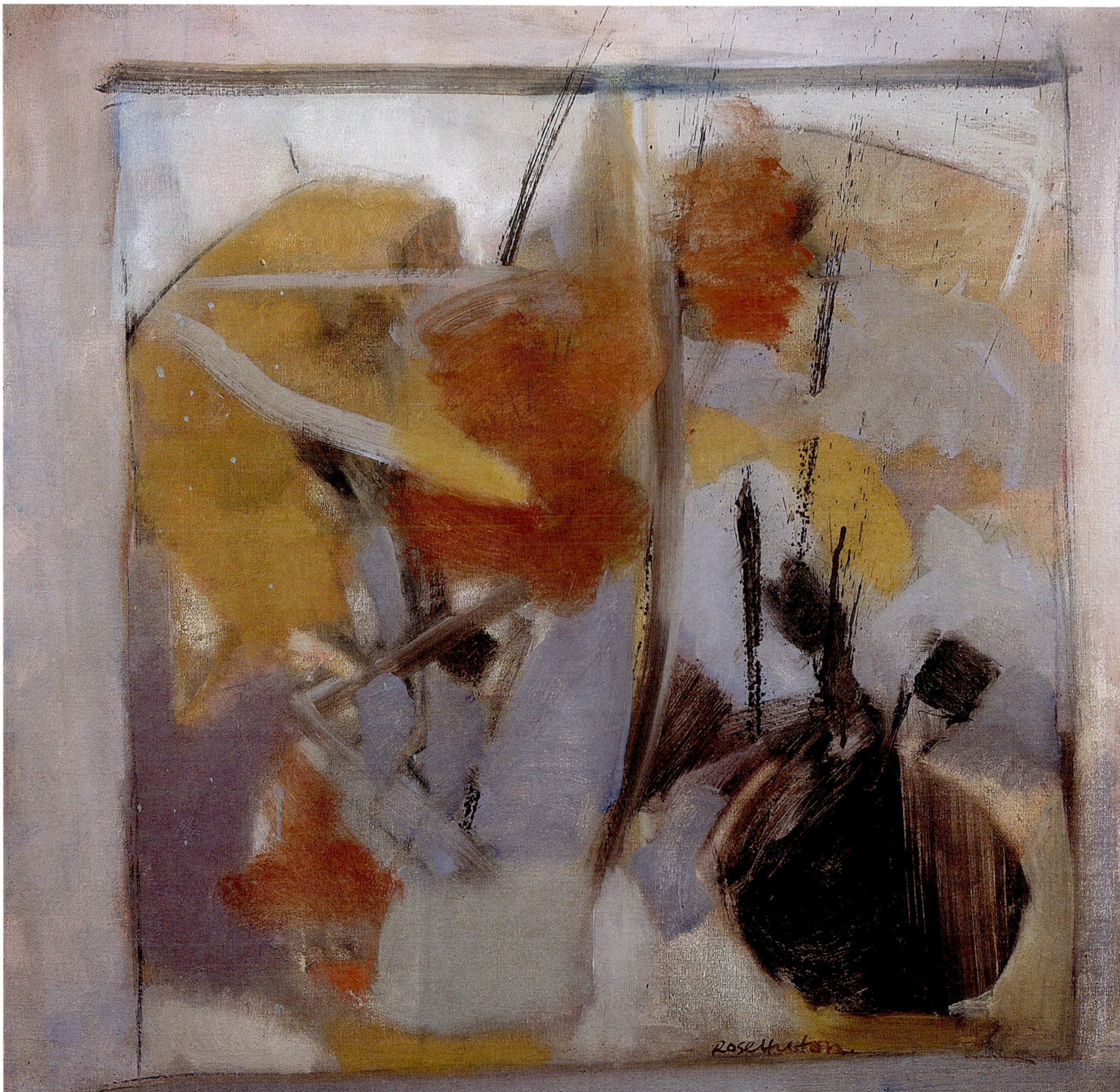

plate 86. ***Grey Still-life***,
1998,
oil on canvas,
76.2 x 76.2 cm (30 x 30 in)

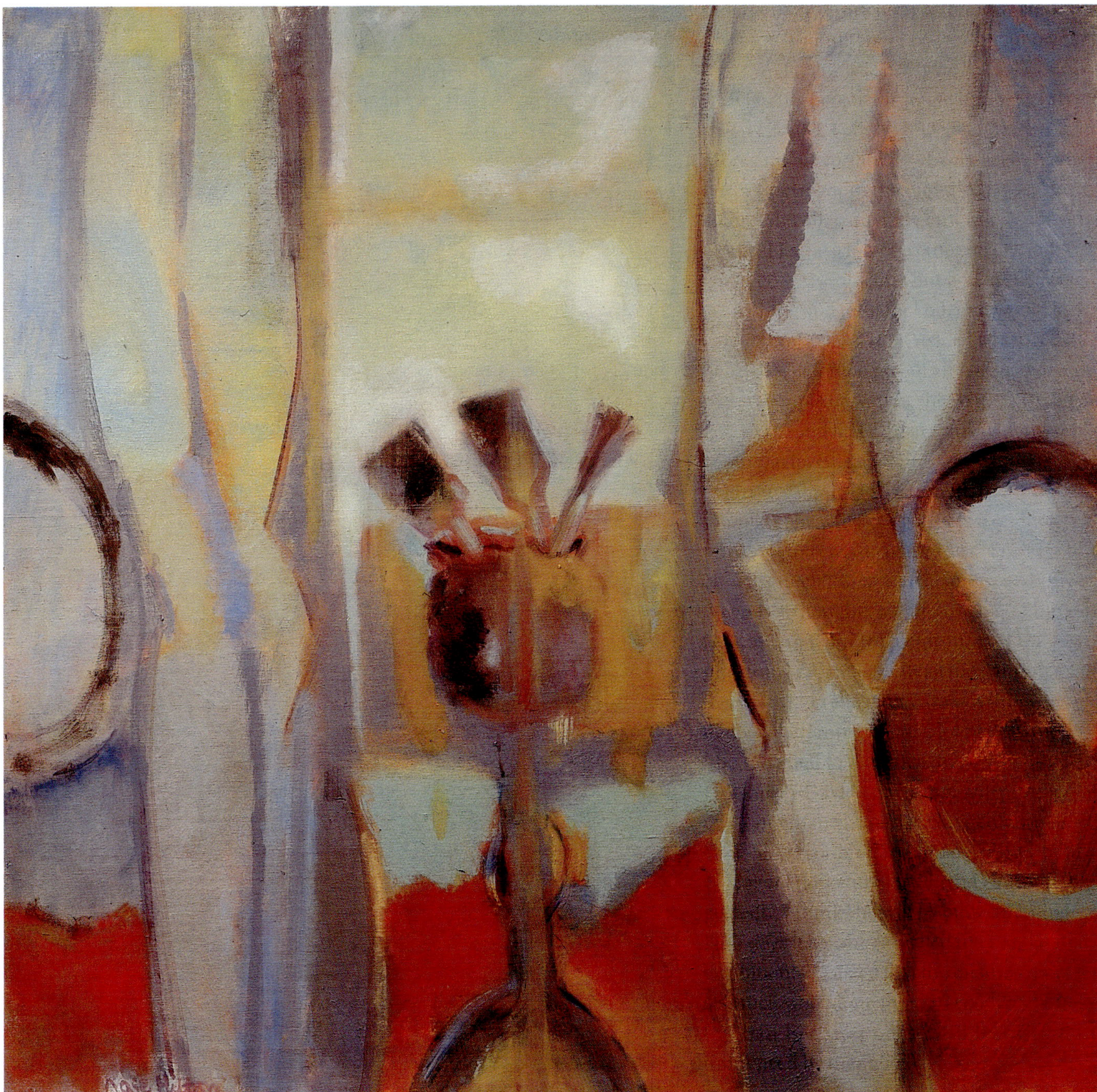

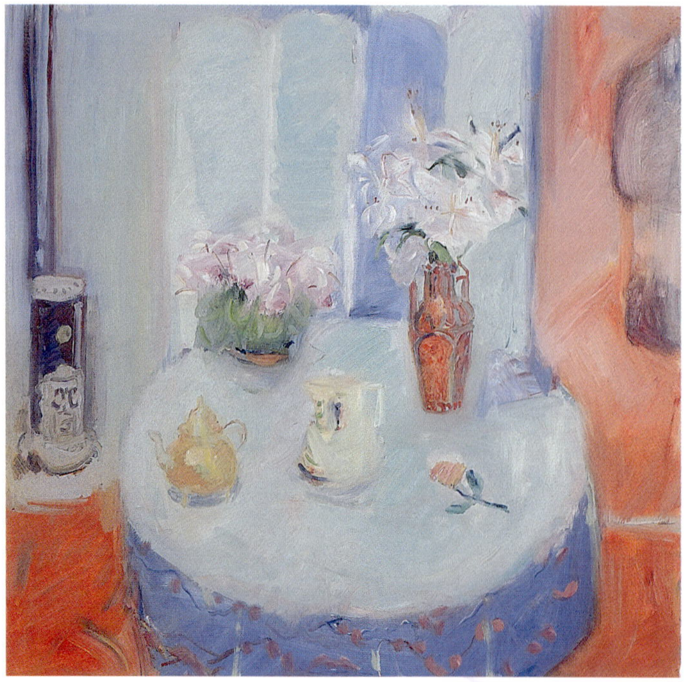

plate 87. ***The Studio Table in Fergie's House***, 1998, oil on canvas, 76.2 x 76.2 cm (30 x 30 in)

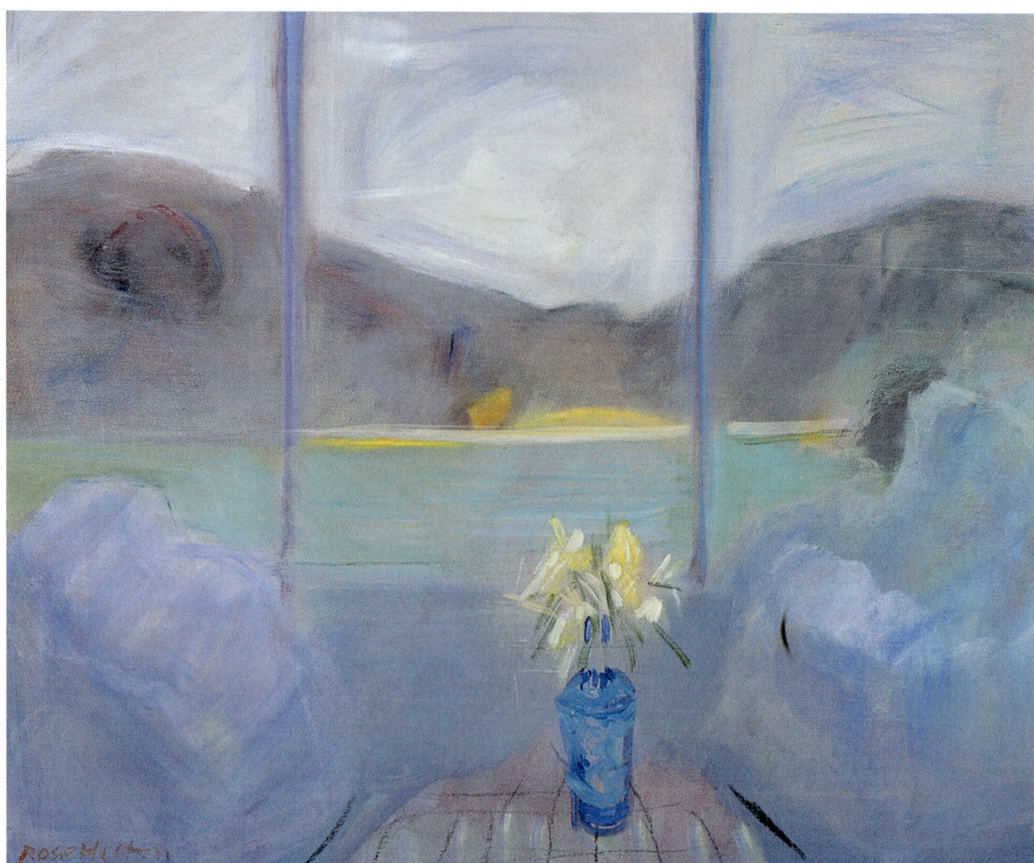

plate 88. ***Misty Day from the Old Boathouse***, 1999, oil on canvas, 50.8 x 61 cm (20 x 24 in)

plate 89. ***Peach Melba***,
1999,
oil on canvas,
76.2 x 76.2 cm (30 x 30 in)

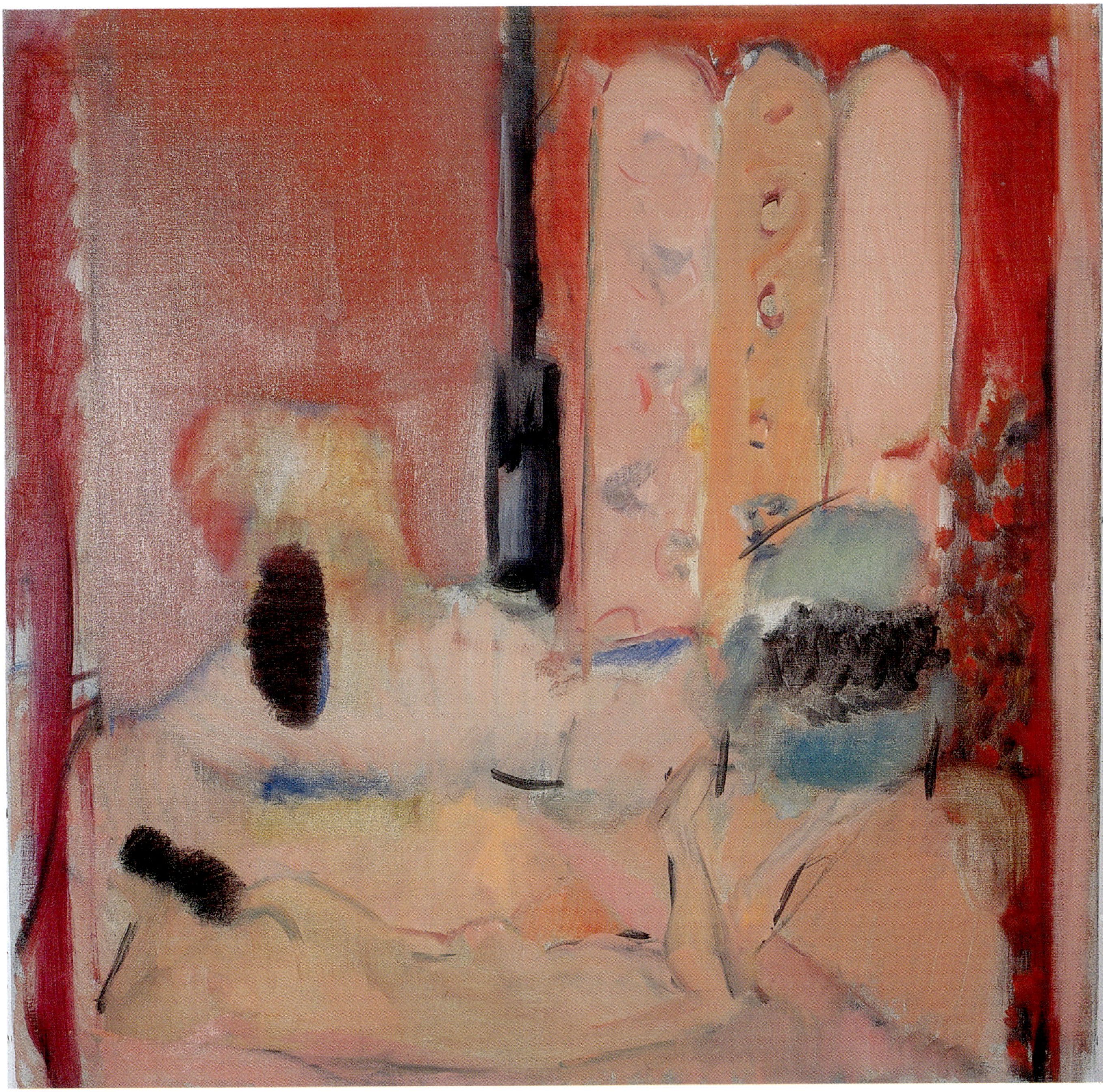

plate 90. ***Girl on Balcony***,
1998,
oil on canvas,
76.2 x 50.8 cm (30 x 20 in)

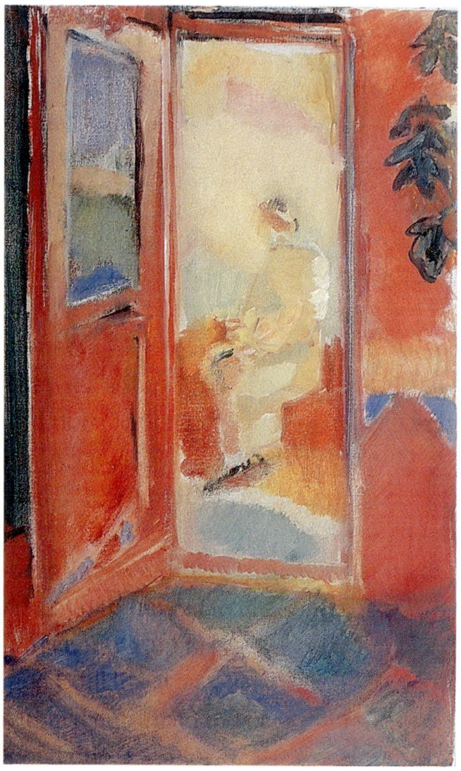

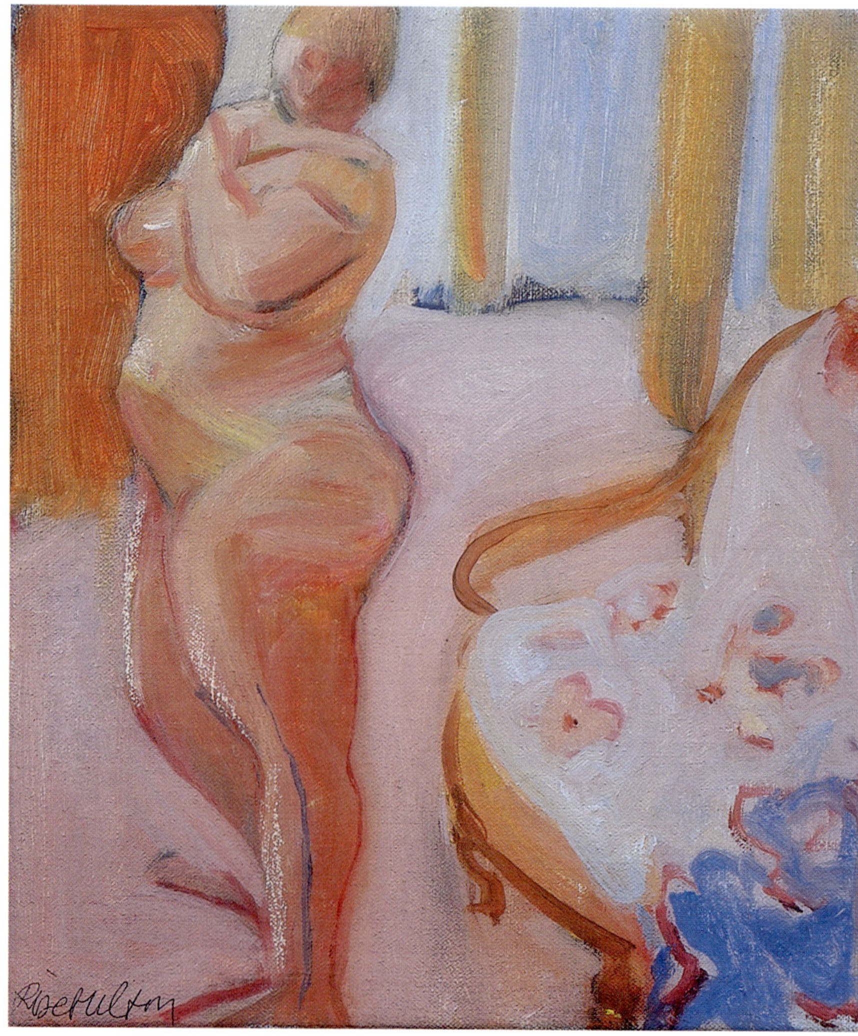

plate 91. ***Sally***, 1999,
oil on canvas,
30.5 x 25.4 cm (12 x 10 in)

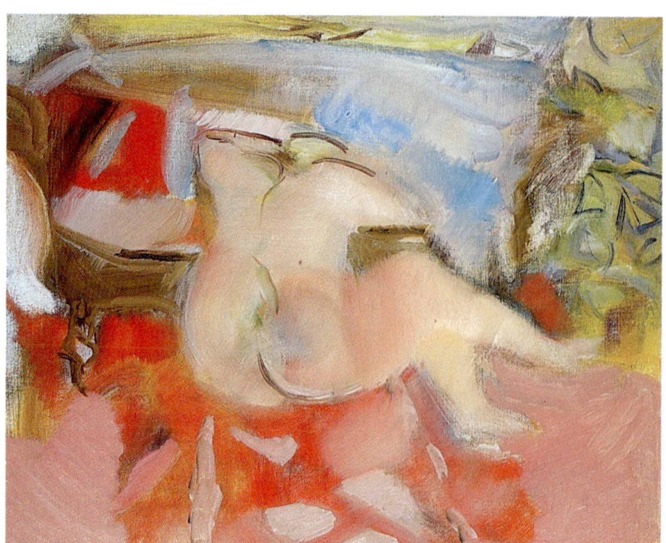

plate 92. ***Figure in Landscape***, 1999,
oil on canvas,
50.8 x 61 cm (20 x 24 in)

plate 93. ***Seated Girl***,
1999,
oil on canvas,
61 x 50.8 cm (24 x 20 in)

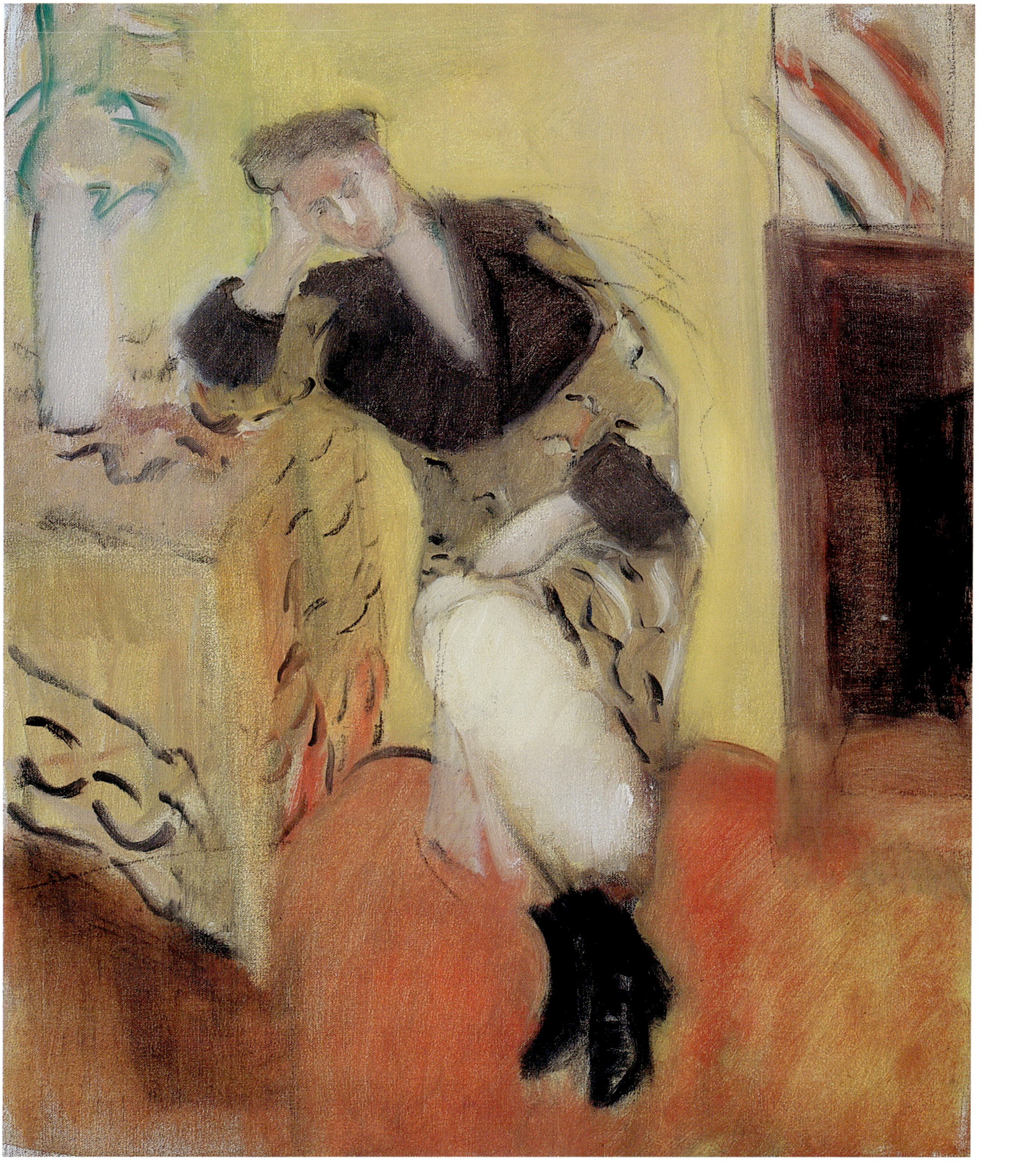

THE NEW CENTURY

On 1 January 2000, Rose writes in her diary: 'A new year, a new century and I am nearly 70 but with the emotions of a younger woman. Needing love and closeness.' Then a note about the really important thing – her work. 'Painting going well, colour relationships getting better.' As is her habit from time to time, she decided to take a studio away from home, once more in St Ives. Then at the beginning of February she was off to India, to stay with Mollie Parkin. Rose writes of her immediate reactions on arrival: 'The impact of the air, the people, the smells, the pace of life is even more powerful than I had been told to expect.'

She later recalled: 'Mollie had a house south of Madras with monkeys in the garden. She lent me a little studio and I painted. I had a great time. I loved being with her. I painted her [plate 96] and sometimes I painted Indian models [plate 97]. I had a relaxing time – it wasn't too hot because it was January.' And in her diary, she privately compares herself to Mollie. 'I am rather more slapdash by nature and in many respects in my living. Only in my painting will I take endless pains to achieve the result that will pass muster with *me*.'

Back in England, Rose was asked to go to Salcombe and give a talk, with questions after-

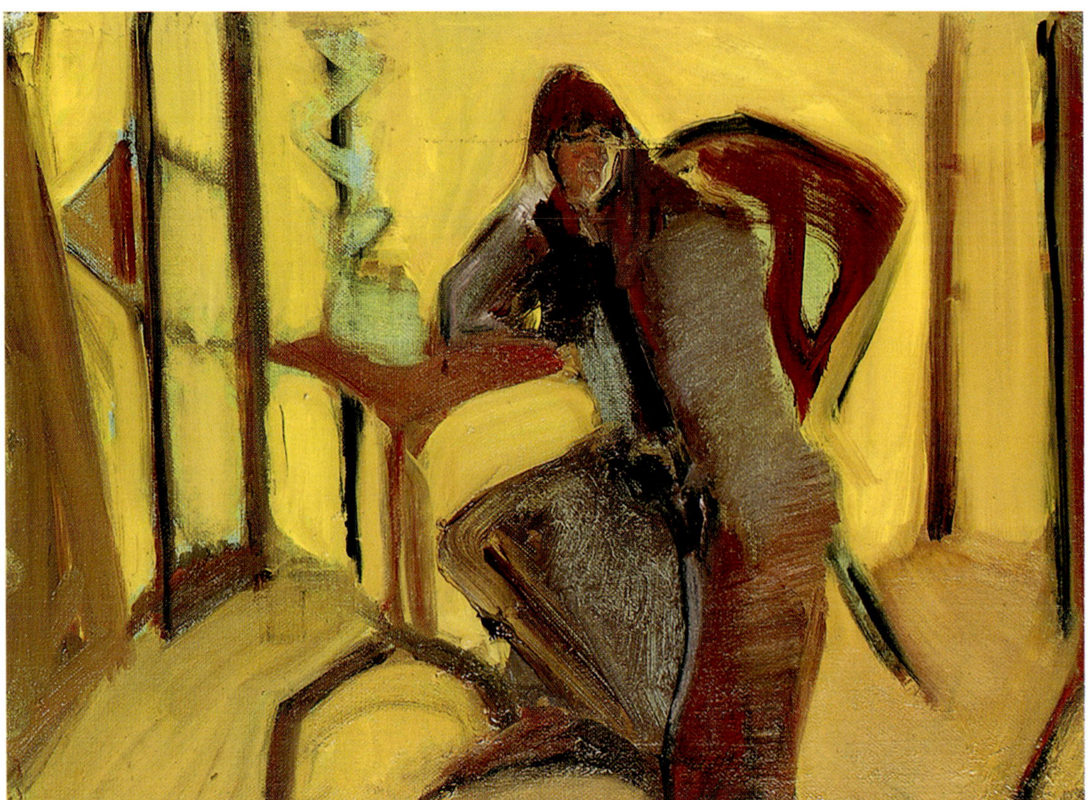

plate 94. ***Girl in Yellow Room***, 2000, oil on canvas, 30.5 x 40.6 cm (12 x 16 in)

plate 95. ***Solitude***, 2000,
oil on canvas,
76.2 x 76.2 cm (30 x 30 in)

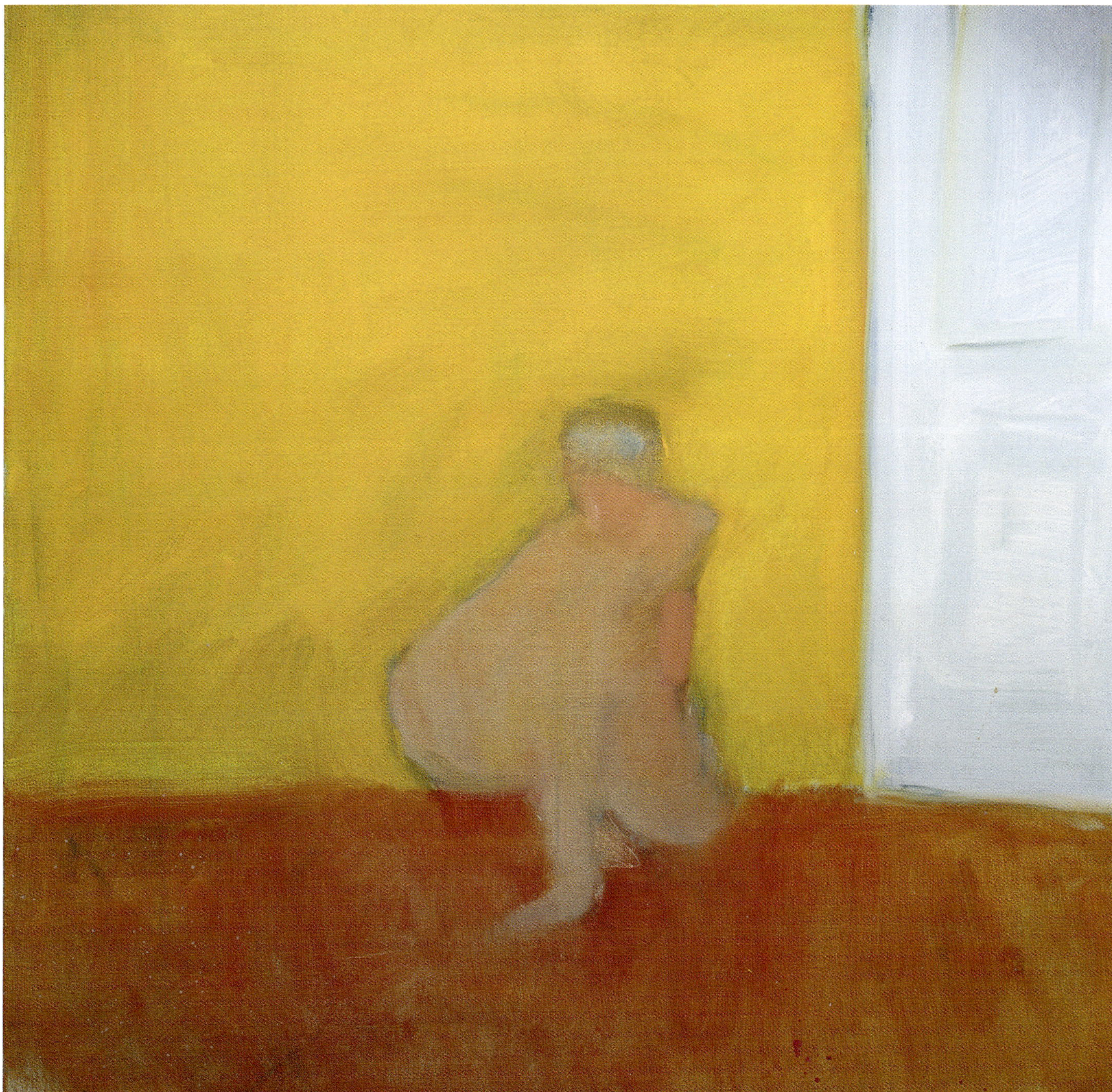

wards, on Roger. She writes: 'It did my psyche and my painting a power of good just to talk about him and read out some of his thoughts about painting and his wild but sane ideas.' In September she gave another talk on his work, this time in the south of France. This continual living contact with Roger's work was a great stimulation and encouragement to her own painting, a further boost to her creativity and confidence.

The church has come back increasingly into Rose's life in recent years. She explains:

I didn't go with Roger or for long afterwards. I missed it, I was unhappy about it. I missed the centring feeling it gave me, and I've always been interested in singing. I do sometimes find it difficult to go along with the Virgin birth and the beliefs of the Church of England, but I do take communion and I like stepping off the busy world for an hour on a Sunday morning and thinking about a greater power than myself. I feel I've done the thing of having a bigger commitment when I was young, when I didn't know what I was doing and perhaps without meaning it. The guilt's all gone now about being one of God's Elect. I don't worry about all that. But I found I couldn't really get rid of the whole belief system completely. I tried but it didn't go. I feel I was born into it. And it's best not to be born into anything fanatical. The thing it's done for me is give me a dedication to painting, a discipline. I wouldn't be happy now if I didn't go on painting. It's a way of worshipping.

The following year, 2001, she went for a holiday in Alba-la-Romaine in the Ardèche region of France in August. She reports in her diary: 'Tried some experimental mark-making paintings. The influence of Alba ...they are rather "on the surface"' (plate 99). Later that year, plans were mooted for a major show of Rose's work at the North Light Gallery, in Huddersfield, to be organised by the critic Lynne Green. This took place in the spring of 2002, and prompted a mood of reassessment. Rose writes critically: 'Some of my paintings are too heavily influenced by Bonnard, Matisse, Hitchens, but seeing them all together they did have a lightness and a luminosity which conveyed good spirits – I have always had better results when my work is seen together.' Then she writes rather touchingly: 'I do not believe all the compliments I have had.'

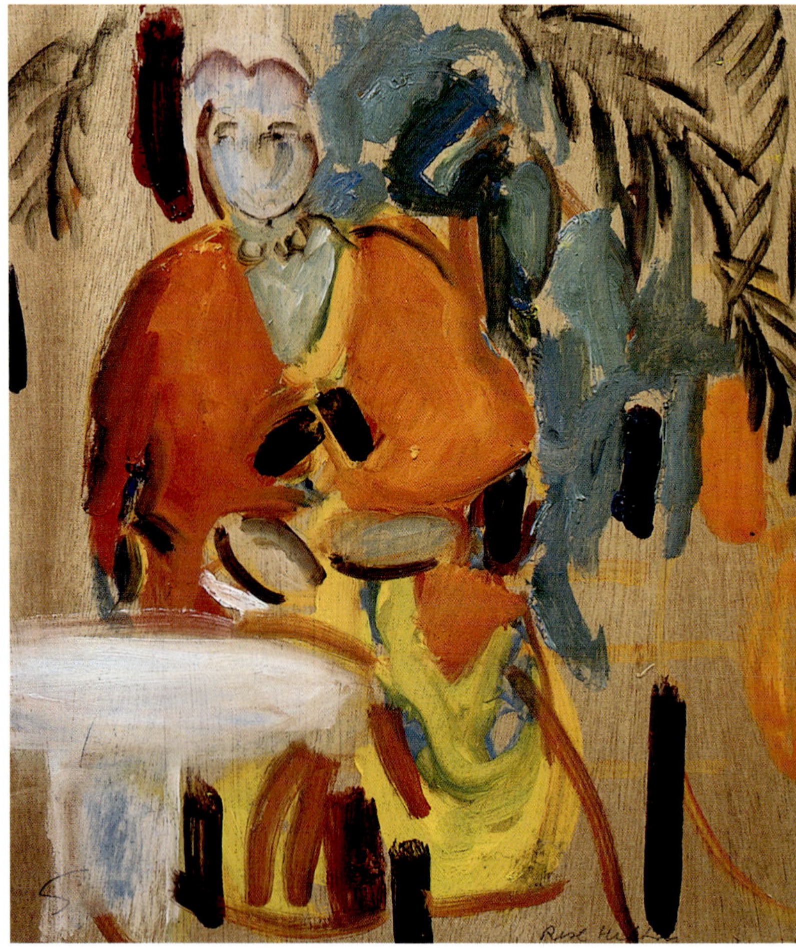

plate 96. ***Molly Parkin, India***, 2000,
pastel on paper,
30.5 x 25.4 cm (12 x 10 in)

plate 97. ***Studio Portrait, India***, 2000, oil on board, 20.3 x 24.1 cm (8 x 9½ in)

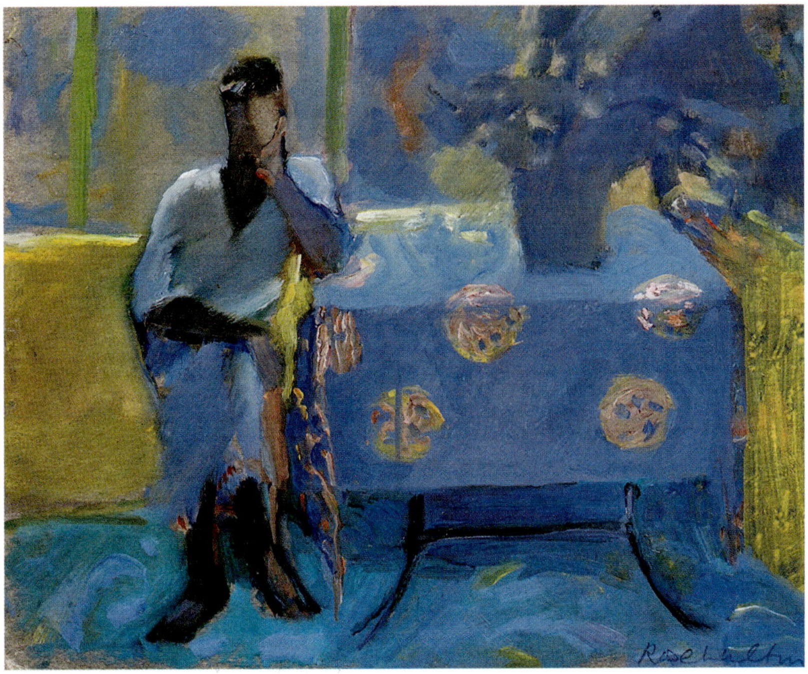

There was sad news in May. 'David Brown died. It is awful to think of the world without him although he got on my nerves at times. He was unique and had enormous courage and brains.' Rose took a teaching job in Patmos (an island that inspires her work) and found herself still getting enjoyable crushes on men. She travelled a fair bit, which she thinks may be a diversionary tactic as all was not well with her painting. 'I cannot see my way forward at present', she writes. 'I just keep going away when really I am running away from painting and the direction of the future, running away from making decisions.'

In August, another friend dies, John Miller. Rose recalls him as 'always an avuncular figure ... It was his greatest gift ... of listening and sharing.' As it often does, death has the effect of making the living take stock. Rose took a long look at herself. She writes: 'I am now 71 and although still have a good figure am beginning to tire and question whether it is in order to expect any more physical contact and beginning to wonder whether I could manage a relationship although I still hunger after sex.' In the same notebook is an entry dated 23 March 2003: 'My generation of friends is beginning to thin out. I have a new studio in Penzance which I like very much ... I am not painting much, but I am hoping to be fired up again'. In May, her first boyfriend (and by this time a distinguished abstract painter), Alan Green died. In August, her friend and model Shoe also died. It seemed a time of melancholy partings.

Meanwhile Rose's relationship with her eldest son, Bo, had grown closer through painting. He set himself up in a studio in St Ives after taking his degree at Brighton College of Art, and mother and son had many conversations about art. Rose writes:

According to him, I was helpful in discussing my approach to painting. He quickly developed his own style, having an inborn sense of tone. Favouring a low-key palette, he produced some remarkable work. For the last 10 years he has been very encouraging about my work, often disapproving if I strayed toward the sentimental (ie girls in straw hats, picnics etc). He fully understood that I was trying to use the subject matter as a vehicle for the marriage of form and colour. I have found him a useful and helpful critic.

plate 98. ***Blue Screen and Figure***, 2002, oil on canvas, 61 x 50.8 cm (24 x 20 in)

plate 99. ***Window in Alba***, 2001, oil on canvas, 25.4 x 30.5 cm (10 x 12 in)

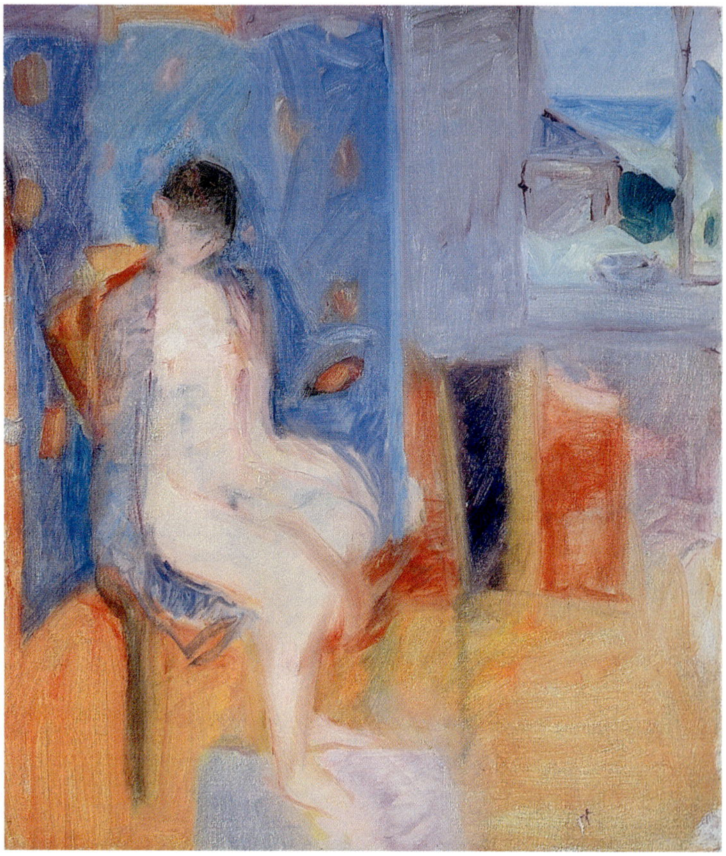

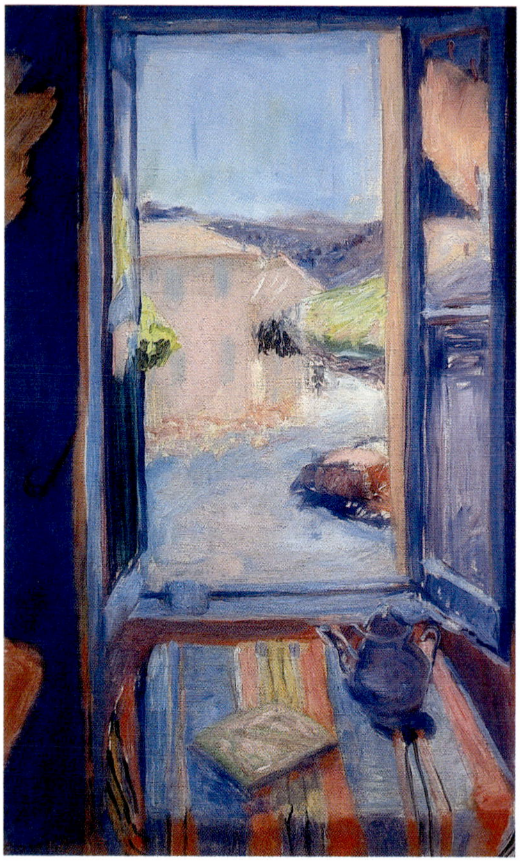

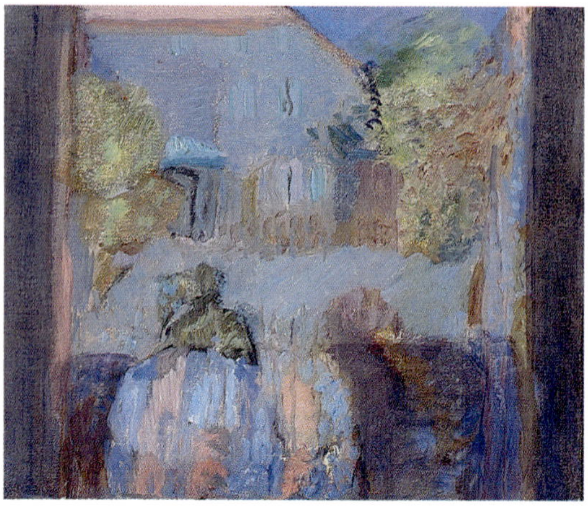

plate 100. ***Studio Window, Ardèche, France***, 2002, oil on canvas, 76.2 x 45.7 cm (30 x 18 in)

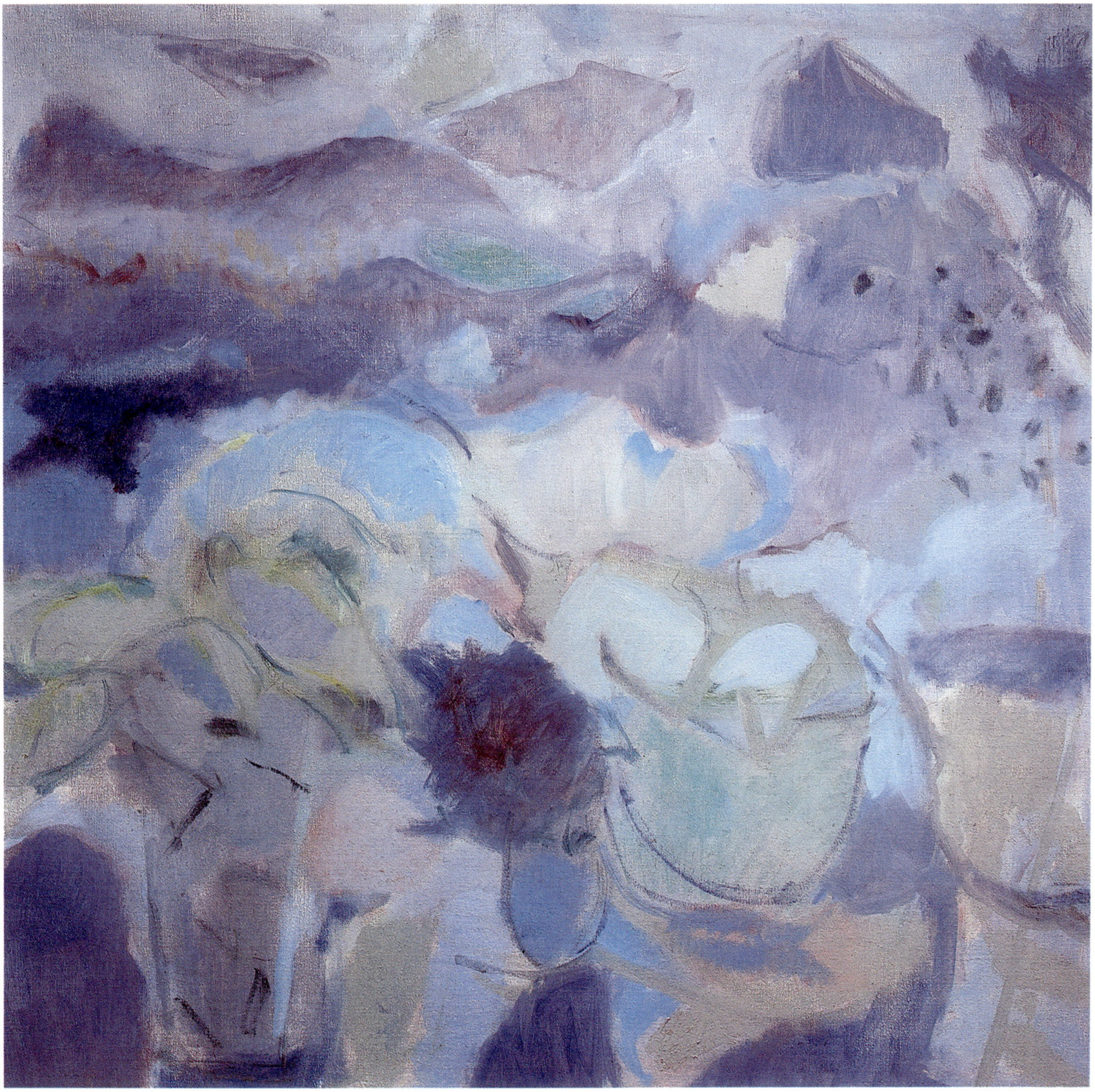

plate 101. ***Patmos Window***, 2002,
oil on canvas,
76.2 x 76.2 cm (30 x 30 in)

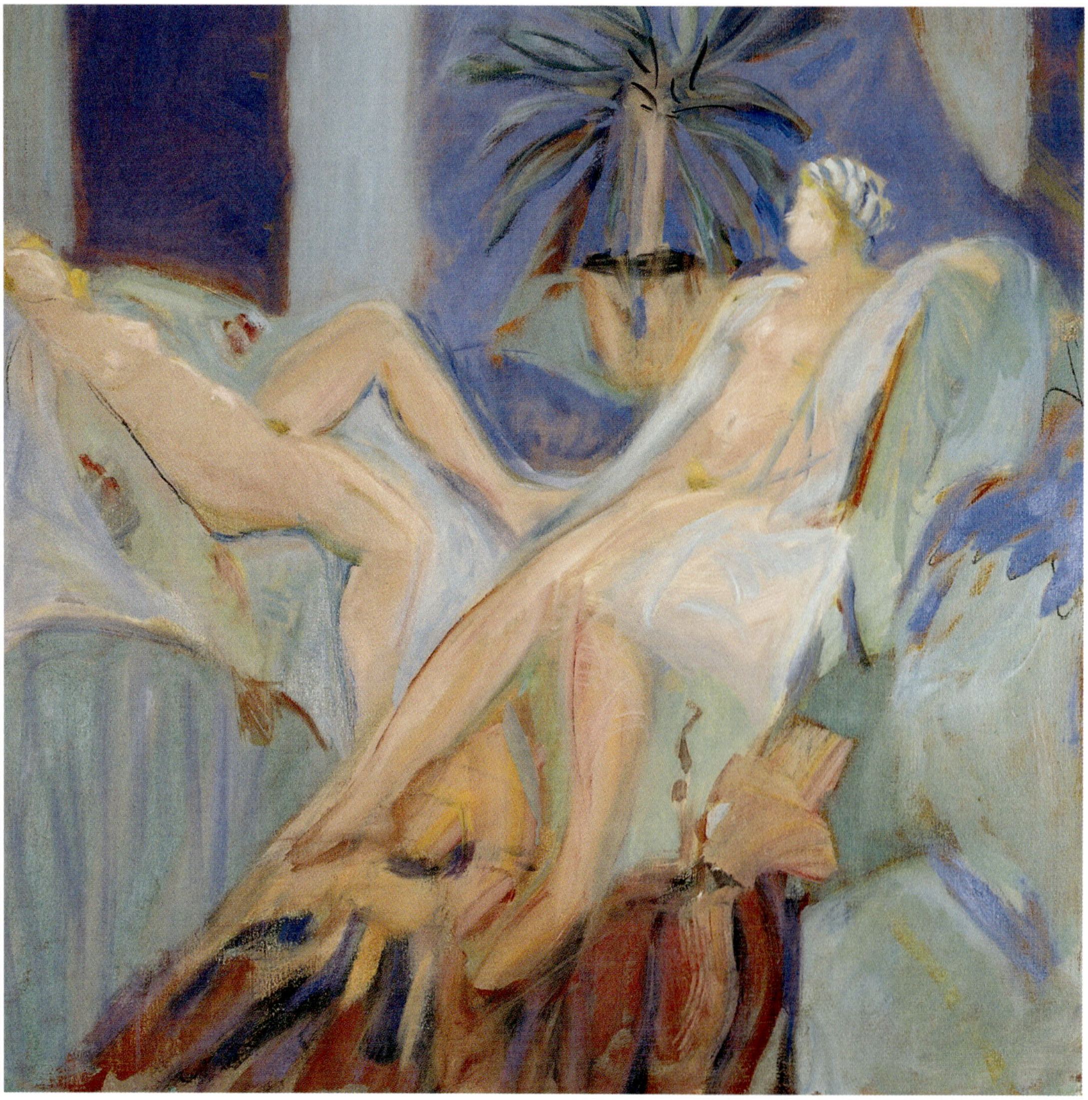

plate 102. ***The Beauty Salon***, 2000,
oil on canvas,
76.2 x 76.2 cm (30 x 30 in)

Then in 2004 a new love interest entered Rose's life, an old acquaintance who had become a friend, and finally a lover. After they went to bed together for the first time, Rose writes: 'It was a wonderful night of love. He is a good lover, a comfortable person and I feel good about it.' After their second meeting she notes: 'I see I have the relationship I have been desiring, however it may work out ... he has style and extravagance and I love him, but I do not want to be dependent or to gush – God help me'.

Meanwhile, art had to go on. Not only her own painting, but also her trips to see what other artists had done. That year she was particularly impressed by a jaunt to Barcelona. She writes: 'Visited Picasso Museum. Very moved by his stunning early landscapes on wood.' She also visited the Miró Museum and the Tàpies Foundation. In London she saw the Philip Guston show at the Royal Academy. She writes: 'Didn't understand the paintings. Only loved the painterly Monet-ish ones UNTIL I read his daughter's book, heard him talking on the video and then I treat him as A HERO. Totally knocked out by the book and his courage.'

Rose's feelings for her new lover loom large

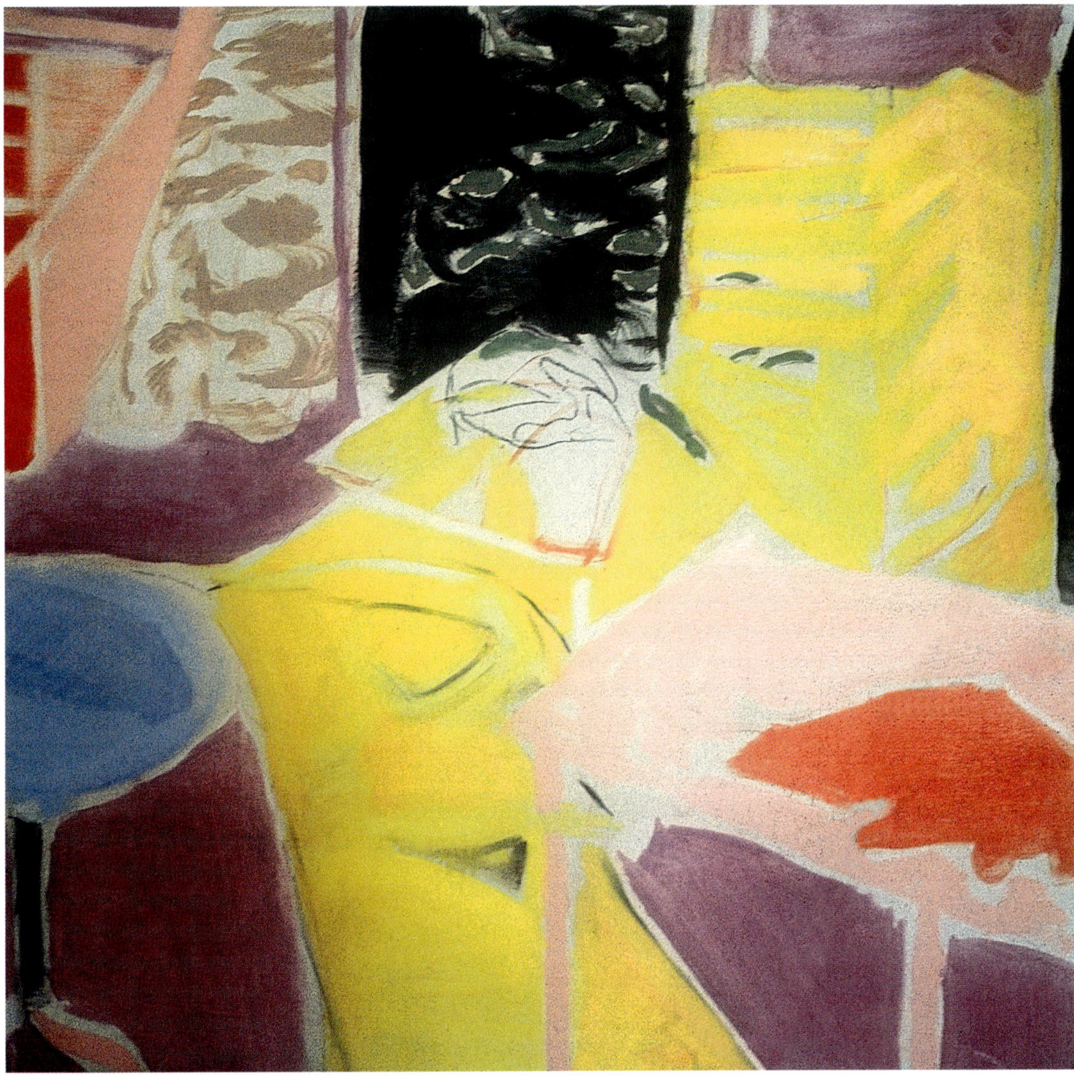

plate 103. ***The Red Interior***, 2005, oil on canvas, 76.2 x 76.2 cm (30 x 30 in)

in the 2005 diary. But he does not live nearby and Rose has long intervals between meetings when her imagination runs riot and her worries multiply. Painting is interspersed with people and travel. Rose notes in June: 'I have two 30" square paintings on the go. The thing to do over this weekend is to work out in pastels how I am going to beat the big canvas and then on Monday and Tuesday do it.' Meanwhile she is riveted by Hilary Spurling's biography of Matisse. In October she visits the Matisse Museum in Nice. 'Wonderful', she writes. 'I felt very stimulated by the paintings, some of them almost a drawing on canvas.' In a later entry that year she talks about her heroes in paint being Bonnard, Matisse, Milton Avery and Hitchens.

2006 opened with further emotional upsets and jealousies. Rose does not seem to be destined for a trouble-free path when it comes to love. But she continued to see her lover and to distract herself with trips abroad and visits to art galleries – the kind of research to which she is still remarkably open. Few people manage this degree of open-mindedness, which does not mean she's uncritical. In February she went to Amsterdam to see the retrospective of

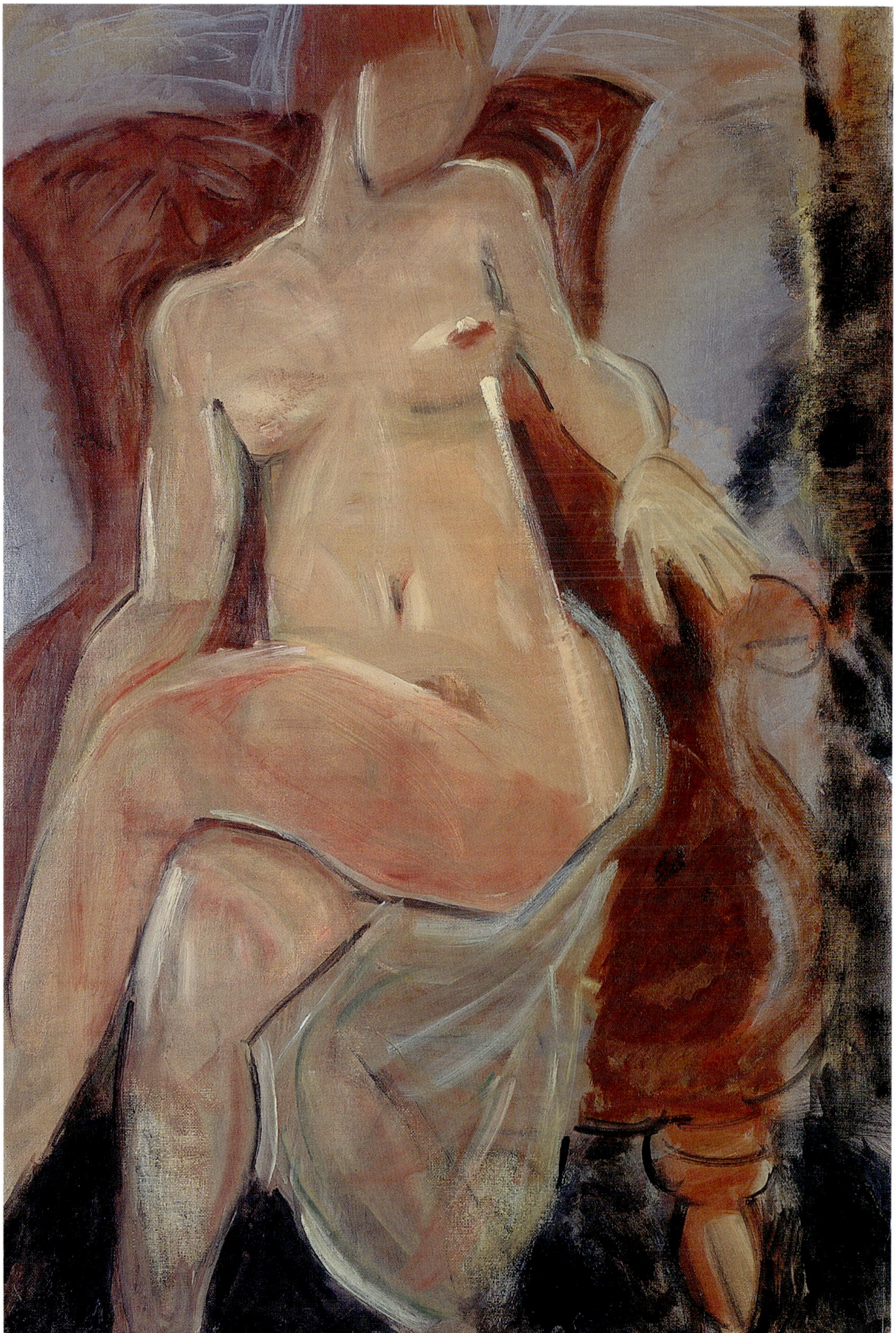

plate 104. ***Valerie***, 2002,
oil on canvas,
76.2 x 50.8 cm (30 x 20 in)

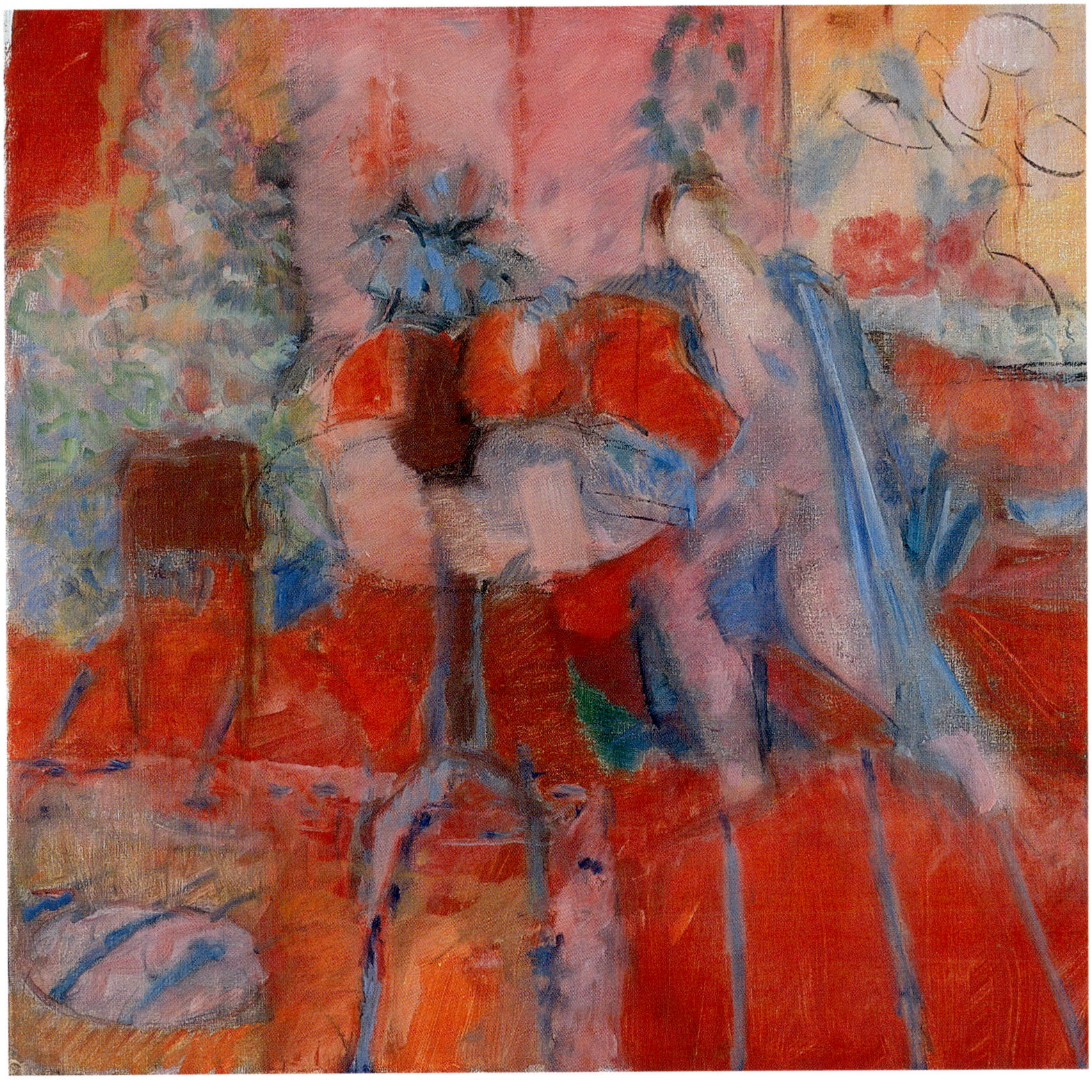

plate 105. ***Conservatory***, 2002, oil on canvas, 76.2 x 76.2 cm (30 x 30 in)

Roger's old sparring partner the COBRA painter Constant. She found it 'very impressive' but 'not much continuity'. She took with her the manuscript of the book I had written on Roger and read it in the friend's flat where she was staying. 'It is very well written evoking Roger, also very moving. It made me cry. I can see clearly what Roger was about now, reviewing his whole life. Before I instinctively knew he was special, fell in love with him, had the good luck to marry him and have 2 kids. *Difficult*(!) But no regrets.'

Back home she was drawing a lot and painting again. From time to time she treated herself to good clothes from designer shops – how she looks will always be a major interest – though she didn't stop hunting for bargains in charity shops. Rose is inventive in her clothes and in what she wears together for good effect. As she says: 'I've always bought clothes from charity shops and dyed them different colours or worn layers of them.' These days, the combinations of colour and texture are sometimes exchanged for a more formal evening outfit of sheer-cut black.

The roller-coaster ride of her long-distance love affair continued, but at some personal cost. In June she visited the art colony at Portscatho, near Truro, for a much-appreciated break. As

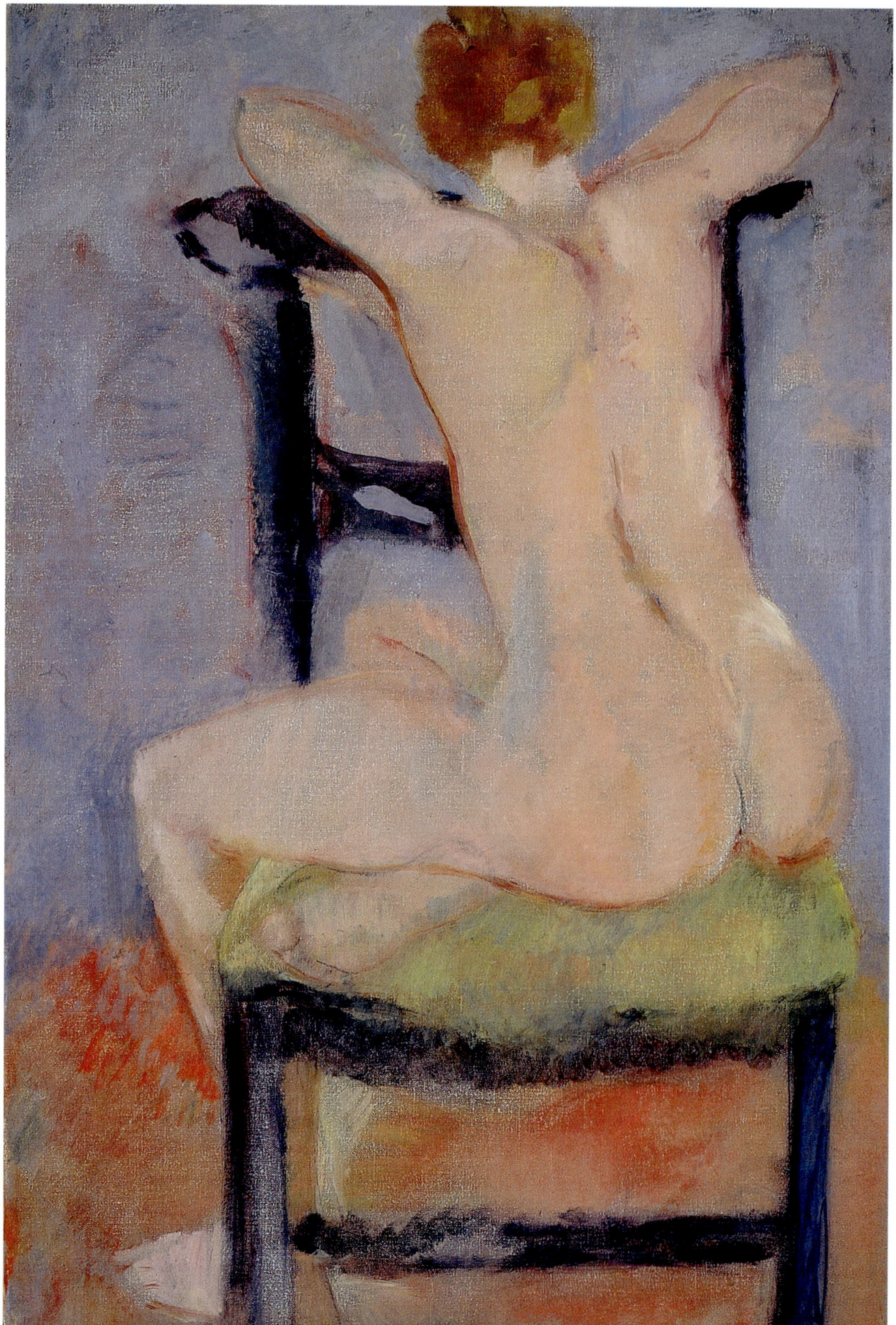

plate 106. ***The Blue Chair***, 2000, oil on canvas, 76.2 x 50.8 cm (30 x 20 in)

plate 107. ***The Green Chair***, 2001,
oil on canvas,
76.2 x 50.8 cm (30 x 20 in)

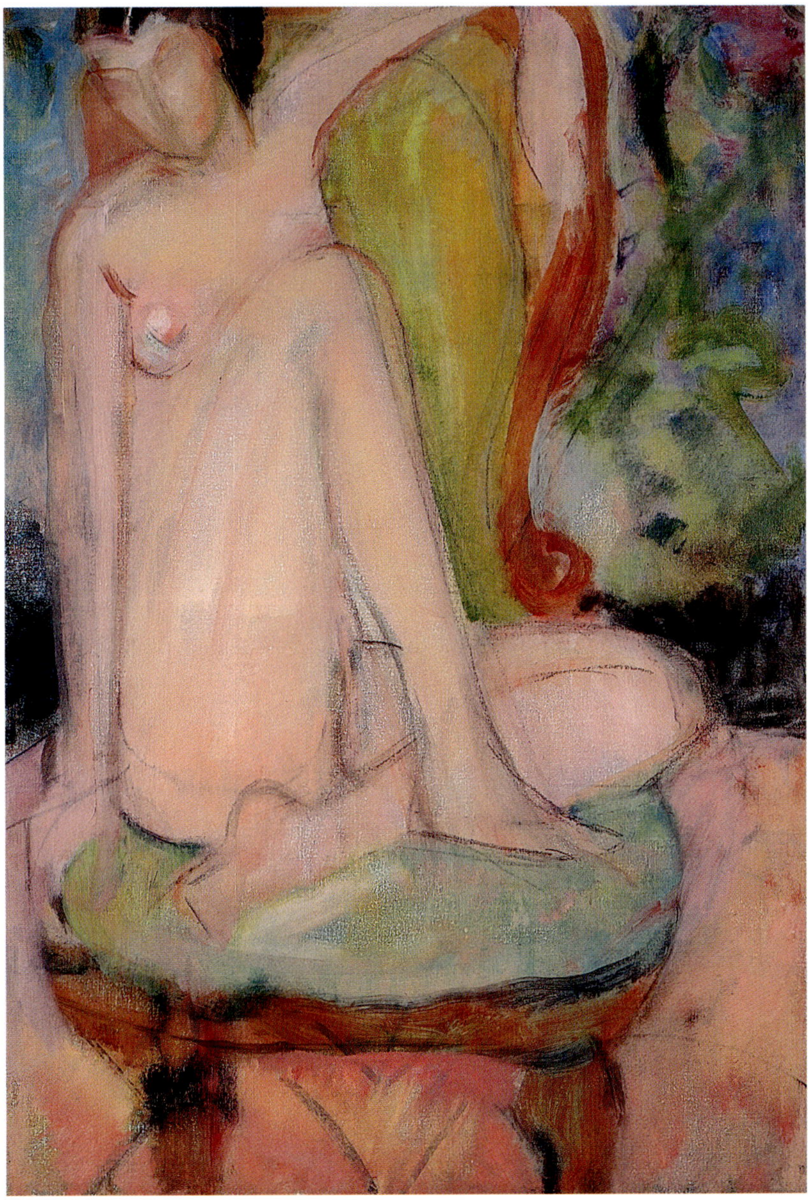

she notes: 'Chris Insoll's place is just what I needed. Full of books paintings encouragement. Enthusiasm.' (She notes again in October: 'Very good talks on painting with Chris.') Back at home, builders were working on an extension to the house. More sad news in August: Sandra died suddenly. Rose writes: 'It can't be true! The fact that she has gone is unbelievable. So full of life and work. The obituaries have been wonderful. Lovely photos of her and her work. She is being truly recognized as a great painter in a decorative abstract way.' It's the end of an era: the person who introduced Rose to Roger in the first place is now gone, though memories of Roger are never far away. Particularly as there's a major retrospective exhibition of his work about to open at Tate St Ives.

As usual, Rose finds the re-connection with Roger useful at a very deep level. She restores her routine and eases back into painting, though these days (she is 75, though hardly looks it) she finds she needs a rest after about three hours. After a 'very successful opening' at Tate St Ives for Roger, talks are opened about a follow-up show there of Rose's work, suggested for 2008. That would certainly be an accolade – a Tate retrospective would really give her the chance of a proper showing and assessment. It's a challenging prospect but a welcome one – something to plan for. The year ends with Rose thinking about Roger, and people's different reactions to his work. Somebody comments that Roger and Sydney were 'intellectuals'. Rose responds: '*They were*, but, as with Einstein, they were a whole lot more – flesh, blood and bone, sexual, jealous, curious, original, creative, loving. VERY MALE.' It seems to sum it all up.

AFFAIRS

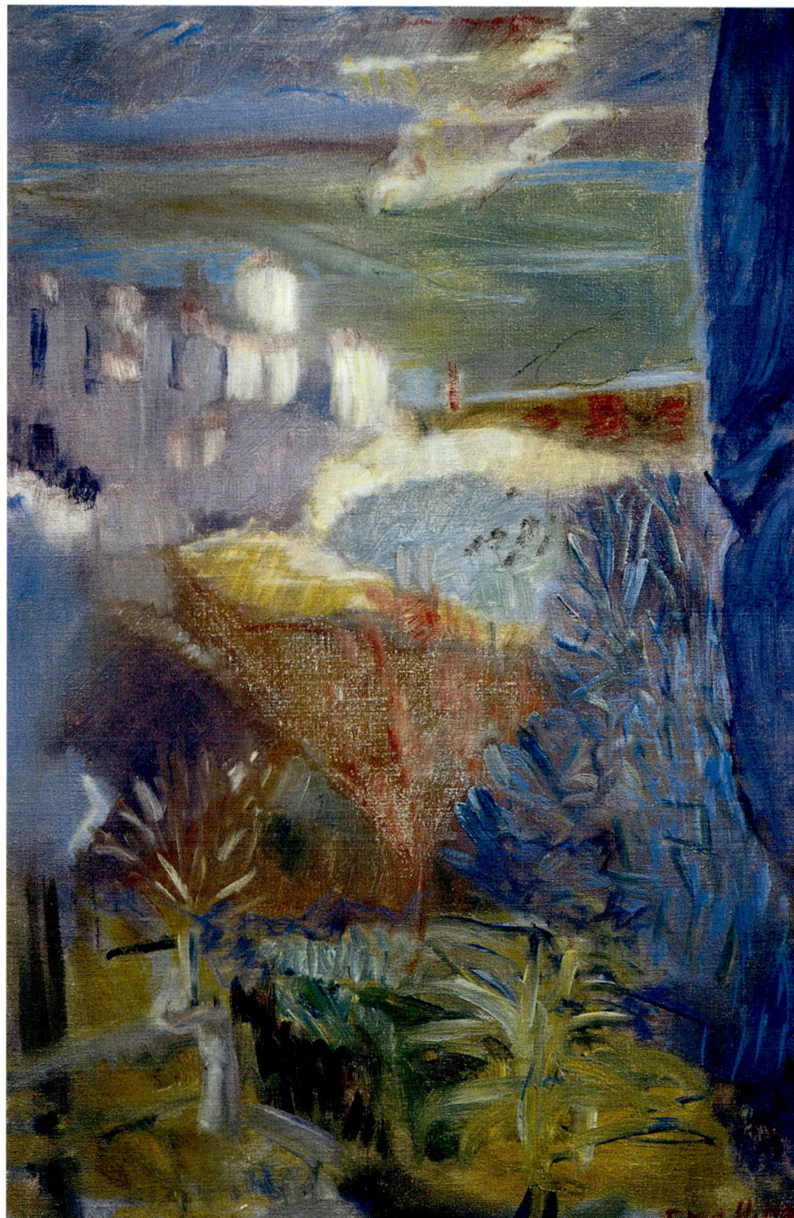

plate 108. *Garden at St Ives*, 2002, oil on canvas, 76.2 x 50.8 cm (30 x 20 in)

ROGER HAD BEEN SO HURT by the Jill Neville affair in 1961 that he didn't stray again once he had decided to be with Rose. It was Rose who did the straying, but as she says, she felt she had to, to keep the balance.

Roger would contradict himself by saying 'I don't want an unhappy sexless woman', and suggesting that I have fulfilling affairs. But when I did, and I told him about it, he didn't like it very much.

Roger didn't want me to leave him. He never forbade me to see anyone. A lot of his life was devoted to his painting and his thoughts about painting, so he wasn't that close to me. We weren't soul mates. In later years, I was his arms and feet, I was his energy.

There is, however, the story about Roger trying to give Rose away in a pub to a fisherman, which Rose tells:

It's a bit like *The Mayor of Casterbridge*, I'm afraid. I did have an affair with a very handsome Cornishman and Roger was jealous. He put on a brave front in the pub and said: 'Do you want to take her on? I'll sell her to you for £2,000.' So the fisherman said: 'Look, I'm not a mean man Roger. Get your cheque book out. I'll accept £1,999.' This amused all the Cornish. It was just bandying jokes. Poor Roger. Sometimes I do have attacks of guilt. I wish I could live all over again and be a better person. It was such a

plate 109. *Life Painting*,
2002,
oil on canvas,
91.4 x 50.8 cm (36 x 20 in)

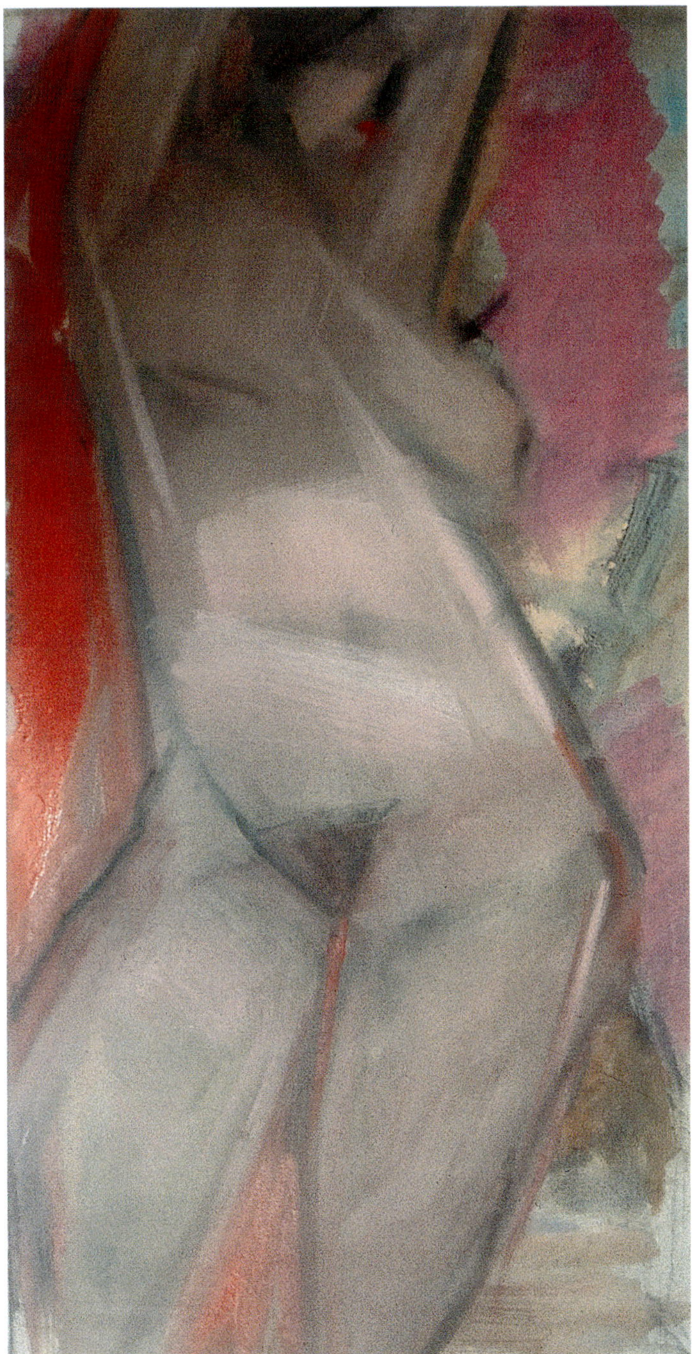

short time we were together and I must have hurt him. Sometimes I have to remind myself how beastly he was to me.

I'd like to say that I've always thought of myself as an artist, and I have, but I've felt that to be fulfilled in life or in art, the seed or the direction had to come from a man somehow. Even in my influences. Then I would respond to it. Some women are at their best when they do have a man as mentor. That's not to say they're inferior artists. But in some deep way they want to get the approval of the mentor. I think I fall into that category. Since Roger died and I've gone on painting I've built up some fans who really like my work – they're mostly women – and now I consider I am an artist, rather than an artist depending on a man as a mentor. I haven't had a mentor since Roger died. I've realized that I was always attracted to the kind of men that bossed me about and the other ones who would have been subservient to me I wasn't interested in. But in order to give my time and energy to painting I haven't had anybody else in my life. I wanted so badly to do my painting I preferred to go it alone.

plate 110. ***Godrevy Lighthouse***, 2003,
oil on canvas,
50.8 x 61 cm (20 x 24 in)

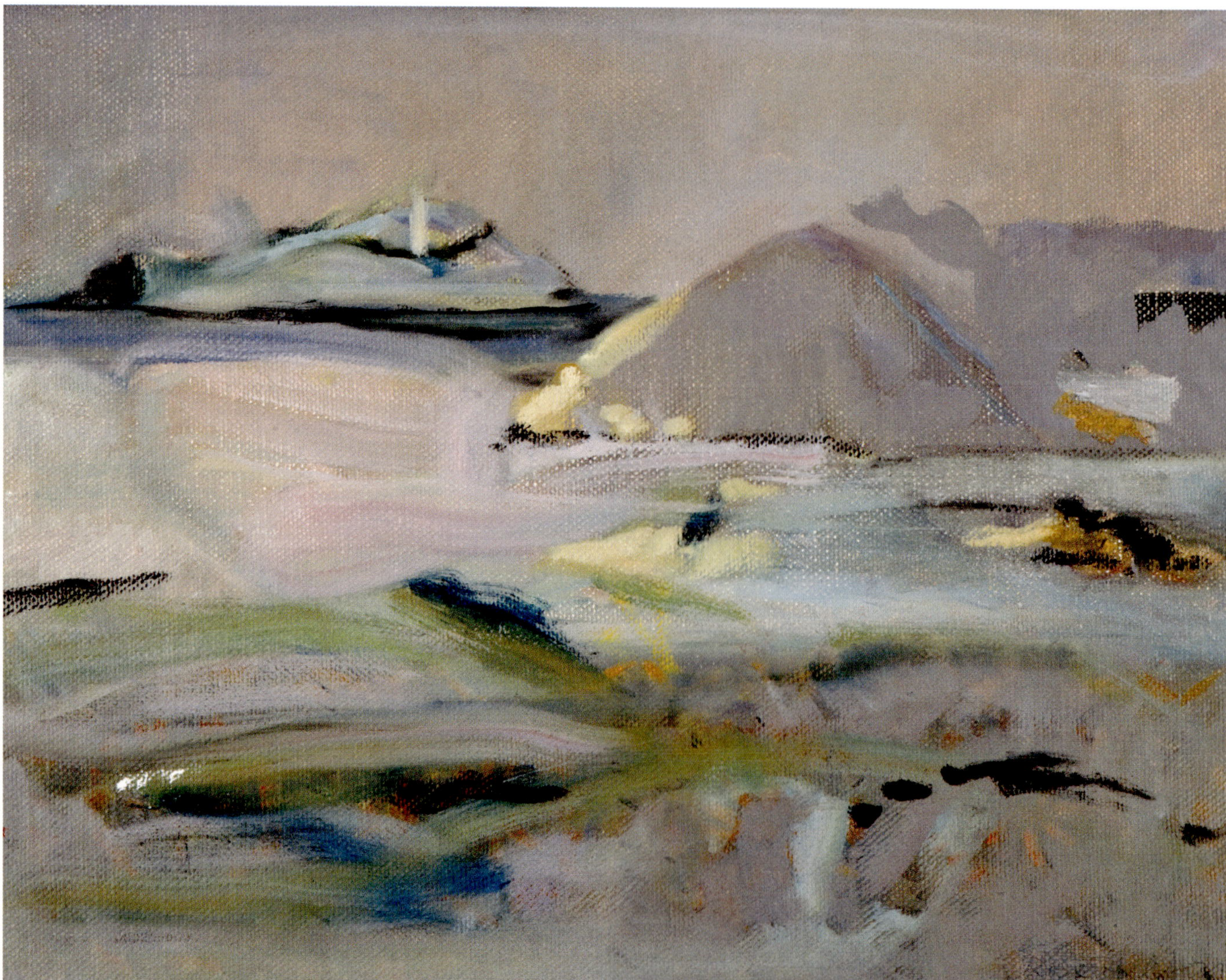

PRINTMAKING

ROSE HAS MADE PRINTS since college days, and has always been particularly drawn to the linocut. Not only does she make an annual linocut Christmas card, but she also makes more complicated lino compositions. *Figures in a Landscape* (plate 53) is a particularly fine example. Rose comments: 'Breon O'Casey loves that linocut – he's got a print of it. It's what's called a "reduction" linocut, like Picasso did. The method is also called "suicide" – you can't go back. You print one layer over another, taking bits off each time.' Her resolution of the image is a triumph of economy and expressiveness.

Etching is a much more technical procedure, in which Rose felt she needed some professional instruction. She first learnt to etch in November 1978 at The Lizard, Cornwall. Later she attended a course on etching at St Ives in April 1996, and subsequently she has worked a lot at Penzance Art School 'just to have the company really'. She went there for about three years and used their press in the afternoons. She has made some superbly evocative line compositions. Look at *The Floral Dress*, for example, a softground etching (plate 111). Rose herself admires it: 'I like the shapes in that', she says. And indeed it is a sophisticated piece of pattern-making, in the way the model's legs and the curves of her arms echo the rhythms of the landscape, and her dress picks up the pattern in the curtains.

In recent years, monotypes have come to the forefront of Rose's printmaking activities. Monotypes are the form of printing closest to painting and it's appropriate that a painterly artist such as Rose should be drawn to making them. Also, you don't need quite so much technical expertise and equipment to produce your own, just a sheet of metal, glass or Perspex to work on, and some paper to print with. The inks can be painted on or applied more freely in any way you want. You can use oil paint, if required. Effects of texture and colour can be pursued through a series of variations, but essentially the monotype is a one-off, handmade print, often very like a painting in appearance. Rose has been experimenting widely in this field, working for instance at Chris Baker's studio in Arundel, Sussex in July 2006, but also at home. She has now set up a small studio with her own press at Botallack specifically to make monotypes. The results have been intriguing and frequently beautiful.

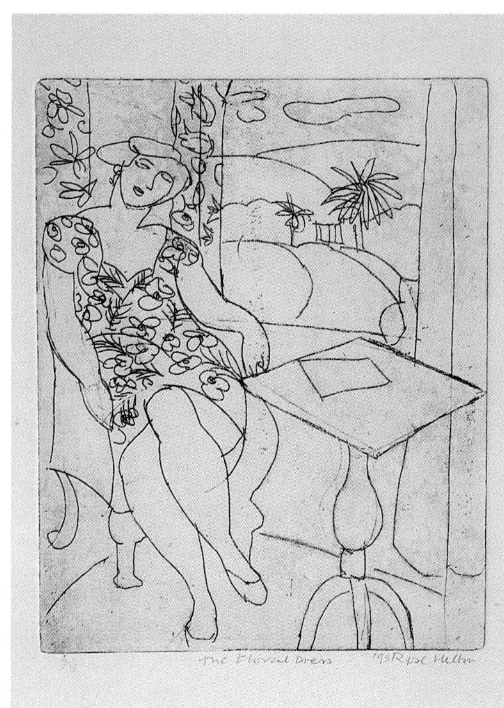

plate 111. ***The Floral Dress***, 1997, soft-ground etching, 25.4 x 19.1 cm (10 x 7½ in)

plate 112. ***Interior, St Ives***,
2003,
oil on canvas,
76.2 x 76.2 cm (30 x 30 in)

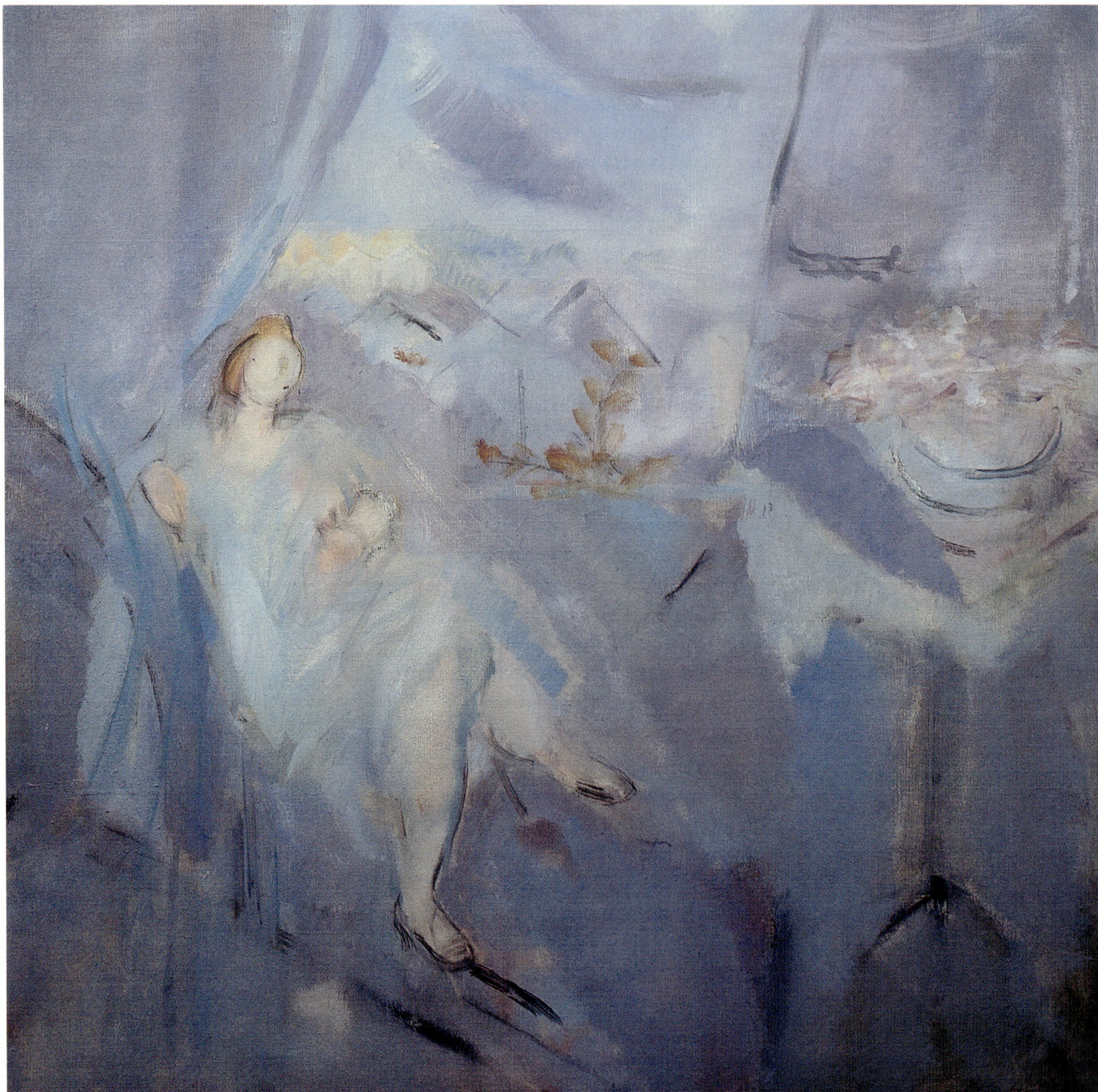

plate 113. ***Summer Afternoon***, 2003, oil on canvas, 76.2 x 76.2 cm (30 x 30 in)

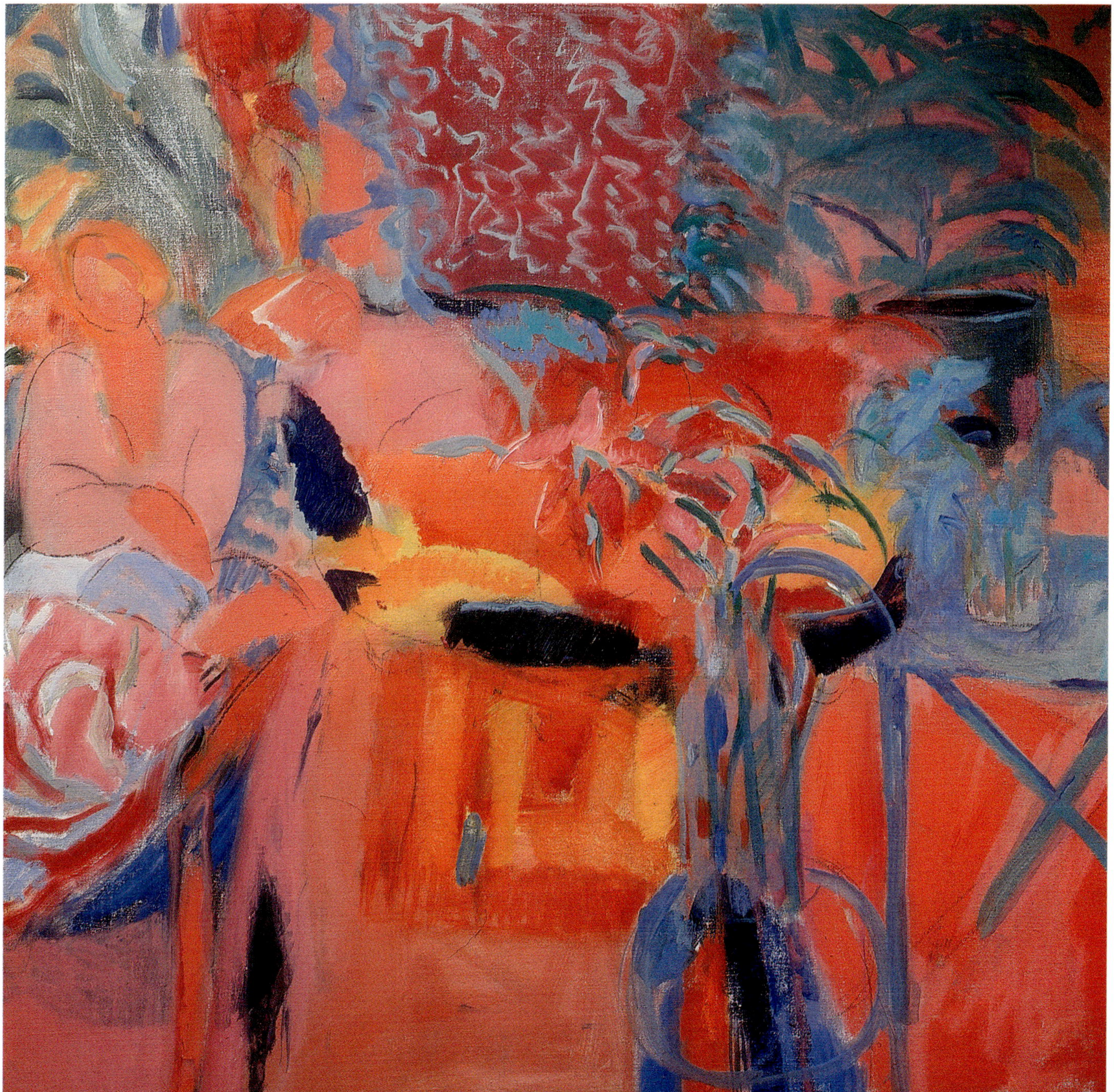

PAINTING PRACTICE

THE ACTIVITY OF MAKING ART is not something that Rose does day in, day out. She finds she gets easily distracted by people, particularly by guests visiting, and has to be very disciplined to maintain her routine. As she says:

I have to stop socialising and clear things out of the way if I'm going to paint. I have to make time and not have too many people coming to stay. I need a lump of time – three or four hours in the studio daily. And then at the end of a three or four month session I can do something quite reasonable – it just slips out. I prefer to work in the mornings. I'll have a rest in the afternoon and then maybe do a bit of printmaking in the evening.

I use my feminine sensibilities in my art but I suppose I have got a masculine drive which enables me to have a bit of discipline about working. I do have to have a bit of an idea when I start a painting, either in charcoal or pastel, which I love more than watercolour, but it does change tremendously. When I'm painting the landscape out here, I would work out the composition a bit before taking my easel out and starting to paint. Then I put a ground down on the canvas. If I had a model sitting, I used roughly to get the shape of the background and then with a wash I'd put the model and the warm colours in green and then all the green bits of the sky would go in red, so they were opposite colours. That I found gave a wonderful glow to the picture. I used that way of working for quite a few years.

The Bonnard influence was to make every bit of the canvas exciting – not just the subject. I found I had to pay attention to all the edges and corners. That's why when you are painting you have to throw yourself into it. You have to think it all the time. Go to bed early. You can't just go up and do a bit and come down again. It's a whole way of life. You need to concentrate on the work and look at it a lot too.

There are certain artists one readily associates with Rose's way of painting – particularly the French masters of the twentieth century, but her interests are much wider than that. Among the Abstract Expressionists, Helen Frankenthaler is perhaps her favourite, but she is also drawn to the light-filled spaces of Richard Diebenkorn and the lyrical realism of the Frenchman Henri Hayden. She has regularly made transcriptions and copies of works by the Old Masters, from the earliest years of her career. Ingres has been an important figure for her, and particularly his famous 1808 painting *The Bather*, which inspired a whole series of variations (see plate 18) She has also found much inspiration in Piero della Francesca and has made copies after Puvis de Chavannes. Matisse has been a constant inspiration and she has made many versions after his paintings. Other artists also pose a challenge. In June 2006 she writes in her diary: 'Trying to do a transcription of Delacroix's *La Femme d'Algiers* in my way. Picasso has done it his way and Matisse I think has had a go. I am finding it difficult.'

Her approach is surprisingly methodical.

I've got a butcher's apron I wear sometimes with big pockets you can put your knife or brush in when you're painting. I don't get covered in paint.

plate 114. ***Red Window***, 2002,
oil on canvas,
76.2 x 76.2 cm (30 x 30 in)

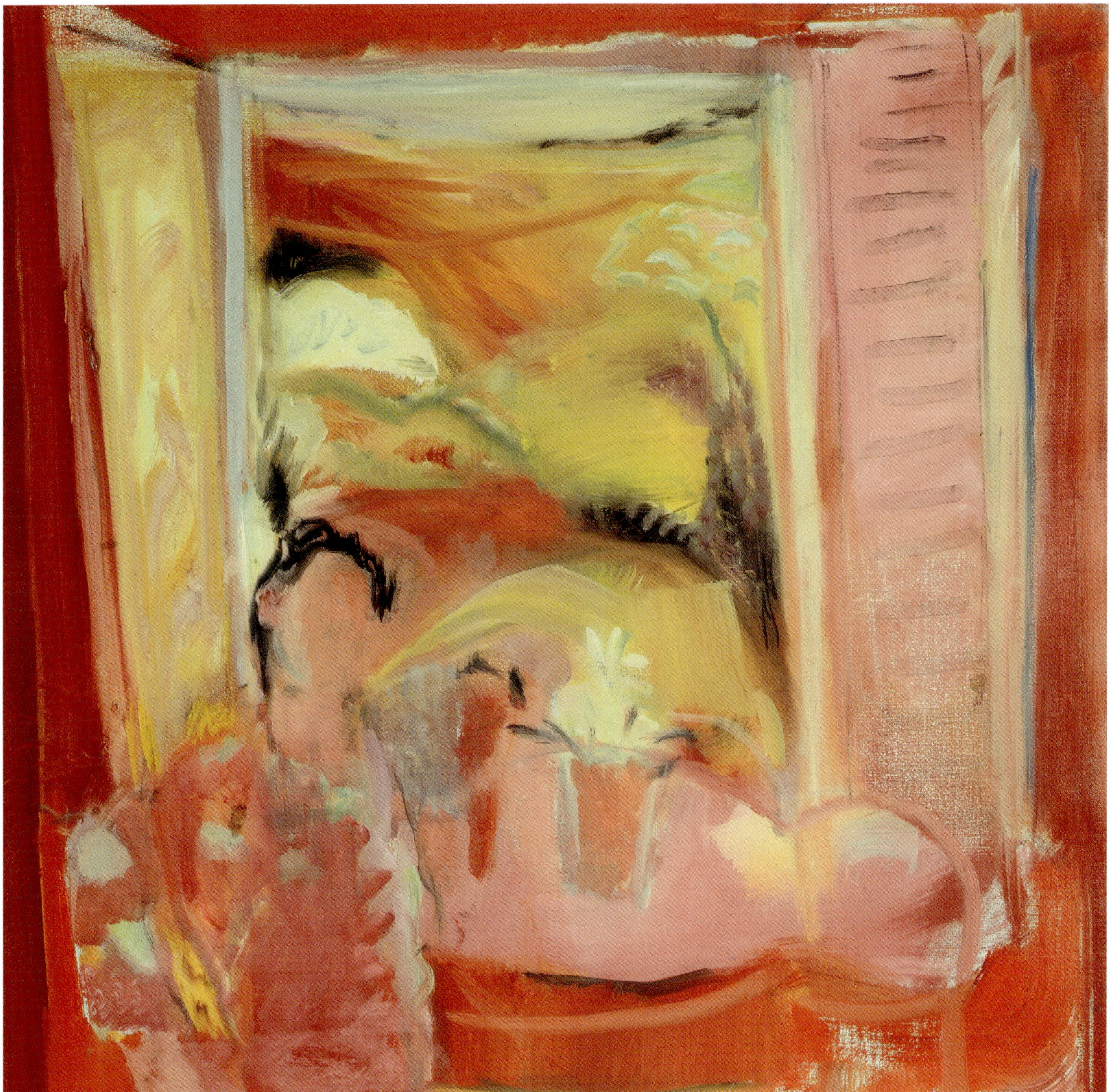

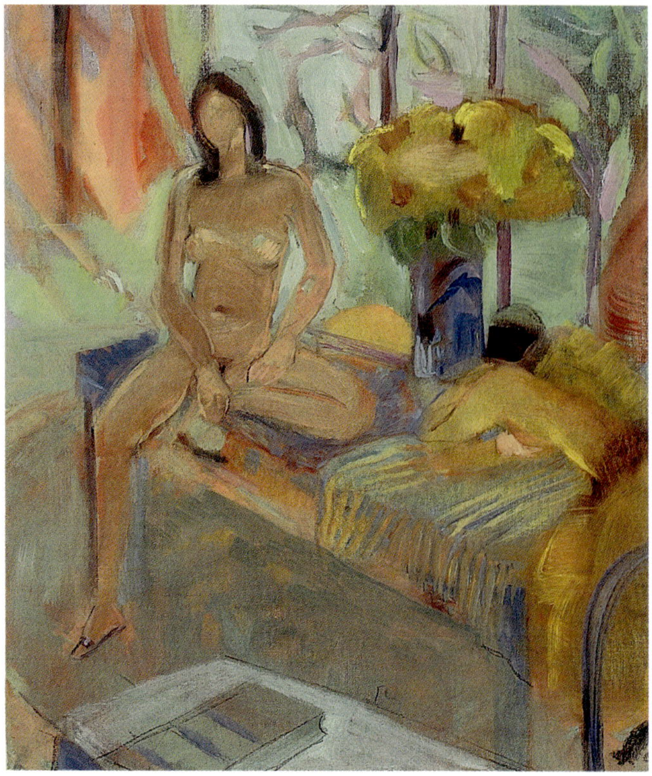

plate 115. ***Chrissie takes a Break***, 2002,
oil on canvas,
50.8 x 61 cm (20 x 24 in)

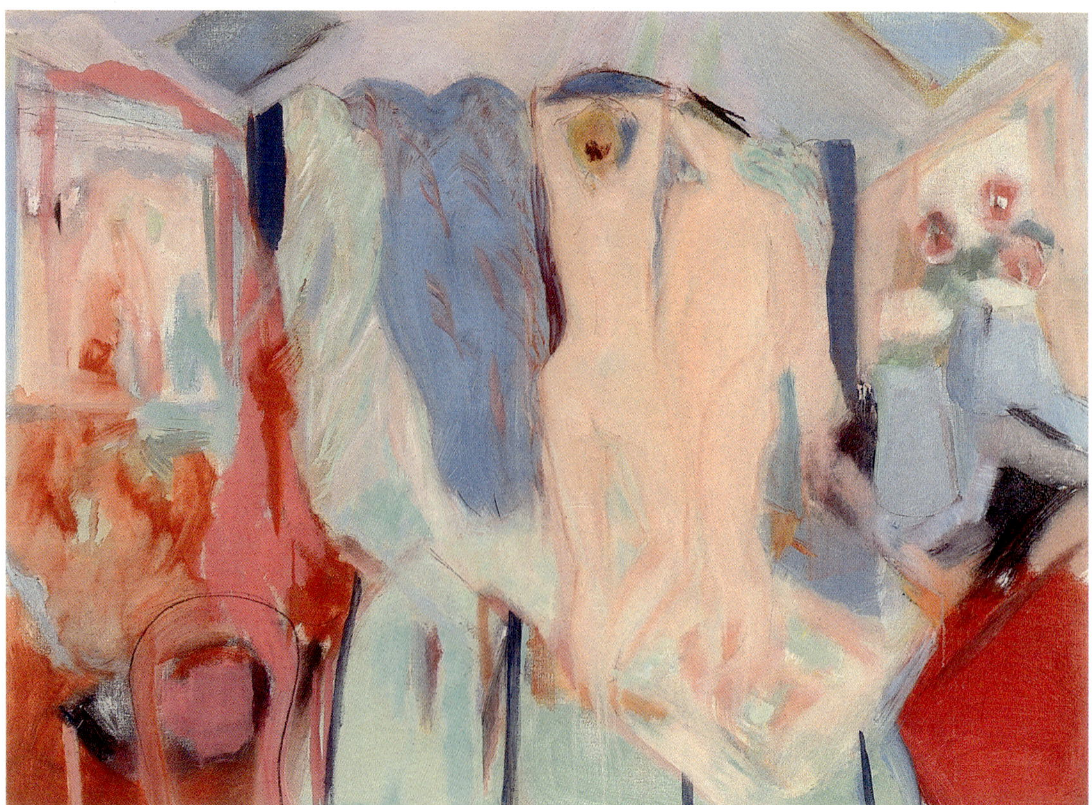

plate 116. ***Girls and Screen in the Studio***, 2002,
oil on canvas,
91.4 x 121.9 cm (36 x 48 in)

plate 117. ***Nude***, 2000, oil on canvas, 50.8 x 76.2 cm (20 x 30 in)

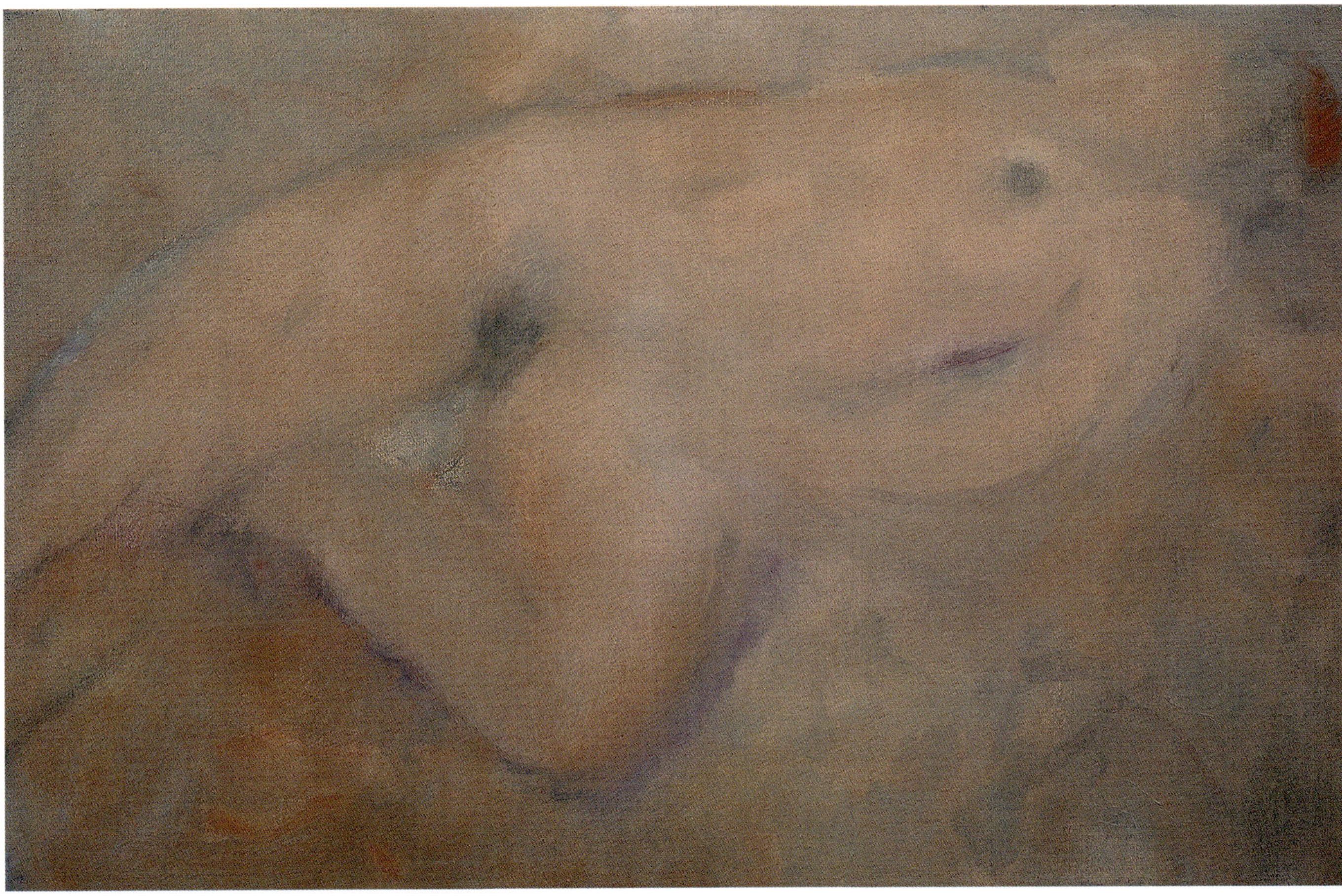

That's something I learned from Roger. I suppose before I was a bit art-studenty and mess didn't matter, but when I noticed he was like a surgeon about his studio, and all the brushes were cleaned and laid out, it had an effect on me. I found I could achieve what I really wanted much easier. For instance, I made my greys rather than depending on having a dirty palette.

Rose is highly critical of her own work and what she calls its tendency to whimsy.

I was so thrilled to have my own gallery and not to have got there via Roger, and then David Messum had a good market for the kind of thing I had a facility for. It was what interested me, so it is a part of me. But I don't like many of those 'frilly' sort of subjects, though they probably do depict the kind of life I think I might have liked.

Now people seem to like my paintings I'm rather confused. I always felt [that in the family] it would be Roger who was recognized. He had

plate 118. ***Winter Botallack***, 2003,
oil on canvas,
91.4 x 101.6 cm (36 x 40 in)

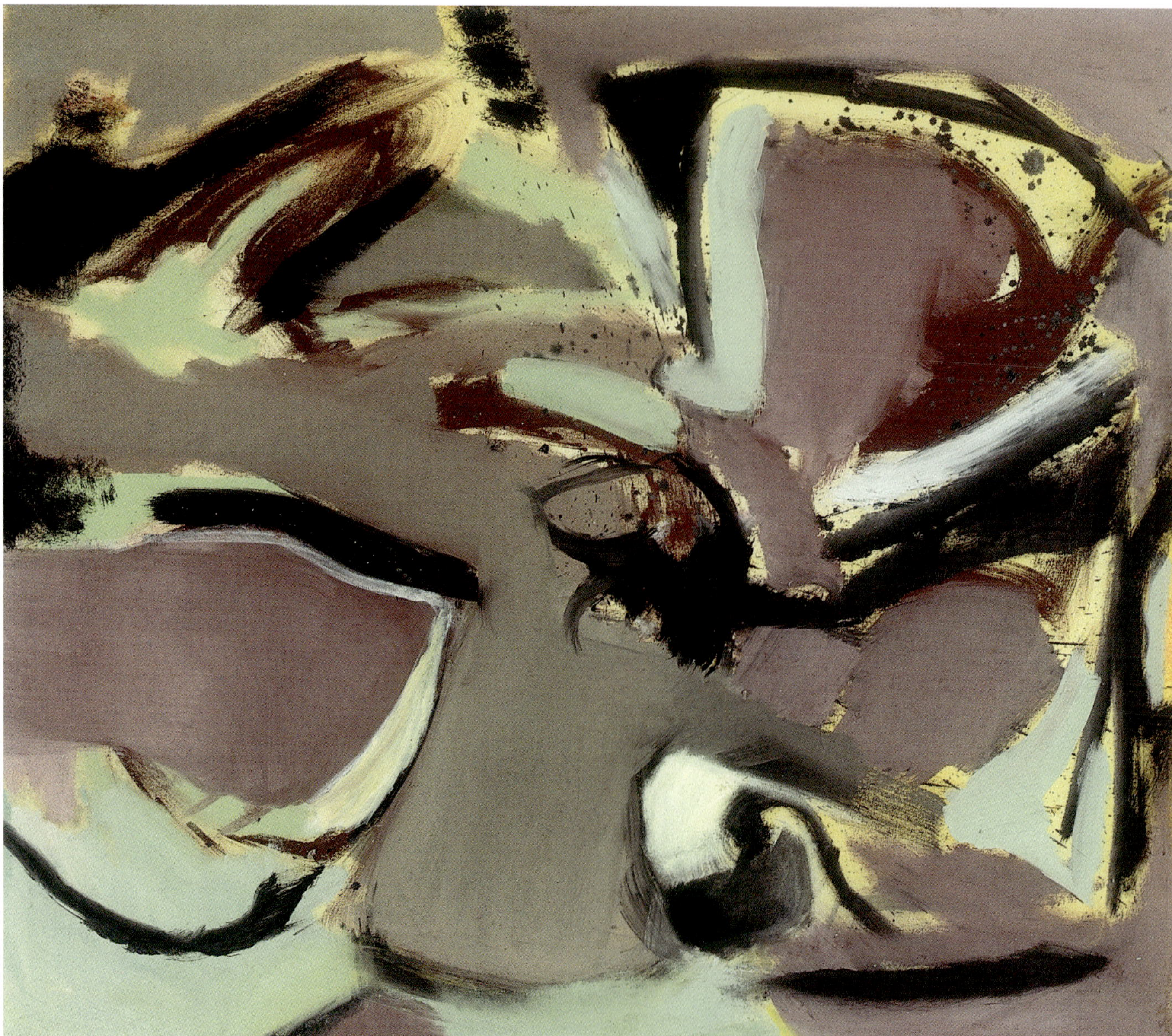

plate 119. ***Studio Window, Penzance***, 2002, oil on canvas, 76.2 x 50.8 cm (30 x 20 in)

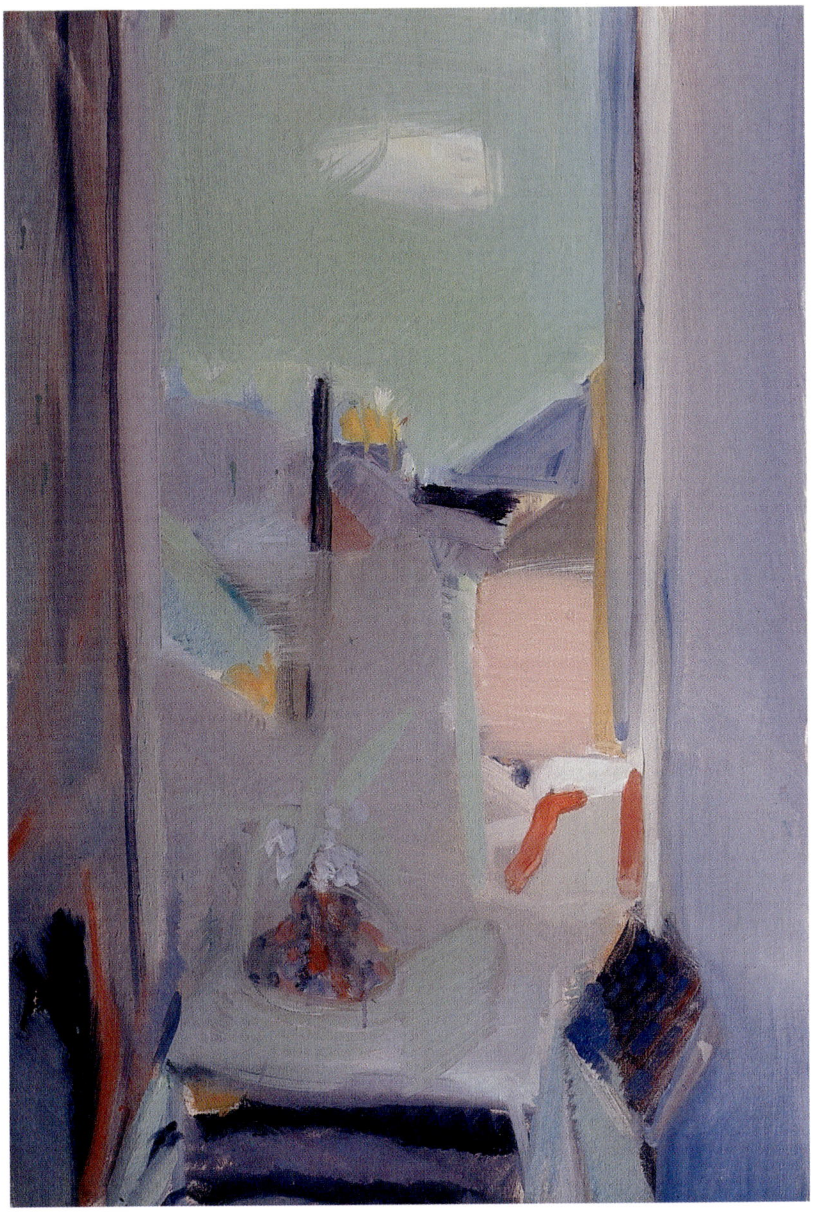

the ideas. I'm still not quite out of that generation that feel that men are IT, you know. I feel I've always looked to a man to find myself. What worries me is that I might have let him down by not being good enough a painter as his partner. After Roger died and I started making my own work, Terry rather hinted that I might be letting Roger down – in the same way that no one in his family could be a representational painter. I think some people may have felt that I should have been more influenced in an abstract way. But I've had to do what I can do.

She said in a talk on women painters given in Scarborough in the late 1990s: 'I think that works of art come from a level of inner truth that transcends gender difference.' She still agrees with that, but continues: 'Having said that, with mine you can tell it's a woman's work. With Sandra's I wouldn't necessarily say so. Or Bridget Riley.' How does she see her own work after this retrospective labour of making a book dealing with her whole life?

Looking back at my early work, I can see I was carving out for myself something I might be able to go on with now. I think, God willing, it's a very exciting time for me, as I've got somewhere and got to know a lot about the shapes and colours that I want to use. And I might be able to simplify them and push it a bit further.

plate 120. ***Music at Botallack***, 2003,
oil on canvas,
91.4 x 121.9 cm (36 x 48 in)

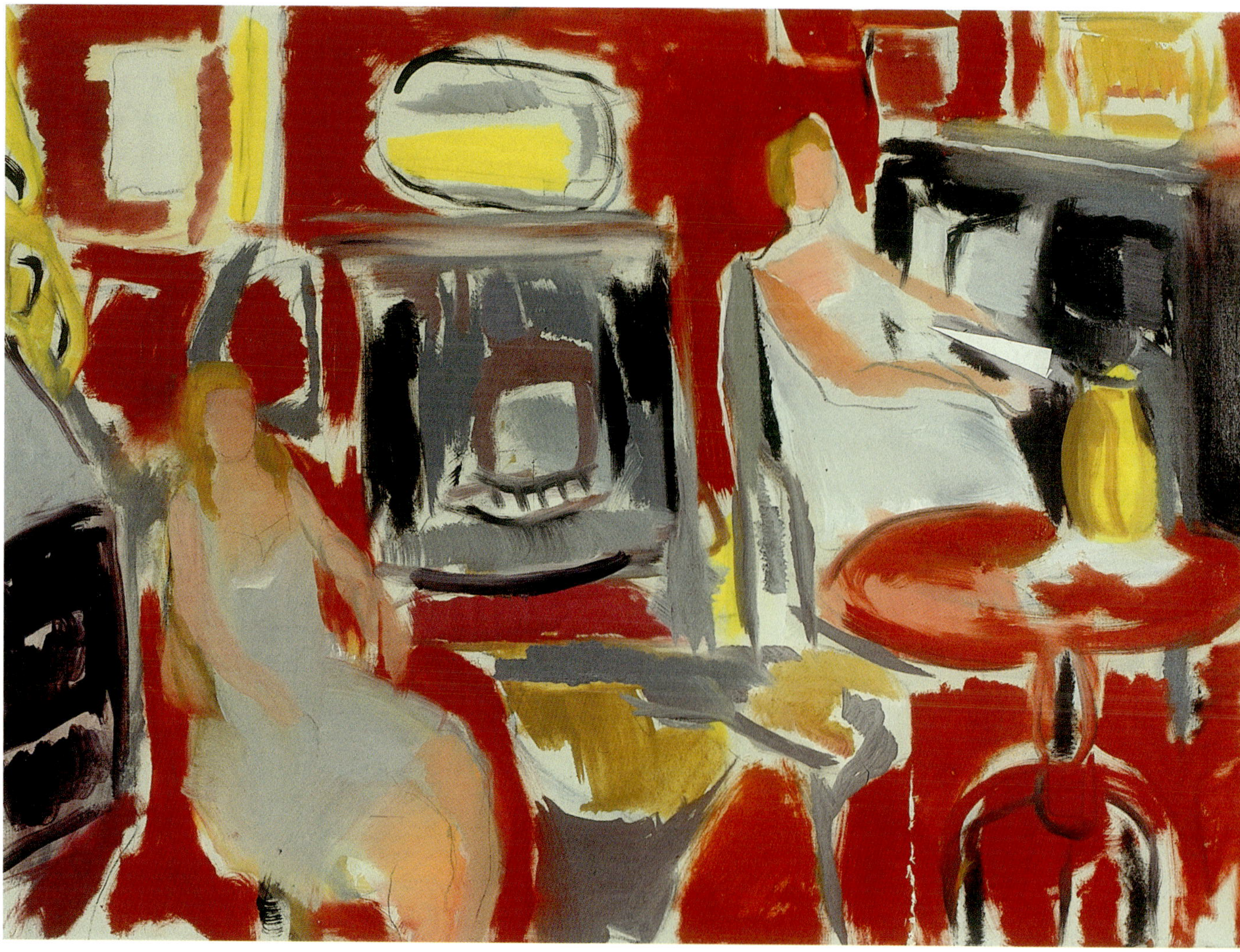

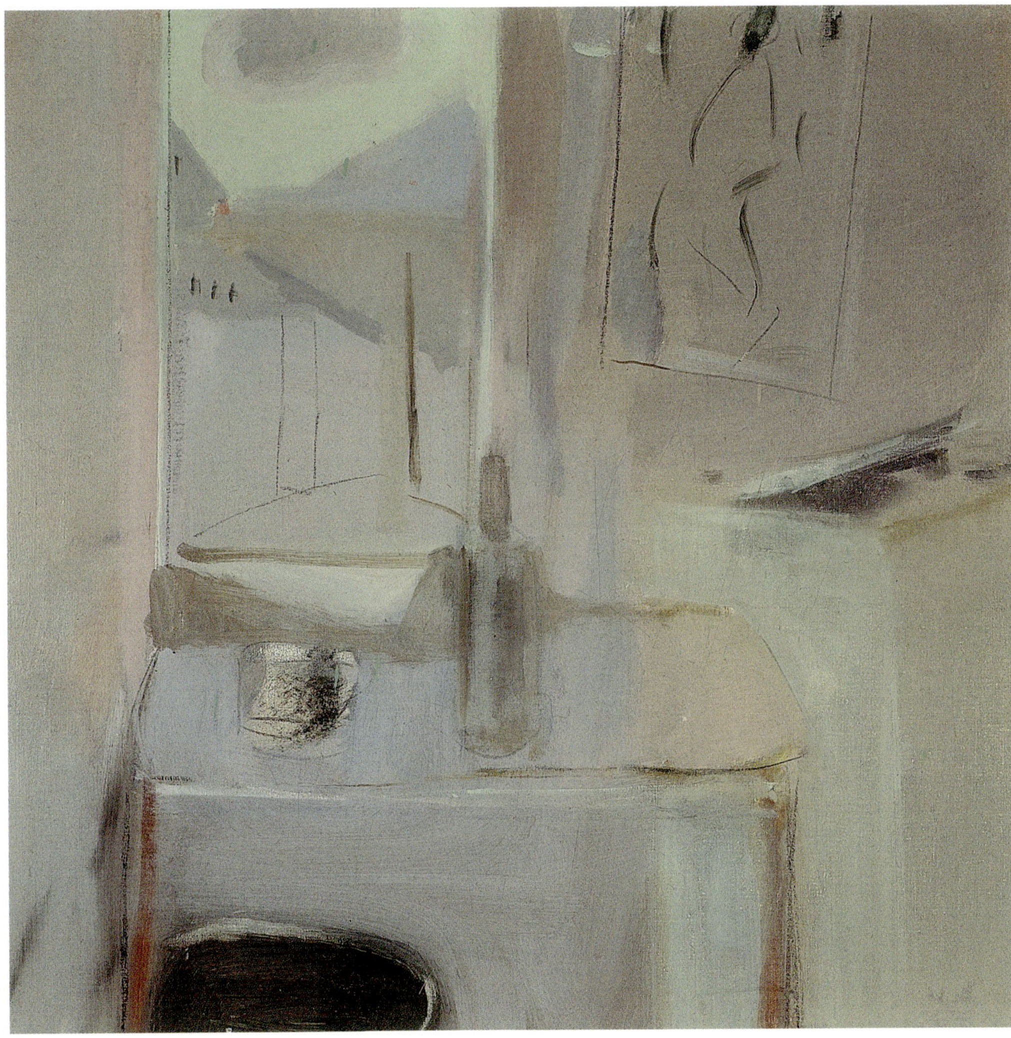

plate 121. ***Grey Kitchen***,
2002,
oil on canvas,
76.2 x 76.2 cm (30 x 30 in)

plate 122. ***Grey Still-life***,
2003,
oil on canvas,
101.6 x 127 cm (40 x 50 in)

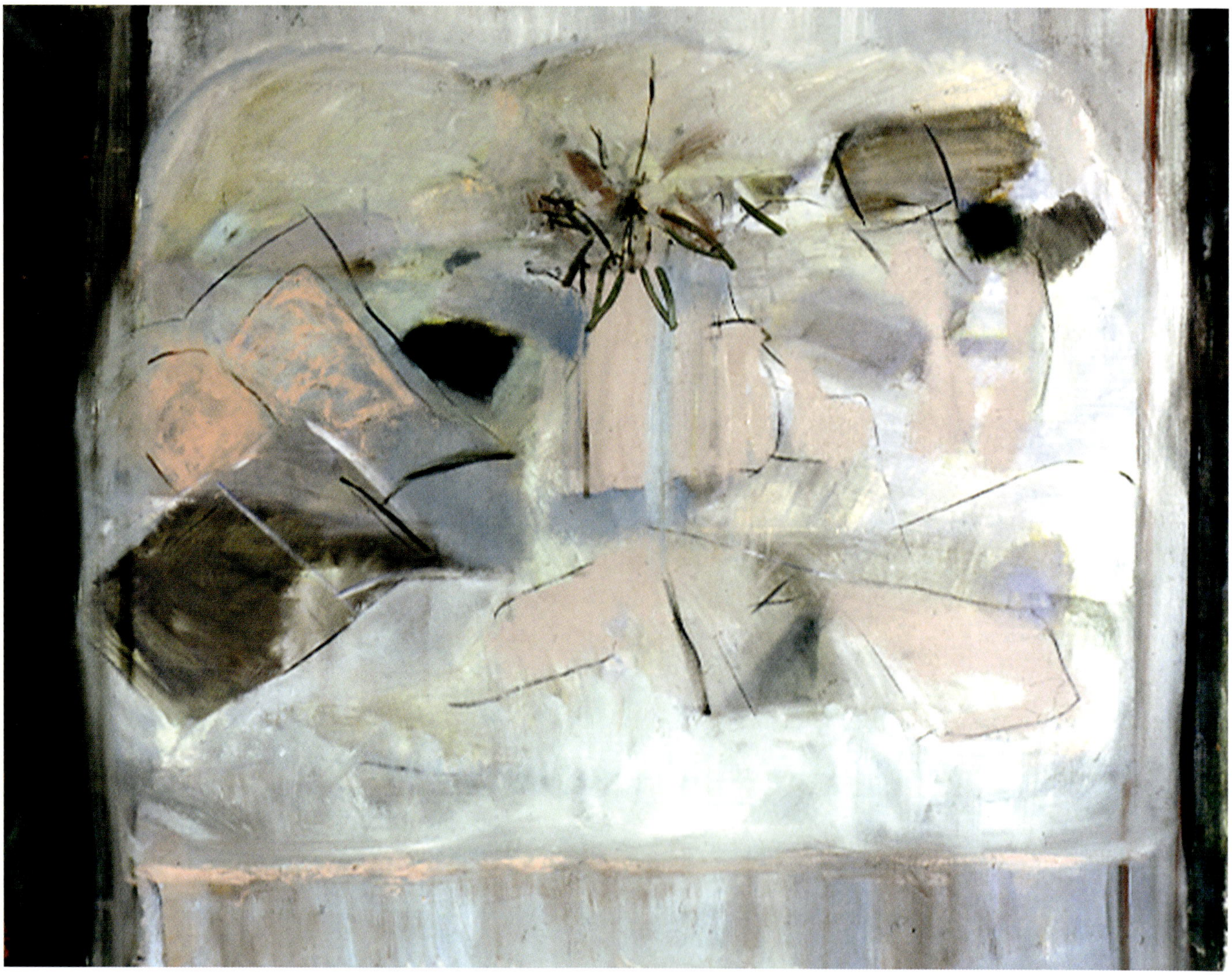

plate 123. ***Susanna and the Elders***, 2003,
oil on canvas,
76.2 x 76.2 cm (30 x 30 in)

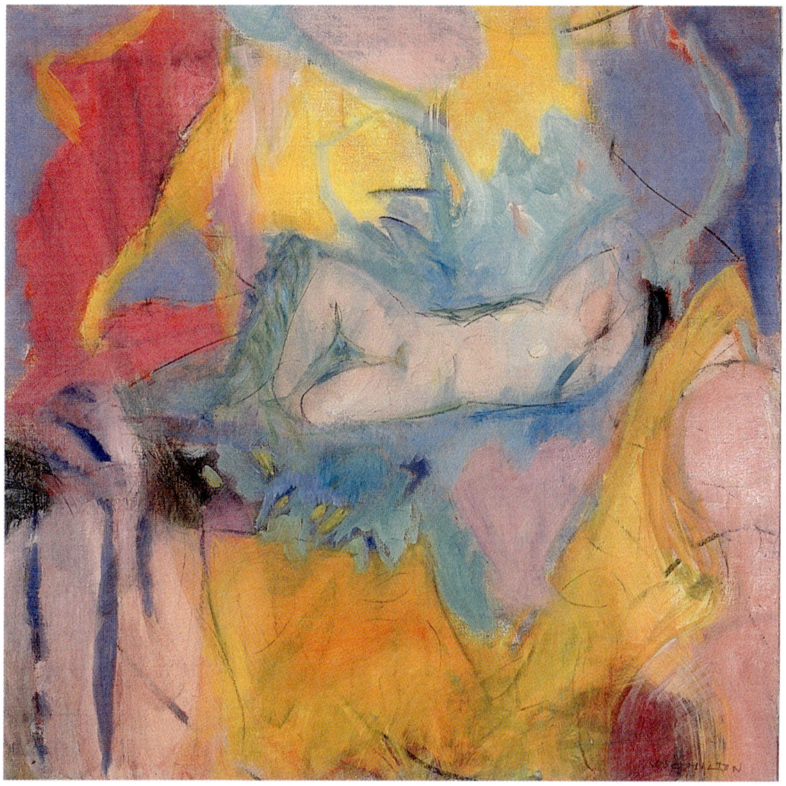

plate 124. ***Stella in the Studio***, 2001,
oil on canvas,
76.2 x 76.2 cm (30 x 30 in)

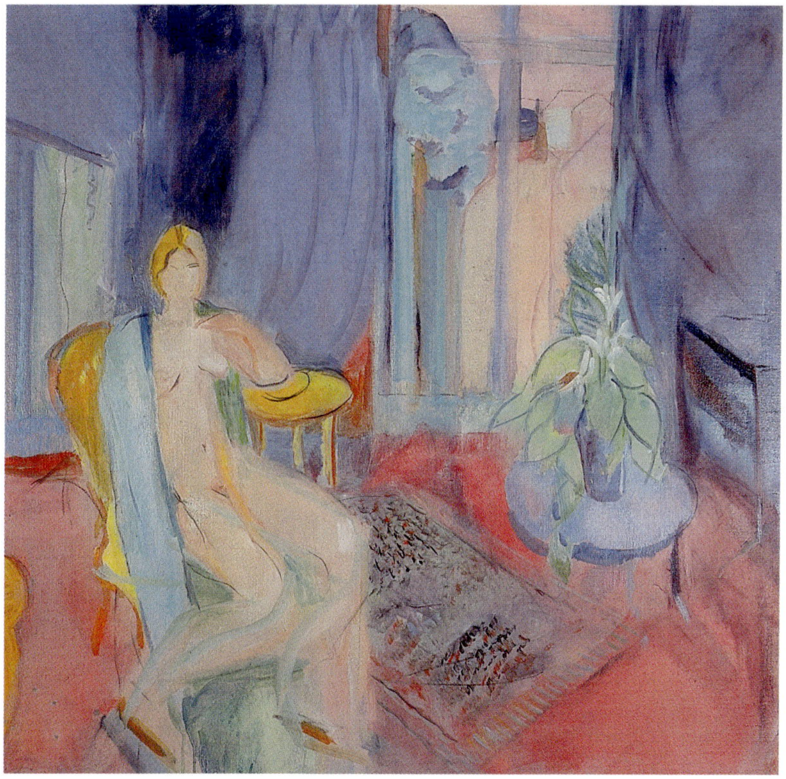

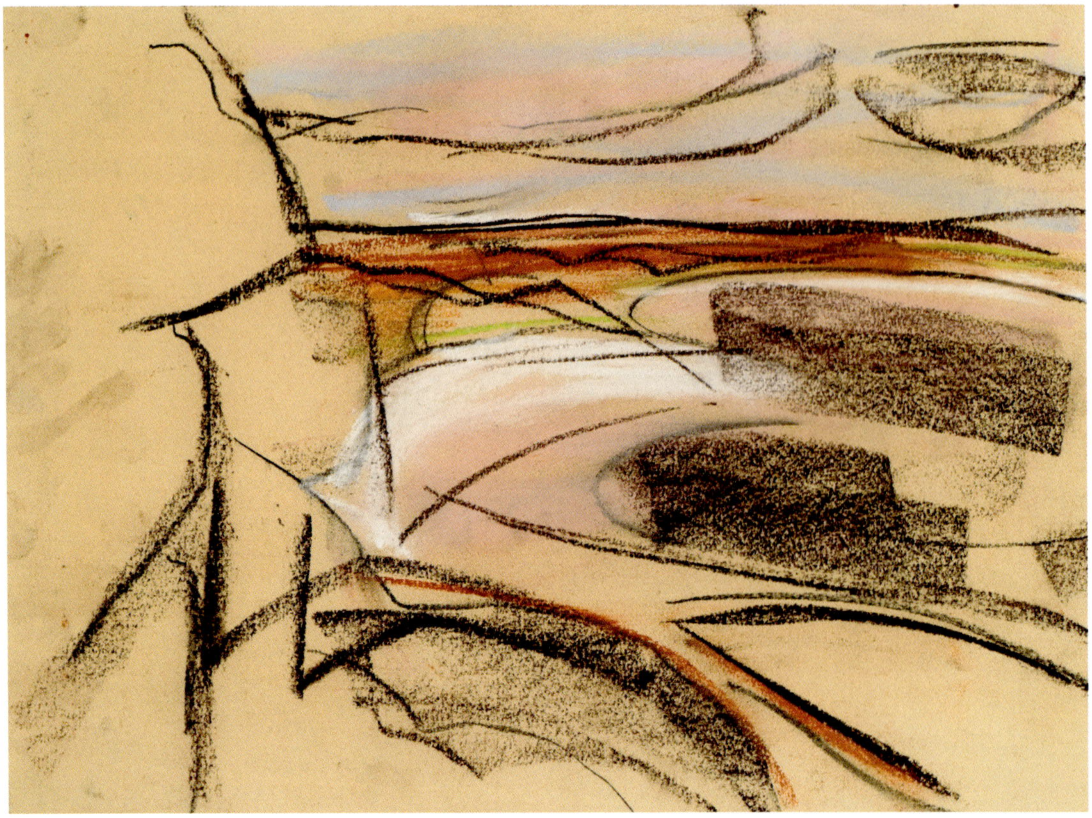

plate 125. ***Scilly Isles, Tresco***, 2004,
pastel on paper,
24.1 x 31.8 cm (9½ x 12½ in)

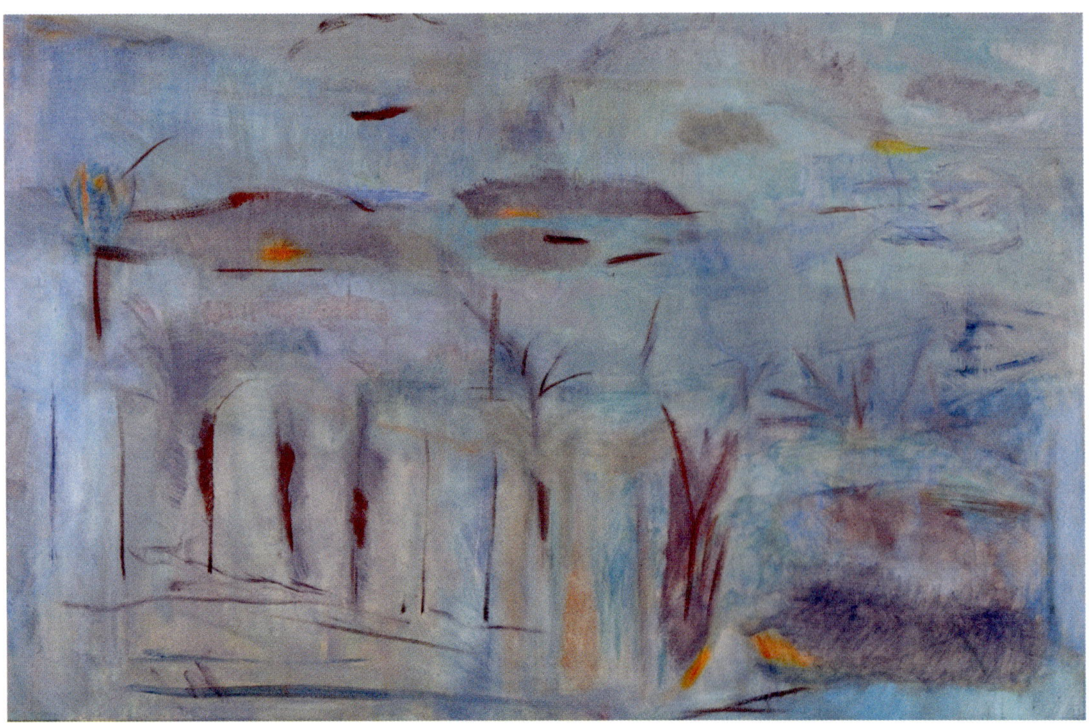

plate 126. ***Kenidjack***,
2007,
oil on canvas,
122 x 182.9 cm (48 x 72 in)

plate 127. ***Dinner Party***,
2007,
oil on canvas,
121.9 x 182.9 cm (48 x 72 in)

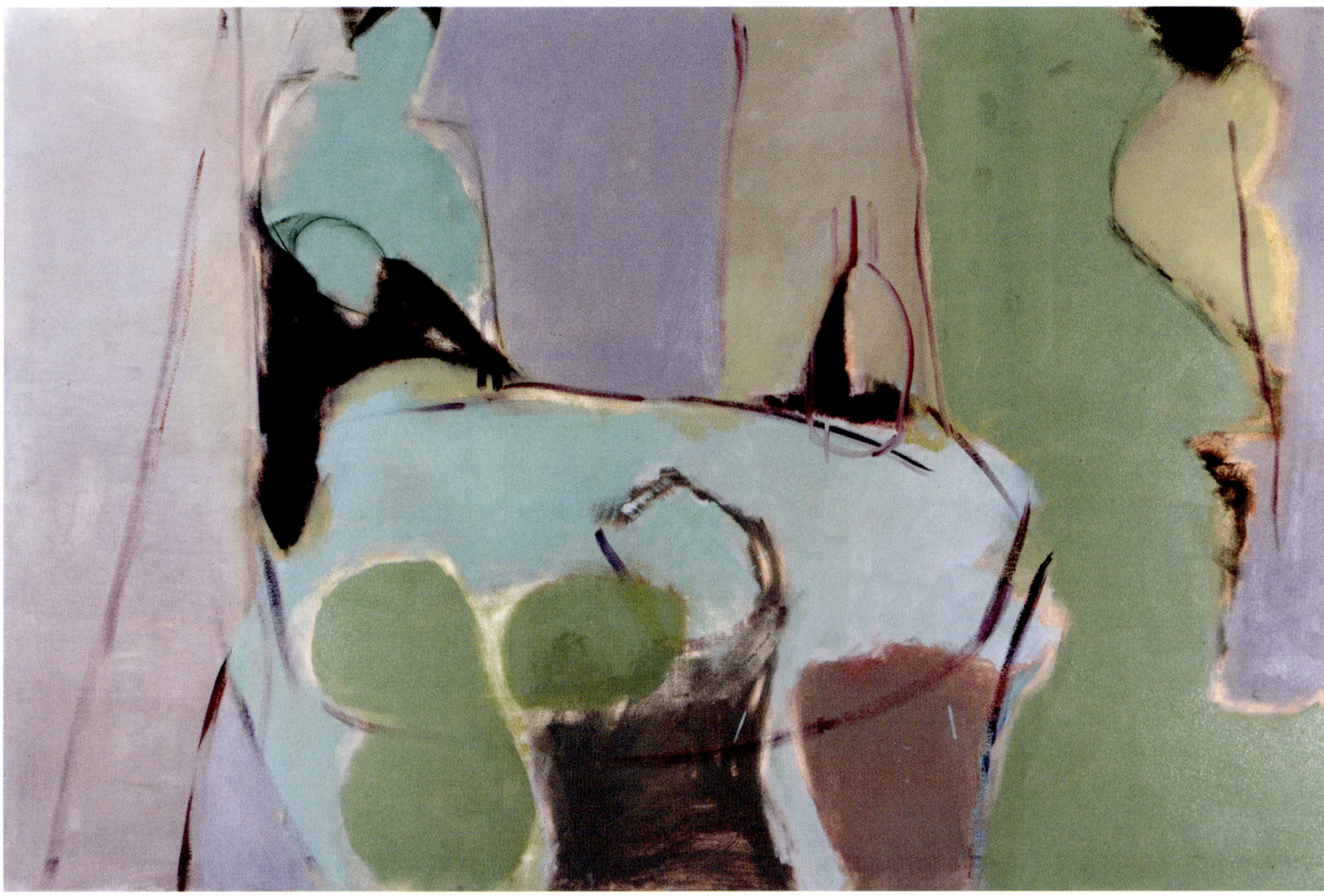

plate 128. *Naxos*, 2007,
oil on canvas,
76.2 x 76.2 cm (30 x 30 in)

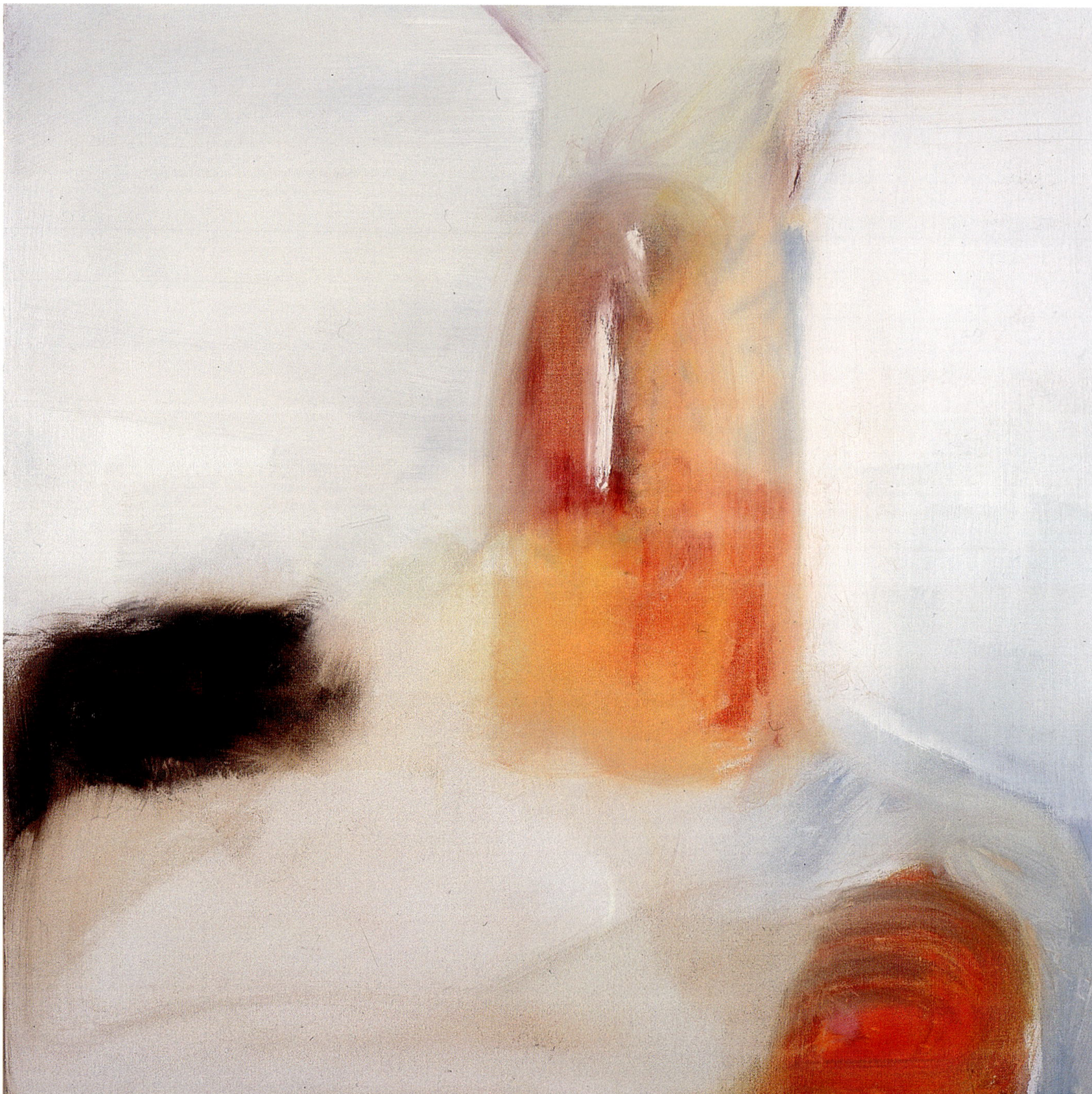

plate 129. ***Botallack Landscape***, 2008, oil on canvas, 76.2 x 76.2 cm (30 x 30 in)

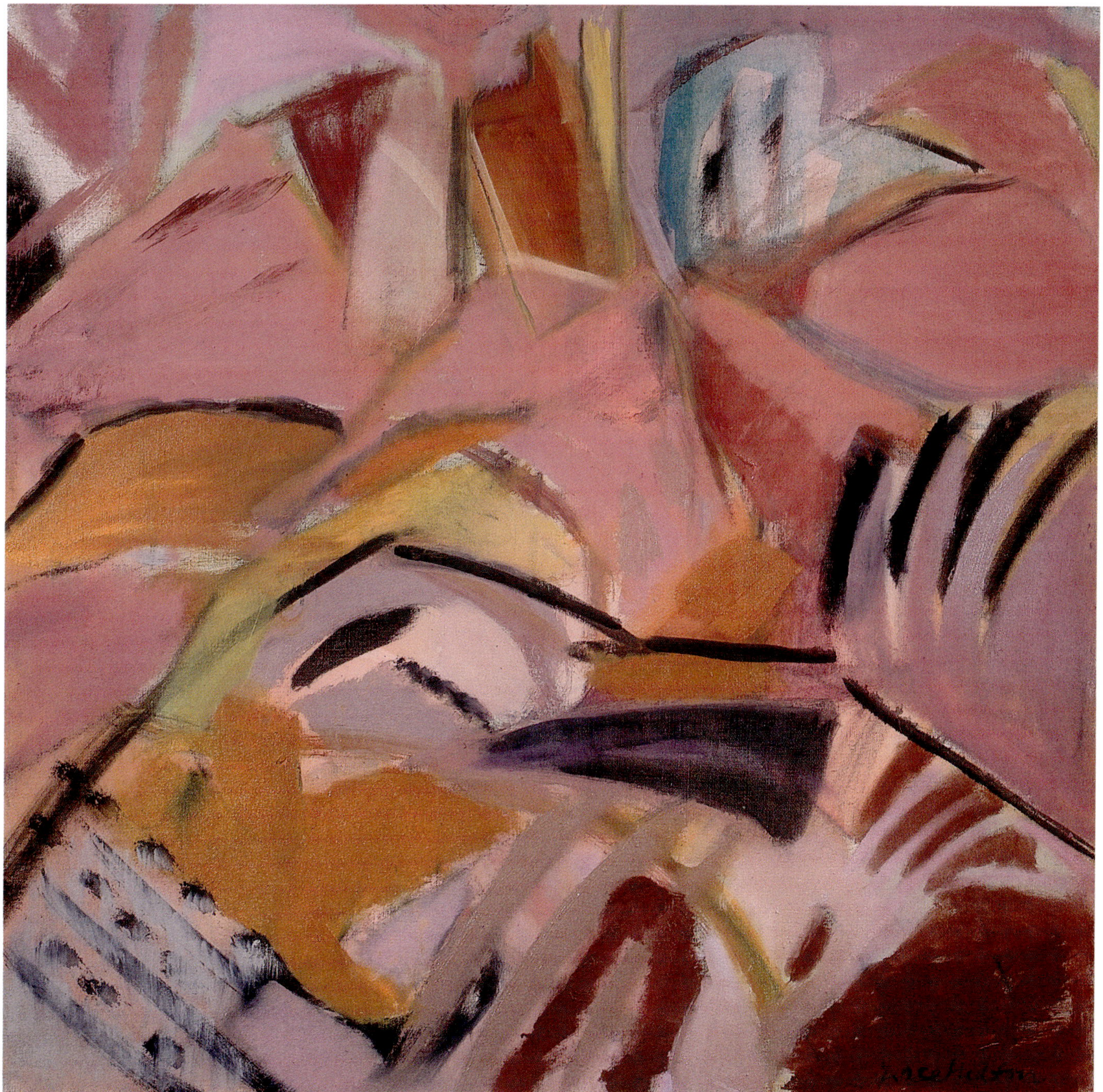

CHRONOLOGY

1931

• Rosemary Phipps born on 15 August, the fourth child of Robert and Julia Louisa Phipps.

1944

• Evacuated to North Wales during Second World War.

1949–53

• Attends Beckenham Art School.

1953

• Takes up place at the Royal College of Art.

1954

• Diagnosed with TB and spends a year at Farnborough Hospital in Kent.

1955

• Returns to the Royal College of Art.

1956

• Enters three paintings for the Young Contemporaries Exhibition at the RBA Suffolk Street, London.

1957

• Graduates from the Royal College of Art with a first-class degree, winning the life drawing and painting prizes.

• Rents a flat/studio on the Fulham Road, London.

1958–59

• Wins the Abbey Minor Scholarship, which allows her to study and work in Rome.

1959

• Rose's beloved brother Robert dies.

• Teaches at Sidcup Art School.

• Meets fellow artist Roger Hilton (1911–75).

• Exhibits at the *Contemporary Women Painters* show in Whitechapel Gallery, London.

1961

• Pregnant with Roger Hilton's child, moves to Paris.

• Returns to London and sets up home with Roger Hilton in Cathcart Road, London.

• Birth of son, Bo Hilton.

From 1961

• Regular exhibitions with Penwith and Newlyn Society of Artists.

1965

• Marries Roger Hilton; family moves to Botallack, Cornwall.

• Birth of son, Fergus Hilton.

1965–75

• Preoccupied with family life including looking after Roger, who is struggling with the effects of alcoholism, and bringing up their sons. Paints purely for pleasure/respite.

1975

• Roger Hilton dies.

1977

• Newlyn Gallery – first solo show.

1978

• Plymouth Art Centre – solo show.

1984

• Has painting accepted by RA, and often shows in successive Summer Exhibitions.

• Enrols in Cecil Collins' drawing class at the Central School of Art.

1987

• Newlyn Art Gallery – solo show.

1988

• The Oxford Gallery – solo show.

1989

• Joins David Messum.

1991

• David Messum Gallery, St George Street, London – solo show.

1993

• David Messum Gallery, Cork Street, London – solo show.

1994

• *Three Painters of Penwith*: David Messum Gallery, Cork Street, London.

1995

• David Messum Gallery, Cork Street, London – solo show.

1997

• David Messum Gallery, Cork Street, London – solo show.

1998

• Messum's, Cork Street, London – solo show.

2000

• Messum's, Cork Street, London – solo show.

2001

- *Twelve New Paintings*: Messum's, Cork Street, London.

2002

- *Painters and Sculptors of the South West*: Messum's, Cork Street, London – group show.
- North Light Gallery, Huddersfield – solo show.
- Messum's, Cork Street, London – solo show.

2004

- Messum's, Cork Street, London – solo show.

2008

- *Rose Hilton, The Beauty of Ordinary Things: A Selected Retrospective 1950–2007*, Tate St Ives.

WORKS IN PUBLIC COLLECTIONS

- British Museum Collection
- Cornwall County Council: Truro Art Gallery
- The Nuffield Collection
- Plymouth Museum and Art Gallery – Permanent Collection
- Royal College of Art Collection

ACKNOWLEDGEMENTS AND FURTHER READING

MY PRINCIPAL DEBT OF GRATITUDE is to Rose Hilton who has entrusted me with presenting the story of her life. For her friendship, optimism and good humour I am much beholden – she has made the task of writing this book a pleasant one.

Among the others who have been instrumental in the preparation of this volume, David Messum, Carol Tee and the staff of Messum's, the gallery which represents Rose's work, have been unfailingly helpful. Thank you to all those owners of pictures by Rose who have allowed their works to be photographed. The photographer Ander Gunn deserves a special vote of thanks for his work on recuperating old photos.

There isn't an extensive bibliography on Rose, apart from the run of Messum's catalogues since 1991 and the Tate St Ives retrospective catalogue *The Beauty of Ordinary Things* (2008), but I would also refer the reader to my monograph *Roger Hilton: The Figured Language of Thought* (Thames & Hudson, 2007) and to Michael Bird's useful survey *The St Ives Artists: A Biography of Place and Time* (Lund Humphries, 2008). Aside from these for background reading, the best course, as always, is to look at the paintings themselves. AL

INDEX OF WORKS